SNAPPING

SNAPPING

America's Epidemic of Sudden Personality Change

Second Edition

FLO CONWAY and JIM SIEGELMAN

STILLPOINT PRESS
New York

In chapter 4, the quotation from Eldridge Cleaver is from *Newsweek* magazine, October 25, 1976. Copyright 1976 by Newsweek, Inc. All rights reserved. Reprinted by permission.

In chapter 5, the excerpt from *73 Poems* by E. E. Cummings is © 1963 by Marion Morehouse Cummings. Reprinted by permission of Harcourt Brace Jovanovich, Inc. The excerpt from "Hanging Out with the Guru" by Sally Kempton is copyright © 1976 by the NYM Corp. Reprinted with the permission of *New York Magazine*.

In chapter 9, the excerpt from *Cybernetics: or Control and Communication in the Animal and the Machine* by Norbert Wiener is copyright 1948 and 1961 by the Massachusetts Institute of Technology. Used with permission of The M.I.T. Press.

In chapter 12, the excerpt from "Choruses from The Rock" is from *Collected Poems 1909-1962* by T.S. Eliot, copyright 1936 by Harcourt Brace Jovanovich, Inc. © 1963, 1964, by T. S. Eliot. Reprinted by permission of the publishers.

In chapter 14, the excerpts from *Helter Skelter: The True Story of the Manson Murders* by Vincent Bugliosi with Curt Gentry are © 1974 by Curt Gentry and Vincent Bugliosi. Used with permission of W. A. Norton & Company, Inc. The quotation from Patty Hearst from "Patty Hearst—Her Story" is © 1976 by CBS News. Used with permission.

Special thanks to John Clarke for his cover, logo and art direction for Stillpoint Press. The chaos curves in chapter 16 were created using Fractint v18.2. Our thanks to Seth Demsey for his technical assistance. Figure 5 was hand-painted on the computer by Mario Henri Chakkour using Painter 3.0 Fractal Design software. Our thanks to Mario for his skill in preparing this illustration.

Library of Congress Catalog Card Number: 95-69831
Publication Data:
Conway, Flo
    1. Personality change—United States. 2. Psychotherapy—United
States. 3. Group relations training—United States.
    4. Conversion—Comparative studies. 5. Experience (religion).
    I. Siegelman, Jim. II. Title.
    Includes illustrations, index (softcover: acid-free paper)

ISBN: 0-9647650-0-4 (previously ISBN: 0-385-28928-6, 0-440-57970-8)

For information address:

Stillpoint Press, Inc.
20 Park Avenue
New York, NY 10016

Printed in the United States of America
First printing—August, 1995

20   18   16   14   12   10   8   6   4   2
    19   17   15   13   11   9   7   5   3   1

Contents

For Hal Conway

With the exception of publicly known figures, the names and identities of all the participants in religious cults, sects, self-help therapies and other groups who are quoted in this book have been changed. Names used for these individuals are fictitious and do not refer to any person living or dead.

Scientists and other professionals whose interviews are partially quoted do not necessarily endorse the authors' views, opinions or conclusions.

Preface to the Second Edition
Frontiers of Freedom in an Information Age

SEVENTEEN YEARS HAVE PASSED since the first publication of *Snapping*. During this time, the world has shifted with speed and drama into the information age. New information technologies have transformed the lives of people and nations. The global communications revolution has redrawn the world's boundaries and reshaped its economies. The tides of change are running high. Yet in all the buzz about the information age and beaming visions of technological utopias around the next turn, there has been almost no serious inquiry into the impact of it all on people.

For two decades, the two of us have been travelers on this frontier. In our work as communication researchers, we've watched the information revolution engulf everyone. We've seen great gains and profound dislocations. We've learned of losses people are enduring that are not just material: losses of time and place, losses of identity and feelings of human worth. We've seen the human moorings of culture, social connection and spirituality that give meaning to people in every society strained and in many ways sundered.

The experiences we document in this book reveal a new truth about the information age that our society has barely begun to confront. It is the meaning of all that information in human terms. The flood of modern messages pouring down on people from so many technical and human sources is a physical force that has an organic impact on the mind and the whole of each individual's personality. This new truth has far-reaching implications for individuals and societies. For, as we have seen, the human mind, the primary resource of an information age, is facing new perils no one ever anticipated, and some that many people are loath to accept, in this exciting, frightening new era.

From the beginning, our focus in *Snapping* has been on these new human terms of the information age and their impact on people in their daily lives. That impact first showed itself vividly to us in the seventies in an epidemic of sudden, drastic personality changes that was being reported by a new generation of spiritual searchers and personal growth seekers. They were the first explorers on the new era's human frontiers. Their quest was not to master the new information hardware, which was then only starting to roll off sleek assembly lines, but to equip themselves inside for coming challenges most could only intuit. They were searching for a new *self*-knowledge, for new personal experiences and illuminating spiritual realms. Instead many discovered the experience we call snapping that took them to the limits of their own minds and their most fundamental human freedoms.

Since that time, the phenomenon of sudden change we explored in the seventies' religious cults and self-help therapies has grown into something much larger. The epidemic has spread far beyond those first questioning college students and trendsetting urban professionals. In the nineties, the snapping phenomenon, with its many bizarre and tragic consequences, has leaped from isolated group settings into wider public arenas. It has transformed the lives of innocent children, whole families and growing numbers of the elderly. It has overtaken entire communities in America and cultures worldwide. It has surfaced among aggressive fundamentalist sects rising in Christianity and every religion, in extremist political groups and ideological movements, in the flourishing "new age" movement and emerging schools of alternative medicine, in the booming global marketplace of commercial sales, motivation, management training and stress reduction enterprises, and in other places where such changes were inconceivable only a few years ago.

The 1978 Peoples Temple tragedy in Jonestown, Guyana, in which a U.S. Congressman, three journalists and more than 900 sect members died in a grisly scene of murder and mass suicide, drew international attention to the dangers posed by the new genre of consuming cults and their uncanny powers of human change and control. The calamitous 1993 siege and conflagration at the Branch Davidian compound near Waco, Texas, where four federal officers were killed and eighty sect members died from gunfire and a blazing immolation, showed how much about this explosive phenomenon has yet to be understood two decades later. Those events are only two in a string of bizarre cult crimes, mass suicides and acts of terror that have transpired worldwide: the Solar Temple murder-suicides in Canada and Switzerland, the Tokyo subway nerve gas attack by members of the Aum Shinrikyo sect, the terror bombing in Oklahoma City allegedly committed by anti-government extremists.

These tragic acts confirm that the phenomenon of snapping is no fad or fluke. They demonstrate the power of artful manipulators to control small groups and large populations, not through coercion, but through the control of information and powerful techniques of communication. And they stand as grim proof of the potential inherent in a widening array of extremist cults, religious sects and political groups for chaos on a scale not witnessed before in America or any other free society.

This new edition of *Snapping* incorporates many insights we have gleaned from our ongoing conversations with people who have experienced sudden changes of mind and personality in cults, sects, therapies, political groups and professional trainings. It also looks deeper into a problem we only glimpsed in the seventies, which we perceived at the time as a wider threat of "snapping in everyday life." In the nineties, this culture-wide strain of snapping has become one of the most troubling aspects of our inquiry. The rise in reported incidents of people snapping suddenly and violently, without the influence of a controlling cult or mind-altering group, has sparked tragedies in America and cultures worldwide. This larger phenomenon is being witnessed more frequently as the compounding stresses of late twentieth-century life break out in sensational crimes, mass slayings and quieter instances of people snapping in everyday life situations. These painful scenes are being played out daily by angry, frustrated citizens, by laid-off workers and disgruntled employees in high-stress jobs and professions, by troubled youths, spurned lovers and desperate family members, and by seemingly well-adjusted friends and neighbors who have been pushed to the breaking point and beyond. In our view, this everyday life epidemic is just one further reflection of the sudden, drastic changes people everywhere are experiencing with the shift into a global information society.

Snapping is on the rise in populations passing through traumatic social, political and technological transitions, in cultures besieged by fanatical mindsets and apocalyptic messages, and the phenomenon seems to be accelerating as a tumultuous millennium approaches. The volatile climate has brought profound confusion over basic freedoms of thought, belief, free speech and association, and conflict in many places over the increasing abuses of those freedoms in religion, politics and other cultural arenas. In some circles, the confusion has grown so acute over these new information age dilemmas of freedom and control that people have become unable to act on, or even to think through, these sensitive issues and the urgent questions they raise.

Travels in the information dimension. Our perspective in this book is different from other treatments of these complex issues. It is grounded, not in traditional psychological or sociological frameworks, but in the new communication sciences that form the foundation of today's global communication culture. Our focus is on the information dimension of this new universe—the intangible domain of human communication where the snapping phenomenon is occurring, where its unprecedented changes of mind and personality are communicated from one person to another, and where their threats to all our freedoms are translated into action. From this vantage point, the sudden changes that have altered so many modern lives can be seen as products of tangible forces moving in the information dimension, in the flow of messages through the air around our heads, in the space between people, and in the interminable appeals of our engulfing mass communication culture.

In *Snapping* we strive to understand not only what is happening to people but *how* it is happening. Our perspective goes beyond Orwellian notions of "brainwashing" and "mind control" as those terms have been applied historically to people in totalist societies. The dramatic changes we have been tracking are products of powerful new methods of human communication that can be observed in countless arenas of late twentieth-century society. This perspective has helped us to understand how profound changes of mind and personality may be brought about by a wide variety of modern messages: by deftly engineered spiritual and personal growth experiences, covertly induced beliefs, subtle suggestions, nonverbal cues, group dynamics, simple mind-altering practices, and other everyday uses of information and human communication.

In the years since *Snapping* called attention to these powerful influences, potent human communication practices such as meditation, visualization, guided fantasy, role-playing and group encounter have brought benefits to many and intense new stresses to bear on others. In many arenas, these communication tools have been refined into precision instruments for remolding every aspect of thought, feeling, belief, behavior and personality in its entirety. In its wider social applications, this new "technology of experience," as we call it, has become an integral player in information age quests for salvation, power and profit that have brought sweeping changes in religion, politics, business, popular culture and the affairs of nations.

This new human communication technology has spread swiftly across America and societies worldwide, its power multiplied millionsfold by electronic gadgets and global telecommunications. Yet this lifechanging human technology and the new knowledge that undergirds it are being disseminated, in almost every instance, without professional standards, ethical guidelines or even the most basic consumer protections.

Our concerns here are not academic. The life processes of the mind, brain and body are intimately affected by this penetrating new world of communication. Those seamlessly connected living systems form the whole of each individual's awareness and personality. Throughout our lives, they are shaped and sustained organically by the information communicated in our day-to-day experiences. And, as we have learned first-hand, like the brain and the body itself, the mind's higher communication powers—of thinking, feeling, awareness, memory, imagination and free choice—are subject to their own organic forces of growth and decay. They are vulnerable to stress and disease and, like every living thing, they can become sick and die.

The bottom line of snapping, we know now, is that there are physical constraints on our human capacities to engage many of today's intense new communication experiences—*organic* limits on the mind's higher powers and serious consequences for those who exceed them. Our inquiry has confirmed with personal testimony and hard scientific data that lasting changes of mind and personality may be brought about by reckless or excessive uses of popular spiritual and personal growth practices and many other modern communication methods. More important, our perspective has enabled us to track the physical impact of those intense experiences and their long-term effects on basic processes of mind.

These findings in the new category of disorders we call "information disease" open a new window into the information dimension of our inner lives and our interactions with one another. They give a first glimpse of the physical limits of human growth and change in today's high-speed, high-stress information society. They also offer hopeful insights for the mind's resilience and ability to adapt to the demands of our era's complex new technologies, changing global realities and shifting spiritual tides.

To bring this larger picture of *Snapping* to our readers, we have added significant material to this edition. We have updated events surrounding many groups and issues we investigated initially, and we have incorporated new information about other religious, political and personal growth enterprises that have attracted large followings in recent years.

In Part I, we have kept most of our original text intact. Those early stories told to us by the first witnesses to snapping when the phenomenon burst on the scene in the seventies continue to instruct and, we believe, will enlighten those who may find themselves in similar situations today and in years to come. In many ways, their testimony gives focus and historical perspective to a phenomenon that will never be so simple again.

In Part II, in a new Chapter 13, we offer findings from our extensive follow-up research on the nature and effects of information disease and related human information-processing disorders. This new research includes findings from a parallel study of American Vietnam war veterans that uncovered striking similarities, in two very different subject populations, between the symptoms of information disease and the newly recognized clinical syndrome known as Post-Traumatic Stress Disorder.

Portions of our "Information Disease" study first appeared in *Science Digest* in 1982. The study was completed during a year-long appointment as visiting scholars with the Project on Information and Social Change at the University of Oregon Communication Research Center. The full findings were presented at the International Communication Association meeting in Honolulu, Hawaii, in 1985 and were excerpted in the international journal *Update*, published in Aarhus, Denmark, in 1986. The complete statistical profile, reprinted in full as a new appendix to this edition, and a graphic presentation of select findings in Chapter 13, are published here in book form for the first time.

Along with our own follow-up research, the information revolution in neuroscience has provided further clues to the organic processes that underlie snapping and information disease. Much of this new research affirms our earlier neuroscientific speculations, and we offer a small portion of those discoveries in the closing pages of Part II. These new insights from neuroscience and molecular biology suggest specific neurochemical changes that may constitute the physical pathways of snapping and information disease.

In many ways, this research supports our initial views that the technical principles of holography and the nonlinear mathematics of catastrophe theory are valuable tools for understanding the personal changes we have heard depicted countless times as a sudden, all-encompassing experience of "snapping." At the same time, the burgeoning fields of cognitive science and computer modeling have produced powerful new conceptual and mathematical tools, and we have drawn on the most relevant advances here.

In a new Part III, we expand our earlier discussion of the social implications of snapping. In particular, in Chapter 16, we have adapted principles from the emerging science of chaos theory to map the complex communication dynamics of the "death spiral" that ran wild at

Jonestown and Waco, and in other fatal cult confrontations. In Chapter 17, we look deeper into the everyday life sources of information stress that appear to be breeding the first cumulative, culture-wide strains of snapping and information disease.

Finally, in a new postscript written for this edition, we explore the latest tragic events in Tokyo and Oklahoma City that have targeted the employees of governments and innocent civilians worldwide in acts of terror by religious-political extremists armed with weapons of mass destruction. The actions of these extremist cults, subcultures and clandestine terror cells conform to their own dynamics of confrontation and chaos, and we offer a first interpretation of this widening public peril.

A Rosetta Stone. Since the seventies, the term snapping has entered the lexicon of human responses to the compounding pressures of late twentieth-century life. Acts of inexplicable madness have become everyday occurrences in American cities, suburbs and towns. New winds of religious-political fanaticism have brought terror to American soil and the specter of whole nations snapping *en masse* on satellite TV.

On this fast-moving frontier, the two of us have felt from the beginning that the cult phenomenon is a modern-day Rosetta stone, a key to understanding the larger crises rising with the information age and its beguiling new techniques and technologies. From the outset, we have seen the closed societies of the new cults, sects and therapies as extraordinary real-life laboratories, controlled environments in which to view and explore *in vivo* the new processes of personal and social change proliferating in the information dimension of our daily lives. These new groups offer unique insights into the life of the mind in society, for they are societies in their own right, sealed off almost completely in their physical environments and, to an even greater degree, in their day-to-day information environments. In their overlapping codes and cultures, we have found invaluable learning tools that help to explain how people in modern societies of every kind may be shaped, changed, influenced, manipulated, utterly controlled and, ultimately, pressed to the breaking point by everyday processes of information and communication.

Through these years, we've come to see the many people we have met on this new frontier of mind as pioneers, first travelers to uncharted realms coming back loaded with precious insights and hardwon lessons to share. With their help, we have worked to illuminate snapping and information disease as extraordinary new disorders occurring in otherwise healthy people—organic disorders of human experience with identifiable communication causes, effects, and cures. Throughout, our aim has been, not to deny the beliefs or experiences of any individual or group, but to bring new understanding that may help to inform and protect the millions of searchers and seekers crowding the nineties' information highways.

As the new century and millennium draw near, the freedoms of these individuals, other Americans and populations worldwide are being endangered by people and groups who have cloaked their activities in the mere trappings of spirituality, personal growth and more extreme ideologies. Many of these forces are flourishing on the strength of the historic freedoms of speech, belief and association guaranteed in the United States Constitution and its counterparts in more than a hundred nations. At the same time, critics of these groups and movements, along with many other balancing voices, have been harassed, intimidated, sued into silence and, in many instances, harmed physically. These threats hanging over journalists, scholars, mental health professionals, government officials and others working to inform the public have had profound chilling effects on the rights of these individuals, on the news media, the marketplace of ideas, and, by those effects, on all our freedoms.

As the information age advances, new ethics must be established to guide the world's diverse peoples, faiths and cultures safely into the next millennium, to ensure that the new era is not one of personal destruction and social regression but one that upholds and encourages human development and spiritual exploration. Ultimately, we believe, every society will be called on to confront the spreading spiritual and psychological abuses of the information age, to resolve the new conflicts building among competing rights and freedoms, and to develop better ways to help the human casualties on this woolly frontier.

On the frontiers of freedom, snapping is a bellwether phenomenon, one striking indicator of the deeper crisis of the mind and spirit fighting for survival in an age cut loose from its human foundations. Our work has strived to help people protect those inner resources from the new threats lurking in the engulfing information environments that now permeate all our lives. We hope this second edition of *Snapping* will continue to provide insights and help point the way to a healthier, safer and more fully human future.

FLO CONWAY AND JIM SIEGELMAN
New York, New York
August, 1995

PART ONE
A New Phenomenon

1 Snapping

Lo! I tell you a mystery.
We shall not all sleep, but we shall all be changed,
in a moment,
in the twinkling of an eye . . .

—*1 Corinthians 15:51 (RSV)*

SINCE THE SIXTIES, America and cultures worldwide have been gripped by an epidemic of sudden personality change.

On the surface, it appears that a new "millennium," a "new age" of enlightenment, is at hand. People everywhere are discovering new faiths, beliefs and personal growth practices that are changing them in ways they never dreamed. Around the country, college students searching for meaning and purpose are joining esoteric cults and fervid evangelical sects. One-time hippies and grown-up baby boomers are flocking to mainline churches and more traditional forms of religious devotion. Upwardly mobile professionals, artists and couples in conflict are taking part in new therapies that root out painful episodes from their past. Hardworking homemakers, executives and workers in every field are learning simple self-help techniques that reduce stress and tension in their daily lives.

Has humankind crossed the threshold of a great new era of personal and spiritual fulfillment? Many people think so. Vast numbers of individuals who have experienced these profound changes in their lives talk of "big breakthroughs," moments of spiritual "rebirth" and "revelation," of "getting it," "finding it" or suddenly "becoming clear." They describe soaring "peak experiences," "ecstasies," and levels of awareness they call "transcendence," "bliss" and "cosmic consciousness." Others boast of miracle cures for lifelong physical ailments and inconsolable fits of depression, while even more report rich new supplies of "inner energy" and creativity. Since the sixties, millions of people in America and elsewhere have set out in search of experiences such as these, exploring new pathways to personal fulfillment and participating in more than ten thousand techniques for expanding human awareness that have been introduced into modern culture. In the seventies, in the United States alone, six million took up some form of meditation. Three million young Americans joined more than one thousand new religious cults and sects; in the eighties, according to conservative estimates, those figures tripled. And they are growing even faster as the century's end approaches.

No doubt in the course of their explorations many people have had powerful new experiences that were the cause or catalyst of some profound improvement in their lives. But there is another side to this epidemic of personality change, a side that has been largely dismissed, downplayed or altogether ignored. It is the dark side of the experience, the side that cannot be described in glowing terms, one that has not been illuminated until now. Yet its signs are painfully familiar to Americans and people everywhere, and its effects have already been dramatically reflected in the headlines.

The news of the late-sixties and seventies was filled with appalling tragedies: the Manson family murders, the Symbionese Liberation Army's kidnapping of Patricia Hearst, the wave of random killings in New York City allegedly committed by a young postal worker, David Berkowitz, who renamed himself "Son of Sam"—and in November 1978, the macabre Peoples Temple cult tragedy in Jonestown, Guyana. What turned the former high school cheerleaders and homecoming queens of the Manson Family into obedient mass murderers? Why didn't Patty Hearst flee her captors when she had more than ample opportunity? What change could have come over Berkowitz, a young man who was almost court-martialed in the army for refusing to carry a weapon, that would prompt him to prowl the streets of New York with a .44-caliber handgun? What strange sequence of events ended in the savage killing of a United States Congressman and three journalists, and the orderly mass suicide of more than 900 men, women and children, at the Rev. Jim Jones' remote jungle commune?

The headlines of the eighties and nineties have been equally bizarre: extremist religious sects establishing vast rural outposts and sprawling international business empires, apocalyptic cults led by self-proclaimed messiahs challenging civil authorities and taking over entire communities; fundamentalist Christian sects moving boldly into politics and government; reports of satanic cults, "past lives" and "recovered memories" inundating law enforcement, mental health and the media—then, in the spring of 1993, the disastrous siege and conflagration at the Branch Davidian compound in Waco, Texas.

And beyond these headlines, countless paradoxes arise in the popular group therapies and self-help techniques that came out of the "consciousness explosion" of the sixties, in the mushroom growth of born-again Christianity in the seventies and eighties, and in the widening controversy over prominent and powerful religious sects in the nineties.

A bright young college student leaves school without warning and is discovered by her parents selling flowers on a street corner. A corporate executive quits his job on a moment's notice to sit on the beach and play the flute. A young mother abandons her family and becomes a foreign missionary after having a "personal encounter with the Holy Spirit." A homemaker in midlife runs away from home to take a month- · long course in levitation. Such stories raise larger and more perplexing questions. Are these changes good or bad? Are they permanent? What's really behind them? Who's susceptible? Me? My kids? Everyone?

For many people today, the quest for personal growth or spiritual fulfillment culminates in an experience that is unmistakably traumatic, an experience that has negative and often disastrous effects on their personalities and their lives. In contrast to the reported pleasures and benefits of the "big breakthrough," for many people sudden change comes in a moment of intense experience that is not so much a "peak" as a precipice, an unforeseen break in the continuity of awareness that may leave them detached, withdrawn, disoriented—and utterly confused. The experience itself may produce hallucinations or delusions or render the person extremely vulnerable to suggestion. It may lead to changes that alter lifelong habits, values and beliefs, disrupt friendships, marriages and family relationships, and in extreme instances, incite self-destructive, violent or criminal behavior.

Participants in esoteric cults and sects, mass-marketed self-help therapies and commercial training seminars vividly confirm the existence of this phenomenon when they speak of sudden changes they have experienced in the process of some sect ritual, therapeutic technique or group dynamic. For the most part, these people are at a loss to explain what happened to them. Many, however, describe it in one graphic, almost visible term. "Something *snapped* inside me," they report or "I just *snapped*"—as if their awareness were a piece of brittle plastic or a drawn-out rubber band. And, indeed, this is often the impression of those who are closest to them: their parents, spouses, friends and colleagues. To these observers, it appears as if the individual's entire personality has "snapped," that there is a new person inside the old one, someone completely different and unrecognizable.

Because this exceptional transformation has not been looked at on its own—although countless numbers have struggled in vain to understand their experience or gone to great lengths to rationalize it—in this book we investigate the phenomenon we call *snapping*, a term which designates the sudden, drastic alteration of personality in all its many forms. We chose this word not only because we have heard it so often from other people but because, to us, it depicts the way in which many of these intense new experiences may affect the mind's everyday powers and physically alter the brain's living information-processing pathways. Our research has confirmed that snapping is not merely a superficial alteration of behavior or belief. It can bring about deeper, organic changes in awareness and the entire structure of personality. And, we have found, it poses more pervasive threats to modern society as a whole, threats that challenge traditional psychiatric, legal and social interpretation.

As co-authors we come to this investigation from widely divergent vantage points. Flo traversed the West Coast in the late sixties and early seventies, observing in the course of her academic and professional work the heyday of America's newborn human potential movement. Out of that historic consciousness explosion came a flood of innovative group communication techniques and radical psychotherapies, among them encounter, psychodrama, Gestalt, primal therapy and guided fantasy, some of which had been used by professionals in clinical settings for decades. Once popularized, elements of these techniques spread quickly throughout the West Coast and into psychotherapy, counseling and crisis centers across the country.

In her doctoral research in communication, Flo studied these new techniques and observed their effects in both clinical and popular settings. She was struck by the proliferation of such powerful tools in the hands of many therapists and group leaders who had little or no understanding of their immediate or long-range effects, and she saw the need for new theory, research and follow-up studies. Throughout those years, her larger commitment, professionally and personally, was to reach a new understanding of human development that would go beyond the prevailing view that all human experience could be wholly explained by drawing analogies to animals and machines. In her effort to validate those aspects of experience that are uniquely human, she developed new methods of interpretation, and before national and international forums, she presented new ways of looking at the profound changes taking place among people and cultures, changes which psychiatry and the traditional social sciences had been unable to explain. Choosing as her foundation the basic principles of the communication sciences, she offered steps toward a new view of the human mind as a living system of communication processes that interact at many physical, biological and human levels. This system contained within its framework the essential elements of traditional theories of personality, new research in the technical sciences of communication—cybernetics, information theory and living systems theory—and exciting new work emerging in the field of humanistic psychology.

At the same time, Jim was taking quite a different tack back East. In his studies of philosophy, psychology and literature at Harvard University and later at Trinity College, Cambridge, he kept bumping into prevailing doctrines which proclaimed that the human "spirit," the human "imagination" and even the human "mind" didn't exist. Like Flo, he was startled to find that, because they were "subjective" and could not be "objectively verified" or "reliably reproduced," these vital human processes had been declared categorically off limits by the reductionist schools of Western science and philosophy that dominated those institutions at that time.

From an academic point of view, Jim was drawn to the mysteries of consciousness that were all around him in the early seventies: the still-rampant use of psychedelics, the growing interest in Eastern philosophy and meditation, the beginning boom of born-again Christianity, and the curious rise of the new religious cults and sects. However, he did not try to crack these riddles so much as humor them in articles he wrote for national magazines and newspapers. He wrote about college classmates who returned from retreats speaking in "tongues," their eyes on fire, and otherwise "blissed out." He told of the public gathering he attended to see a film that would reveal how anyone could attain a state of "perfect knowledge." (The presentation was delayed two hours because no one in the sponsoring organization knew how to run a movie projector.) But that was before anyone had begun to question what was going on in America's new cults, sects and therapies.

By 1974, the situation wasn't funny any longer. The Children of God, one of the first new cults of "Jesus freaks," was being investigated by the Attorney General of New York. The Hare Krishnas and the Moonies had taken to the streets, and people were being jailed around the country for attempting to "deprogram" cult members who had allegedly been "brainwashed." To add to the confusion, a new breed of entrepreneurs had begun mass-marketing human awareness on a nationwide scale, like fast food, in slick, prepackaged mass-group therapies and instant self-help techniques.

That year, the two of us joined forces in New York while working for a new national magazine. There we compared notes and personal experiences and immediately noticed some disturbing common patterns in what we'd been seeing all around us. The closer we looked, the more some of these profound breakthroughs people were talking about appeared quite different from what they were being called. Moreover, when we viewed our findings through the lens of Flo's perspective in communication, it became clear at deeper levels that many techniques being used to create intense personal and spiritual experiences posed hidden threats to fundamental processes of the mind. In the months that followed, Jim, too, became a serious student of communication, immersing himself in the major texts and seminal works of the field. Then, together, we forged a joint framework for further exploration.

We focused our investigation on America's most conspicuous and aggressive cults, sects and therapies, threading our way through their various doctrines, rituals, techniques, philosophies and private jargons to reach what we believed to be their common threat to people's minds and personalities. Early in our research, we came to the conclusion that the new religious and therapeutic groups should be viewed together because they used nearly identical methods of manipulating the mind and because, since their initial outcroppings in the sixties, many of them had become impossible to categorize. Some used sophisticated therapeutic methods yet called themselves religions and claimed tax exemptions. Others invoked the names of Hindu deities yet advertised their medical and scientific credibility. For many, refined strategies of mass marketing and mass persuasion were helping them to reap huge sums of money on a national—and international—scale. Nearly all relied on the legal sanctions of the First Amendment and similar laws in other countries that protected religious groups from government intervention; while others defied both government regulation and consumer protection through the establishment of diversified charitable trusts, foundations and nonprofit institutions.

We traveled to dozens of cities and towns to get a cross-section of opinion and experience. Like most cultural trends in America, the new sects and therapies began in the major centers of media and population on both coasts and then moved quickly inland to the heart of the country, where popular religions and grassroots movements have always found fertile soil. The largest cults established centers and temples in every major city, in many smaller towns and on most college campuses. The most popular therapies claimed scores of outlets from coast to coast and were rapidly expanding into remote regional and international markets.

In our travels, we talked with hundreds of people and heard innumerable testimonials about wonder cures and instant renewals and revelations. However, as we probed deeper, many of these accounts broke down in nonsense or contradiction. More often, we were told vivid—and surprisingly similar—stories about individual quests for personal growth and spiritual fulfillment that culminated in what we call snapping. Time after time, we heard about people who were transformed "in a moment, in the twinkling of an eye," people who, at the time, had no idea what had happened to them except that somewhere something inside them had "snapped." We heard as well about individuals whose transformations were only relatively sudden and slightly less dramatic, people who slid not instantly but in the course of a weekend or a month into states of mind that were equally baffling and, often, even more bizarre.

In this book, the people who have undergone these sudden changes speak for themselves. Our effort to understand their experiences has led us to a new perspective on the nature of personality—what it consists of, how it is formed and how it can be transformed. Here we use the term "personality" in the largest sense of the word: the living system of the human mind in its combined individual and social nature, which finds its outward expression in the unique qualities observable in every human being. On this basis, we range freely through the various levels of this system, and whether we refer to the organic process of "awareness" in terms of the more philosophical notion of "consciousness" or use the more subjective term "mind" in place of "personality," our concern always is to deal with the larger system of personality as most people use the term in its everyday sense.

We offer our perspective with one immediate goal in mind: to point out what we consider to be the hidden dangers in the communication techniques and other ritual practices employed by many new cults, sects and therapies. Given a comprehensive picture of these dangers, the reader may better determine the difference between a cult and a legitimate religion and may find some criteria for establishing when a worthwhile therapeutic method is being put to potentially harmful use.

On a broader level, however, this investigation of snapping addresses questions that touch the whole of modern society. Today, everyone is vulnerable to snapping, even if he or she has never considered participating in a cult, sect or self-help therapy. In recent years, many practices employed by these new groups have come to permeate every level of modern society, from mainline religion and mass media, to government and business, to our daily social interactions. Yet most people have little understanding of the extent to which each of us—not only our beliefs and opinions but the whole of our personalities—may be shaped and changed by these pervasive communication practices and by things we experience every day.

In the course of our work, we have encountered only one objection to our method of investigation. "Why," some people have asked, "don't you participate in these new sect rituals and therapeutic practices yourselves? You can't possibly understand them unless you have actually *experienced* them." To that charge, we take no stand in defense of objectivity or of maintaining our professional detachment. We realized early on that we would be unable to gain any perspective at all if we subjected ourselves to each of the sect rituals and therapeutic techniques described in this book. Even if we did, it wouldn't work. No investigator, journalist or social scientist who heads into a group in search of "the experience" can possibly capture the experience of those who have made a personal commitment to that group.

In another sense, however, each of us has already experienced the new sects and therapies in ways no cult member or group participant ever could. We have known close friends and colleagues to return from cult retreats and group training seminars as complete strangers. We have been personally confronted on the streets, where our donations were solicited and our beliefs assaulted. We have attended private dinners and intimate gatherings at which we were matter-of-factly condemned to hell and told that we were agents of "Satan's world." And for two decades now, we have watched with growing concern the widening exploitation and abuse of our fundamental American freedoms expressed in the First Amendment to the U.S. Constitution, and the turmoil spreading in many nations around those same fundamental human rights and freedoms.

The phenomenon of snapping has changed the news, the law, the meaning of religion, and the people we live with and work around every day. In the pages that follow, we will explore this extraordinary phenomenon in detail: the attitudes it grew out of, the techniques those attitudes gave rise to, the experiences produced by those techniques, and the deep-reaching effects of those experiences on individuals and societies. We turn first to the search for self, America's legacy from the sixties, which was transformed into something very different in that enigmatic decade, the seventies.

2 The Search

*The office of those who seek new worlds is to stumble upon
those they never expected to find.*

—*Cervantes*

IN THE SIXTIES, with the rise in leisure and affluence, the advent of
psychedelic drugs and the rediscovery of Eastern thought, millions of
Americans set out to explore the underused, often dormant powers of
thought, feeling, imagination, self-expression and relationship that have
come to be known as their human potential. In the process, they crossed
new thresholds of sensation and discovered the "high"—the privileged
domain of peak experience attainable through drugs, encounter groups,
meditation and other paths to transcendence. For the first time, many
people recognized this experience as a missing link in their development and were drawn to it. The search was on: for the highest high,
the tallest peak, the deepest reach of experience.

Beyond their immediate physical and emotional rewards, the tools
and techniques of the "human potential movement" held a greater promise of release: from childhood traumas, undesirable habits, conditioned
roles and social expectations. Inevitably, however, this rich new world
of personal growth became subject to exploitation and abuse as un-
learned, uncommitted amateurs moved in to till the field. Without warnings or guidelines, America's searchers, in their earnest longing to find
something higher and their sincere desire for self-improvement, had
no way of interpreting their new experiences, of separating the truly
spiritual from the sham, or of distinguishing genuine personal growth
from artificially induced sensation.

Soon, not surprisingly, people started getting hurt, set back financially and personally.

It's not easy to locate those who have been hurt, for they rarely
want to talk about it. The gains derived from the search arc by nature
a personal matter, and so its losses too become a torturous private

ordeal. Often, people are reluctant to admit that their best efforts yielded something less than the stunning breakthrough they were seeking. Many are deeply embarrassed at what they consider to be a personal shortcoming or insurmountable flaw in their capacity for growth. Some may be unable to overcome the fear and confusion that linger for months, even years, following the traumatic climax of their quest. Others who have sought psychiatric care, even briefly, are obscured forever within the confidentiality of the doctor-patient relationship.

When we began our investigation of sudden personality change in the mid-seventies, we quickly learned that the traditional channels of communication would be virtually useless for our purposes. Then we passed a quiet word through the extended grapevines of the human potential movement and a large network of contacts opened up to us, revealing beneath the jubilant surface of the movement a substratum teeming with shocking, often tragic tales of snapping.

A woman we will call Jean Turner was only one of an inestimable number of people of all ages who strayed into the shadows of the human potential movement. The man who told us about her was a respected psychologist who had been active in the movement from its beginning, but he later became troubled by some of the paths down which it had wandered. He had known Jean Turner for several years. When he gave us her name, he explained that she had had an "extreme reaction" to one of the mass therapies we discussed, but he said that he did not want to prejudice our conversation. He just told us to call her and we did. She offered to come out to the small house we had rented for our initial round of interviews on the West Coast.

When she appeared at noon the next day, our first impression was of a tall, attractive, middle-aged woman whom we might have met anywhere. Her shyness, even apprehensiveness, as she sat down with us seemed quite normal under the circumstances of our meeting. After brief amenities we told her about our project and our backgrounds. She nodded, smiled, and said she would try to help us in whatever way she could. She told us she was fifty-two, a college-educated mother of three, recently divorced, just visiting the West Coast from her home in a city some distance away.

She had read a newspaper article that provided her with a term for her current social status. "Displaced Homemaker," she said. "There are so many of us and nobody has paid much attention to this group of women who, after years of raising children and husbands, come out middle-aged and without a skill. What do you do then? You have no money, no security, nothing. Who are you?"

She smiled again, but her eyes were glistening with tears.

"I had raised my children through every kind of crisis imaginable," she said. "When they were grown and healthy I felt pretty good about it, but it was as though the most important part of my life was over. I had to find meaning. That's when I started to search."

Her search for meaning first led her into a new experience she was hearing about in the media and from friends: Transcendental Meditation. The invention of Indian guru Maharishi Mahesh Yogi, TM in the seventies became the largest and most widely known of the new mass-marketed self-help techniques. It was hailed as a nonchemical means of relieving nervous tension, and its relatively low cost made it an ideal point of embarkation for the practical-minded or casual seeker.

Its initial impact on Jean Turner was profound.

"TM gave me glimpses of what it was like to be living on a different level. After a four-day residence course, I came back home and for two weeks my body and mind were completely one. I was just working and going about things, but every day would seem to fly by. I would look back and say, *what an incredible experience to be moving on this level.* That was the beginning; it really opened me up to the search."

Through TM, Jean told us, she found relief from stress, as the technique promised. She experienced enjoyable physical sensations of relaxation and bliss. These initial moments of fulfillment spurred the expansion of her search. For a while, she continued to pursue the Maharishi's path of exploration, attending several TM weekend retreats and enrolling in a TM "Science of Creative Intelligence" course. Then a friend invited her to participate in another new experience, a small-group encounter session.

"I didn't know what an encounter group was. I had no idea—" She smiled. "I even stopped and bought a notebook thinking I was going to hear a lecture." Then she turned serious. "At first it was too much for me. I saw all this closeness and touching. I'd had no exposure to anything like that before, and at one point I just ran out of the room. Then a lovely young woman took me aside and we talked for an hour. I had never known what it was like to be close with another woman."

After she got over her initial fear, Jean's first encounter-group experience turned out to be a pleasant one. There was nothing mystical about it, she explained, no overwhelming effects, but the experience of "sharing" touched something in her and prompted her to investigate other encounter groups.

In the next one, she found a form of transcendence that surpassed anything she had become acquainted with in TM.

"I thought I must be getting in touch with my psychic energy. How else could you explain it? It was all mind, nobody was doing anything or saying anything, and I just got high. I got so high I didn't know what to do with it. It was a beautiful feeling of well-being, warmth and loving. It was so strange, at first, because nobody seemed to be making it happen to me. I went home and all night long these warm feelings kept coming up in my body. I felt that I either wanted to have fantastic sex or be a four-year-old child."

The "encounter high," as it has been called, the first great revelation of the consciousness explosion, not only gave Jean Turner new sensations of warmth and inner peace; it opened her to new dimensions of experience through intimate encounters with other people in later groups and in her daily life during the next few years. When she heard about the mass-group therapy called "est," she said, she was far from naïve about the powerful effects of meditation and encounter.

Est—Erhard Seminars Training—was the most successful self-help therapy of the seventies. Described as "sixty hours that transform your life," the original est "training" served 250 people at a time in four marathon sessions, usually held over two consecutive weekends. Trainees gathered in a hotel ballroom or other large meeting area and signed agreements not to leave their seats without permission or to speak unless called on. No eating, smoking, drinking or use of drugs was permitted. Bathroom breaks, which came every twelve hours in the beginning, were later increased because of frequent accidents.

As our conversation turned to est that day, Jean Turner stiffened. Up to that point she had answered our questions with relative ease. Now she became guarded and oddly remote, as if suddenly threatened and wondering whether or not she could trust us.

She hesitated, then recited a phrase we had heard frequently from others: "Let me say first that I feel est was one of the most positive things I've ever done."

We said nothing. She looked back and forth between us, appeared to change her mind, and began again.

"Est was extremely different from anything I had ever been in," she said, her voice low and shaky. "I say that because I was personally encountered by the trainer and taken through a lot of trauma. I'm still afraid to talk about it, because I haven't found people to be very understanding."

We assured her that she was not the first person we had talked to who had expressed reservations about est. This seemed to help, and gradually her story emerged. It came out in jumbled sequence, in rushes of words interspersed with emotionally charged pauses and, occasionally, tears. It was as if her est experience still lay in fragments in her memory. Now and again we asked gently for clarification, but we did not try to force the pace or confront her with our own conclusions. Ultimately we got a chronological picture of her story.

Est, she said, had been for her a grueling physical ordeal. "During the first body process—it was a meditation technique—I experienced a great deal of pain in my legs," she said. "After that first full day of training, we left very late and I had this terrible pain from my knees down. The next day I was scared. If I hadn't paid two hundred and fifty dollars I wouldn't have gone back. I was tired. I was on the verge of tears, but I made myself go back. The first thing I did was tell the trainer how I felt. I said, 'I'm scared. I have some idea of what this is all about, getting things up from my past, but do I have to experience my whole life here?' That was when the trainer came over to me and encountered me, taking me back through the first time I ever experienced pain in my legs. Of course, it went back to when I had rheumatic fever as a child. I've always had weak legs. There were days when I couldn't walk to the bus stop because of the pain in my legs. I had been treated for arthritis over the years and I was in pretty bad physical condition when I started the training. The doctors had said they couldn't do anything for it. They said I had to live with it."

She told us that her est trainer had wasted no time in excavating buried experiences and emotions from her past.

Then—"I had a healing," she said. "When the trainer focused on all that, it was indescribable. It was too much. The pain in my legs was so intense. Then I felt waves of heat come over me and all the pain went away. I wouldn't choose to go through that pain again, but since that day I haven't had a single pain in my legs."

Presumably, the intensity of that confrontation broke through something deep and painful that had plagued her all her life. The resulting cure was real and dramatic, and it left Jean Turner in a state of physical ecstasy that kept up throughout the following week. Toward the end of her next est weekend, however, she said she experienced a second overwhelming—but very different—emotional reaction.

"It came up in me like a ball," she told us, her voice rising. "I thought I was going to be sick. At the same time I experienced a release from my body as though somebody had pulled a ripcord in me. It just shot up and unraveled out of my body. That whole day I hadn't known where I was. Then suddenly I found myself screaming at the trainer. I was calling him a son of a bitch. It came out at him, I don't know why, except that the sound of his voice was getting to me. He was encountering someone else when it came up and I let go. When I sat down, my body was just flooded with feeling. I think the fact that all this anger had come up in front of two hundred and fifty people must have had some effect. I was so humiliated. It just kept coming and coming in great waves. I felt all this heat in my wrists and I felt like I couldn't move my arms. But I sat there with it because I knew there was going to be a break soon, and I said to myself, *I'm getting out of here.* And I did. I managed to leave the training at that point."

Here was the phenomenon we call snapping in its most intense physical form.

"I walked out of est," she continued, "and I walked about a mile home and just went to bed. When I woke up the next morning, I was disoriented and scared to death. I didn't want any part of est. I called the city's mental health service and they sent out a crew. They stayed with me for about an hour. They seemed to understand what I was going through. One of them asked me if I had blown my mind and I said, 'Yes, I don't know what that means, but it sounds like what's happened.' I was afraid. I felt very shaky. My son was coming in that night and I didn't think I could drive out to meet him. After the first weekend of the training, I had sent him this incredible note: *Get your ass over here! I have to clean up my shit!* He'd never heard any of this language. It was est jargon and I was full of it."

Later that day, she did decide to make contact with est.

"I called their office. I never talked to the trainer, but the manager told me this had happened because I hadn't gone to the very end of the training. Something was unfinished. So I agreed to do the second weekend over in the next training, which was a month away."

In the interim, she experienced "the most marvelous body feelings I had ever known," she said. "I had never felt so good. Something was going on that I didn't want to interrupt. I was just high all the time."

Finally, overtaken by the urge to share her feelings, she went to the est office.

"I walked in and shouted, *IF YOU DON'T GET IT, THEN YOU AIN'T GOT IT!* The secretary looked at me as if to say, What's going on with you? I walked into the manager's office and he hugged me."

When the month's wait was over, Jean Turner completed her est training without further incident. Afterward, her physical high continued and spilled over into other realms.

"After seven more days of experiencing these body things, I began fantasizing," she recalled. "It was beautiful. I was out of touch with reality; it was as though I could see on a different dimension. I experienced an intense joy the whole time."

Then her state of mind took an even more startling upturn.

"I reached a point where the fantasies became real," she said. "It was poetical. I was speaking in biblical languages. At times I couldn't open my mouth, but when I did it came out in verse. I was alone in my apartment for a week. I felt like I was getting a whole new body, a renewal. I was extremely active. I couldn't stop dancing. I didn't want to stop, it was too good. My body just felt so powerful."

Then her high topped out and veered sharply downward.

"I can't explain it except that I became afraid," she told us. "Somewhere I knew this behavior wasn't right and I started feeling fear. So I called the est office and the manager asked me where I was and I told him. He said, 'We can't help you, but we can *assist* you.' He told me to come to a seminar that night, but I needed help right then."

In panic, she called a friend—the man who later put us in touch with her—who arranged for her to go into a psychiatric hospital. She spent two weeks there and then was released at her own request without further medication or professional care. Not long afterward, however, her delusions returned and she was readmitted to the hospital. The second time she was released on thorazine, a powerful tranquilizer. For the next ten months she underwent weekly psychiatric care and was put on antidepressant drugs.

Est became the most controversial of the new mass therapies. In the seventies, it was the subject of countless magazine articles, several best-selling books and endless hours of talk-show discussion. Celebrities who numbered among est's first 100,000 graduates included entertainers Valerie Harper, Cher, Cloris Leachman, John Denver, astronaut Buzz Aldrin, and Watergate political figure John Dean.

The est package was put together in 1971 by Werner Erhard, a man whose personal background quickly assumed mythic proportions. Born Jack Rosenberg in Philadelphia, Werner Erhard started his career as a used-car salesman. In 1960 he left his job, his wife and four children and headed west to California. On his way, the legend had it, he read an article in *Esquire,* "The Men Who Made the New Germany," and pieced together a new identity for himself from biographical threads of Werner Heisenberg, the formulator of the Uncertainty Principle of modern physics, and Ludwig Erhard, who served as economics minister in postwar West Germany. As the new Erhard, he arrived in California, where he spent some time training encyclopedia salesmen and began experimenting with the various techniques emerging from the consciousness explosion. Eventually, he began working for Mind Dynamics, one of the first consumer enterprises to package the discoveries being made in the still-experimental stages of the human potential movement. Then, in 1971, Erhard fused all his newly acquired knowledge into est, a conglomeration of techniques and principles from such scattered sources as encounter, psychodrama, Gestalt therapy, Scientology, Zen Buddhism, Dale Carnegie—and marine boot camp.

The actual title of est was reputed to have come from a science-fiction novel, *est: The Steersman Handbook,* by a now untraceable author named L. Clark Stevens. Stevens' est stood for *electronic social transformation.* His book foretold the rise of the "est people" a generation of postliterate men who would bring about the transformation of society. Not long after he formulated est, Erhard was said to have had his own great catalytic experience while driving in his Mustang. Somewhere along the highway, he "got it"—est's term for its own brand of enlightenment—in a moment of insight that informed him that "What is, is," and "What isn't, isn't." This experience led Erhard to further revelations. He said later, "What I recognized is that you can't put it together. It's already together, and what you have to do is experience it being together."

For the most part, the early est training consisted of endless hours of lectures on the nature of reality, perception and belief systems. The lectures were intertwined with a series of est "processes," mental exercises aimed at erasing the trainee's "tapes" (est jargon for patterns of thought and feeling that, est said, prevent one from fully experiencing life). The course of the training was laced with direct verbal assaults in which trainees were dubbed "turkeys" and "assholes" and drawn into "personal encounters" with the est trainer. During the course of those early weekends, many trainees cried, fainted, vomited or lost sphincter control. At the end of the training, trainees were supposed to "get it" in a moment of sudden realization that they alone were responsible for creating everything in life that happened to them.

Like many graduates, Jean Turner failed to "get it" in the est fashion. The pain in her legs vanished as a result of the intense physical outpouring she experienced, and for this she could be grateful. For a brief time, too, she had a taste of est's often-stated goal: "to transform your ability to experience living so that the situations you have been putting up with clear up in the process of life itself." But the fulfillment she sought in est never came about. When we met her, almost two years after the training, she seemed confused and vulnerable.

Jean's story naturally raises two important questions: Might she have been unusually vulnerable or, as some might claim, predisposed to a severe episode in the aftermath of the est training? Was her experience a rare exception among est graduates? We could not say with certainty that Jean's est training was solely responsible for what happened to her. Inevitably today, questions of vulnerability arise. No statistics were made available on the later lives of est graduates. There was, however, documented evidence which showed that Jean Turner was not the only est trainee to have undergone an emotional disturbance extreme enough to require psychiatric treatment.

Not long after our conversation with her, we read an article in the *American Journal of Psychiatry* titled "Psychiatric Disturbances Associated with Erhard Seminars Training," the first such report in the professional literature. There three psychiatrists described five cases that "represent a segment of est trainees who came to our attention in a variety of emergency psychiatric settings." Each of these experienced reactions very similar to, or even more extreme than, Jean Turner's; four of the five cases had no record of previous psychiatric disorder.

At the end of our interview, Jean Turner admitted that she was still anxious—and still searching.

"Lately I've been experiencing some discomfort and tension in my body," she said, "and I've been waking up with feelings of anger. But I don't want to go back on the drugs they gave me at the hospital. I want to deal with it.

"I went to see this doctor who does acupuncture," she said as we escorted her to her car. "He gave me a book and I'm reading it now. It sounds like something I will pursue."

In 1985, riding the waves of the eighties, Erhard changed est's name to the more businesslike handle "The Forum" and raised the price to $525. He replaced est's boot-camp encounters and harsh training rules with more accommodating "dialogues" and training "requests." But according to many customers, the new package contained essentially the same product. Forum participants were often given sickness bags in case of vomiting. Some trainees were designated "body-catchers" to catch those who fainted, and there were more serious casualties. A 25-year-old Connecticut man dropped dead during a Forum session. His attorney said the otherwise healthy man died of fright. In 1992, a federal judge ordered Erhard to pay $380,000 to a Maryland woman who, like Jean Turner, suffered bouts of euphoria, anxiety, manic behavior and, then, a full-fledged mental breakdown after her Forum training.

In the face of mounting business disputes, an IRS inquiry, a messy divorce action, and claims of physical and emotional abuse by his daughters, Erhard left the United States in 1991. He reappeared in Russia, set up a network of foreign entities and financial accounts, and proceeded to expand his diverse training enterprises in the fertile markets of Eastern Europe.

3 The Fall

Theseus and his comrade Pirithous in their descent to Hades to bring back the goddess of the underworld . . . sat down to rest for a while, only to find that they had grown to the rocks and could not rise.

—*Carl Jung*
Modern Man in Search of a Soul

THE CHILDREN OF the seventies set out on a different search. The great cultural upheaval had subsided, and in lieu of self-realization their goal became spiritual fulfillment, a headier destination and one with deeper pitfalls along the road.

By mid-decade, as the smoke from the sixties, Vietnam, and Watergate began to clear, those pitfalls became apparent with the emergence of a new subgroup of Americans. They were the first of a new generation of "cult" members, young people who had left home and school in pursuit of those rare moments of insight and meaning sought by us all. What they found were organizations such as the Unification Church, the Children of God, the International Society for Krishna Consciousness, the Divine Light Mission, the Forever Family, the Church of Scientology, the Love Family, the Assembly, the Body, the Way, the Farm, the Church Universal and Triumphant, and the Tony and Susan Alamo Foundation. In the beginning, the new cults gave little cause for concern. Their disciples were few in number, and whether they went barefoot, shaved their heads and chanted, or wore dark suits and ties and passed out leaflets, they were all simply variations on a familiar American theme: law-abiding citizens exercising their constitutional right to freedom of religion. If those citizens seemed a little strange, at least they didn't get in anyone's way. At worst, the early cult members were mere loose threads in America's colorful social fabric.

As they became more numerous, their various faiths and practices began to blur in the public eye. The question of whether someone was a follower of the Swami, the Reverend, the Perfect Master, the Guru, the Yogi, His Holiness, Krishna or even Jesus became less important to those the disciple approached than the flowers, incense, books, peanut brittle, cookies, vacuum cleaners or other items he or she was selling. For in addition to their earnest looks and tireless proselytizing, many of the new young cult members had taken up fund raising in a big way. They had learned to solicit door-to-door in residential neighborhoods, to set up folding tables outside suburban shopping malls, and to make intensely personal approaches in bus and train stations and airport terminals coast to coast and worldwide.

This industrious and charitable public image often bore no relation whatsoever to the bizarre stories being told reporters, judges, doctors and anyone else who would lend an ear to a distraught parent or jilted lover. These stories told of people who had changed completely, almost overnight. While they claimed to have found true happiness and fulfillment, many seemed to have lost their spontaneity and humor, their free will and their individuality in the process. They had become estranged, presenting themselves in odd postures ranging from stiff to animated, ecstatic to withdrawn. There was something eerie about them, but it was nothing you could put your finger on.

None dared call it crazy, not in any clinical sense. In some ways, cult members functioned even better after their conversions. Most could not be accused of even the most familiar frailties or conceivable vices. They had stopped smoking and drinking; often they had given up drugs and sex as well.

Nevertheless, alarmed by the changes they were witnessing, desperate parents began to take extreme measures to rescue their children. They sought help from "deprogrammers" who would kidnap cult members and attempt to free them from the groups' effects. Then the legal battles began, as young people sought to prosecute those who had tried to prevent them from practicing the professed religion of their choice.

A young married couple whom we will call Lawrence and Cathy Gordon made the front page of their hometown paper when their parents managed to recover them from South Korean Rev. Sun Myung Moon's Unification Church. The article described the organization's wealth, tax status and political affiliations, and gave a detailed history of Lawrence and Cathy's involvement. But the newspaper account didn't reveal what it was like to go through it all. Despite extensive media coverage of the cults, little attention was given in those early days to the personal impact of the cult experience.

Soon after we started our research, it became clear to us that America's growing fraternity of ex-cult members held the key to the phenomenon of snapping. They alone had gone through the most bizarre forms of sudden personality change and come back to tell the story. With the goal of unraveling this mysterious experience, we traveled to the small midwestern town where Lawrence and Cathy Gordon then lived and worked.

Like the Displaced Homemaker who ventured into TM, encounter groups and est, the Gordons were everyday people—good, decent, healthy. They were also typical ex-cult members, college-educated and from upper-middle-class homes. Lawrence was a strapping, fair-haired, all-American type. Cathy was diminutive and vivacious, an outdoorswoman with long strawberry-blond hair and a cheery smile.

Cathy began. She took us back to her first close encounter with the energetic recruiting forces of Moon's church.

"I was standing outside the public library when this guy who was about six feet tall came up to me," she said. "He seemed to be very happy, like he had a lot of answers to things. He said they had a group called the New Age Fellowship, just a group of people who would come together and sit around and talk about different things."

For Cathy, who had earned her degree in sociology, the idea of an evening of intellectual stimulation was appealing. She explained that she and Lawrence had spent some time traveling around the country after his thwarted attempt to get into medical school, and they had only recently returned to town and were just starting to become socially established after their long absence. In this casual and friendly context, the "Moonie's" invitation was attractive. To Cathy, it sounded like a way for Lawrence and her to meet people like themselves.

Yet something odd about this Moonie struck her.

"He seemed to be in a different place than most people," she told us. "There was an aura about him. At the time, he seemed kind of spiritual. He asked me to this dinner they had and I felt strange. I had to lean against the wall. He seemed to be a very powerful person."

Lawrence, who arrived on the scene later, was unmoved by that initial meeting.

"When I drove up," he said, "this guy was talking to her and I shouted, 'Come on, Cathy!' Finally she broke away from him and he came running up to my car in the middle of the street. He said, 'Hey, I just invited your wife to this dinner where we sit around and talk philosophy and sing songs.' I said, 'Sure, sure, thanks a lot.' I just wanted to get home. But a couple of days later, when we were talking about it, we said, 'What the heck, let's go check it out and see what it's all about.' "

First encounters with cults are rarely anything extraordinary. People may sense something strange about cult members, but the decision to check out the cult is usually a casual one. When Lawrence and Cathy attended their first Unification Church gathering, however, the Moonies' impact on them was much less subtle than before. This time Lawrence felt it more than Cathy. He leaned forward in his chair as he described it.

"We went to the dinner, and there was a funny feeling in the room," he recalled. "I couldn't pinpoint it, but the people seemed to be putting on an act. It wasn't something I wanted to think about. They kept the ball rolling; then this speaker came up. He was a very, very dynamic person; he just radiated when he talked. He started off normal and calm. Then he got more into it and his eyes just glowed. It was amazing how much power his eyes had. We sat there glued to him as he communicated this urgent message to us about saving the world. As he talked, he walked around. Every muscle was involved. He was talking to us with his whole body. Because of him we decided to take up the invitation to the weekend workshop in the country, to find out what made him so enthusiastic."

Cathy put in, "My initial reaction to these people was, *I don't know what they have, but I want it.* They all seemed serene, ecstatic or very, very loving."

"That Friday, all the way up to the workshop we were singing," Lawrence remembered. "Like we were going to summer camp or something. They woke us up at six o'clock the next morning and made us hurry to the lectures. We did exercises—stretching, shouting, singing, running through the trees—then had breakfast and toured the camp. There was a lecturer who introduced himself and then began talking about something called the Principles of Creation. You couldn't deny the first lecture. It was about God's love for man —it was perfectly in line with Catholicism in every way. Lecture Two was the Fall of Man, which was a very heavy lecture. It made you feel guilty for the way you were living and the general attitudes of society. It had a lot to do with sexuality."

After each lecture, the Gordons and about twenty or thirty other new recruits were assigned to small groups where church members answered their questions.

"I kept asking about Masters and Johnson," Lawrence told us, with a boyish grin, "but they said you should totally deny all your sexual feelings and your feelings for other people. I didn't believe it right away, and they said, 'Didn't you feel that way when you were young? Didn't you feel guilty and want to cover yourself up?' I said, 'No, I didn't,' and the Moonies all said, yes, they did."

Cathy had been more affected by the exhortations of the second lecture.

"When they were talking about the Fall of Man," she recalled, "they said that we all had Satan's blood spiritually in us. I felt really dirty, and I had this sense of shame that made me feel even worse."

The final lectures were a mixture of traditional religious references and themes from history, philosophy and American politics.

"They went through Hellenism and the Reformation," said Lawrence. "Then they arrived at this twenty-one-year period of history—which was supposed to be what Jacob went through—when Communism would be at its peak because Vietnam was a failure and the American people hadn't rallied behind Nixon, which was an indemnity thing because MacArthur didn't save Southeast Asia from the Communists because of President Truman."

Cathy picked up the original thread. "At the end of the weekend workshop," she said, "they left us with the idea that Christ could be coming very soon. In fact, he could already be here. You say to yourself, *Wow, could this be true? Could it be?* But they still hadn't even mentioned Reverend Moon."

Then, according to Lawrence, just before that weekend of much talk and little sleep came to an end, the church leaders made their first direct attempt to bring the two of them into the fold.

"They spent two straight hours trying to talk us into staying," he said. "They told us that when we went back down into the regular world, Satan would invade us. I'd never believed in Satan before, but somehow they got to me. When we left and were driving down, I felt really weird, and it kept up the whole next day while we were getting our business done so we could go back up."

Even though at this early stage the Gordons could feel the "weird" effects of Moon's conversion technique, they were unable to focus their impressions. As Lawrence described it, he and Cathy returned to an everyday world that had grown alien and sinister.

"When we came back down, we thought we were still in control of ourselves," he explained, "but when I look back on it now I can see how heavy their influence was. As soon as we walked into the house, my mom and dad looked at us and said, 'What's wrong with you? What's wrong with your eyes?' But we had been told to anticipate this, that the rest of the world would see us as different because we knew the truth. I just thought, *Aha! Maybe I'm getting spiritual or something!*"

Cathy explained the resolution of that first confrontation with Lawrence's family.

"We had been told that a lot of times people will get sucked back into the real world and Satan through their families, and you had to cut that emotional tie and look at your parents objectively. Lawrence's mother got frantic when she realized we were going back; she ran out to the car crying, but we remained very cool and untouched by her. As we drove away, I said, 'It must be hard for you to see your mother like that.' And Lawrence said, 'That's not my mother. That woman who is crying and carrying on is not my real mother.' And I was proud of him then, for seeing things the way they were."

Lawrence and Cathy drove back to the Moon camp, confident that they were at last seeing the world in its proper perspective. Once formally in the cult and swayed further by repeated fervid lectures, they became totally engulfed.

"I remember looking in the mirror one time," said Cathy. "We were told not to look in the mirror, because it was such a vain thing, but I just glanced at it as I was walking by and I saw my eyes and I thought, *Oh, boy, my eyes are on fire. I'm really high, spiritually high!*"

Then they described the same kind of high that led to Jean Turner's emotional breakdown in est, which grew for them into a sustained alteration of awareness.

"By the end of the next week, I remember feeling objective about the world, really detached from it," said Lawrence. "The first day of that seven-day workshop, the lecturer had said to us, 'By the end of the week, you're all going to be just like me. You're all going to be walking around smiling.' And we were."

Along with the other new converts, the Gordons experienced not just one but frequent peak moments when they felt as if they were receiving a revelation.

"Two other people and I were asked to pray for all the new members," Cathy recalled, "so we prayed out loud for three hours. At the end of the prayer, the leader came in and said, 'You've been praying long enough. Why don't you break it up in a few minutes.' I realized that I had one more minute to make this prayer really count, so I prayed even harder and just then I felt like everything I was saying was being sucked into a vacuum. When I stood up, I felt like thin air; I had to brace myself. I felt this energy, it was kind of an ecstasy. It just flowed through me like a sensation of tingling. It sent shocks through me, and I equated it with divine love."

Here again was the moment of snapping in an intense physical form. Lawrence reported having a similar experience, "when I felt my spirit opening up."

"One day I started to have doubts, so I said to myself, *I have to go out and pray about this,* because that's what you're supposed to do when you're weak. So I went out and prayed just like Cathy did, and after—I don't know how long, I have no recollection of time—I started to get strong again. I felt a tingling in my back like raindrops, and I thought, *Wow, this is a sign!* It felt cool; it lasted about ten seconds, like God was about twenty feet above me with a little sprinkler."

Soon after they moved into the church, Lawrence and Cathy were separated. Cathy's participation remained largely subservient, the woman's fate in many cults, while Lawrence was sent halfway across the country to begin fund-raising activities. Securely anchored in his altered state of awareness, he returned to the everyday world, dressing up in the plain dark suit and tie worn uniformly by male Moonies in the seventies to begin solicitations that would often keep up twenty hours a day. Now, on the streets, the same power Cathy had noticed when she met her first Moonie had become an unmistakable feature of her husband's own demeanor.

"I felt a rush when we were out campaigning, a real high," Lawrence told us. "I was bursting with joy. People would open the door in a humdrum mood and as I talked they would get high with me."

According to Cathy, the effect was contagious.

"When we came back from a weekend workshop, Lawrence talked to his sister for a couple of hours. She was affected for days. People where she worked noticed it all week."

But the high that communicated itself so effectively was frequently marred by the Gordons' discomfort and personal misgivings.

"Every day of fund raising people would make comments to me," Lawrence said. "I was getting all the negativity that the church predicted, but it was supposed to be Satan attacking me. We were told to be humble toward people and say, 'I'm sorry you feel that way.' But many times doubts came up in my mind when I was fund raising. I'd think, *Do I really want to go into this plush restaurant and bother these people who are having a nice dinner with their family? Do I want to do that and make a fool of myself?* But the church said, *Try always,* and I'd find myself at banquets, going from table to table asking people for money." He accomplished his goal. The first year he was in the Unification Church, he raised $50,000.

Exhaustion was a more pervasive problem in the Gordons' life in the Unification Church. According to church doctrines, it was considered a sin to be sleepy. Another former Moonie we interviewed later told us more about this problem.

"I'd be out fund raising in a parking lot somewhere, feeling very heavy, having trouble keeping my eyes open, and I'd go back somewhere and lie down," he said. "One time some people called the police. They thought I was dead. I saw other members fall asleep while they were talking, just leaning in a car window, right in the middle of a sentence.

"Anyone who can't stay awake is said to have *sleep-spirit* problems," he went on. "Sleep spirits were supposed to be the spirits of people who had died. They were very low—they came from Satan's world—and if church leaders found someone with sleep-spirit problems, they would treat him very badly. One time at their training center in Barrytown, New York, a Japanese member slugged me very hard. When we would get tired, they'd tell us to go take a cold shower. Sometimes they would use squirt guns to keep people awake."

The Unification Church holds a special place among the cults. With a membership once estimated to be as high as 60,000 to 80,000. It remains one of the largest, richest and most active cults in America and more than a dozen other countries. Despite numerous questions raised by private citizens and government investigators regarding its tax-exempt status and worldwide religious, political and business operations, the church has survived virtually unscathed every claim made against it. Despite many legal battles over the kidnapping and deprogramming of its members, it continues to operate virtually without restraint on college campuses, in small towns, big cities and major world capitals.

The Rev. Sun Myung Moon, the founder of the Holy Spirit Association for the Unification of World Christianity, is a wealthy Korean industrialist turned evangelist. While church members usually state publicly that Moon makes no claim to be the Messiah, former Moonies we interviewed told us that while they were in the church he was openly referred to as the Messiah and that he himself claimed to be a divine being sent to earth to finish the work of Jesus Christ, which he saw as the breeding of the "ideal race." The sect appears to have taken steps toward that breeding program in its infamous mass marriage ceremonies involving thousands of Moonies, many of different races and nationalities, and total strangers to one another, reportedly paired by Moon or other sect leaders.

Since it was founded in Korea in 1954, the Unification Church has grown to enormous proportions and accumulated immense wealth. In addition to his munitions interests in Korea, Moon owns factories that produce ginseng tea, titanium products, pharmaceuticals and parts for automatic rifles; yet four decades after the sect's founding, Moon church members still could be seen selling flowers on street corners. In the seventies, church monies were used to make sizable investments in American real estate, including a huge retreat in Barrytown, New York—Moon's primary American residence—and the old New Yorker Hotel in midtown Manhattan, purchased for a reported $5 million in 1976, which was made the church's national headquarters. In 1994, sect leaders announced plans to reopen part of the historic structure as a hotel.

Through the seventies and eighties, the Unification Church conducted many of its American recruiting activities under the name of CARP, the Collegiate Association for the Research of Principle. The church repeatedly denied reports that it operated through dozens of other organizations, among them the International Federation for Victory Over Communism, the Professors Academy for World Peace and the Little Angels of Korea. Until they were exposed publicly in the mid-seventies, Moon had church members doing volunteer work for many members of the U.S. Congress.

In 1978, a congressional inquiry found that the multi-pronged Moon organization had systematically violated federal tax, immigration, banking and Foreign Agents Registration Act laws. It also found evidence of long-standing links between the Unification Church and the South Korean Central Intelligence Agency, which had reportedly sought to use the sect in the U.S. to influence American public opinion and government policies toward South Korea. In the eighties, a Moon enterprise launched a daily newspaper in New York City, which assumed the name of the defunct *New York Tribune*, and a Spanish-language daily, *Noticias Del Mundo*. In 1982, another Moon-affiliated business bought the fallen *Washington Star* newspaper in the nation's capital and revived it as the *Washington Times*. The ultraconservative *Times* won wide favor in the capital during the years of the Reagan and Bush administrations. Also in 1982, Moon was indicted and convicted in New York on federal charges of tax evasion, conspiracy, obstruction of justice and perjury. After serving eighteen months in federal prison, he was released early for good behavior and went on to become a generous supporter of "new right" and "religious right" political activities in the U.S. and worldwide.

The Moon empire now encompasses commercial business, mass communications and ideological operations throughout the U.S., Latin America, Europe and Asia. In 1987, the name of one Moon organization, CAUSA, the Confederation of the Associations for the Unification of the Societies of the Americas, reputed to be the political arm of the

Unification Church, was found on a secret White House organizational chart surrendered to Congress during the "Iran-contra" investigation. CAUSA and other Moon groups reportedly contributed significant sums to the Nicaraguan *contra* rebels and went on to play active roles in U.S. presidential campaigns and domestic political debates.

Participants in Moon groups describe patterns of recruitment, conversion and ritual practice that have become more subtle and sophisticated, but which have remained surprisingly consistent over the years. Yet, with the growth of power and political influence of the sect and its affiliated enterprises, concerns about the reported psychological manipulation of Moon sect members have largely vanished from public discussion.

In our opinion, the Unification Church remains among the most troubling of the new cults in both its public activities and its personal conversion processes. To further Moon's diverse causes, the sect's efforts are reported to keep up virtually around the clock. Former members have reported consistently that they were not given adequate time to rest or even to begin to think about anything other than the urgent mission of the church. For weary sect members laid low by exhaustion, doubt and fear of the outside world, relief appears to come only in the form of infrequent snapping moments.

Before our meeting with the Gordons came to an end, we heard another account of this extraordinary phenomenon. We were struck by its frightening resemblance to the many vivid descriptions of death and dying that have been published in recent years. For us, it indicated an equally significant form of personal dissolution.

"Once we were in the vans and our fuel pump broke and I curled up on the back seat to go to sleep," Lawrence said, still obviously baffled by the experience. "Then I felt my body was numb, going away, and I had many sensations all at once, like I was physically dying but spiritually being pulled out of my body. At the same instant, this thing was opening up before me. I could see a light and feel something coming toward me to get me or help me. Then I heard this heavenly singing, all different kinds of ranges and pitches, like *Ahhhhh!* But because I felt my body physically dying I became petrified and pulled myself back together and sat up."

To us, Lawrence and Cathy's year and a half in the Unification Church sounded like a waking nightmare, a winding descent into a world devoid of free will, where personal survival loses all meaning, feelings for others disappear, and the outside world takes on dark, supernatural dimensions. Back in those early years, we found few people who got out of the Moon church or any other cult on their own; and as the new groups have matured, their controls have only become more subtle. In many groups, members are warned to fear invasion by Satan. In some, they are told that leaving the group will result in reincarnation as an insect or in death to a family member. To ardent cult members, these threats are totally believable, and many are help-less to act against them.

Can this state of mind possibly be contained within the meaning of the terms "personal growth" and "religion" as we know it? Were the ongoing highs experienced by Jean Turner and the Gordons the result of true enlightenment or revelation? Before we could draw any conclu-sions about the phenomenon of snapping, we needed to examine these intense experiences within their original context of religion, and then to traverse the new cultural ground that underlay both these psycho-logical and spiritual transformations.

4 The Roots of Snapping

*Religion claims to be in possession of an absolute truth;
but its history is a history of errors and heresies. It gives
us the promise and prospect of a transcendent world—
far beyond the limits of our human experience—and it
remains human, all too human.*

—Ernst Cassirer,
An Essay on Man

THE MIRACULOUS HEALING of Jean Turner's legs in est and the moments of ecstasy and revelation experienced by Lawrence and Cathy Gordon in the Unification Church have their counterparts throughout history in every culture and civilization. In ancient Greece, audiences experienced catharsis, a moment of purgation and purification, at the height of Greek dramas and religious rituals. To this day, in Nepal, Sufi dervishes whirl around until they are overcome with religious fervor. Voodoo tribes in Africa and Latin America pursue the same moment in fiery, drum-beating, earth-pounding black masses. In each instance, the activity gives way to a moment of overwhelming physical sensation.

But physical sensations alone do not account for the violent upheaval Jean Turner experienced in the aftermath of her est training or the abrupt change that overtook the Gordons in the course of their initial three-day Unification Church retreat. Modern culture has never witnessed transformations of precisely this kind before, although there have been similar examples throughout the history of religion. In the infinite richness and variety of religious experience, people have perceived almost any sudden, extraordinary refocusing of awareness as a great spiritual breakthrough—spiritual because, although it is felt "in the flesh," it cannot be directly linked to any immediate physical cause. Lacking understanding and with no reliable method for investigating the phenomenon, people through the ages have grappled imaginatively with their experiences, looking to some higher order and ascribing these abrupt changes in awareness to a source outside the body. They have been explained as messages from beyond or gifts of revelation and enlightenment, personal communications that could only be delivered by a universal being of infinite dimensions, a cosmic force that comprehends all space, time and earthly matter.

In the course of human development, every culture has recognized this spectacular phenomenon. The Greeks called it the *kairos* or divine moment, because since ancient times it has been characterized by awesome sensations and celestial visions. Every major religion, including Islam, Hinduism, Buddhism and Zoroastrianism, stems from the similar experience of its founding figure. Among Western religions, Judaism is replete with the moment in the divinations of its prophets and seers, and the stories of Christianity overflow with incidents of "revealed truth." The pages of history tell very little about the actual circumstances surrounding these incidents, but they provide undeniable proof of the universality of the experience.

While not a commonplace occurrence, the experience of enlightenment is a completely natural one. Stripped of its supernatural components, it is simply a moment of fundamental human growth, of overwhelming feeling and understanding when an individual pushes through to those higher levels of consciousness that distinguish us as human beings. For the prophet, the genius and the average citizen alike, life moves forward in such sudden leaps, peak moments and turning points.

In the course of our own travels and interviews, we spoke with many people who told us they had experienced this same "divine moment" of enlightenment. Collecting their stories, we were amazed to find the variety of contexts in which these experiences occurred—from huge public gatherings to lonely roads, in childhood and old age alike. The changes of mind and personality people described ranged from the dark transformations we are primarily concerned with in this book to glorious breakthroughs that seemed to us truly spiritual in the highest sense of the word.

The most beautiful and moving example of this latter experience was told to us by a woman we will call Helen Spates. A devout Christian in her late forties, she was a gentle person with rich black hair and wide, youthful eyes. We came upon her in the South, where we sat in her kitchen and drank tea as she recalled the circumstances that led to her first spiritual awakening at an early age.

"I had my own personal experience as a child," she told us. "I really came into the awareness that there is something higher that is wonderful and beautiful. My mother died and I was very despondent. I just wanted to die along with her because she was a part of me; she was the one I loved. Here I was in the first grade and the children in school would throw rocks at me and just add to my loneliness. Then one day I was underneath a tree, a big cottonwood tree on our farm, and I was spread out just lying there in an old wagon, looking at the sky and the white clouds. Their beauty overwhelmed me, and from the cottonwood tree I saw these beautiful, shiny leaves, and I thought, *New life, new life, how can there be such beautiful creativeness? There must be someone that brought all this about. There must be.*"

She looked at us, searching our faces. She explained that she was embarrassed to have such an intimate part of her life tape-recorded, but then, eager to share with us, she went on.

"I was just overwhelmed with everything," she said, "and I started singing my problem to God. I just blurted out to him exactly how I felt. I told him that my father was a drunkard and my mother was dead, and I was an orphan child and I just didn't know where to lay my head. Then I stopped singing and just lay there and I felt something real warm overwhelming me. It was in just a moment, yet it was like an eternity. No sooner did I become aware of this warm peace overwhelming my little body when a joy, such a joy hit me with such tremendous force that I jumped out of that wagon and ran. I ran past an orchard, I ran on a ditch bank, I ran and ran. Then finally I stopped. I looked at my dad's acreage of alfalfa in full bloom and the butterflies dancing overhead, and I raised my arms and sang, *My heart is taking over. It's learning how to love!*"

Helen Spates' profound personal experience had apparently released her from the enormous emotional stress she had been forced to contend with as a young girl—the loss of her mother, the insults of her schoolmates, the torments of an alcoholic father—and had signaled the resolution of those conflicts. Of all the stories we heard, hers stands as the most unchallengeable instance of genuine enlightenment. It was a moment in which she broke through to a new level of awareness; it took her beyond her painful emotions to an understanding that left her with new feelings of joy and love.

We spoke with others who had experienced this natural moment during their adult lives. For each of them, as well, the experience marked the end of a period of personal torment from which they had found no release. Another woman, a recent convert to Christianity, told us about a crisis that was resolved in an instant and led directly to her conversion.

"When I finally accepted Christ I was in a desperate situation," she confessed. "I had fallen and gashed open my head, and I thought,

Nothing is accidental. I thought that I had done this to myself. I was going crazy thinking that I had these self-destructive impulses. My mind was going on and on like that and I was really scared. I was afraid I was going to throw myself off a cliff and not be able to stop it. I thought, *How can I stop this craziness?* and said, *God, if you can make this go away I'll serve you.* And instantly I felt calm. I felt really crazy, then I felt really calm."

As this woman described her experience, it seemed to us that a sudden physical shock had set off a reaction which nearly snowballed into tragedy. Yet, in contrast to Helen Spates, in the calm that followed, this woman had the sensation, not simply of newfound feeling and awareness, but of having entered a whole new state of being, a transformation of personality on its most intimate level.

Among Christians in America, this powerful experience is often called being "born again" and, in the United States, it is a surprisingly widespread occurrence. Gallup polls consistently report that half of all adult Protestants, or nearly one third of all Americans, say they have been born again.

Some have made their private experiences public. One of the more astonishing born-again conversions was that of Charles Colson, former White House counsel and aide to President Richard Nixon in the Watergate era. Colson vividly described his experience in his best-selling autobiography, *Born Again.*

"Something began to flow into me—a kind of energy," Colson wrote, recounting an event that came on him suddenly while he was sitting in his car. "With my face cupped in my hands, my head leaning forward against the wheel, I forgot about machismo, about pretense, about fear of being weak. Then came the strange sensation that water was not only running down my cheeks, but surging through my whole body as well, cleansing and cooling as it went. They weren't tears of sadness nor of joy, but tears of release. I repeated over and over the words, *Take me. . . .* Something inside me was urging me to surrender."

And Colson did surrender, cooperating fully with federal prosecutors in one of the most baffling personal turnabouts of the Watergate scandal. As in the two previous accounts, Colson's spiritual metamorphosis could be linked to tangible circumstances. The intense physical sensations he experienced often accompany the born-again moment, and they were confirmed by many other born-again Christians we interviewed. A tingling of energy is common, along with alternating feelings of heat and cold. Frequently, a person will have the impression of a cleansing flow of water, often accompanied by an uncontrollable surge of tears.

Another unlikely figure, former sixties-era Black Panther leader Eldridge Cleaver, said that he, too, was born again while hiding overseas from prosecution in the United States on charges of assault and intent to murder. In an interview in 1976, Cleaver described a mystifying feature of the born-again experience: the divine vision, which may be a powerful spur to life-changing action.

"I was looking up at the moon," said Cleaver, "and I saw the man in the moon and it was my face. Then I saw the face was not mine but some of my old heroes. There was Fidel Castro, then there was Mao Zedong. . . . While I watched, the face turned to Jesus Christ, and I was very much surprised. . . . I don't know when I had last cried, but I began to cry and I didn't stop. I was still crying and I got on my knees and said the Lord's Prayer. I remembered that, and then I said the Twenty-third Psalm because my mother had taught me that, too. It was like I could not stop crying unless I said the prayer and the Psalm and surrendered something. . . . All I had to do was surrender and go to jail."

In the aftermath of his divine vision, Cleaver gave himself up to foreign police and was returned to federal custody in the United States.

Skeptics have questioned the sincerity of dramatic conversions such as those of Colson and Cleaver, but there can be no doubt about the extensiveness of the born-again moment in the United States. In the stressful situations just described, being born again was an intensely private, personal experience. For many other Americans, their rebirth took place in a group religious gathering held by one of America's numerous branches of evangelical Christianity.

This public spiritual experience dates back as far as human society, and it has been a vital feature of religion in America as well. The first Great Awakening of Colonial America in the 1740s was led by the Puritan minister Jonathan Edwards, whose fire-and-brimstone sermons reached peaks of emotion that sparked a "New Light" among whole assemblies of colonists. In the 1800s, Baptists, Mormons and other large religious groups joined in frenzied services of devotion that rivaled the ecstatic rituals of the more esoteric Quaker and Shaker sects. With the turn of the twentieth century, amid the emergence of American evangelicalism's bombastic Holy Rollers, the experience of divine enlightenment reached out to touch great masses of Americans. Long before the human potential movement began hailing encounter highs and peak experiences, America's diverse fundamentalist, pentecostal and charismatic Christians set off a grassroots revolution of their own. With the rise of the Reverends Billy Sunday and Aimee Semple McPherson, evangelical Christianity grew quickly into an international movement spanning a broad spectrum of Christian sects and world-wide revival crusades.

The ecstatic charismatic revival is generally acknowledged to have begun on the first day of the year 1901, when the long-established tradition of Christian evangelism, the ardent preaching of the gospel, was itself reborn in a new and potent form. In a Bible school in Topeka, Kansas, directed by the Methodist minister Charles Parham, people "laid hands" on one another and prayed that the Holy Spirit might be given to them with the sign of "speaking in tongues."

Even to most born-again Christians, the experience of speaking in tongues remains shrouded in a mystery. Historically, it has its origin in the New Testament, in the Acts of the Apostles. According to that passage, at Ephesus, in what is now Turkey, the early Christian Paul came upon some Christian disciples who had not received the Holy Spirit according to Christ—they had only received the baptism according to his cousin John. In that first recorded instance of the Christian charismatic experience, Paul told them about the baptism according to Jesus: "On hearing this, they were baptized in the name of the Lord Jesus. And when Paul had laid his hands upon them, the Holy Spirit came on them; and they spoke with tongues and prophesied."

In that ancient moment, according to the Bible, those who felt the spirit spoke in a language unknown to humankind; and in the wake of that experience, their lives were instantly transformed. Their awareness underwent a sudden change, which they attributed to the spirit of Jesus Christ, and they became devout followers of Christianity, their faith confirmed by intense physical sensation.

In the same tradition, the Holy Spirit did in fact appear to Parham's congregation in Topeka, first overwhelming a young woman student and then visiting others in the assembly. From Topeka, the charismatic movement has spread around the world to an estimated fifteen million communities. Other modes of religion require great leaps of faith on the part of their followers. The more straight-laced fundamentalist movement focuses strictly on the literal words of the Bible and generally eschews the exotic "tongues" experience. In contrast, the charismatic movement, as one tract describes, sees itself as "a powerful new sign of the spirit adapting to the needs of our modern era." In keeping with the core tradition of evangelicalism, which promises personal renewal through the "living experience" of Christianity, the charismatic movement strives to bring its adherents to frequent personal encounters with the Holy Spirit. Strengthened by that experience, the individual is then sent forth into the world with a newfound joy, inner peace and—as one minister described it—"a love for God and neighbor." From then on, in many charismatic sects, a major focus of the new convert's devotion becomes the activity of "witnessing," or giving personal testimony of his experience, in the hope of winning new converts to the movement.

As with Helen Spates' natural moment of enlightenment, we found many instances where the Christian form of group "personal encounter" proved to be a source of genuine personal growth. The potential benefits of this mode of worship were poignantly demonstrated to us during a conversation we had with a gentleman we will refer to as Martin Young, a thoughtful husband, loving father of two small children and, for many years, a successful businessman in the Midwest. A Roman Catholic all his life, he joined in the late sixties the burgeoning charismatic movement within the Catholic Church, which has sparked controversy in recent years between traditional and more venturesome Catholics. In contrast to the older image of charismatics as Bible-thumping religious extremists, we found Martin Young to be a polite, easygoing individual, a short, handsome man who was happy to share his first experience of "baptism in the Holy Spirit." He ushered us into his living room one afternoon, built a roaring fire in the fireplace and poured three glasses of white wine.

"There were about seven of us and we went into a prayer meeting," he began solemnly. "After the regular meeting they asked if some of us would like to come upstairs and pray together. We went into the upper room. There were other people laying hands on and I was kneeling in the circle. I just knelt—I wasn't asking for it—and all of a sudden I came into a chant in tongues. Now I'm not much of a singer, but it came out a very beautiful chant. My wife was standing beside me observing, and she received tongues without even knowing it."

As Martin Young described it, he and his wife had a personal experience of the presence of the Holy Spirit in their small charismatic prayer group. Along with other members of the group, they uttered sounds which have no meaning in any modern or ancient language, but which they interpreted as part of the traditional Christian scriptures. The tongues chant, Young told us, had often been likened to ancient Middle Eastern and Asian dialects, but extensive scholarly research had failed to establish its derivation or even a definite vocabulary or grammar. Regardless of its origin, speaking in tongues appeared to be a profoundly compelling group experience which, Young said, may visibly affect both participants and observers. He tried to convey to us the essence of the charismatic ritual that had become so familiar to him.

"When you come into a prayerful atmosphere," he said, "anyone can sense a different feeling. If you walked in here when we were having a prayer meeting with a smaller group, you could feel the intensity of the fervor with your whole being—your heart, your mind, everything. You can see the reverence of the people. You can tell which people have been in the prayer group before; you can feel that they are immersed in the spirit of God."

Following his first charismatic encounter, as others had professed after their born-again moment, Martin Young experienced a sudden refocusing of awareness which he anchored to the established doctrines of Christianity. From his own account, it became clear to us that strict adherence to this traditional body of moral teachings and guidelines for living enabled him to grow socially as well as personally. He explained how his awareness was altered for the better as a result of his tongues experience.

"After you have received tongues," he said, "you are transformed. You come with new eyes, the eyes of God. You look for new ways of liking people; instead of focusing on their weaknesses, you find something good about them. You turn to the positive, to the beautiful—this is living Christianity. I'm not saying that we are not still weak and creatures of habit, but walking with the Lord is a process. It's a journey. It's a mode of change."

From our point of view, Martin Young's understanding of his transformation seemed remarkably perceptive, although, as he described it, the entire experience was contained within the framework of his firm religious belief. Traditionally, religion in America has facilitated and encouraged this kind of personal growth through spiritual belief. It took the born-again movement, however, to fuse religious faith and physical experience into an organized program of personal renewal that offered a prescribed path of daily life and worship for those in search of one.

For the most part, the expressed doctrines and values of evangelicalism are in keeping with the spiritual ideals of American life. They do not depart greatly from other religious traditions that have played autonomous but integral roles in this nation's social and political development. Yet, unlike America's other historic religions, we found numerous sects within the diverse born-again movement that seem to share many characteristics with more extreme religious cults and self-help therapies. Ecstatic moments are sought after and intense. Conversion is sudden and profound. The movement boasts miraculous cures for lifelong ailments and engages in zealous recruitment of new members. Moreover, like many cults and therapies, in recent years the born-again movement generally has multiplied its enormous wealth and following through the use of sophisticated mass-marketing techniques, bringing its heavily advertised crusades to prime-time television, and linking satellite-cable television, radio and print media across the country into sectarian networks that promote fund raising, proselytizing and political action.

This use of modern marketing strategies and mass communication technologies has been the trend in twentieth-century evangelicalism, but in the past few fast-moving decades it has become the movement's primary mode of recruitment and conversion. It is in this leap of that "old-time religion" into new arenas of big business and high technology that the new evangelicalism crosses paths with the phenomenon of snapping in America—and raises some of the most difficult and sensitive questions of our investigation.

In the seventies, the most visible signs of this new attitude could be seen on highways across America, where huge blue billboards and innumerable bright yellow bumper stickers proclaimed the simple phrase "I Found It." This vague message soon became the catchphrase of America's mushrooming born-again movement, yet few Americans were aware of the heavily financed and well-coordinated public relations campaign behind it. The creation of a Harvard Business School graduate and former adman for Coca-Cola, the seventies' I Found It campaign placed the number of recruits it won for Jesus at 600,000 in two hundred cities.

The organization that sponsored I Found It, Campus Crusade for Christ International, Inc., had become, since its founding in 1951, the largest born-again missionary organization in America and, with operations in more than one hundred countries, perhaps in the world. In one of Campus Crusade's many copyrighted pamphlets, *Jesus and the Intellectual,* the group's president and spiritual leader, Bill Bright, drew quotes from the Bible to bolster his argument for the "surrender of the will"—the same act of surrender that both Colson and Cleaver testified to in their born-again stories. According to Bright, the key to becoming a Christian is "the surrender of the intellect, the emotions and the will—the total person." Only then, as it is stated in Corinthians, does an individual become a "new creature" in Christ, as "old things are passed away" and "all things are become new." In its similarity to the appeals of so many cult recruiters and lecturers, this traditional Christian doctrine and the suggestion contained in it took on new and ominous overtones.

Was Campus Crusade, and the born-again movement as a whole for that matter, a "cult"? When we began our investigation in the seventies, we were asked that question by many traditionally religious people, including a number of ardent born-again Christians. At the time, we dismissed the idea as an impossible charge, for our initial acquaintance with the new Christian crusaders revealed none of the prominent features we had come to identify with cult behavior. Most rank-and-file born-agains we met did not cut family ties or leave school to live in communal homes. They did not work around the clock in sect fundraising efforts or turn over their possessions and life savings to born-again organizations. Nor did they engage in arcane rituals and erratic behavior or demonstrate an inability to communicate with the world at large. And besides, it seemed, this movement with so many prominent adherents in positions of high social and political standing was just too big to be considered a cult.

In our early interviews with dozens of born-agains around the country, we found many to be as amiable as Helen Spates and Martin Young: aware, concerned, delightful people who were actively engaged in furthering the lives of their families and communities. Others, however, shocked us considerably. There were those who, at the end of what we thought was an open and genuine discussion, declared flatly that we would be condemned to hell for the opinions we expressed and the beliefs we held. One young woman implied that our project was foolhardy because it was contrary to "God's plan." "It's the intelligent people, like yourselves who have such difficulty coming to Christ," she informed us. Another crusader handed us a little booklet written, she said, "just for our Jewish friends," copyrighted by the American Messianic Fellowship. It excerpted Hebrew scriptures from the Old Testament to verify that the "Messiah Jesus" would cleanse the reader "from all your filthiness." In our travels, we were also astonished to see how many born-again Christians, many of them members of Campus Crusade and other aggressive evangelical groups, had become completely absorbed in their newfound faith, devoting the bulk of their lives, their time and their money to organizations whose most visible charitable activities appeared to be soliciting donations and recruiting new members.

What is the line between a cult and a legitimate religion? In America today, increasingly, that line cannot be categorically drawn. In the course of our investigation, however, it became progressively clearer to us that many born-again Christians indeed had been effectively severed from their families, their pasts and society as a whole after their profound personal transformations. It was not the purpose of our inquiry to examine the far-flung evangelical movement in its entirety, but our research raised serious questions concerning the techniques used to bring about conversion in many evangelical groups. To further our understanding of those techniques, we paid a visit to a renowned American charismatic leader, Holy Roller and faith healer—retired.

Marjoe Gortner was the first evangelical preacher to blow the whistle on his profession. In his Oscar-winning documentary film *Marjoe,* made in the late sixties, he revealed age-old tricks of the trade and exposed some of the entertainment aspects of the movement that have made it big business.

If he lives forever, Hugh Marjoe Ross Gortner will most likely always be "The World's Youngest Ordained Minister." Born January 14, 1944, Marjoe was almost strangled during delivery by his own umbilical cord. The obstetrician told his mother that it was a miracle the child survived, and thus "Marjoe"—for Mary and Joseph—the Miracle Child took his place at the end of a long line of evangelical ministers.

From the beginning, his preaching skills were meticulously cultivated. Before he learned to say "Mamma" or "Poppa," he was taught to sing "Hallelujah!" When he was nine months old his mother taught him the right way to shout "Glory!" into a microphone. At three, he could preach the gospel from memory, and he received drama coaching and instruction in every performing art from saxophone playing to baton twirling. On Halloween, 1948, at the age of four, Marjoe was officially ordained and thrust into a wildly successful career as the Shirley Temple of America's Bible Belt, the sprawling nongeographic community of strict adherents to the Christian Scriptures. In the following decade he preached to packed tents and houses coast to coast, as enthusiastic audiences flocked to see the Miracle Child who allegedly received sermons from the Lord in his sleep. Owing to his mother's careful training, harsh discipline and indomitable ambition, Marjoe's sermons were flawlessly memorized, right down to each perfectly timed pause and gesture. Frequent Hallelujahs and Amens punctuated his performances, which were cleverly promoted with titles such as "From Wheelchair to Pulpit" and "Heading for the Last Roundup," which Marjoe preached wearing a cowboy suit.

Marjoe's captivating sermons rarely failed to fill the church collection plate to the brim, and his renowned healings were miraculous even to him. In his teens, however, Marjoe grew disenchanted with the continued deception of his "divine" powers, and he left the evangelical movement in search of more legitimate means of employment. He spent time in a rock band, trying to move with the times; then he returned to the revival circuit to make his revealing motion picture. *Marjoe* is one of those frank films that delve deeply into sensitive areas of American morality that slip over the line into profiteering.

We found Marjoe in Hollywood on a secluded hilltop estate in Laurel Canyon. After we drove up the winding dirt road leading to his lofty home, Marjoe greeted us cordially and ushered us into his sunken living room, where he pointed out some familiar features of the sprawling southern California landscape visible through his wall-sized picture window. We told him that we had come to hear about his miraculous powers of "saving" and "healing," trade secrets that neither his film nor his subsequent biography unraveled satisfactorily. Tall, handsome, with lion-colored curls and a penetrating stare, even in T-shirt and faded jeans Marjoe had an air of power about him. From the outset of our talk, however, he quashed all notions we might have had that his talents were in any way extraordinary.

"I don't have any power," he started off, just to set the record straight. "And neither do any of these other guys. Hundreds of people were healed at my crusades, but I know damn well it was nothing I was doing."

Yet, Marjoe admitted, he remained somewhat baffled by the thousands of souls he helped to "save" and the numerous illnesses he seemed to have cured. His own insight into his preaching skills was on a decidedly earthly level. Based on his years of training and experience, he located the source of his divine power squarely out among the flocks who assembled to receive his gifts.

"You start with a guy who obviously has a problem," he explained. "You've got to begin on that premise. Things haven't worked out for him or he's looking for something or whatever. So he goes to one of these revivals. He hears very regimented things. He sees a lot of people glowing around him—people who seem very, very happy—and they're all inviting him to come in and join the clique and it looks great. They say, 'Hey, my life was changed!' or 'Hey, I found a new job!' That's when he's ready to get saved or born again; and once he's saved, they all pat him on the back. It's like he's been admitted to this very special elite little club."

Marjoe downplayed his own role in the proceedings. As he saw it, the real show was in the audience. He served primarily as a conductor.

"As the preacher," he said, "I'm working with the crowd, watching the crowd, trying to bring them to that high point at a certain time in the evening. I let everything build up to that moment when they're all in ecstasy. The crowd builds up and you have to watch that you don't stop it. You start off saying you've heard that tonight's going to be a great night; then you begin the whole pitch and keep it rolling."

For Marjoe, who had seen it a million times, the divine moment of religious ecstasy had no mystical quality at all. It was a simple matter of group frenzy that had its counterpart in every crowd.

"It's the same as a rock-and-roll concert," he asserted. "You have an opening number with a strong entrance; then you go through a lot of the old standards, building up to your hit song at the end."

The hit song, however, was spiritual rebirth, the product of a time-tested recipe for evangelical religion to which the preacher and every member of the audience contribute some small but active ingredient. Afterwards, according to Marjoe, the only fitting encore to the over-whelming moment of being saved is a personal demonstration of the power of that newfound faith. This is the motivating factor that prompts speaking in tongues, also known as the "receiving of the glossolalia." As Marjoe explained it, this well-known evangelical tradition required even greater participation on the part of the tongues recipient and the entire audience.

"After you've been saved," Marjoe continued, "the next step is what they call 'the infilling of the Holy Spirit.' They say to the new convert, 'Well, now you're saved, but you've got to get the Holy Ghost.' So you come back to get the tongues experience. Some people will get it the same night; others will go for weeks or years before they can speak in tongues. You hear it, you hear everyone at night talking in it in the church, and they're all saying, 'We love you and we hope you're going to get it by tonight.' Then one night you go down there and they all try to get you to get it, and you go into very much of a trance—not quite a frenzy, but it is an incredible experience.

"During that moment the person forgets all about his problems. He is surrounded by people whom he trusts and they're all saying, 'We love you. It's okay. You're accepted in Christ. We're with you, let it go, relax.' And sooner or later, he starts to speak it out and go *dut-dut-dut*. Then everyone goes, 'That's it! You've got it!' and the button is pushed and he will in fact start to speak in tongues and just take off: *dehandayelomosatayleesaso* . . . and on and on."

Marjoe paused. We were dumbfounded by his demonstration, al-though he hadn't gone into the jerking, trancelike ecstasy that is com-monly associated with the tongues moment. His movie contained dozens of real-life instances of the purported mystical experience. Yet even in this restrained demonstration, he seemed almost uncannily to be trig-gering some innate releasing or babbling mechanism. We asked him how he brought it about.

"You'll never get it with that attitude," he joked. Then he went on to explain the true nature of the experience. His perspective showed it to be a process that requires a great deal of effort to master.

"Tongues is something you learn," he emphasized. "It is a releasing that you teach yourself. You are told by your peers, the church and the Bible—if you accept it literally—that the Holy Ghost spake in another tongue; and you become convinced that it is the ultimate expression of the spirit flowing through you. The first time maybe you'll just go *dut-dut-dut-dut* and that's about all that will get out. Then you'll hear other people and the next night you may go *dut-dut-dut-UM-dut-DEET-dut-dut* and it gets a little better. The next thing you know, it's *elahandosatelayeekcondelemosandreyaseya* . . . and it's a new language you've got down."

Except that, according to Marjoe, it's not a real language at all. Contrary to most religious understanding, speaking in tongues is by no means passive spiritual possession. It must be actively acquired and practiced. Although the "gift" of tongues is a product of human and not supernatural origin, Marjoe displayed tremendous respect for the experience as an expression of spirituality and fellowship.

"I really don't put it down," he said. "I never have. It's just that I analyze it and look at it from a very rational point of view. I don't see it as coming from God and say that at a certain point the Holy Spirit zaps you with a super whammy on the head and you've 'gone for tongues' and there it is. Tongues is a process that people build up to. Then, as you start to do something, just as when you practice the scales on the piano, you get better at it."

Already, we could see the difference between Marjoe and some of his modern-day fellow preachers and pretenders. Unlike many cult, group therapy and evangelical leaders, Marjoe always held his congregations in high regard. During his years on the Bible Belt circuit, he came to see the evangelical experience as a form of popular entertainment, a kind of participatory divine theater that provided its audiences with profound emotional rewards. Marjoe realized that his perspective would not be shared by most born-again Christians.

"The people who are out there don't see it as entertainment," he confessed, "although that is in fact the way it is. Those people don't go to movies, they don't go to bars and drink, they don't go to rock-and-roll concerts—but everyone has to have an emotional release. So they go to revivals and they dance around and talk in tongues. It's socially approved and that is their escape."

Within that context of social entertainment, Marjoe took pride in his starring role as a traveling evangelist.

"It was my duty to give them the best show possible," he said. "Say you've got a timid little preacher in North Carolina or somewhere. He'll bring in visiting evangelists to keep his church going. We'd come in and hit the crowd up and we were superstars. It's the charisma of the evangelist that the audience believes in and comes to see."

What got to Marjoe, he explained, and eventually drove him out of the business were many of the same disturbing aspects of the evangelical movement we had noticed in our own travels.

"When I was traveling," he said, looking back on the old days, "I'd see someone who wanted to get saved in one of my meetings, and he was so open and bubbly in his desire to get the Holy Ghost. It was wonderful and very fresh, but four years later I'd return and that person might be a hard-nosed intolerant Christian because he was better than anyone who drinks and better than the world because he had Christ. That's when the danger comes in. People want an experience. They want to feel good and their lives can be helped by it. But then as you start moving into the operation of the thing, you get into controlling people and power and money."

Marjoe shook his head sadly. Indeed, he didn't strike us as the type of person who would be comfortable in that role. In the sixties, while he was exploring new outlets for his talents, he watched his former profession grow to vast international dimensions. Since then, he had followed the curious rise of the new religious cults, among them Moon's Unification Church.

"Moon is doing the same thing I do," said Marjoe, "only he's taken it one step further. He's suggesting to people that he *is* the Messiah. In my religion, the old-time religion, it's total blasphemy to suggest that. Moon has gone too far, but that's a very heavy number on people, because everyone wants to meet a Messiah."

Marjoe was quick to point out that Moon's preaching powers, like his own, were by no means divine or even innate. Marjoe acknowledged that his power over an audience derived primarily from the skills he perfected as a child, techniques of rhetoric and public speaking that have passed down from the Greeks. These tools have long been in the public domain, and they make up the stock-in-trade of everyone whose work involves personal contact with other individuals and groups.

"It's the same whether you're a preacher, a lawyer or a salesman," he told us. "You start off with a person's thought processes and then gradually sway him around to another way of thinking in a very short time."

As he approached midlife, Marjoe restricted the use of his talents to his acting career and to social causes he believed in deeply. Foremost among those causes was informing the public about some of the rhetorical techniques that were being used to manipulate their thoughts and emotions. Many of the techniques he commanded were simple and age-old, but so effective that they proved equally powerful even when an audience had been explicitly forewarned of their use. Toward the end of our conversation, Marjoe told us a story that revealed the fineness of his skills. In contrast to the massive physical experiences, intense group rituals and intimate personal crises that we had identified as major contributors to the snapping moment, Marjoe demonstrated how words alone, artfully manipulated, may be used to influence groups and individuals, even to the point of evoking the overwhelming emotional response of being "saved."

"I lecture in about twenty colleges a year," he began, "and I do a faith-healing demonstration—but I always make them ask for it. I tell them that I don't believe in it, that I use a lot of tricks; and the title of the lecture is 'Rhetoric and Charisma,' so I've already told them how large masses are manipulated by a charismatic figure. I've given them the whole rap explaining how it's done, but they still want to see it. So I throw it all right back at them. I say, 'No, you don't really want to see it.' And they say, 'Oh, yes. We do. We do!' And I say, 'But you don't believe in it anyway, so I can't do it.' And they say, 'We believe. We believe!' So after about twenty minutes of this I ask for a volunteer, and I have a girl come up and I say, 'So you want to feel better?' And I say, 'You're lying to me! You're just up here for a good time and you want to impress all these people and you want to make an ass out of me and an ass out of this whole thing, so why don't you go back and sit down?' I really get hard on her, and she says, 'No, no, I believe!' And I keep going back and forth until she's almost in tears. And then, even though this is in a college crowd and I'm only doing it as a joke, I just say my same old line, *In the name of Jesus!* and touch them on the head, and wham, they fall down flat every time."

5 Snapping as Something New

OUR CONVERSATION WITH Marjoe gave us a rare view of the ways rudimentary rhetorical skills could be used to manipulate the emotions of individuals and audiences. But it did not explain what happened to Jean Turner in est or to Lawrence and Cathy Gordon in the Unification Church. To understand those experiences we need to take a closer look at America in the much celebrated, much maligned decade of the 1960s. It was an era that began with a burst of powerful new therapeutic techniques and spiritual practices and ended in a runaway, mind-altering technology of experience.

The Technology of Experience. The wheels of this new technology began to turn in the fifties, when America was still on its rollicking course of postwar affluence and conspicuous consumption. By the end of that decade, the simple high of material splendor had begun to flatten out. Across the country, people awoke from the American Dream in a cold sweat of "existential despair," as the triumphs of business and applied science that had showered America with mere things was overpowered by a crying hunger for new and meaningful *experience.*

The first steps in that direction were taken by the poets and writers of the Beat Generation, who set off to mine the rich spiritual lodes of the East. Zen Buddhist practices first cropped up in the poetry and literature of Allen Ginsberg and Jack Kerouac. The benefits of meditation were laid out in the popular writings of Alan Watts; his book *The Way of Zen* opened the East to a stream of traffic that has been bumper to bumper ever since. Perhaps the most influential figure of all was

British author Aldous Huxley, whose short, brilliant essay *The Doors of Perception*, as far back as 1954, linked emerging trends in Eastern thought to psychedelic drugs and blasted a gaping portal in our Western notion of reality. (Its title, drawn from a poem by eighteenth-century visionary William Blake, later inspired the name of the sixties' rock group The Doors.)

These sparks touched off the consciousness explosion, a cultural revolution that brought Timothy Leary, Richard Alpert (a.k.a. Baba Ram Dass) and LSD out of Harvard and led an entire generation to "turn on" to new modes of thought and experience. Before long, in California's fertile climate of open enjoyment and experimentation, these new ritual and therapeutic practices blossomed into a full-fledged movement for exploring humankind's untapped potentials.

Abraham Maslow, father figure of the new movement and its related discipline, humanistic psychology, set the upper limit of that potential when he marked off the realm of peak experience. He identified it as the "core-religious" or "transcendent" experience, the nucleus of every known high or revealed religion—the mystical, revelatory, ecstatic moment that was universally endowed with supernatural significance. Maslow's intention, however, was to view this peak objectively. He proposed that this new category of experience be examined on its own merits, free of religion. He cited the promise of psychedelic drugs as just one manner in which all human beings could investigate moments of peak experience for themselves.

Maslow's endorsement of peak experience sounded the keynote of the sixties. It became the pot of gold at the end of the search, the breakthrough for which all that vague despair of the fifties had been longing. At the Esalen Institute in Big Sur, California, cradle of the newborn movement, innovative techniques for creating intense sensory and intellectual experience were experimented with in a receptive atmosphere. There objective knowledge of how mind and personality may be affected by intense experience was pushed forward many decades in only a few years. Along the way, Esalen's spiritual and psychic voyagers spent extended moments in realms of consciousness human beings had only dreamed of until then, or mentioned cryptically or cloaked in metaphor.

In no time, Eastern practices and psychedelics became high fashion among scientists and casual experimenters alike. The fledgling movement spurred an outpouring of new therapeutic techniques from what had been largely private, professional settings into loudly public, experiential arenas. The encounter group or T-group, as it was originally called, one of the first to appear, was born at the National Training Laboratories of Bethel, Maine. Soon a glut of radical therapeutic techniques—some old, some new—came out of the woodwork. Among them were psychodrama, a role-playing therapy developed in the twenties by a Viennese physician; psychosynthesis, a combination of individual and group therapeutic techniques developed by an Italian psychoanalyst; guided fantasy, a systematic daydreaming technique outlined in the forties by a French psychotherapist; bioenergetics, a body therapy from the fifties developed by American psychiatrist Alexander Lowen, a former student of maverick European Gestalt psychologist Wilhelm Reich; and rolfing, a form of deep-muscle manipulation pioneered in California by Dr. Ida Rolf, a biologist turned therapist.

Suddenly, it seemed, the intangible stuff of human experience itself had been captured and harnessed. Now it could be reliably reproduced and put to work in systematic techniques, and powerful individual and group communication dynamics. This new technology of experience worked by subtle verbal and nonverbal means. In its attempt to evoke some desired experience by manipulating human awareness at basic physical and psychological levels, many of its new methods bypassed vital processes of reason and conscious decision-making. By its nature, the new technology operated, not on critical thinking, but on deep reservoirs of feeling. Sometimes the feelings were negative ones that played on people's confusions, anxieties and fears of rejection. More often, however, the technology of experience acted by positive means, through words, gestures, images, ideas, intimate group dynamics and other interactions that made people feel good about something. Along the way, however, much of that hardwon knowledge and technical know-how was turned into precarious new methods of manipulating and controlling the world within people themselves, impelling many to act in ways they never would have considered and, under any other circumstances, would stop to question.

Each new technique was fully capable of producing an emotional high, peak experience or other dramatic personal breakthrough. Through the sixties, they were intermixed ad-lib, along with drugs and Eastern practices of zen, yoga and many forms of meditation, to bring about profound adventures in awareness; however, in the era's free-for-all of experimentation, these powerful techniques were frequently applied without even the most general guidelines, professional standards or consumer warnings. As a result, amid all their peaking, bursting and mind-blowing ecstasy, many people broke through boundaries of everyday awareness into unforeseen—and unruly—reaches of consciousness. One man's outburst of screaming and violence became another's "release of blockages" and still another's "cosmic vision." Yet, at the time no one, not even the new methods' inventors themselves, could say with certainty who was doing what to whom, and with what, and how.

The only indisputable interpretations were spiritual ones, for the new field of humanistic psychology, still in the process of defining itself, was unable to supply sufficient alternative explanations; and in the late sixties the movement began a slow strip-down to its theological underpinnings. The notion of transcendence became entangled in its fundamentally Eastern, Hindu roots, and the theory and practice of encounter edged closer to its revivalist forerunners.

By the end of the decade, the human potential movement had become a potpourri of therapy and religion, science and mysticism, the avant-garde and the occult. In the fog, the golden age of Esalen and the human potential movement began to tarnish. The drugs got out of hand, the techniques went awry, and the vision of humankind emerging to meet its destiny grew nearsighted. In the early seventies, with the souring of so many counterculture themes, the voyage to self-awareness lost its way. The Aquarian dream hit the skids during the final agony of the Vietnam war and bottomed out with the nightmare of Watergate. In that time of social and political upheaval, the energy and excitement of the sixties were consumed, and the lively culture of that decade fell into a state of aimlessness and torpor. It took just one more hammerblow to drive the last nail into the coffin.

That blow landed hard in the consummate American element of mass marketing, as the methods of big business were brought into the movement, took it over and changed its character altogether. Mass-marketed therapies led the way, pooling bits and pieces of psychoanalysis, psychodrama and other old techniques with the new group techniques of encounter, guided fantasy and Eastern meditation practices. The first conglomerations of techniques were neatly packaged and distributed nationwide under names like Mind Dynamics, Arica and Silva Mind Control. Transcendental Meditation was already being peddled like speed reading. Scientology's Dianetics had been mass-marketing its own pop therapy since the fifties. At the same time, America's religious cults got in the swing, fanning out quietly across the country in massive fund-raising and recruitment drives. Cults such as the Hare Krishna, Divine Light Mission and Unification Church cleaned up their images and outfits, honing their sales techniques to razor sharpness and making use of expert business and legal counsel.

As the human potential movement spread outward into society, self-styled "new age" entrepreneurs, social scientists in the private sector and specialized experts of every hue began adapting its revolutionary concepts and methods for more conventional commercial ends. Mass-marketing programs were engineered by top experts from Madison Avenue. The Hare Krishna hired its own admen. Like Campus Crusade, est gave a top position to a former Coca-Cola executive. The campaign clicked. The right buttons were pushed and Americans let their appetites for experience run hog-wild. Suddenly, without apology, as if another world war had just ended, the seventies saw Americans take to meeting their own needs for experience and little else. It was the coming of what social analyst Peter Marin termed the New Narcissism, an era pop-critic Tom Wolfe dubbed the "Me" Decade. In their eyes, the noble desire for self-realization had turned into simple self-indulgence.

What no one noticed was the important change taking place at a more fundamental level. With the spread of the technology of experience and its popular practices that had profound effects on the workings of the mind, people were not merely changing their beliefs and indulging their egos in the seventies—they were snapping. And, as a direct consequence of that dissemination, they have been snapping in America and every culture the technology of experience has touched ever since.

The cults are a Rosetta stone: they offer countless vivid examples of how the technology of experience has been used to bring about fundamental alterations of personality. For many cult members, snapping is the product of a systematic assault on their awareness. During the first moments of contact, potential converts may be manipulated with precision by the rhetorical ploys Marjoe so deftly demonstrated: conversation, rapport building, group lectures, confrontation and other modes of persuasion. Once they have been drawn into the cult, they may be bombarded with ideas and religious doctrines they cannot fit together and led through ceremonial rituals that induce intense emotional highs and overwhelming peak experiences.

Converts may then be subjected to more personal encounters in which their new experiences are given prescribed cult interpretations. During this period, new converts are instructed in intensive repetitive rituals such as chanting and meditation that may induce a physical and psychic high, stop the mind's natural processes of thinking and feeling, and further weaken their resistance to suggestion and command. In many groups, throughout recruitment, conversion and initiation, converts are given specific orders to refrain from doubt and told not to question the wisdom of cult doctrine.

Inevitably, under the cumulative pressures of this sweeping physical, mental and emotional blitz, self-control and personal beliefs give way. Isolated from the world and surrounded by exotic trappings, converts may rapidly absorb the cult's altered ways of thought and daily life. Before they realize what is happening, while their attention is diverted by contrived spiritual conflicts, repetitive rituals and, in many groups, impaired further by lack of food and sleep, the new cult members may slide into a state of mind in which they literally are no longer capable of thinking for themselves.

In our view, this comprehensive assault strikes at the heart of consciousness, undermining the basic processes of thought and feeling essential to individual awareness and volition. Yet to zealous cult members this new state of mind often has another name: happiness. Their characteristic public pronouncement is that they have found true happiness, fulfillment on both personal and spiritual planes, in the simple life and labor of the cult. Their everyday state is a constant high, an emotional peak that maintains itself. When it falters, for whatever reason, cult members may simply intensify any number of techniques of meditation, chanting or fervent prayer in which they have been studiously instructed, all guaranteed to return them to the state of bliss that is their reward for unquestioning devotion.

Except for the religious component, most self-help therapies use the same basic methods. They recruit their participants through similar informal channels—telephone and mail solicitations, word of mouth, and casual interactions among friends, relatives and colleagues. By these means people are drawn into intimate group settings and therapeutic sessions in the hope of having some life-changing breakthrough. Then, as in est, that profound experience may be created by various personal "processes" and group "training" techniques. Group leaders may instruct participants in therapeutic meditation or guide them through vivid fantasies and visualizations. They may give interminable lectures filled with psychological and scientific jargon, or sow intense conflicts spanning the range of people's life experiences, from infancy through childhood and adolescence to current work and family relationships.

Caught in this crossfire of verbiage and long-buried emotion in the context of a grueling group ordeal, a person may reach a state of explosive overstimulation or emotional collapse. In the aftermath of this overwhelming new experience, he or she may enter a state of mind that is perceived as a renewal or rebirth and which may be, in fact, an ongoing physical and emotional high. Successful self-help therapy graduates often achieve a sustained state of euphoria, their problems solved because they have, in effect, stopped worrying about the things that were bothering them.

At the present time, our language has no term for this new way of coping with the problems of life. We can describe the process as one of shutting off the mind, of not-thinking. In our view, this is the underlying appeal of countless cults, sects and therapies operating in America and worldwide, as well as the unstated attraction of many branches of born-again Christianity..

Dream Time. What kind of cultural environment breeds this widespread need to shut off the mind? It could be argued that the need is universal, that everyone—from Athenians to Sufis to voodoo tribesmen to modern Americans—must have some periodic release from the ordeal of being human. In that sense, the rituals and techniques which throughout history have been used to create peak experiences and moments of enlightenment may be looked on as vital sources of rest and relaxation for the mind, momentary breathing spells that hold great powers of insight, healing and renewal.

But what value can there be in engineering these experiences to shut down the workings of the mind *altogether,* to persistently stunt the processes of thought and leave people numb to their own feelings and the world around them? Throughout history, this systematic stilling of human awareness has proved an efficient method of controlling members of tribes, societies and whole nations in which little value is placed upon individuality. The state of mind it produces has a tradition that dates back to the dawn of civilization.

In the remote bush country of Australia, aboriginal tribes still engage in rituals perfected more than 16,000 years ago to induce a state of mind in their adolescents that is surprisingly similar to the plight of many of society's brightest youth today and people of all ages. Joseph Chilton Pearce described the technique in his 1971 book *The Crack in the Cosmic Egg.* Around puberty, the young male of the Ananda tribe of central Australia is taken from his mother, isolated in the wilderness and deprived of food for a prolonged period of time. He is kept awake at night in a state of constant fear by the eerie, whirling sound of the bullroarer, a native hunting device, until the combined physical and emotional stresses reach their maximum effect. At that moment, the elders of the tribe converge on the terrified youth wearing grotesque masks and covered with vivid body paints and proceed to subject him to a painful ritual of initiation into manhood. If he survives the ordeal, the young man emerges from the ritual in a drastically reduced state of mind, his awareness continuing at a level only sufficient to allow absolute adherence to the strict laws and taboos of the tribe. The adult Ananda tribesman may spend his entire life in this altered state the natives call Dream Time. He will stand on one leg for hours, completely motionless, in a waking trance so deep that, as Pearce reported, flies may crawl across his eyeballs without causing him to blink.

In recent years, aboriginal Dream Time has been hailed as a state of profound sophistication in human awareness. Anthropologists point to the aborigine's physical endurance, spiritual satisfaction and telepathic powers as marks of advanced evolution in a tribe that may represent humankind's longest unbroken line of cultural development. However, they make the error of implying that this efficient and admittedly remarkable form of social control in a primitive, unchanging environment holds some promise for the future of our vastly more complex and fast-changing technological society. After a breakthrough decade like the sixties, it is ironic to find Americans who seek greater awareness and self-determination accepting instead a contemporary counterpart of Dream Time. What turn of events could have struck such an ancient chord in our modern time?

In the sixties, people rebelled against another modern version of Dream Time: the corporate mentality of the fifties which turned so many active, imaginative individuals into soulless "organization men" and women. But the consciousness explosion that ripped through the sixties' society unleashed more awareness than many people were prepared to deal with: awareness of the empty rewards of many jobs and careers, of the confinement of many traditional marriages, family relationships, worn-out sex roles and social stereotypes, of the dangers of nuclear war, environmental pollution, dwindling energy resources, and of the moral bankruptcy of so many modern political institutions.

In the sixties, millions of people worldwide took action on all these fronts and won major victories, politically, culturally and environmentally. But there were problems that would not yield to mere awareness, the best intentions or even aggressive action. In the seventies, people found themselves confronting a new world of overwhelming trade-offs: environmental quality versus technological progress, international diplomacy versus basic principles of human rights, the freedom and independence of the single life versus the sharing and loving of intimate relationships. These uncompromising dilemmas and others gave rise to still another kind of expanded awareness, one born of a maturing realism rather than the youthful idealism of the sixties.

In the wake of the fifties' postwar era of American omnipotence and economic supremacy, and of the sixties' colorful, space-age decade in which people lived their dreams and accomplished the impossible without blinking, the new realism that crash-landed in the seventies was a tangle of lowered sights and diminished expectations. Old traditions and institutions had been shattered but no new ones were evolving. In too many places, the life of the individual seemed to be less important than the demands of a runaway consumer society. The problems, pressures and pace of modern life were snowballing. The worlds seemed to be turning into a maze of pollution, inflation, political tensions and, at the personal level, exhaustion, loneliness, boredom and frustration.

For many people, the way out of this nightmare was to stop worrying altogether, to plunge into work or play with the hope of finding something that would bring results or, at least, a temporary diversion. So in the seventies, as others watched, millions of Americans took off on a mindless pursuit of happiness. Panicky college seniors forged rationalized "practical" career goals that exempted them from the commitments of their sixties' counterparts. Young couples settled for "realistic" relationships that freed them from their earlier ideals and desires. Runaway husbands and wives spun intricate webs of faulty logic to excuse themselves from their prior commitments and adult responsibilities. Late-blooming hippies and disillusioned political activists set off on escapist back-to-nature expeditions and wilderness retreats. While businessmen in "midlife crisis" and mothers with "empty-nest syndrome" sought ever greater material indulgences to disguise their own lack of meaning and direction.

Today this enduring shift in attitudes, opinions and lifestyles continues to feed a social and cultural environment that offers heady rewards for not thinking. How easy it is to be carried aloft and swept along by God's "revealed plan" or to buy some technique that causes problems to "cure up in the process of life itself." Shutting off the mind in this way provides instant relief from anxiety and frustration. It evokes pleasure by default, salvation through surrender and, even better, its simple happiness is self-perpetuating.

Indeed, the moment when we stop thinking may be one of overwhelming joy, the moment when the search at last comes to an end. Journalist Sally Kempton, writing in *New York* magazine when this new attitude was still in its infancy, described a series of personal and professional crises that brought her to an audience with the Swami Muktananda, one of the less mercantile of the post-sixties' wave of Eastern guru-entrepreneurs. Sitting quietly before Muktananda along with a hundred other devotees, Kempton sought enlightenment from the Swami. She found it in a single, casual remark that epitomized the new cultural trend we were tracking.

"And finally," she wrote, "out of the welter of questions about lights and visions and experiences of transcendental love, came the one question that seemed to apply to my situation: 'What do you do about negative emotions?' a woman asked, and Muktananda said, 'Let them go.'"

That simple instruction may have been more propitious than profound, yet it set off a chain reaction of mind and emotion that led to one of the most vivid accounts of snapping to reach the media:

Perhaps it wasn't what he said that struck me, but how he said it. Or maybe it was both. One of my deepest assumptions was that the thing to do about negative emotions was figure out where they came from, talk them over with your friends, work them out, *deal* with them. The last thing I had ever thought to do about negative emotions was to let them go. But Muktananda's words did something to me. It was as if they entered my mind, sinking through my assumptions like a kind of depth charge. It sounds strange, but for a moment I felt as if his words had actually knocked the voices of irritation out of my mind. I hadn't even realized they were there, those voices, until I noticed how good I felt without them. And for the rest of that intense and dream-like afternoon I sat feeling empty and absorbent, until at last Muktananda picked up a large tambourine and banged on it, and I sat up with a start. A chant was beginning, sweet and melodic, and also rhythmic; and five minutes into the chant I noticed a warm ache in my throat and liquid in my eyes, and wondered why I was crying. I didn't feel at all sad.

Driving home on the freeway afterward, I noticed that I had a lot of energy. In fact, I had so much energy that I didn't quite know what to do with it, and so I went home and ate a huge meal and talked loudly for two hours with my friend Jane, and then went into my room and lay down on my bed and closed my eyes and the whole thing started.

What it made me think of was Alice falling down the rabbit hole. I felt as if a huge pool had opened in my heart *(Oh, God, I thought, it's all true what those creeps were saying),* and the pool was full of soft air, and I was floating on it. It was the most intensely sensual feeling I had ever had. It felt so good that my first reaction was a sharp pang of guilt, a feeling that I had stumbled into some forbidden region, perhaps tapped a pleasure center in my brain, which would keep me hooked on bodyless sensuality, string me out on bliss until I turned into a vegetable . . . then I forgot about thinking and just let myself drift on it.

6 Black Lightning

I do not doubt that in the course of time this new science will be improved by further observations, and still more by true and conclusive proofs. But this need not diminish the glory of the first observer.

—Galileo
*(writing in praise of William Gilbert,
pioneer in the study of magnetism)*

IN ALL THE WORLD, there is nothing quite so impenetrable as a human mind snapped shut with bliss. No call to reason, no emotional appeal can get through its armor of self-proclaimed joy.

We talked with dozens of individuals in this state of mind: cult members, group therapy graduates, born-again Christians, some Transcendental Meditators. After a while, it seemed very much like dancing to a broken record. We would ask a question, and the individual would spin round and round in a circle of dogma. If we tried to interrupt, he or she would simply pick right up again or go back to the beginning and start over.

Soon we began to realize that what we were watching went much deeper. These people were not simply incapable of carrying on a genuine conversation, they were completely mired in their unthinking, unfeeling, uncomprehending states. Whether cloistered in cults or passing blindly through the world, they were impervious to the pain of parents, spouses, friends and lovers. How do you reach such people? Can they be made to think and feel again? Is there any way to reunite them with their former personalities and the world around them?

A man named Ted Patrick developed the first remedy. A controversial figure dubbed by the cult world Black Lightning, Patrick was the first to point out publicly what the cults were doing to America's youth. He investigated the ploys by which many converts were ensnared and delved into the methods many cults used to manipulate the mind.

He was also the first to take action. In the early seventies, Patrick began a one-man campaign against the cults. His fight started in Southern California, on the Pacific beaches where, in the beginning, organizations such as the Hare Krishna and the Children of God recruited among the vacationing students and carefree dropouts who covered the sands in summer and roamed the bustling beach communities year round. The Children of God approached Patrick's son there one day and nearly made off with him. Patrick investigated, was horrified at what he found, and immediately set out on a course of direct action. His first-hand experiences with cult techniques and their effects led him to develop an antidote he named "deprogramming," a remarkably simple and—when properly used—nearly foolproof process for helping cult members regain their freedom of thought.

Before long, Ted Patrick was in action all over the country on behalf of desperate parents. Through the seventies, he made front page headlines in the East for his daring daylight kidnappings of Ivy League cult members. He made network news for his interstate car chases in the Pacific Northwest to elude both cult leaders and state troopers. And eventually he made American legal history. In his ultimate defense of the U.S. Constitution, Patrick challenged the confusion of First Amendment rights surrounding the cult controversy and drew an important distinction between Americans' guaranteed national freedoms of speech and religion and their more fundamental human right to freedom of thought. In precedent-setting cases, U.S. courts confirmed Patrick's argument that, by "artful and deceiving" means, the new cults were in fact robbing people of their natural capacity to think and choose. To that time, it was never considered possible that a human being could be stripped of this basic endowment.

In many courtrooms, however, Ted Patrick lost his case for freedom of thought, gathering a stack of convictions for kidnapping and unlawful detention. In unsuccessful attempts to free cult members from their invisible prisons, Patrick was repeatedly thrown into real ones, in New York, California and Colorado. In July 1976, during a time when Americans were celebrating their two hundredth year of freedom, Patrick was sentenced to serve a year in prison for a cult kidnapping he did not in fact perform.

Early in 1977, we first visited Ted Patrick in the Theo Lacy Facility of the Orange County Jail to learn about deprogramming from the man who coined the term. It was dark when we arrived, and we had to squeeze past the evening's incoming offenders at the main desk and make our case for seeing a prisoner after hours. Theo Lacy, we were told, was not half as bad a place as some others Patrick had seen. Yet upon showing our credentials, we were ushered into a glaring, airless cubicle under fluorescent light and constant surveillance. Minutes later, Patrick joined us.

Sturdy, round-faced, with dark skin and close-cropped hair, he conveyed little of his notorious reputation through his physical appearance. He wore large dark-rimmed glasses, a plain white prison shirt and baggy trousers. Yet even in this depersonalizing environment, he projected an unmistakable presence. There was a sense of command about him and even a measure of charm in his guarded smile.

When we told him about the nature of our investigation, Patrick seemed to warm to our visit. In a sentence, he ticked off the physical and emotional stresses that make up the basic cult technique as he saw it. "They use fear, guilt, hate, poor diet and fatigue," he said. We had heard that from many people, we told him. What we had come for was his perspective on the way those techniques may affect the mind. Suddenly, our interview came alive.

"The cults completely destroy the mind," he said without qualification. "They destroy your ability to question things, and in destroying your ability to think, they also destroy your ability to feel. You have no desires, no emotion. You feel no pain, no joy, no nothing."

Patrick confirmed our own perspective when he described the method of control used by many cults, beginning with the moment the recruiter hooks his listener.

"They have the ability to come up to you and talk about anything they feel you're interested in, anything," he said. "Their technique is to get your attention, then your trust. The minute they get your trust, just like that they can put you in the cult."

It was the classic sales pitch, carried off so smoothly that it amounted to what Patrick called "on-the-spot hypnosis." Then, he said, once the potential member is hooked, the cult keeps up a steady barrage of indoctrination until conversion is complete.

"When they program a person," said Patrick intently, "they use repetition. They give him the same thing over and over again, day in and day out. They sit up there twenty-four hours a day saying everything outside that door is Satan, that the world is going to end within seven years, and that if you're not in their family you're going to burn in hell. When a person goes under, he feels guilty if he goes outside in that bad, evil world. He is terrified of what will happen to him out there."

Patrick stopped. His version was almost identical to the experiences Lawrence and Cathy Gordon had reported, although they had not been deprogrammed by Patrick but by one of his former clients. He leaned forward, resting his powerful arms on the table between us as he continued.

"There's just so much the human mind can take. You can stay up just so long without sleep. You can hear the same thing over and over and then it breaks you down. I went into one of the cults with the intention of staying a week. I stayed four days and three nights, and if I'd stayed six more hours I would have been hooked. I'd have never left."

It was in 1971 that Patrick infiltrated the Children of God, the cult that had tried to recruit his son, Michael, one Fourth of July on Mission Beach in San Diego. His initial concern over the cults was personal but it also had a public side. Worried parents had already appealed to him for help in his official capacity as head of community relations for California's San Diego and Imperial counties. Patrick had moved to the area years earlier and become active in local politics working against discrimination in employment. During the Watts riots in Los Angeles in 1965, he helped calm racial unrest in San Diego. His public service caught the attention of then California's Republican governor, Ronald Reagan, who appointed Patrick, an active Democrat, to the community relations post.

In his brief encounter with the Children of God, though he was alert to the cult's tactics, Patrick found that he was not immune to their effects.

"You can feel it coming on," he explained. "You start doubting yourself. You start to question everything you believe in. Then you find yourself saying and doing the same things they are. You feel like you're sinking in sand, drowning—sometimes you get dizzy."

Here, according to Patrick, was that moment when the individual first goes under, when he may experience the overwhelming emotional release of snapping. From then on, the new member is taught daily rituals of chanting and meditation which effectively prevent him from regaining control of his mind, or wanting to.

"Thinking to a cult member is like being stabbed in the heart with a dagger," said Patrick. "It's very painful, because they've been told that the mind is Satan and thinking is the machinery of the Devil."

Having gained personal insight into the manner in which that machinery may be brought to a halt, Patrick developed his controversial deprogramming procedure, the essence of which, he explained, was simply to get the individual thinking again.

"When you deprogram people," he emphasized, "you force them to think. The only thing I do is shoot them challenging questions. I hit them with things that they haven't been programmed to respond to. I know what the cults do and how they do it, so I shoot them the right questions; and they get frustrated when they can't answer. They think they have the answer, they've been given answers to everything. But I keep them off balance and this forces them to begin questioning, to open their minds. When the mind gets to a certain point, they can see through all the lies that they've been programmed to believe. They realize that they've been duped and they come out of it. Their minds start working again."

That, according to Patrick, was all there was to deprogramming. Yet since Patrick began deprogramming cult members, both the man and his procedure had taken on monstrous proportions in the public eye. Patrick's legendary kidnappings, a tactic he employed only as a last resort, often brought him into physical confrontation with cult members who had been warned that Black Lightning was an agent of Satan who would subject them to unimaginable tortures to get them to renounce their beliefs. Cult members who managed to escape their parents and Patrick before being deprogrammed frequently ran to the media with horror stories about the procedure. One young woman charged on national television that Patrick had ripped her clothes off and chased her nude body across the neighbors' lawns. Other active cult members claimed to have been brutally beaten by Patrick, yet no parent, ex-cult member or other reliable witness we talked to ever substantiated any of those charges. In truth, Patrick told us, and others later confirmed, many of the distortions that had been disseminated about deprogramming were part of a coordinated campaign by several cults to discredit his methods. In the end, he said, the propaganda only worked to his advantage.

"The cults tell them that I rape the women and beat them. They say I lock them in closets and stuff bones down their throats." Patrick laughed. "What they don't know is that they're making my job easier. They come in here frightened to death of me, and then, because of all the stuff they've been told, I can just sit there and look at them and I'll deprogram them just like that. They'll be thinking, *What the hell is he going to do now?* They're waiting for me to slap them or beat them and already their minds are working."

In the beginning, Patrick admitted, he developed his method by trial and error, attempting to reason with cult members and learning each cult's rituals and beliefs until he cracked the code. Refining his procedure with each case, he came to understand exactly what was needed to pierce the cults' mental shield. Like a diamond cutter, he probed with his questions the rough surface of speech and behavior until he found the key point of contention at the center of each cult member's encapsulated beliefs. Once he found that point, Patrick hit it head on, until the entire programmed state of mind gave way, revealing the cult member's original identity and true personality that had become trapped inside.

As Patrick loosened up, his spirit and confidence came through more freely. We asked him to describe a typical deprogramming from the beginning and, then, how he knew when a person had been deprogrammed, that is, when he could say for sure that he had done his job.

"The first time I lay eyes on a person," he said, staring at us intently, "I can tell if his mind is working or not. Then, as I begin to question him, I can determine exactly how he has been programmed. From then on, it's all a matter of language. It's talking and knowing what to talk about. I start challenging every statement the person makes. I start moving his mind, slowly, pushing it with questions, and I watch every move that mind makes. I know everything it is going to do, and when I hit on that one certain point that strikes home, I push it. I stay with that question—whether it's about God, the Devil or that person's having rejected his parents. I keep pushing and pushing. I don't let him get around it with the lies he's been told. Then there'll be a minute, a second, when the mind *snaps*, when the person realizes he's been lied to by the cult and he just snaps out of it. It's like turning on the light in a dark room. They're in an almost unconscious state of mind, and then I switch the mind from unconsciousness to consciousness and it *snaps*, just like that."

It was Patrick's term this time—we hadn't said the word—for what happens in deprogramming. And in almost every case, according to Patrick, it came about just that suddenly. When deprogramming has been accomplished, the cult member's appearance undergoes a sharp, drastic change. He comes out of his trancelike state and his ability to think for himself is restored.

"It's like seeing a person change from a werewolf into a man," said Patrick. "It's a beautiful thing. The whole personality changes, the eyes, the voice. Where they had hate and a blank expression, you can see feeling again."

Snapping, a word Ted Patrick used often, is a phenomenon that appears to have extreme moments at both ends. A moment of sudden, intense change may occur when a person enters a cult, during lectures, rituals and physical ordeals. Another change may take place with equal, or even greater, abruptness when the subject is deprogrammed and made to think again. Once this breakthrough is achieved, however, the person is not just "snapped out" and home free. Deprogramming always requires a period of rehabilitation to counter-act an interim condition Patrick called "floating." To ensure that cult members did not return to their cult state of mind, Patrick told us, he recommended that his subjects spend some time living in the home of a fully rehabilitated deprogrammee. He felt that the best way to keep a person from "backsliding," as he called it, was to return him to everyday life and normal social relationships as quickly as possible. In that environment, the individual must then actively work to rebuild the fundamental capacities of thought and feeling that have been systematically destroyed.

"Deprogramming is like taking a car out of the garage that hasn't been driven for a year," he said. "The battery has gone down, and in order to start it up you've got to put jumper cables on it. It will start up then, but if you turn the key off right away it will go dead again. So you keep the motor running until it builds up its own power. This is what rehabilitation is. Once we get the mind working, we keep it working long enough so that the person gets in the habit of thinking and making decisions again."

Deprogramming added a whole new dimension to the already complex mystery of snapping. In one sense, deprogramming confirms that some drastic change takes place in the workings of the mind in the course of a cult member's experience, for only through deprogramming does it become apparent to everyone, including the cult member, that his actions, expressions and even his physical appearance have not been under his own control. In another sense, deprogramming is itself a form of sudden personality change. Because it appears to be a genuinely broadening, expanding personal change, it would seem to bear closer resemblance to a true moment of enlightenment, to the natural process of personal growth and newfound awareness and understanding, than to the narrowing changes brought about by cult rituals and artificially induced group ordeals.

What is it like to experience the sudden snap of a deprogramming? As a result of Ted Patrick's efforts, and others, there are now thousands of answers to the question. Patrick claims to have personally deprogrammed more than two thousand cult members; thousands more have been deprogrammed by other deprogrammers and professional "exit counselors" who have since entered this fledgling field. In our first round of cross-country travels, we spoke with dozens of ex-cult members, many of whom had been deprogrammed by Patrick. As far as we could see, his clients showed no scars, either physical or mental, from their deprogramming experience. Most seemed to be healthy, happy, fully rehabilitated and completely free of the effects of cult life.

In contrast to the many tales of cult conversion that we heard, which after a while began to sound virtually identical, each story of a Patrick deprogramming was its own spellbinding adventure, rich with intrigue and planned in minute detail. The first step in the process was almost always to remove the member from the cult, which might be accomplished by abduction, legal custodianship or, as Patrick seemed to prefer, simply a clever subterfuge. One of the more suspenseful examples of this tactic was told to us by a young woman we will call Lynn Marshall, a former member of the Church of Armageddon, also known as Love Israel, one of the early Christian cults of the Pacific Northwest. She described her shanghaiing by Patrick and her family.

"I was kidnapped at the prompting of my parents," she told us. "My mother invited me to have lunch with her, but you weren't supposed to go anyplace by yourself in Love Israel—especially not with somebody from the outside world—so a guy went with me, the one we all called Logic, who in real life was the son of Steve Allen from television. We went out with my mother and had lunch. She was with a man she said was a friend of the family. They had a rented car and were going to drive us back, and when we got in the car they had me sit in the back seat with my mother while Logic sat in the front seat with her friend. We headed off in the wrong direction, and Logic said, 'We're going in the wrong direction,' and my mother's friend said, 'Well, I have a friend to visit.' He started to get on the freeway and he stopped to pick up this guy who was hitchhiking. I thought to myself, *He's going to pick up a hitchhiker with my mother in the car?* They made Logic get out because they said they wanted the hitchhiker to sit in the middle. Then when Logic got out they closed the door and left him standing there on the on-ramp. I thought my mother had gone crazy, but we sped off and my mother said, 'We're taking you home.' The hitchhiker was Ted Patrick."

Not all of Patrick's legendary kidnappings proceeded like clockwork. Another ex-cult member we spoke with, Tom Koppelman (not his real name), a former Hare Krishna "devotee," recalled his abduction; then he went on to describe the deprogramming process itself.

"They didn't talk about the deprogrammers much in Krishna," Koppelman said, "but I remember one devotee was about to leave once with his parents, and this guy mentioned that you had to be careful because there are people parents hire called deprogrammers and they beat you up and make you eat meat and parade prostitutes in front of you and put ice on the back of your neck to keep you awake."

With those fears instilled along with other fears of the outside world, Koppelman did not go gently into his own intricately planned deprogramming several months later.

"My father had the idea to tell the Krishnas that they were going to take me to the dentist to get my teeth checked," he recalled. "My mother picked me up and I went alone because my cult leader said I could. So we were driving the right way to the dentist, and suddenly my mother pulled behind this car and I asked, 'Why are you stopping?' and I looked up and these big guys got out of this Pontiac. They lifted me right out of the front seat into the back seat. I was scared to death. I was sure I was going to get taken to a motel and beaten up. So I started kicking and shouting and chanting *Hare Krishna* in the back seat."

When a cult member first realizes that he may be confronted in a deprogramming, some extreme reaction often follows. He may chant or pray until he sees the futility of his efforts, or he may appear to cooperate, but that does not mean the person has come out of his cult state of mind. Koppelman's response was typical of many we heard.

"I stopped shouting when they said they weren't going to do anything to me," he remembered. "They said they were only going to talk to me and that was all. Then I relaxed completely. I said to myself, *Boy, here's my chance. I'm going to convert all these people.* I also remember thinking, *This is sure going to make a great story when I get back to the temple.*"

From the first moment, the deprogramming process was under way. At the outset, Koppelman faithfully defended his sect, but just by listening to the deprogrammer and observing other people in the world outside, he started to sense the strangeness and alienation of his cult state of mind. It was his first inkling of doubt after months as an unwavering devotee.

"First I felt very strong," he recalled. "Then they got me to the house and I started to feel very small, like a withdrawing feeling."

Surprisingly, to deprogram this ascetic follower of Krishna, a Hindu God, Patrick used the same tool he might use on a Moonie or a Jesus freak: the Bible.

"Patrick knew a great deal about religion and I respected that," said Koppelman. "He started pulling out verse after verse from the Bible that really cut down the Krishna movement. I think the last one was 1 Timothy 4, which said, essentially, *There will be those who depart from the faith and with consciences as if seared by a hot iron will command not to marry and forbid the eating of meats, which God hath put on this earth to be taken with Thanksgiving*—something like that. That really got to me; it blew the groundwork out of the whole vegetarian business."

Here, as Patrick himself had described to us earlier, he determined from his initial questions that the core of Koppelman's bond to Krishna was the cult's argument against killing and eating animals, a belief held universally by Hindus and, in recent years, by growing numbers of Westerners of many faiths. In Koppelman's case, the belief was intricately tied to the cult's doctrines of self-denial and reincarnation, and to the extended ritual meditation practices that served as the group's primary technique of mental control. Patrick pressed the issue until he broke through Koppelman's main line of defense.

"Then something happened in my mind," Koppelman said. "I was sitting there and it was like there was this tremendous chasm that went way down. It looked like it was endless. Here I was on one side and I knew this side wasn't right. Things were just going around in my brain. I was still on the Krishna side at this point, but I could feel myself rushing toward this edge which I was crossing over. I was scared. I really wanted to say, Well, who do I follow now? But suddenly, *bang,* I was on the other side. In my mind, I could actually see myself leaping over this chasm. It was very vivid. There was a dark mist and this deep chasm. I moved toward it and hesitated at the edge, then I sort of went over. It's like in a dream when you jump and everything is in slow motion and then suddenly you wake up. I just snapped out of it completely and immediately got my sense of being human back. Instantly. Bingo!"

For Patrick, it was a familiar moment of confirmation. He noticed the change immediately, as did Koppelman's parents, who were present throughout the deprogramming. For everyone assembled, final proof came seconds later.

"The first thing I said was, 'Where are the prostitutes? I'm disappointed.' That was the first time I'd cracked a joke in six months."

As we listened to Koppelman's story, it became clear to us that he certainly had not been asleep all those months, nor had he been unconscious. Yet his state of mind was a deep "chasm" apart from our usual notion of awareness. He was conscious the whole time, but not thinking; as Patrick said, he had been robbed of his *freedom* of thought. Immersed in a fantasy world, Koppelman was cut off from that vital quality philosophers and theologians in the West used to refer to as "free will." Without it, he was a different person altogether, blank and humorless, until the deprogramming procedure broke through the shell of his less than fully human existence.

Bill Garber, as we will call him here, an ex-member of the Divine Light Mission, another Hindu cult founded in the early seventies by a rotund teen-age guru named Maharaj Ji, painted a slightly different picture of the deprogramming process.

"Ted took me to the limits with a series of questions," he told us, "and I found myself wondering what was going on, since I supposedly had a monopoly on truth and love and he didn't, and I was not supposed to be able to be talked out of my faith. Ted's questions had to do with people in other groups. He asked me what made me think that I had the only true way when they all felt that they had the only true way. I knew I couldn't handle that one, so I just started meditating and waiting for the guru to send me the answer. Then Ted said, 'Meditation is okay, but not when someone is using it to control your mind. You have been brainwashed without your knowledge or consent.' I stopped meditating and a few ideas popped into my head. I began thinking about the interrelatedness of selling techniques and brainwashing. Ted didn't know it, but I had been an encyclopedia salesman some years before."

As Garber described it, the moment when he snapped out was more abstract than wildly dreamlike. Yet for him, as for Tom Koppelman, its abruptness was unforgettable.

"The effect was something like whipping through a deck of IBM cards," he remembered, drawing an image from those dawning days of the computer era. "A couple of ideas fell together with a kind of a *zap*. It was the first imaginative thinking I'd done in a considerable period of time. Everything came together with such a suddenness that Ted didn't even know what he had done."

And for Garber, the moment when his mind switched back on was accompanied by extraordinary physical sensations.

"I sat there with this dazed look on my face," he said. "I was jolted, as if by a shock, and there was a momentary visual distortion which was part of the overwhelmingness of it, like having a zoom lens built into your eyes. All of a sudden, Ted's face went *zip-zip*. I never experienced that before, and I haven't experienced it since."

One puzzle of snapping that the deprogramming process illuminates is the enormous amount of mental activity that takes place in the unthinking, unfeeling state many cult members are drawn into. Ironically, most people we spoke with fought desperately to preserve their blissed-out states, although they often were saturated with fear, guilt, hatred and exhaustion. In the beginning this seemed to present a disturbing contradiction: How could an individual whose mind has apparently been shut off, who has been robbed of his freedom of thought, display such cunning and initiative? What the deprogramming process demonstrated is that cult members do not simply snap from a normal conscious state into one of complete unconsciousness (and vice versa during deprogramming). Rather, most pass from one frame of waking awareness into a second, entirely separate, frame of awareness in which they may be equally active and perceptive.

We talked with an ex-member of the Church of Scientology, one of the oldest and cagiest of America's cults, who took steps to preserve his cult frame of mind during his deprogramming, until Patrick's adept conversational skills caught his attention and he snapped out.

"I tried to pretend that I was listening," this former Scientologist told us, "but I also tried to stay spaced out and not really pay attention. Occasionally, something would go *pop* and I would suddenly be listening to him. The feeling was mainly caused by his continuous talking and changing the speeds of how he was talking. He made his own rhythm and his own changes of high-pitched and low-pitched tones that was really refreshing. From his continuously talking like that, he just snapped me out of the spaced-out state I was in. All of a sudden I felt a little flushed. I could feel the blood rushing through my face."

To further our understanding of deprogramming and its controversial inventor, we looked into Patrick's background and, during our interview, asked him questions about his childhood, discovering a depth of experience that gave clues to his insights into the tactics used by the cults. Born and raised in Chattanooga, Tennessee, young Theodore Roosevelt Patrick had even more social handicaps to overcome than just being poor and black. The man who came to work wonders with words was born with a speech impediment that brought him into contact, at an early age, with many dubious forms of religion.

"My mother carried me to every fortune-teller, faith healer, Holy Roller, false god, prophet, voodoo and hoodoo—every one that came into town; but you could hardly understand a word I was saying," Patrick told us. "My sister had to interpret for me. Then suddenly it came to me. I thought, *Are you asking God to do something that you are not willing to do for yourself? Have you tried?* And I knew I hadn't."

So Patrick cured himself.

"I'd always been afraid of words," he confessed. "I was unable to say a lot of words because I was afraid they'd come out wrong. So I started correcting myself over and over again, out loud. Even when I was in church, my mind would be correcting itself over and over again. That's how I got to the point where I can talk now."

After overcoming his initial disadvantages, Patrick progressed through ten years of public school, leaving high school to embark on his career of social activism in defense of minority rights. Later, when he began his battle against the cults, it must have seemed ironic to many who knew him that he had become passionately engaged in what superficially appeared to be a fight against the rights of individuals and minorities. When he first began deprogramming, Patrick was well aware that he was technically violating the First Amendment freedoms of the cult members he abducted. In view of the circumstances, however, and the observable changes that had come over the cult members, Patrick was led to draw his fine and hotly debated distinction between constitutional and human freedoms.

"When you're born into this world, you're born into the laws of nature," Patrick asserted, "and only then are you introduced to the laws of the land. Anytime someone destroys your free will, when they take away your mind and your natural ability to think, then they've destroyed the *person*. As long as you remain in that condition, you have no more constitutional rights to violate."

From the beginning, Patrick spoke out boldly in defense of freedom of thought, knowing that his new procedure would cost him his job and his own freedom as well. Although he had been deprogramming cult members full-time for years, Patrick remained a deeply moral and religious man. Nevertheless, in his deprogrammings, he took great care never to impose his own religious beliefs, or anyone else's, on the young people he rescued.

"When I deprogram people," he stressed, "I don't make any mention of a church or whether or not I even believe in God. That's beside the point. My intention is to get their minds working again and to get them back out in the world. I've been through the Bible, I know it backwards, but I didn't begin to understand the Bible until I got out of school, when I hit the streets and started studying people. That's the only way to use the Bible; you must relate it to everyday life. When the twenty-fourth chapter of Matthew says, *There will be many coming in my name, saying, I am Christ; and they will deceive the very elect,* then people should relate it to all these false gods today."

There were signs that some people were beginning to understand. By the late seventies, as other deprogrammers started working around the country, most former clients or self-confessed imitators of Patrick's style, they benefitted greatly from the trailblazing efforts of Patrick and Sondra Sacks, the mother of a young Hare Krishna member Patrick had deprogrammed, who worked closely with Patrick through the seventies. That evening, as we prepared to leave the cramped visitors' cubicle in the Orange County Jail, Patrick told us of his plan to write a manual of deprogramming, one that would clear up some of the public and professional confusion surrounding his technique and place it in a broader framework that might be of value in treating other mental and emotional disorders. Patrick grew philosophical as we touched upon the implications of his work.

"A lot of people who are in mental hospitals have nothing wrong with them," he said. "They just don't know how to accept life for what it is and not what they want it to be. Like in here, for instance, I adjust myself to this jail. I enjoy myself in prison because I'm stuck here." As he continued, his powerful dark eyes began to twinkle. "I got them organizing here," he confided. "It's been booming the past week. One hundred and five inmates signed a petition requesting a grand jury investigation of my case."

After eight months in prison, apparently, Black Lightning was back in action.

Three days after we left him, he was released from jail.

Through two decades of his legal battles and repeated periods of imprisonment and probation, few people spoke up in defense of Ted Patrick or the pioneering work he was doing, ultimately, at his own great personal and financial expense. No mainstream mental health organization or established social institution has yet taken a stand on behalf of his concept of freedom of thought. Part of the problem, especially in those early years, was attributable to Patrick's manner of action. In his single-minded focus on rescuing cult members, he minced no words and wasted little time on social niceties. As a result, he often irked and alienated those parents, clinicians and law enforcement officials who might otherwise be his natural allies.

Yet, regardless of his style, the grave questions Patrick first flamboyantly brought to public attention are not ones we can choose to like or dislike—nor will they simply go away if we ignore them. Is an individual free to give up his freedom of thought? May a religion, popular therapy, political movement or any other enterprise systematically attack human thought and feeling in the name of God, the pursuit of happiness, personal growth or spiritual fulfillment? These are questions that Americans, perhaps more than others, are not prepared to deal with, because they challenge long-standing constitutional principles and cultural assumptions about the nature of the mind, personality and human freedom itself.

In the months after our trip to the Orange County Jail we spoke with many people about Ted Patrick: parents, ex-cult members, attorneys, mental health professionals and others who, at the time, were only dimly aware of the building controversy over some alleged forms of religion in America. Some denounced him as a villain and a fascist, others hailed him as a folk hero and dark prophet of what lay ahead for America. Yet Patrick himself showed little concern for titles or media images.

We met with him again during the summer of 1977, in Colorado, where he had gone voluntarily to serve out the last few weeks of an earlier kidnapping conviction in that state. He greeted us warmly in a private visiting room at the Denver Jail, his hands and shirt covered with bright-colored paint from work he had been doing in the prison workshop. Our talk turned to the cult controversy and his own worsening legal and financial situation caused by a flood of lawsuits filed against him by several large, wealthy cults. In a statement more prescient at the time than either of us knew, Patrick became somber, concerned over what he saw as the public's growing apathy in the face of the cult world's increasing wealth, power and social legitimacy.

"The cult movement is the greatest threat and danger to this country that we have ever had," he said gravely, "but the people won't wake up, the government, Congress, the Justice Department won't wake up until something bad happens."

With regard to his own work, he said, he felt a greater urgency than ever, and he was already marshalling his forces to go back into battle upon his release. He said he would try to stay within the law wherever possible in the future, but if it became a question of crossing the line to save a cult member's captive mind, he had no doubt what his priority would be. Patrick assured us he would continue to appeal to government and the mental health establishment for their help, although he saw little hope of winning support for his efforts.

"Sooner or later, they're going to have to recognize deprogramming as a profession," he said. "They're going to be forced to. But right now they don't believe that this is something that can happen to anybody. Everybody's vulnerable. I want to make people aware of that."

We crossed paths with Patrick many times in the years that followed. We interviewed him for *Playboy* just days before the 1978 Jonestown cult massacre, and we shared a podium with him and other cult investigators at a joint U.S. House-Senate committee hearing on the cult phenomenon convened in Washington in 1979. He was convicted on another kidnapping charge in 1980 and spent a year in two more California prisons in the mid-eighties for violating his probation on that conviction. He survived another criminal indictment in Washington State and weathered two dozen civil suits for claims totaling more than $100 million.

Through the eighties, Black Lightning remained a lightning rod, a target of aggressive counterattacks and disinformation campaigns waged against deprogramming by major cults and more mainstream fundamentalist Christian sects. By the mid-nineties, he was widely presumed to be out of commission, but Patrick was still active, working mostly on voluntary deprogrammings and rehabilitation counseling. In the interim, swayed by a changing religious, political and social climate, courts across the country grew cold to deprogramming. Another pioneering deprogrammer, New York cult counselor and private detective Galen Kelly, was prosecuted on criminal charges in two separate cases in the same federal court in Virginia. Kelly won the first case but was convicted and spent more than a year in prison on the second before an appeals court overturned his conviction.

Those cases and others brought a global chill. In the new climate, judges were deaf to the pleas of the parents and families of cult members, and the precarious deprogramming profession was largely eclipsed by the efforts of the new generation of cult "exit counselors." Exit counselors we talked with, many of them one-time sect members themselves who had gone on to acquire clinical training and credentials, were testing a wide range of eclectic approaches, some more successful, some less so. Many were generalists, counseling cultists and families across America and, increasingly, in other countries. Some specialized in counseling ex-Moonies, members of Eastern cults, or controlling charismatic groups and extreme fundamentalist sects.

Most confirmed a pattern we, too, had noted: the new methods of voluntary deprogramming and exit counseling, while far less controversial and much safer from a legal standpoint, prompted fewer cult members to experience a sudden "snapping out" of their controlled states of mind. Instead, most experienced a slower process of emergence, or as Rick Ross, an exit counselor from Arizona, called it, a gradual "unfolding" from the cults' ingrained altered states. Afterwards, many required additional counseling, specialized rehabilitation and, for some, ongoing psychotherapy to recover their personalities and regain full control over their impaired powers of mind.

At the Wellspring Center in southern Ohio, one of the few organized post-cult rehabilitation centers, Paul Martin, Ph.D., himself an ex-member of an extreme Christian sect who went on to earn a clinical degree in psychology and doctorate in counseling, became the first exit counselor to develop diagnostic tests of cult effects and systematic methods to help departing cultists traverse the difficult steps of emergence and re-entry into society. He and other exit counselors worked productively with the media and interested clinicians to bring the spreading phenomenon of cult control to higher levels of public and professional concern.

But, two decades later, public understanding and professional support were still in short supply.

7 The Crisis in Mental Health

The present crisis of psychology (which, however, has already lasted for some 30 years) can be summarized as the slow erosion of the robot model of man.

—*Ludwig von Bertalanffy,*
General Systems Theory *(1968)*

IN THE EARLY YEARS, Ted Patrick made repeated appeals to the mental health community. The professionals, however, almost totally ignored his insights into cult techniques and effects, and they flatly refused to become involved in the public controversy over deprogramming. But Ted Patrick was not the only person who was brushed aside. A much less controversial figure, William Rambur of Chula Vista, California, was similarly disregarded in his efforts to bring the cults' new threat to personality to the attention of mental health specialists.

Wanted: Professional Help. William Rambur went to bat for the perplexed, embarrassed, angry, heartbroken parents of America's cult members who had been legally handcuffed in their efforts to rescue their sons and daughters. In 1973, he helped organize the Citizen's Freedom Foundation and became its first president. The group, later renamed the Cult Awareness Network, soon claimed thousands of active members and became the nationwide umbrella for dozens of parent, ex-member and concerned citizen groups combatting destructive cults. Since CAN's founding, its small staff and many volunteers have helped to locate and rescue cult members who have disappeared from their schools, homes and city streets. They have published newsletters, given lectures and worked actively with local media in an ongoing program of public education. And they have traveled repeatedly to Washington to ask for government investigation and prosecution of alleged cult abuses.

In our initial swing through Southern California, we stopped at the group's first office in Chula Vista, near San Diego, where we spent an emotional afternoon that stretched into evening with William and Betty Rambur. There we heard one of the most appalling stories of our investigation.

As with Ted Patrick and many others who have taken up the fight against destructive cults, sects and therapies, theRamburs' activism was born of painful personal experience. In July 1971, theRamburs' daughter Kay vanished abruptly from her job as a registered nurse. Soon after her disappearance, William and Betty Rambur received a letter from their daughter informing them that she had joined a group called the Children of God and that she had decided to devote her life to the service of Jesus Christ. Kay had always been a religious girl, but given no further explanation, the Ramburs were baffled by her decision. After repeated attempts to find her, they finally located Kay on a Children of God farm in Texas, where they were horrified to see for themselves all the signs of the cult state. As we sat surrounded by great bins of mail in the burgeoning cult network office, William Rambur, firm but mild-mannered after his many years as a high school teacher, told us what it felt like to see his daughter in that condition.

"You know how when you look at people," said Rambur, "you look them in the eye and it seems like they're looking back at you? In the case of the cult members, you look in their eyes and they're not looking back. It's a strange thing, especially when it's your own daughter, and you look in her eyes and remember how she looked the last time you saw her, and now there's nothing, no emotion or anything left. It's just like a void, and you look in other people's eyes who are in these cults and you see the same thing. It's scary."

On the COG farm, Rambur told us, he walked with his daughter in a field and persuaded her to return home to Chula Vista. As they were driving away, several COG members sped up in another car and blocked them from leaving. Without a word, Kay unlocked the car door and went back with the other members. Several months later, Rambur finally managed to talk Kay into returning home for a weekend. Once she was free of the closed cult environment, Rambur said, he and his wife succeeded in questioning Kay and reasoning with her until they effected a crude deprogramming of sorts.

"Finally she came out of it," Rambur recalled. "She seemed like her old self again. She was happy. She said, as far as the Children of God were concerned, they could go to hell, she was out of it."

When Kay snapped out of her altered state, she gave her father some very specific instructions.

"She said, 'Dad, all of those people in there need help,' " said Rambur, "but we've got to help them from the outside, because nobody can help themselves from inside.' She said, 'Dad, don't ever give up fighting, because if you ever give up fighting, they'll never get out by themselves.' "

But Kay Rambur's amateur deprogramming was far from complete. For the next few days she lingered in the precarious "floating" state, a twilight zone of uncertainty and vulnerability to suggestion. During that time, Kay and her father attempted to free Robert, another cult member who had been married to Kay by cult leaders in what Rambur interpreted as an attempt to remove her from her father's legal jurisdiction. Rambur and his daughter phoned Robert to invite him to spend a few days at their home. Rambur told Robert that he was welcome, and he heard his daughter say, "Robert, it's beautiful, you've got to come." Then he and his wife left the room to let Kay talk to Robert alone.

"That was our mistake," Rambur said sadly, "but that was before anyone really knew."

While Robert and Kay were talking, Betty Rambur picked up the phone to extend her welcome to Robert. She heard him tell Kay, "If you leave the Children of God, you'll be responsible for the deaths that follow. The blood will be on your hands."

Astounded by what she was hearing, Betty Rambur told Robert that he was welcome in their home, but that she wouldn't tolerate that kind of talk. Then she put down the receiver, and a few minutes later Kay emerged markedly transformed.

"When Kay came out of that back room she was just a different person," said Rambur. "She was only on the phone a couple of minutes, but when she came out she was like a zombie again."

The nightmare that followed was as incomprehensible as it was horrifying. Rambur said that just after Kay talked to Robert, two neighbors received anonymous telephone calls warning them that if they didn't stop associating with the Ramburs they would be killed and "there wouldn't be enough bones left to bury." Children of God members lined the Ramburs' street in trucks and vans, and Kay rushed out screaming that the Devil was in the house. As Rambur and his son brought Kay back inside and tried to calm her, Kay wrestled her brother to the ground and started to choke him. She hit one of the Ramburs' neighbors across the neck and kicked another in the groin. Finally, the Ramburs called the police, who responded promptly, restored peace, and recommended that Kay be hospitalized. At this point, Rambur had his first confrontation with the mental health profession.

"When we got to the hospital there was a woman doctor who we later discovered had been contacted by the Children of God," he said. "They called the hospital when they found out we were coming and told her that an upset father was trying to bring his daughter in to have her committed. When we walked in there, the first thing she said to Kay was, 'You're not crazy, are you?' She refused to admit her to the hospital. She said, 'There's nothing wrong with her. I think it's the father who is upset. He's the one who needs help.'"

At the time, Rambur couldn't believe his ears. He said, "Look, if you think that's how it is, put me in, too! Put us both in here." But the admitting doctor steadfastly refused.

"We just didn't know what to do," said Rambur, reliving the scene. "This whole episode had gone on for close to a week, and most of us had had no sleep during that time and we were getting pretty distraught. We'd reached the end of the line, so I told my daughter, 'Look, you think I'm persecuting you? I'll not persecute you. I will not try to find you, but I want you to remember this: If you ever need me, I'll come.'"

They left her there, got into their car and drove home and went to sleep. After about an hour, however, William and Betty Rambur woke up and said to each other, "Why are we doing this? How could we abandon her?" Desperate, they called the hospital and talked to the chief of staff, who told them a psychiatrist had examined Kay, found nothing wrong and released her.

"That was six years ago," said Rambur, looking over to his wife, then back to us, "and no one has seen her since."

In the years that followed, police in twenty-seven countries were unable to trace Kay Rambur's whereabouts. William Rambur remembered his daughter's plea, however, and traveled around the United States to help other parents find their children and free them from cult control. Time after time, Rambur appealed to the mental health community, but the strange new disorder he brought to their attention posed a peculiar dilemma for their expertise.

"I phoned many psychologists and psychiatrists and asked if they would help; if we could get a youth to come to them, would they give us some insight into the situation?" Rambur remembered. "Several said that they would try. Once, after getting the youth there, the psychiatrist called me and said, 'Look, we're wasting our time. That person has to admit that he has a problem'"—which is something few cult members are prone to do under any circumstances.

Later, Rambur took his plea to other professionals, only to meet with a similar lack of comprehension. "I spoke to a group of sociologists and explained to them what was happening," he told us, exasperated. "They could follow me up to a point; then we got to this threshold that I couldn't make them go beyond. They wouldn't believe this is something new that they should study. They said, 'Why don't you parents go home and relax, and after a certain period your children will come back to you and everything will be fine.' They wouldn't entertain the possibility that what is going on is very different."

Rambur did not dismiss the traditional responses he heard from clinicians and academicians. As a teacher, he was among the first to admit that parental upbringing and social pressures were often important factors in cult conversion. But these simplistic explanations, he felt, begged a larger and more immediate question concerning cult conversion techniques.

"Psychologists and psychiatrists who are not aware of what is happening will try to base their opinions on past behavior," said Rambur, "and they lose sight of the fact that there is a new element here that they know nothing about."

Rambur asked us to convey a message to the professionals.

"We've reached the threshold of something new and different," he repeated. "Now we have to add to what we knew before and go beyond that into a new area of study of the mind."

He spoke eloquently but he knew, like Ted Patrick, that without proper credentials, he would get no one to listen. After six years, William Rambur's voice of experience had grown hoarse.

"They've studied cases in their textbooks," he said with a measure of resignation, "but I've studied the real thing. You would think that psychiatrists and psychologists would sit down and talk to me."

As frustrated as parents are who have been unable to secure help for their children, the situation is immeasurably harder for many cult members who have themselves sought professional guidance. We spoke with one young man we call Paul Davis who was a rare figure among America's early ex-cult fraternity. After spending nearly two years in the Unification Church in the mid-seventies, Davis left the Moonies on his own, first choosing to visit his family for a weekend, then simply deciding not to return to his life in the sect. Davis never underwent deprogramming, however, and he never snapped out of his cult state. For three months after he left the group, he endured an excruciating mental and emotional ordeal. His encounter with a psychiatrist was typical of the quality of professional help received by growing numbers of casualties of the new cults and therapies.

"I had an uncomfortable feeling in my head," Davis recalled the

day we met, his voice still shaky. "I was unable to focus my consciousness or my thoughts. I couldn't differentiate between what was true
and what was not. It was a very emotional thing. I was almost in a
state of shock. I was unable to relax, always spaced out. My pupils
were dilated; I couldn't focus on anything or talk to anybody in a normal way. So I went to a psychiatrist and told him I was in very bad
trouble. He couldn't comprehend it. He said someone had planted unconscious things in my mind."

Unconscious things. We catalogued many professional interpretations of "the cult syndrome" that were passed on to us in those early
years by parents and ex-cult members. According to America's mental
health establishment, the sudden personality changes people experienced in the cults were caused by "serious failures in family life," "underlying anxieties" and "guilt-ridden insecurities." They were the
product of "ego conflicts," "masochistic reactions" and "emotional im-
maturity." They could be traced to "environmental factors," "anteced-
ent conditions" or "deep-seated subconscious needs."

Two decades later, we were still adding to our catalog. Despite
much public testimony to the phenomenon, and mounting clinical evidence of the cults' altered state and its persisting effects, ex-cult members commonly reported being diagnosed by respected professionals as
suffering from "paranoid schizophrenia," "bipolar manic-depressive disorder" and even "temporo-limbic epilepsy." The new diagnosis attributed that age-old neurological disorder to modern youths and adults
whose speech or behavior showed an "obsessive preoccupation with
religion."

Fortunately, such verdicts were not unanimous. Beginning in the
late seventies, a small number of clinicians around the country began
cult counseling efforts of their own. In some cases their clinical background proved helpful, providing trained counselors with effective keys
to unlock captive minds. Yet in many instances their professional concepts and jargon served only to obscure the main objective: which was
to help cult members regain their ability to think for themselves. In
many cases we heard about, powerful psychoactive drugs were prescribed that have never been tested, or even investigated scientifically, for their potential value or drawbacks among people suffering
aftereffects of a traumatic cult experience.

In fact, as public concern has mounted over the visible dilemmas
of the cult phenomenon, and as growing numbers of people fall victim
to mass-marketed therapies and more extreme cult-like movements,
America's mental health professionals and their colleagues in related
academic disciplines have contributed little to public or professional

understanding of the problem. Their old models fail to match up with the new facts; their analyses are based on concepts left over from eras that bear little resemblance to late twentieth-century America or any other advanced society. Above all, while family members and cult casualties themselves cry out for support, America's mental health community has shown little sign of assuming the leadership role that would seem to be its responsibility on such matters.

In 1984, the national office of the Cult Awareness Network received more than 5,000 inquiries from individuals and families affected by destructive cults, sects and self-help therapies. By 1994, that number had climbed to more than 22,000 calls and letters yearly—more than seventy requests for help each working day.

The Robot Model Unplugged. America's epidemic of sudden personality change is itself a symptom of a deeper crisis in the mental health of the culture as a whole. This crisis, long building below the surface, first became evident during the consciousness explosion of the sixties, which had a profound impact on mental health practice across the country and on the lives of many mental health professionals as well.

Until the early sixties, Western psychological thought cleaved neatly along two theoretical lines: the Freudian, or psychoanalytic, and the behaviorist, often called Skinnerian or positivist school. The psychoanalytic school separated human personality into a set of mental subdivisions called ego, id and superego, which were believed to be governed largely by the "unconscious." The behaviorist school dealt solely with observable behavior, insisting that mental activity and "internal states" were of little significance in human affairs because they could not be observed or reproduced experimentally.

The psychoanalytic and the behaviorist schools of psychology are still generally considered to be diametrically opposed to one another in both theory and therapy. The first looks inside the psyche to the realm of unconscious mental processes; the other stands back to validate only the observable product of behavior. Yet both models share a common assumption about human beings: that an individual's conscious experience of the world around him is, at best, of secondary importance in the development of his personality and the determination of his behavior. In the Freudian tradition, the unknowable and unreachable unconscious governs personality. In behaviorist theory, an indeterminate number of environmental forces automatically condition an individual's responses. This common assumption unites the traditional forces of psychology in contemporary culture; both relegate an individual's power over his thoughts, feelings and actions to some form of hidden internal or external control beyond the reach of everyday awareness. Taken together, the two traditions, one inner, one outer, comprise the "robot model" of man, the theoretical base of psychology upon which our technological society has evolved.

In this century, application of the robot model has become a major preoccupation of modern society generally and the free enterprise system particularly. The business world has developed perhaps the most sophisticated fusion of the two schools. Its mass-marketing and advertising strategies target basic human needs, wants, desires and personal insecurities in order to create and fulfill consumer demands with scientific predictability. Throughout our society, the conscious control of unwitting human beings remains the focus of powerful institutions. It is taken for granted by many in politics, religion and mass media. It is the subject of continuing experimentation in offices, factories and other work environments. The same mentality has prospered commercially in a spate of best-selling books advising readers how to exploit tactics of "body language," "assertiveness," "power dressing," "winning through intimidation" and countless other methods for turning the unawareness of others to one's own advantage.

Yet, as predominant as the robot model of man has been and continues to be in modern life, there has always been an alternative force in psychology, and it, too, has gained strength and popularity in recent years. In the fifties, splinter groups from the main trunks of Freudian and behaviorist theory began to coalesce into a new school of thought on human nature. This so-called "Third Force" in psychology was made up of many of Freud's early disciples and later rivals, among them Alfred Adler, Otto Rank and Freud's protégé Carl Jung. These towering figures were joined by emerging existential and humanistic psychologists such as Gordon Allport, Gardner Murphy, Rollo May, Carl Rogers and Abraham Maslow, and by dynamic social psychologists such as Kurt Lewin. By the early sixties, after many of its founders had died, this Third Force became one with humanistic psychology, the new discipline that would lead the way in the exploration of humankind's uniquely human capacities. In recognizing the mind's unlimited creative potentials, the new force unplugged the robot model and gave primacy to human awareness and the shaping power of human experience.

The new humanistic therapies offered impressive demonstrations of that power. They used a person's own experience as a tool to help the individual to alter, not simply patterns of behavior, but his state of awareness, even his whole personality. Almost overnight, the new psychology and its offspring, the human potential movement, transformed popular attitudes toward mental health beyond recognition, first on the West Coast, then spreading quickly eastward. Suddenly, people drastically reduced their participation in psychoanalysis, psychotherapy and traditional group therapy—small weekly groups led by a psychiatrist or psychologist devoted primarily to talk along traditional lines. Instead, they entered into weekend encounter groups, extended marathons and more radical therapies that used intense physical and emotional experiences, including arm wrestling, body massage, verbal attacks and prolonged confinement, to produce those now familiar peak experiences and breakthrough moments.

In the beginning, the new humanistic methods received a cool reception from tradition-bound clinicians. Encounter group therapies contradicted almost every rule of traditional mental health practice. By urging personal confrontation and, sometimes, physical contact among group leaders and members, they trampled on sacred accords of the doctor-patient relationship and overturned inviolable canons of professional detachment. Yet the first results achieved by the new techniques were difficult to ignore. Often people returned to their traditional therapy sessions raving about the fun they had in an encounter group and declaring that they had accomplished more in one weekend than they had in years of private analysis. As the consciousness explosion took off, despite their skepticism, many professionals were forced to pay attention to this personal testimony.

Before long, however, the new experimental climate turned heedless, and many searchers strayed into no-man's-lands of awareness. Growing numbers found themselves cut loose from their mental moorings, set adrift, run aground—and they began to react accordingly. Across the country, some people began to snap visibly, "flip out" and go crazy, engaging in violent and self-destructive behavior. Others snapped quietly and flipped inward, dropping into states of fantasy, delusion, disorientation and psychic terror that were, in those early days, unforeseen and wholly inexplicable.

Predictably, the burden of treating the new casualties of the consciousness explosion fell on the shoulders of the psychiatric profession, on the medical doctors who manned the nation's emergency rooms, crisis units and psychiatric wards, and who were the first to see those people in most urgent need of professional help. However, psychiatry was not prepared to deal with this new monster of "experience," nor was it capable of treating the unusual disorders of personality it was spurring. In the sixties, when clinicians first identified this new category of mental and emotional disturbance caused neither by known neurological dysfunctions, childhood traumas nor recognized environmental factors, they found they could not diagnose it as either medically based mental illness or traditional psychological malaise. Many described it simply as a "critical situational response," a crisis brought on by some new and intense experience, such as psychedelic drugs, encounter groups, Eastern ritual practices—or by everyday social problems of indefinable origin.

The traditional tools of psychiatry proved ineffective for diagnosis and treatment, and slowly the old approaches began to give way to new systems of interpretation. For the first time, psychiatrists began to look beyond the clinic, the couch and the laboratory. New insights from humanistic psychology were incorporated into existing models and practices. By the late sixties, revolutionary approaches to mental health, such as family therapy and community counseling, were being applied to the new problems affecting individuals in all kinds of groups and everyday life situations. Along with psychiatrists and psychologists, other mental health professionals—clinical social workers and rehabilitation counselors—began to serve in front-line positions and play new supporting roles to help cope with the greatly increased numbers of adults, adolescents and even young children who had begun using counseling services, drug rehabilitation facilities and crisis centers from coast to coast.

But not all the changes taking place in the mental health field were confined to questions of patient treatment. By the late sixties, professionals at the forefront of American psychiatry and psychology were themselves immersed in experimentation, exploring the new techniques personally in search of alternate modes of insight and understanding. Yet, like anyone else, they were not immune to the new techniques' effects. Many professionals from traditional backgrounds found themselves ill-equipped to deal with new humanistic notions of creativity, play and spontaneity, and unprepared for the moving peak experiences and alterations of awareness they encountered.

By the mid-seventies, surviving traditionalists in the ranks of psychiatry continued to mind their own business while others in the profession were growing overloaded and exhausted. Many younger members fled the field for alternative careers. The profession ignored its social responsibility to issue warnings, establish guidelines and set other criteria that might aid the millions who were searching indiscriminately for some ill-defined personal or spiritual breakthrough. By the end of the decade, the mental health establishment had pulled back almost completely from the wave of experimentation still coursing through the culture. In an effort to reassert itself as a field of scientific inquiry and clinical practice, psychiatry retreated to its medical foundations. Psychiatrists turned increasingly toward pharmacological treatments for mental and emotional disorders. In many areas, professionals simply abandoned their clinical commitments and public service activities. In the transition, tens of thousands of institutionalized patients were given maintenance doses of medication and sent out on the streets to fend for themselves. Major psychiatric institutions, along with other vital clinical, counseling and rehabilitation services, were dramatically reduced in size or cut back financially, prompting the public in general to seek out alternative religious and commercial versions of those much-needed services.

Left without leadership, the rest of the mental health community remained silent while powerful new group techniques, radical therapies, and other tools for altering human awareness and personality slipped into the hands of cult leaders, spiritual empire-builders and self-help entrepreneurs.

8 Beyond Brainwashing

"At Panmunjon the American imperialists and their running dogs and lackeys, the British capitalist ruling clique, are holding up the peace talks. In the imperialists' prison camps they are torturing, starving and killing the Korean and Chinese prisoners, but we will remain calm and will never torture or kill you. You are safe with us. We shall always self-consciously carry out the Lenient Policy and thus shall continue to give you the chance to study and learn the truth, and see how your leaders are catching the people in a web of lies and preparing to extend the Korean conflict, and unleash a third world war."

—Commandant POW camp in Korea, 1954
(quoted in a British chaplain's account
of his imprisonment)

WHILE THE MENTAL health establishment was grappling with the consciousness explosion, "critical situational response" and the changing mental health of the nation as a whole, the appearance of the new "cult syndrome" with its total transformation of personality posed an added and unwanted challenge. Sudden personality changes had been taking place in American religious arenas for decades, but they had been practically ignored by the mental health field, first because they posed few legal or social problems but also because religion and psychiatry, like church and state, had traditionally refrained from crossing into one another's territory. With the rise of the new cults and the growing legal concern for the constitutional rights of cult members, some members of the mainstream mental health community, with considerable caution and reservation, began to examine this bizarre form of personality change.

In the late seventies, a small group of professionals from across the United States—psychiatrists, psychologists, social workers and lawyers working on mental health and legal forefronts—began to acknowledge that what was happening to America's cult members was indeed something new. Their newfound national organization, the American Family Foundation, marked the first professional attempt to understand the cult experience, to aid cult casualties, and to help cult parents and family members in their own needs for professional support and treatment. What these professionals were first forced to admit was that their traditional tools of analysis and treatment were woefully inadequate to those tasks at hand.

In the beginning, there was one man, Dr. John G. Clark, Jr., an assistant clinical professor of psychiatry at Harvard Medical School and Massachusetts General Hospital, who co-founded AFF in 1979 and served as its first resident scholar. Several years earlier, walking point on the issue, Clark had testified before a special committee of the Vermont State Senate investigating "the effects of some religious cults on the health and welfare of their converts." In his statement, he cited the known health hazards, both physical and psychological, and noted that limit beyond which his profession had been unable to go. Said Clark:

> The fact of a personality shift in my opinion is established. The fact that this is a phenomenon basically unfamiliar to the mental health profession I am certain of. The fact that our ordinary methods of treatment don't work is also clear, as are the frightening hazards to the process of personal growth and mental health.

Soon a few other concerned professionals rose to the challenge, among them psychologist Margaret Singer, Ph.D., of the University of California at Berkeley and Dr. Louis Jolyon West of the UCLA Neurosychiatric Institute, both of whom became charter members of AFF and, along with others in the group, soon became embroiled personally and professionally in the mental health debate. In their efforts to account for this new kind of "personality shift," these professionals and others turned to the only body of knowledge that was recognized at the time as research related to the phenomenon: the inquiries conducted decades earlier into the way the human mind responds in situations of extreme physical and psychological duress. A generation before, this topic took on international urgency with the discovery of extreme examples of sudden shifts in belief, behavior and personality which came to be identified with a process known as "brainwashing."

Brainwashing. The term brainwashing entered the vernacular in the early 1950s. Then it served as a vivid description of the technique

Chinese communist revolutionaries employed in their long march to power to change the beliefs and behavior of the mainland population. They called the process re-education or remolding—in Chinese literally "cleansing the mind" or "washing the brain." The same technique was applied systematically by North Korean forces to extract allegedly voluntary confessions of war crimes from U.S. airmen downed in the Korean war. When it was first brought to light, this new, uncanny and sinister method of inducing personal change seemed to have sprung out of nowhere, having no comparable tradition in the West and no apparent foundation among the ancient rituals of the East. Threatened and intrigued, the U.S. government supported a number of research projects aimed at unraveling the mystery.

Of many early studies of brainwashing, the most widely recognized was that of psychiatrist Robert Jay Lifton, then affiliated with Yale University, who was among the first American doctors to examine victims of the process, both soldiers and civilians. In his book *Thought Reform and the Psychology of Totalism,* published in 1961, a compilation of studies he had published earlier in professional journals, Lifton analyzed the method of brainwashing as it was developed by the Chinese communists during their political takeover in the late forties. Approaching the subject from an essentially psychoanalytic orientation, Lifton described the various physical and emotional stresses used by the Chinese to induce feelings of "guilt anxiety" and create a condition of "ego-destruction" in their subjects, after which they proceeded to "re-educate" them in accordance with the principles of Chinese communism.

Then, going well beyond Freud, Lifton took the first steps toward an alternative approach. He described how the totalist process of "depersonalization" was accomplished by repeated attacks on the individual's sense of self, overt death threats and establishing complete control over the surrounding "milieu" or environment, followed by a sudden offer of reprieve—lenient treatment in return for full cooperation. He described the traumas individuals suffered in symbolic "death and rebirth" mirrored in the subject's confession of past wrongdoing and subsequent reindoctrination. He parsed the communist re-education process with its spurious science and its own tacit mysticism. He even noted the familiar "thousand-mile stare" that often characterized brainwashing victims.

From these insights, Lifton went on to distill eight distinguishing features of the totalist thought-reform process: "milieu control," "loading the language," "demand for purity," "confession," "mystical manipulation," "doctrine over person," "sacred science" and "dispensing of existence."

Lifton's work was significant. His phrase "ego-destruction" accurately described the sweeping effects of brainwashing on personality, and his alternative approach staked out the symbolic components in the process. But like the colorful metaphor of "brainwashing" itself, his analysis offered few insights into the underlying organic mechanisms by which the brainwashing process remolded the minds of his research subjects. Another approach, in line with the growing trend in psychiatry, was to seek medical answers to questions of brainwashing and "personality shift"; for although psychiatry could·say very little with scientific certainty about how brainwashing affected the mind, it had discovered a great deal about how it affected the body.

By the time the new cults came on the scene, the physiology of both brainwashing and religious conversion was already a well-established subject of medical inquiry. The pioneer in this field was British psychiatrist William Sargant. In his seminal work, *Battle for the Mind,* published in 1957, he explored in detail the role of intense physical experience in bringing about sudden changes in religious and political belief. In support of his argument, Sargant cited his own work with battle-weary soldiers during World War II, research in psychotherapy using drugs, electroshock and neurosurgical methods, and experiments on laboratory animals, to draw an elaborate picture of what happens to the central nervous system during rituals of brainwashing and religious conversion.

Sargant addressed questions of central importance to our investigation. His book shed light on two distinct sets of physiological factors that may be involved in the creation of spiritual or revelatory experiences. The most common techniques produce states of overexcitement in the nervous system, which, according to Sargant, can be accomplished by means of drumming, dancing, singing, praying, or "by the imposing of emotionally charged mental conflicts needing urgent resolution." Sargant identified these techniques in the black masses of voodoo tribes and the dances of Sufi whirling dervishes, as well as in American religious practices such as those of the Shaker dancers of Connecticut, the snake-handling Christian sects of rural Tennessee and the fiery preachers of evangelicalism. His second set of physical factors was nearly opposite in every way. The sensation of enlightenment or newfound awareness, said Sargant, could also be produced by practices that, in effect, reduce or inhibit the activity of the nervous system, such as fasting, meditation and other forms of sensory deprivation. He noted the ubiquitous use of these techniques among practitioners of Eastern religions.

In each case, Sargant held, the dramatic conversions that follow these experiences are the product of a physiological "dysfunction" of the brain which renders it receptive to new ideas and physically incapable of judging or evaluating the wisdom or correctness of those ideas.

Sargant's argument was impressive but, as he acknowledged, by no means original. The first scientific data on the subject were compiled early in this century by the Russian neurophysiologist Ivan P. Pavlov. Pavlov's studies of the effects of stress on the higher nervous systems of dogs provided Western science with a new terminology of psychological malaise. He accurately mapped the successive stages of "protective inhibition" of brain function as a response to overwhelming stimulation, and he described the physiological and behavioral effects that resulted from it.

Years later, following in the steps of Sargant and Pavlov, medical professionals investigating the cult experience confirmed the physiological effects of recognized physical stresses such as reduced sleep and caloric intake on the nervous systems of cult members. Verifiable links were discovered between the cult state of narrowed awareness and a decrease in peripheral vision. Connections also were established between physical stress, poor diet, fatigue, and disruptions of the endocrine system found among cult members that often caused women to stop menstruating and men to lose secondary sex characteristics such as facial hair and a deep voice. Those insights proved helpful in treating physical damage to the body caused by extended periods of cult life, but in the larger picture we were assembling, they led away from—not toward—a fuller understanding of the effects of cult techniques on the mind.

The medical approach also ignored situations in which sudden conversions and other intense spiritual experiences were brought about in individual and group settings that presented no physical stress or deprivation whatsoever. Our own research offered numerous examples: Jean Turner's first encounter high and, most spectacularly, Sally Kempton's audience with the Swami. In both cases, the only elements that could be identified as triggering those overwhelming reactions were a few well-placed words or, at most, some intangible quality in a rather exotic and alien environment.

The two dominant theories of brainwashing, Lifton's and Sargant's, offered no suitable explanation for these experiences. The only relevant insights in the brainwashing literature could be found in a lesser-known study by social psychologist Edgar Schein. Schein, like Lifton, participated in the first army studies of brainwashing. However, in contrast to his psychiatric and medical colleagues, he focused on the dynamic force inherent in the group processes used by the Chinese to change beliefs, attitudes and opinions. He based his theory of "coercive persuasion" on models of small-group interaction developed by M.I.T. social psychologist Kurt Lewin, who was widely recognized by humanistic psychologists as "the father of the encounter group." However, like other brainwashing theories, Schein's model placed overriding emphasis on the element of coercion—a feature that rendered his theory, like the others, of only marginal value to our investigation.

In the end, all theories of brainwashing, while historically significant, fall short of explaining the phenomenon we call snapping. The Chinese thought reform program was designed to change political beliefs and induce cooperation among Chinese citizens and captive Westerners. The situation in America and cultures worldwide today is very different. Instead of physical coercion and threats of death, the minds of the young and free people of all ages are being swayed and changed by the promise of exciting new adventures in spiritual fulfillment and human awareness. While some of these dramatic experiences no doubt are created by group pressure and physiological stresses, no one yet has been able to explain the profound personality shifts and other odd effects they so often produce: the disorientation and delusions found among many self-help therapy participants, the sensation of experiencing mystical realms of consciousness widespread among practitioners of Eastern meditation methods, the ongoing ecstasies common to self-help buffs and born-again Christians alike, and the bizarre trance-like states that characterize so many modern cult members.

Hypnosis. The only other tool that begins to explain these responses in terms familiar to professionals and the public is hypnosis, a widely used but still little-understood technique for influencing the mind in extraordinary ways. The concept of hypnosis, however, only compounds the problem at hand, for the age-old art remains the black sheep of Western science. Although the methods and effects of hypnosis have been widely demonstrated, scientists have yet to explain the prodigious power of suggestion that enables a skilled hypnotist to put people in trance states where they may perform feats of superhuman strength, demonstrations of complete imperviousness to pain, and acts of memory and imagination that defy all waking capability.

Many have tried and failed to explain hypnosis in scientific terms. As early as 1755, F. A. Mesmer, the Viennese physician who pioneered the practice, offered a theory of "animal magnetism" to explain the hypnosis phenomenon, for which he was condemned as a fraud by the most revered minds of his day. Many scientists, including Pavlov, have tried to explain hypnosis in terms of animal behavior. However, the effects of hypnosis have nothing to do with humankind's animal nature. In fact, animal response to hypnotic techniques is almost exactly *opposite* to that of human beings in every instance. While fear and physical stress may produce a temporary state of catatonic immobility in dogs, sheep and other animals, it has been shown repeatedly that this effect has nothing to do with hypnosis.

As scientists have come to understand hypnosis a little better, most of their earlier beliefs about it have been rudely overturned. The myth of the somnambulent trance state has been shattered—the old notion that a person must be put to sleep to be hypnotized has been categorically disproved. Similarly, the dangling watch fobs and swirling spirals of the stage mesmerist have been shown merely to distract their subjects' attention, rendering them more susceptible to suggestion and command. Gone, too, are the naïve convictions that hypnosis cannot be put to harmful use and that a person will not perform an act under hypnosis that is contrary to his conscious nature. Historically, hypnosis practitioners have exercised extreme caution and responsibility in the use of their mysterious skill, but many admit that, through lies and carefully contrived suggestions, a hypnotist could prompt his subject to commit any action, even a crime, in the firm belief that he was performing the act to accomplish some greater good.

In these newer findings about hypnosis and the power of suggestion there are important clues to the destructive effects of many cult and group techniques, but—like "brainwashing," "ego-destruction" and "coercive persuasion"—the term "hypnosis" alone tells nothing about the dramatic alterations of mind and personality we learned of from participants in the new cults, sects and self-help therapies. The techniques employed by most cult and group leaders bear no resemblance to the classical induction of hypnosis, nor are the effects confined to simple trance states or feats of memory and imagination. Their attack is comprehensive and profound, not simply altering belief and behavior as in brainwashing, but producing *ongoing* changes in the underlying workings of the mind. And, as we heard described repeatedly, their tools are not arcane conjuring devices but the tools of everyday human communication—ordinary skills and natural abilities that have been honed to the sharpness of precision instruments.

Communication. Almost invariably today, a person's involvement in a cult, sect or self-help therapy begins with voluntary participation. He or she reads a handbill, engages in a conversation, attends a free lecture or introductory session, accepts an invitation to a group dinner or cult feast. Then come further offers to attend a weekend seminar, workshop or spiritual retreat. At any time during these early stages of recruitment—and throughout participation in the cult or group—the individual's actions and responses may be artfully controlled without physiological stress or any physical means whatsoever. In lieu of coercion or hypnosis, most cult and group leaders use an altogether different class of strategies: they may misrepresent their identities and intentions; they may lie about their own relationships to their organizations; they may display false affection for the potential member; they may radiate spiritual fulfillment and happiness to the point where it has a profound impact on the individual they are confronting; they may train people in trance-inducing self-hypnotic techniques called by many mystical, contemplative and health-promoting names; or they may merely provoke discussion and debate, creating what Sargant calls "emotionally charged mental conflicts needing urgent resolution."

However, none of these ploys depends on any physiological dysfunction of the brain or nervous system to be completely effective and produce its most dramatic effects. On the contrary, whatever the ploys, their effectiveness depends on the normal functioning of the human brain in its infinite capacity for communication—without that, they would not work at all. At every stage of involvement, from initial contact through conversion to the most profound states of surrender and submission, every consequence of cult and group participation that has been explained as a product of physiological stress may also be produced with equal intensity and reliability by means of simple techniques of human communication: age-old tools of rhetoric and religious ritual, refined methods of persuasion, propaganda and mass marketing, still little-understood elements of group dynamics, nonverbal communication, and the many other new spiritual and personal growth practices that make up modern culture's burgeoning technology of experience.

In most instances today, there is nothing casual in the way these sophisticated techniques are employed, nor is there anything mysterious in the way they achieve their most predictable and profound effects. Like the distracting watch fob of the mesmerist, the well-known physical stresses used by cult and group leaders serve only to weaken people to suggestion and command. Their subsequent thoughts, actions, expressions and even states of awareness, however, are controlled by identifiable processes and products of human communication. They are controlled by the specific ideas, beliefs, opinions, emotions, suggestions and direct orders people receive from cult recruiters, sect leaders, self-help trainers, pop therapists, born-again preachers and others, in personal conversations and group rituals delivered amid the atmospheres of warmth, love and total acceptance common to each of these diverse interactions.

The process of communication reaches far beyond the mere exchange of spoken and written messages among individuals. This complex and sophisticated process controls both our bodies and our minds. Communication, in fact, governs everything we experience as human beings. It is the basic organic process that regulates the everyday operations of the human brain and nervous system, and it is the main channel through which the new cult methods of change and control turn inward and take root in the mind. The principles of communication that underlie Marjoe's rhetoric, Moon's propaganda and Erhard's group dynamics are one with the natural laws that direct and control the flow of experience throughout the body, brain and mind. By this common process, acts of speech, from sermons to hypnosis to casual conversations and every other form of communication, may affect biological functions at their most rudimentary levels and human awareness in its highest states of consciousness and spirituality.

With the widening exploitation in modern cultures of sophisticated new communication techniques and technologies, we believe, a new perspective is in order, one rooted in the universal process of communication that has come to play such a tangible role in our daily lives. Since the days of Freud and Pavlov, research on subconscious processes and animal behavior has made important contributions to scientific understanding of elementary human responses, but that knowledge alone no longer provides the broad base necessary for contemporary psychological, social and legal interpretation. Inevitably, theories based on the study of unconscious processes and lower organisms are doomed to fail as explanations for events and activities that are uniquely human. Very often they obscure our understanding of individual and social phenomena that have no counterparts in other times and species. Snapping is such a phenomenon, and in order to understand it, we must first recognize that human beings today do not grow and develop in an unconscious world of childhood influences and unvarying animal behavior; they do so in an ever-changing world of experience that, from their first breath of life to their ultimate encounter with death, shapes their awareness, their personalities and every aspect of their lives.

To reach the core of society's spreading epidemic of sudden personality change, we must go beyond brainwashing and hypnosis, beyond physiology and psychology, to the living process of communication by which human beings exchange thought, feeling and experience itself with one another. Communication processes caused Jean Turner's first "encounter high" as well as the roller-coaster ride of ecstasy, fantasy and horrifying delusion she experienced after est. They charted the entire course of Lawrence and Cathy Gordon's participation in the Unification Church, from Cathy's feelings of strangeness when she met her first Moonie to Lawrence's vision of death while out fund raising. Communication offers new ways to understand Marjoe's seasoned ability to sway an audience to the point of emotional collapse and explains why Sally Kempton snapped in response to a few empty words from the Swami Muktananda. It also explains how thousands of cult members have regained their ability to think for themselves after answering pointed questions put to them by Ted Patrick and other cult counselors.

In recent years the term "communication" has been used to signify an expanding universe of activities, encompassing disciplines as varied as computer science, speech pathology, broadcast journalism and public relations. Our aim, however, is not to explore communication in the catch-all sense. From here on in this book we use the term to refer to a set of distinctly human processes that may be better understood in the light of new knowledge in biology, mathematics, electrical engineering and brain science. With the aid of these basic sciences and the breakthrough insights of humanistic psychology, we can now forge a new perspective on the phenomenon of snapping. We can build a bridge from our culture's unconscious robot models of personality and behavior to a new view of human beings based on dynamic, organic processes of human awareness and experience.

The foundation of this bridge is anchored in the technical sciences of communication—cybernetics, information theory and living systems theory. And the first step in building it requires that we update our understanding of how those universal communication processes shape the living workings of the human brain and nervous system, the basic biological machinery from which our minds and personalities emerge.

PART TWO
A New Perspective

9 Information

Information is information, not matter or energy.

—Norbert Wiener,
Cybernetics

IRONICALLY, CYBERNETICS AND information theory, the new technical communication sciences that gave rise to the information age explosion of high-tech hardware and automated technology, offer a natural point of departure from the robot model of psychology. It is this world of sophisticated machines, not the world of animals and lower organisms, that has been constructed in humankind's image. From its raw materials, its basic principles and processes, we can begin to refine our understanding of snapping.

In every form of the phenomenon we can identify a common element, whether it be the most intense personal growth experience or the most evanescent spiritual moment, the most profound thought, the deepest emotion, or the most mundane phrase or fleeting image that sets off some massive, life-changing human response. It is that wondrous, elusive stuff called *information*. Information is what human beings are made of, not simply information in the technical sense—news, facts, computer data, telecommunications signals—but information in human terms, the living force and substance that flows through every reach of our minds, brains and bodies. Information, not matter or energy, is the stuff of human consciousness. It is the soul of communication and the key to the phenomenon of snapping.

Before we can fit together the different pieces of the puzzle, we must first understand what information is and how human beings take in and make sense of the stuff. In recent years scientists have begun to comprehend this amazing process and, as it turns out, it is not at all as they once suspected.

CYBERNETICS. The concept of information grew out of the science of cybernetics, one of the new tools of understanding developed in the second half of the twentieth century. Cybernetics is not simply an advancement in older sciences. It is a whole new field of inquiry, born in America during World War II when teams of scientists from diverse disciplines were brought together in all-out efforts to solve the practical problems of modern warfare. Out of such concrete engineering tasks as computing intricate enemy flight trajectories and designing tracking mechanisms for antiaircraft artillery emerged the first principles for the scientific study of communication.

Cybernetics, succinctly defined as the study of "communication and control in the animal and the machine," developed quickly into a broad science of automatic control systems: mechanical, electronic and biological structures that regulate their own internal processes and correct their own errors in operation. The word cybernetics—coined by Norbert Wiener, the brilliant mathematician from M.I.T. and the acknowledged father of the science—comes from the Greek word *kubernêtês*, for steersman or governor, and commemorates the earliest known cybernetic device: the automatic steering mechanisms used on ships which monitored the disturbances of wind and waves and adjusted the rudder accordingly to keep the ship on a steady course. In Wiener's terms, the vital "feedback" which guided the ship's tiller, like the beams of radar waves bouncing off enemy targets which fed instructions to the automatic antiaircraft guns he helped develop, supplied a "measure of organization" to the system that he identified as "information."

Following the war, Americans began to receive the first fruits of these once top-secret labors, as a new generation of automated hardware and appliances came to the marketplace to ease all sorts of daily chores. Early arrivals included automatic washing machines, self-triggering toasters and electronic supermarket doors, each employing simple feedback devices that responded to some tiny measure of information. Yet, despite these practical beginnings, the notion of information remained one of the slipperiest concepts to hit modern science since the theory of relativity. Engineers in America tended to view information in terms of "organization," "order" and "organized complexity," while their British counterparts preferred to view it in terms of "selectivity" and "variety."

INFORMATION THEORY. The first technical definition of information was proposed in 1949 when Dr. Claude E. Shannon, a research mathematician at the Bell Telephone Laboratories, published a paper with Dr. Warren Weaver, then of the Rockefeller Foundation, entitled "The Mathematical Theory of Communication," in which they set out the physical requirements and limits to the communication and transmission of messages. In this initial scientific attempt to give form and substance to that indefinable flux coursing through Ma Bell's sprouting networks of long-distance telephone lines, the mother of today's information highway, Shannon and Weaver introduced the concept of the "bit" (short for *binary digit)* of information, the simple on-off, heads-or-tails choice which they defined to be the smallest amount of information any message may contain. Then, armed with the bit and simple mathematical logarithms, they went on to derive a way of calculating the amount of information contained in *any* message. This scientific reckoning with the intangible provided no insight whatsoever into the meaning in human terms of any particular communication, but by avoiding ancient, endless debates over the nature of words and numbers, it offered engineers a new way of speaking simply—and only—about the math and physics of transmitting that information as quickly and efficiently as possible.

Together, cybernetics and information theory led to major breakthroughs in engineering and technology, from the mastery of vast telephone and television networks to the lightning logic of the computer. From the beginning, the new sciences helped electrical engineers reduce chaos and complexity to order, but for laymen these new technological triumphs seemed only to increase the complexity and confusion of daily life. In a few years, high-speed telecommunications and electronic data-processing systems began supplying people with ever-increasing quantities of information at speeds far beyond their human capacity to process and organize: instant news from around the world, intimate glimpses of remote cultures, close-up images of natural disasters, wars, social problems and political crises as they happened. Before long, in countless arenas, human performance was being pitted against the extraordinary capacities of the computer and the near-limitless speeds of electronic gadgetry.

How were people to cope with the inundation? Were there no limits to the amount of information people could take in and make sense of? Or was there a built-in barrier—a physical point of "information overload"?

Many scientists, including Wiener himself, raised such questions about the impact of the new technologies on human beings, and their concerns seemed urgent enough to warrant serious investigation. Hundreds of projects were launched in the United States and other countries, all aimed at determining the precise nature and physical limitations of human information processing. The human nervous system was quickly found to be a marvel of cybernetic engineering, converting every sight, sound, smell, taste and touch into its own distinct pattern of information. Every printed word, every musical theme, every life experience sent its own unimaginably complex flow of information from the body's sense organs to the brain.

The human brain, however, presented insurmountable barriers to scientific understanding. Acclaimed as the most sophisticated computer in the world, it was generally assumed to process information in the manner of telephone switching systems and electronic data processors, but its exact information pathways were far too complex for experimental observation or even the best computer analysis available at the time. So, alternatively, researchers borrowed technical concepts of information transmission, "channel capacity" and "storage and retrieval," and attempted to "input" massive quantities of information to the brains of their test subjects. They staged elaborate experiments designed to measure the quantity of words, numbers and other signals people could process before their information-processing powers began to break down. Their findings were remarkably consistent: researchers across the board identified common patterns of human response that seemed to describe a distinct condition of "information overload."

Like so much science and scholarship in the fifties, however, those initial inquiries into human information processing were strictly behavior-oriented. Most studies were motivated by practical concerns and failed almost completely to address basic questions about the *kind* of information people were being asked to absorb, the *intensity* of the information—the sheer physical impact of it all—and the *meaning* of the information in human terms.

Information Stress. Psychologist James G. Miller, a pioneer in human information-processing research, assessed the results of several hundred studies on the subject in a retrospective published in 1978. Miller uncovered disturbing responses caused by information overload and a related condition he referred to as one of "information stress." Those distinctive stress responses started with impaired work performance and progressed to more severe "pathological effects" that bore strong resemblance to the symptoms of overstimulation described by Sargant— and to the lengthening list of human responses we were hearing described as tell-tale signs of snapping. These included predictable emotional responses such as feelings of fear, guilt, frustration, anger and anxiety, physical effects on the body such as nervousness, high blood pressure, exhaustion and insomnia, and all-encompassing responses of apathy or surrender.

However, when it came to the impact of information stress on the mind itself, Miller had little to report. Amid their rigors, researchers had all but ignored the problem from the most obvious aspect of concern: the cumulative effects of the new stress on the mind and its underlying workings in the brain. Nor were they able to explain or treat the new information stress symptoms that were beginning to appear, not merely among volunteers in controlled laboratory studies, but among people confronting overwhelming amounts and kinds of information in their day-to-day lives.

And there were more serious scientific problems. To their amazement, researchers studying the physical limits of human information processing were startled to find that, through various memory enhancement techniques and simple methods of grouping or "chunking" long sequences of words and numbers, human storage and retrieval capacities became virtually limitless! Evidently, human beings did not process information in the manner of telephones and computers. Yet, faced with the indecipherable complexities of the human organism, psychologists were forced to treat the mind and brain together as a vexing "black box," an engineering term for a sealed device with internal workings that remain inaccessible and unknown.

The black box was by no means impenetrable. Modern biologists and neurologists had been roaming its inner corridors for decades, but most were unable to decode the organic actions they found there. Scientists probing the brain's internal information-processing operations encountered orders of complexity that ran circles around Shannon's straight-line signal transmission theory and the simple feedback loops of Wiener's rudimentary cybernetic mechanisms. For, as Wiener himself recognized early on, human beings do not only transmit information. They also *transform* it in extraordinary actions that required whole new ways of thinking about the process of communication. As the brain's communication secrets began to yield, researchers discovered that the organ's inner workings perform intricate transformations of information that change the stuff from mere signals into moving biological patterns that play fundamental roles in the processes of life. The discovery gave scientists their first girder across the gaping brain-mind chasm, linking information in the technical sense with the living force and substance coursing through the body's biological and neurological communication channels.

LIVING SYSTEMS. By the late fifties, biologists building on Wiener's and Shannon's groundbreaking theories and new findings in their own field were starting to grasp the real nature and incredible complexities of human information processing. Their new "living systems" approach grew from basic principles of biological organization and the idea of ascending levels or "hierarchies" of biological activity into a new picture of how human beings and living systems generally grow and change. Somehow, amid the physical world's relentless forces of randomness and decay, an opposing tendency of nature managed to bring order out of chaos and create these organized entities that maintained stable internal states, thrived on their surrounding environments and reproduced themselves generation after generation—and the key to the entire process was information. In fact, the most up-to-date definition of life itself, often expressed by systems scientists as a pattern of self-sustaining, self-reproducing "organized complexity," was virtually identical with Norbert Wiener's first definition of information!

The systems approach opened a new worldview to science. In the sixties, it spawned new schools of interdisciplinary study and the fledgling science of "ecology" that made societies aware of the interdependence of all living things and the fragile environment of the earth as a whole. Yet, when it came to the life of the mind and the new stresses people were experiencing in the changing world around them, like the sciences before it, the systems approach fell mute.

COGNITIVE SCIENCE. Since those dawning days of the information age, the study of the brain's living information-processing capacities has grown into a specialized science of its own. At universities and research institutes across America and worldwide, whole centers for "cognitive" information processing have begun to decipher the unique manner in which human beings order their daily fare of information.

In their first investigations, the new cognitive scientists determined that the eye alone has over one hundred million information receptors. Using new computer modeling methods and advanced brain imaging technologies, they traced the bulk of those signals along the optic nerve to specialized cells and networks deep in the brain's visual information-processing centers. And gradually they began to understand how the brain converts the bombardment of photons on the retina into shapes that change in space and brightness over time and then forms those patterns into objects—trees, chairs, recognizable faces, words, etc.—that have some usefulness to the individual.

What the new science had yet to determine, however, was how all those incoming signals come together to create the phenomenon of awareness: how the individual *experiences* that information and makes meaning of what he sees. In its first triumphs, cognitive science made important discoveries about how our nervous systems transform everything we experience into progressively more complex patterns of information, but the field had yet to connect the physical facts of information in its biological, neurological and ultimately neurochemical form with the phenomenon of consciousness that has eluded investigators throughout the glorious course of Western science.

Early in our collaboration, the two of us found ourselves confronted with this same dilemma. We had been observing and hearing about extraordinary snapping moments, intense spiritual and personal growth experiences that produced profound changes in people's awareness and personalities. People's religious beliefs notwithstanding, and contrary to popular fashions which tended to attribute extraordinary human events to the supernatural, mystical or cosmic forces, our research had convinced us that, ultimately, all these experiences could be traced to entirely natural processes occurring in the living workings of the human brain. Our goal was to account for those extraordinary experiences in concrete communication terms and to determine what impact they might have on the brain's living information-processing capacities. Yet we recognized that even the most cautious speculation would draw us to the edge of scientific understanding—and beyond to a new, distinctly human communication perspective on the mind.

The Way to Awareness. From the start of our travels in search of people who had experienced the snapping phenomenon, we also visited with prominent scientists across the country, respected figures working in the hard disciplines of mathematics, physical and electrical engineering, new researchers in systems theory, cognitive science and "bioinformation" studies, and neuroscientists who had spent their entire careers studying minute aspects of brain function. Many scientists we spoke with expressed dismay over the enormous gaps that continued to separate the new knowledge blossoming in their respective fields from practical understanding of the mind's everyday communication operations. The space between, they said almost unanimously, was filled with irreconcilable contradictions in the life of the mind that collided head on with the laws of nature and modern physics.

One fascinating view of these contradictions came in a conversation we had in the late seventies with Dr. John Lyman, then a professor of engineering and psychology at the University of California at Los Angeles. Lyman was among the first of the new mind scientists. He began his career in the hard sciences, then went on to apply his engineering knowledge to the task of exploring the human factors in the information equation. In two meetings with him—one in his office and one at his cliffside home overlooking the San Fernando Valley— we discussed our investigation of sudden personality change and our developing communication perspective. He told us that in the early sixties he had the good fortune to meet almost daily for several hours with his long-time friend Norbert Wiener during the last summer of that great scientist and philosopher's life. In their conversations, he and Wiener debated the question of what they called "epochal" or life-changing events in human development. As Wiener told Lyman, the subject was of great personal concern for, as a diabetic, he frequently battled the sudden reversals of emotion and mood characteristic of the disease. Yet both men recognized that the complexity of the problem extended beyond their learned speculation. Lyman shared some of the questions that emerged from their discussions which continue to confront scientists working in his field.

"The human being is more than just a supercomputer," said Lyman. "The principles from which computers have been developed are certainly very similar to the way human beings process information, but human beings do a lot of things that no one has found out about yet."

According to Lyman, human information processing takes place at chemical speeds of roughly 300 feet per second, neural speeds far less than the 186,000 miles per second that marked the speed of light and the upper limit of any electronic device. Yet human beings regularly perform feats of memory and recall at speeds unmatchable by any computer available at the time—or since.

"We don't know how it's done," said Lyman. "We have some ideas involving hierarchies of information-processing levels, but this is something that's just beginning to be worked on in computer design."

The problem of time, Lyman noted, was a plaguing dilemma for both technical and human scientists. In human information-processing activities, for example, there were numerous instances in which the brain seemed to function independently of time altogether.

"When you start measuring dream lengths in relation to their content," he said, "you observe much more dream content than would seem possible in the length of time sleep is going on. The rates of dreaming don't seem to be time-bound—literally, in sequence. The brain appears to restructure things simultaneously. Another example of this phenomenon is when a person sees his whole life flash before him when he's drowning."

To help us understand this peculiar simultaneity of the brain, Lyman offered the analogy of a motion picture reel. Every frame of the picture sequence is already present on the reel, and when the film is run, the images appear to occur in time. The activity of the brain would be equivalent to slicing up the film and spreading out all the pictures side by side. The illusion of motion disappears and all the information is present simultaneously.

"I don't know if it's true," said Lyman, "but it's possible that when you tell somebody your dream, you may be describing the dream as a sequential thing, whereas when you had the dream, it was like that, like a *snap*"—and he snapped his fingers.

Our word again, but we hadn't mentioned it to Lyman.

"I can't give you any details," he continued, "except that dreams and the time they cover don't match up very well. Most evidence is that dreams apparently covering hours or days of detail take place in a few seconds."

Lyman didn't see time as much of a factor in the basic functioning of the brain. In his view, the time element mattered only when the functioning of the brain was translated into action.

"We are time-bound by our ability to express," he said. "Everything we do requires muscular activity, including the movement of our vocal cords. All our outputs to the world are muscular in nature, and the very nature of muscular response is that it has to be temporal, it has to occur in sequence."

As a living information-processing organ, Lyman noted, the brain has no moving parts and its activities need not be stretched out over time. As a cybernetic system, however, the brain has its own built-in structural limitations. According to Lyman, rather than being time-bound like the rest of the body, the brain is *space-bound* or unable to imagine anything outside its three dimensions.

This question of space led us into another perplexing quandary. Exactly where, in any sense, did these extraordinary phenomena of mind occur? The bulk of information-processing activities were generally conceded to take place in the brain, but beyond that humankind's subjective experiences had yet to be located. Specific neurological activities had been traced to particular regions of the brain, but neuroscientists had been unable to establish precise information-processing pathways similar to those wired into computers. They could only trace brain function down to vast "aggregates" of neurons, interwoven "neural networks," and quantum neurochemical actions that could not be precisely determined. In fact, in many areas of brain function, more minute dissection led, not to clearer understanding of how the organ worked, but to greater confusion at elementary levels of chemistry and physics.

Lyman acknowledged the delicacy of the problem.

"There are a lot of subjects that you have to step very carefully on," he said, "because there are many phenomena physics has not put into order yet."

For Lyman, the final challenge to the study of the mind lay not in biology but in modern physics, which had yet to extricate itself from the paradoxes of relativity and quantum mechanics. He pointed to the perennial paradox of light, which scientists continued to conceive of and work with practically in terms of both particles and waves, despite the fact that the two models contradicted each other in fundamental ways.

"The traditional concepts of physics are being profoundly questioned by our own methods," Lyman told us. "Nobody's willing to go mystic and say, 'Okay, we admit that logic doesn't exist.' On the other hand, science is starting to recognize that there's a lot more to relativity than Einstein ever put together."

In Lyman's view, questions of human consciousness would remain unanswerable until those elementary problems of physics were resolved. As he saw it, the breakthrough that was required could not be of greater conceptual proportions.

"We had Newton and we had Einstein," said Lyman appreciatively, "but now we need somebody to carry us to the next stage. We need someone to take us beyond $E=mc^2$."

At Stanford University in California, Dr. Karl H. Pribram was taking his own steps beyond $E=mc^2$, making giant strides on the way to understanding the ultimate phenomenon of human awareness. In the course of his lifelong investigation of the brain, this internationally acclaimed neuroscientist had developed a new model of the brain's higher information-processing activities that, potentially, was the stuff of which scientific revolutions are made.

Pribram's work spanned wide areas of brain research. He had made fundamental discoveries about the ways nerve cells communicate with each other, how the brain filters the input it receives from the senses, and the brain's role in higher psychological processes. His most stunning achievement, however, was a new model of brain function that shattered many previously accepted notions of basic cognitive activities such as perception and memory. Since its introduction in the mid-seventies, his model had provoked widespread excitement and controversy in the scientific establishment, and in many camps it had been hailed as a major breakthrough in scientific theory.

Following threads of research teased out by founding figures in modern neuroscience, many of whom he had known and worked with, Pribram took on the fiercest challenge in the field: the mystifying problem of how memory is stored and retrieved in the brain. His approach was boldly innovative. Instead of looking for specific bits of stored information, as most of his predecessors had done, he abandoned this file-drawer model in favor of a new approach to information storage suggested by Dr. Karl Lashley, a legendary figure in American brain research. Lashley, who gave up in despair after an unsuccessful thirty-year search for specific memory traces, proposed that memory was not stored in discrete units but rather in intersecting patterns of information flow within the brain. As Pribram was pursuing this avenue of exploration, he came upon a close-fitting mathematical and physical model called the *hologram*, at the time a curious new invention of the science of optics. Today holography is well known as a revolutionary new form of three-dimensional photography, a novel way of assembling a graphic information "store" from which a lifelike visual image can be reconstructed. What Pribram saw in it was an elegant demonstration of his new theory of memory and perception. In technical terms, the three-dimensional holographic image represents the "emergent" product of the stored interference pattern created by two intersecting beams of light—and patterns of light, of course, are not only waves and particles but, more important, a visible form of information.

To create a hologram, a beam of coherent light (light waves of a single frequency, in phase, traveling in the same direction) produced by a laser is split through a mirror that is partially silvered and partially transparent. Half the light goes directly to a photographic plate; the other half, the information half, is reflected off the person, object or scene being photographed (in this case, *holographed)* and then it too converges onto the photographic plate. The plate records not the actual image, as in conventional photography, but the interference pattern formed by the two beams of intersecting light. The plate or film (also called the *holograph* as distinct from the image itself, the hologram, although the two terms are often used interchangeably) displays only a pattern of dots and swirls that means nothing to the naked eye. To recreate the hologram, the holograph has to be illuminated by another beam of coherent light, which produces an image with true three-dimensional perspective, an image not *on* the film but somewhere behind or in front of it. By looking at the holograph from a variety of angles, the viewer can see the image from below, above or either side, perceiving it as though he were looking at the original object itself from several different positions.

Holography is more than just a photographic gimmick for use on plastic credit cards or in cinematic special effects. It is also an incredibly efficient and sophisticated method of information storage. By use of different frequencies of light, many interference patterns can be superimposed on a single holographic plate. In technical experiments as far back as the seventies, a record-setting 10 billion bits of information were stored holographically in one cubic centimeter of space. More important than the capacity of the hologram to store enormous quantities of information, however, is the truly astonishing manner in which that information is stored.

In holography, the information or light reflected off each point of the object being holographed is spread out and distributed across the entire surface of the film. The holographic film can then be cut into small fragments and each fragment, when illuminated, will generate the *entire* image. Damage to any part of the film, even to the majority of it, will not affect the film's ability to reproduce the whole image.

In his research, Pribram seized on the hologram concept as a remarkably appropriate model of how the brain functions in perception. In the process of vision, for example, information traveling to the brain over its vast number of separate channels comes together at several levels to form interference patterns. The result is a "brain representation" (akin to the photographic holograph) that registers beyond the retina (the photographic plate of the eye). The subjective experience is the image created when that visual representation is projected holographically deep within the visual areas of the brain. As in holography, the image is projected outward from the representation and is perceived as an object in the individual's field of vision. The impression of distance, also known as depth of field, is another holographic effect, a phenomenon called parallax, caused by the intersection of the twin inputs brought to the brain by the left and right eyes.

Similar processes take place in relation to other sense impressions— as Pribram noted, the principles of holography are not dependent on the physical presence of light waves. Another common form of holography is stereophonic recording. The two channels of sound coming from separate stereo speakers create an interference pattern caused by intersecting waves of vibrating air. The product, a three-dimensional "auditory image," seems to be coming not from one speaker or the other but from somewhere in between—which is, in fact, exactly where the stereophonic image is located. The same stereophonic hologram is an exact model for the way our two ears function in the process of hearing. More recent research suggests that similar processes occur with our other senses of taste, touch and smell. Those sensations are not only projections of the enormous quantities of information received by each isolated sense. In many instances, they are products of *synesthesia*—information patterns intersecting from two or more sensory systems at once. Taste impressions, for example, are so heavily dependent on the sense of smell that without the latter many foods would be indistinguishable.

Beyond sensation, the holographic model also resolved the conceptual dilemmas of time and space that arise in both memory and dreaming. The hologram's ability to distribute information and retrieve it without searching through endless strings of data bits helped to explain the brain's remarkable speed of memory. The brain's memory mechanisms appeared to operate on principles similar to the holographic process of storing many images within the same space or film on varying communication frequencies. One wavelength of information will illuminate only one specific image or memory; multiple sources will generate many images simultaneously. The same principle also seemed to account for the simultaneity of memory in dreaming. In a sense, it enabled the brain to relive an entire event from memory or, to use Lyman's image, to slice apart the separate frames of its time-bound motion picture and, in effect, lay them out side by side, making all the information available at one time. This versatile scheme suggested explanations for other uncanny mental processes, from the mind's boundless capacity for free association to the complex integrative and creative processes that produce the mind's highest works of art and imagination.

A supremely sophisticated and eminently practical form of information processing, Pribram's holographic brain model seemed to us a highly attractive and entirely plausible alternative framework for understanding the phenomenon of snapping. Its scientific soundness had been carefully worked out and verified mathematically; the holographic distribution of information had been shown to take place in accordance with precise mathematical "spread functions." In addition, the applicability of the model to the brain had been confirmed experimentally by researchers working independently of Pribram. In hundreds of operations conducted in the seventies, researchers at Indiana University successfully "shuffled" the brains of salamanders—excising, grafting and literally scrambling their structure and contents—in studies that strongly supported the notion that memory storage does in fact conform to holographic principles. With Pribram's breakthrough, it seemed, science had at last produced a credible theory, mathematical and experimental proof and, in the three-dimensional holographic image, a working model of consciousness itself.

We drove into Palo Alto one cloudy afternoon in the spring of 1977 to discuss with Karl Pribram the implications of his holographic model. Silver-haired but youthful, even sprightly, Pribram possessed an ageless quality that mirrored the timelessness of his work. For two hours, he breathed life into his model of the brain, augmenting his views with photographs, diagrams and his colorful manner of expression.

"Holograms do deal with conscious awareness," he said. "When I light up a hologram, the image I see is not on the photographic film. It's somewhere beyond—it's a projection. If the brain is holographically organized, conscious experience will be similarly projected when the right input comes in."

Throughout our talk, Pribram was careful not to state conclusively the implications of his theory, for he was quick to admit that the brain was much more complex and specialized than a simple hologram, combining multiple modes of information storage, distribution and organization across diverse regions of brain function. Nevertheless, he cited research suggesting the broad applicability of his model; and he seemed delighted to surmise about its countless fascinating ramifications: new holographic principles that appeared to resolve long-standing paradoxes of mind and other notions which, we suspected, held vital clues to the mysteries of sudden personality change we were investigating.

Most intriguing to us, in the light of countless descriptions we had heard of instant changes in awareness and seemingly timeless mystical states, was the paradox that the brain does not appear to be time-bound in its function yet meets the temporal demands of every human activity and real-world function. Pribram accounted for this contradiction with little difficulty, transporting us beyond our traditional notions of space and time into the inner world of the brain.

"Now if the hologram is something that is for real in the brain," he cautioned, "it means that we can store things in our brains in terms of various frequencies of information. Then we can read out the information in either linear or spatial fashion. The linear way is sequential, over time, and the spatial is simultaneous. Space and time are not in the brain; they are *read out* of it."

As we contended with this new idea that the brain may be, in fact, the master of its own time and space, Pribram recounted the brief history of the hologram. He pointed out that although his model was a radical one for both biology and psychology, proposing an explanation for intangible qualities of mind in exacting technical terms, scientists and philosophers had been thinking along similar lines for centuries, developing more and more sophisticated concepts to help them grasp the complexity of the world around them. Pribram explained that the first formal principles of holography were introduced in the late forties and fifties by British mathematician Dennis Gabor, whose intention was to improve the resolution of electron microscopes, high-powered optical devices that magnify objects to the limits of visible light. Gabor was hoping to find a way to sharpen those infinitesimal images, the same way American scientists sought and soon succeeded in "deblurring" early photographic images received from satellites in space. To do this, he drew upon complex mathematical equations called spread functions, which describe the precise manner in which information is spread out around the entire holographic plate. They also determine how that information is gathered up again to reproduce the original holographic subject.

Pribram cited important historical connections to the mathematics of the hologram.

"The mathematics Gabor used were differential equations, the integral calculus," he said, "and if you go back in your philosophy, you get to Leibniz, who invented calculus. Leibniz first proposed the idea of *monads,* elementary units that contained the entire image of the universe. At the time, everybody thought, *Well, Leibniz is getting old. He's trying to talk about God again, just to make sure he gets into those portal gates of St. Peter.* They thought he was going soft, but it turns out the hologram is nothing but a bunch of monads! In other words, every part of the hologram has the attributes of a monad. It includes everything. All the information is there, from a slightly different window or viewpoint. Nonetheless, each part represents the whole and that, of course, is Godlike, isn't it?"

He let that idea sink in as our minds raced to make connections. We thought about all the people we had talked to whose experiences with various cults, therapies and mind-altering drugs had given them overwhelming sensations of oneness with the universe, or of stepping into other dimensions of reality in which they saw the world "through a different window." We thought about the immensely popular, free-wheeling fiction of Kurt Vonnegut, whose characters frequently came "unstuck" in space and time. And we thought about an astrologer we had interviewed in New York who, in his own nonscientific way, had attempted to convince us that each individual's life is influenced by the entire configuration of the solar system at the instant of his birth. All these ideas, if not holographic truths, were at least holographic possibilities, as was the way our own imaginations leaped from one tantalizing association to another. Already we were beginning to grasp the new understanding of human information processing and human experience itself that could be derived from Pribram's holographic model. Pribram shared our enthusiasm and helped us ground it in more practical matters as well.

"The holographic notion applies to all of the spiritual ideas we've ever had," he said nonchalantly, "but it also applies to everything we know about social organization."

We had already begun speculating along those lines, for we knew that our developing communication perspective could not separate the individual from his greater social nature. The hologram infused new meaning into ideas of social relationship and the interdependence of living systems to which modern societies had only recently turned their attention. In the new framework, each individual could be viewed as a living hologram of his culture and his time, at once a record and reflection of his life experiences—his childhood upbringing, education, work, family and personal relationships—and, in a larger sense, of his society as a whole.

From a communication standpoint, the social implications of the hologram shed new light on the intricate human dynamics of all group activities, from marathon encounters to religious revivals, and gave tangible form to the complex information, sensations, relationships and other palpable communication forces that come together in the individual's all-encompassing experience of a group. The same holographic principles were reflected on a greater scale in the flow of information through mass society. Like the rush of sensation to the brain, the flood of mass communication—each day's news, ideas, entertainment and speeding electronic messages—is multiplied hundreds of millions of times over, as in each human eye, then spread out and distributed to every individual, with each person receiving and interpreting his unique mix of that information from his own distinctive holographic "window," be it his television, computer screen or real-world vantage point.

It seemed to us that, in contrast to the world of matter and energy, the entire universe of information and communication—the "information dimension," as we had begun to call it—from the smallest flashes of human awareness to the palpable dynamics of people in groups to the broadest disseminations of mass culture, was governed by its own set of natural laws and physical properties which appeared to conform in significant ways to the math and physics of the hologram. Could that same hologram offer ways to resolve more baffling paradoxes of physics and modern science? Pribram addressed this larger concern we had heard voiced by so many scientists.

"We've got to get into a different frame of reference," he declared. "We need a math and physics that will allow us to ask the right questions. We're not asking them now. We're not anywhere near them, and we can't reach them as long as we're stuck within the old Cartesian deterministic coordinates of time and space.

"Look at what is happening in nuclear physics," he went on, making reference to the subatomic particle called the tachyon, which had been discovered only recently. "You have a particle leaving here and getting there before it left. Something's wrong! Someone may get a Nobel prize for putting that in diagrams that have time running backwards, but if you ask him what he means by that, he'll say, 'What do you mean, *what do I mean?* I can describe it mathematically but I haven't the slightest idea what it's all about.' Somehow, we've got to switch to an entirely different way of thinking. Not that the ordinary way is wrong—I'm not giving up the idea that this is a flat floor, but that doesn't mean that the world isn't round."

Pribram's holographic model was not the ultimate, world-changing "theory of everything" many scientists were looking for, yet in less than a decade, it had made major inroads into scientific thinking about fundamental processes of memory and perception. It suggested new ways of looking at everything from particle physics to social relationships and even shed light on intangible aspects of the human spirit.

"All of a sudden these things are no longer mere wisps of imagination," Pribram said with a smile. "They turn out to be, mathematically, precisely describable ideas."

He spoke modestly, but his confidence and enthusiasm came forward in a forthright manner. As we prepared to leave, Pribram reaffirmed his belief in his model and its potential scientific contribution.

"I think the hologram notion is in fact a real change in our scientific paradigm. It makes studiable by scientific tools all the things that have been dismissed as mystical and subjective and so on. In other words, here is an explanatory device that turns the corner."

In the years after we visited him at Stanford, Pribram expanded on his holographic model, assembling piece after piece of new scientific data from his own research and independent investigations. Other neuroscientists uncovered further details about the holographic actions of specialized brain cells and the precise frequencies by which different sense perceptions are parsed and distributed in localized brain regions; and the debate intensified among scientists vying to explain how the brain binds all that dispersed information back into specific images and other sensations. We kept tabs on the alternatives: prominent cognitive science theorists put forth intricate "neural-network," "parallel-processing" and quantum-mechanical models. But, from our vantage point, Pribram's model remained vastly superior to competing theories—and the only one to plausibly explain and physically reproduce the experience of consciousness itself.

10 The Laws of Experience

Just as no man lives or dies to himself, so no experience lives or dies to itself.

—John Dewey,
The Need of a Theory of Experience

WE LEFT STANFORD confident that Karl Pribram's innovative holographic model offered our investigation one new window we had been looking for into the subjective world of human awareness. Through it, we could see the human mind in a way it had not been viewed before, unclouded by material paradoxes that once posed insurmountable barriers to understanding. Suddenly, the brain's lightning speed and versatility became more compatible with the laws of nature. The miracle of memory, so effortlessly accomplished, and the mystery of perception dropped into new positions in the larger puzzle we were working.

No longer was the term "information" simply a lifeless engineering concept, a procession of signals, a tally of messages directing the performance of computers and other robots. With the aid of the hologram, we could better understand the meaning of information in human terms. In the brain, information bursts alive in vivid projections of the sense impressions that create our experience of the world, superimposing one on another at many different levels and frequencies of awareness. Intermingled with those projections are the private sensations of thought and feeling, what Pribram called "introjections," that make up our experience of ourselves as human beings. Following the direction set by Pribram's insights, it became possible for us to start drawing together the separate elements of our own perspective and, cautiously, begin sketching a new picture of the mind in communication terms—a mind that became even more amazing when viewed as a living product of information.

As we had come to understand it, the human mind was not some abstract concept, some inaccessible *epi*phenomenon or subjective "ghost in the machine." In communication terms, the mind could be described more accurately as a *living information mix,* an organic whole of billions of interacting perceptions, sensations, thoughts and feelings coming together, not in a cold computer store of discrete memories or hard-wired neural networks, but throughout the brain's richly interwoven tissue. Within this compact but infinitely complex arena, an individual may focus his attention on any portion or detail of his mind in the manner of a hologram. He may approach the overall perspective from many different windows or points of view, or he may zero in on any particular focus of thought, feeling, memory, imagination or perception. In holographic fashion, we could envision every purported state of consciousness, from everyday awareness to those altered psychological or mystical states, not as disconnected planes of alternate "realities" but simply as different slices of mind innate within each individual's holographic reach and flexibility.

However, to fully understand the experience of snapping and the alterations of mind that may follow from it, we found it necessary to go further still. We had to integrate our new insights into the mind and brain with a larger understanding of human experience itself and its role in the mind's lifelong process of growth and change.

The Way to Experience. For all the breakthroughs that had been made in the technical processing of information, despite the explosion of computers, telecommunications, and the new technology for engineering life-changing spiritual and personal growth experiences, little progress had been made in understanding information in human terms—in the living form of experience.

In our research, we counted more than a dozen divergent uses of the word. Scientists historically used the term experience to refer to any external event or object perceived by the senses. Many used the term to describe biological actions that were wholly unconscious and might be ascribed as easily to animals and even to plants, for that matter, as to human beings. For strict Freudians, experience seemed to end in childhood. Many cognitive scientists, like the behaviorists before them, used the term interchangeably with learning and memory to describe any knowledge, acquired trait or other information pattern retained over time. For those modern minds, as for scientists in earlier eras, the principle of reduction remained their primary tool for cutting down experience to manageable dimensions, but with each reduction, something vital and distinctly human was lost. As with consciousness and the mind itself, the well-trenched scientific paths led away from the insight we were seeking into the intense experiences that gave rise to snapping.

For us, the answer lay at the crossroads, at the intersection where the new technical sciences of cybernetics and information theory met up with the new biologically-based science of living systems, with the new research in neuroscience and the new knowledge of human communication that coalesced in humanistic psychology. Together, the combined discoveries of these new sciences pointed to a fact as obvious as human nature itself: that human beings comprise an entirely different order of organization in nature, one that thrives, survives and adapts, not from pre-programmed genetic codes, unconscious processes or conditioned behavior, but from a ceaseless flow of experience that shapes every aspect of our minds and our day-to-day lives.

With that basic insight and the new tools at our disposal to explore it, the separate pieces of our puzzle began to fall into place. Finally, the monster of experience, the beast that had come charging into popular culture in the sixties, devouring the reigning traditions of psychology and loosing an epidemic of sudden personality change in its wake, could be understood scientifically in communication terms. And slowly we began to see how information in the living form of experience— whether that experience was an overwhelming spiritual or personal growth experience, a grueling weekend training retreat, a spontaneous rush of emotion or simply a well-timed earful of the right words— could have the power to shape and dramatically alter human awareness and personality.

That information might be communicated in words, gestures, images, ideas, beliefs, commands, suggestions, and other verbal and nonverbal messages. It might be packaged and delivered in controlled information environments and applied human communication techniques and technologies. In the day-to-day flow of information, this ubiquitous force and substance comes at each individual from every direction in moving currents of sights, sounds, scents, tastes and touches falling on the eye and ear and skin, passing from one person to another in fluent streams of language, signs, symbols, personal interactions, group dynamics, social relationships, and other everyday communications.

Once that information comes into contact with human beings, an awesome transformation occurs. The mind in its infinite capacity for communication converts that tide of information into the highest and most complex form of organization in nature. Experience, in our perspective, was not just another name for information. It was the living embodiment of the stuff in human terms, the active form in which people come to know and *feel* the flood of information they take in and process daily. They experience the information every moment, over the countless communication channels of the human system that weave the mind, brain and body together in a unified, seamless whole. Each thought, feeling and everyday event is not only a bit of information in the technical sense, but a living *piece* of experience. Each piece adds some small measure to the greater whole of the mind, and each becomes an ongoing part of that individual's awareness and personality.

Those same life-giving experiences, from the most extraordinary moments to the most commonplace occurrences, supply the vital information that shapes and sustains the living workings of the human brain itself. Each moment the brain receives and processes billions of bits of raw experience in the form of minute electrochemical impulses. This torrent of incoming information flows through the brain's 100 billion living cells called neurons, sparking slowly through the minute fibers of the synapses, the winding, tangling junctures of weblike interconnection that link each brain cell to many others. In these synapses information mixes freely, creating a teeming pool of mental activity that takes place at many conscious and unconscious levels. The mix is a multisensory kaleidoscope, a swirl of sights, sounds and sensations, from direct impressions, such as a punch in the face, to the most subtle human experiences, such as the veiled signals each individual picks up and gives off through body language and other nonverbal communications. In holographic fashion, this teeming flow of information is then physically spread out and distributed throughout the brain and nervous system. Feelings of sadness and loss may come to rest in the pit of a person's stomach. Shocking news may stab him in the chest; an awesome spectacle may leave him breathless. In this way, the things we experience every moment as human beings deposit traces of information throughout our brains and our bodies, literally informing our lives from that moment on.

The Metabolism of Experience. This organic process in the brain may be compared to the way the body digests food. The powerful chemical and biological machinery of the digestive system breaks down the food we eat into its basic nutritional components, which are then made available to the rest of the body. In this same sense, the human brain physically *metabolizes* experience through its natural capacity for transformation, converting its rich diet into diverse forms of information which it then uses to fuel the human system's diverse communication operations. Like the other organs of the body, the heart which runs on blood, the lungs which run on air, the human brain—the seat of the mind and main stage of awareness—runs on experience.

The analogy is not simply a vivid organic metaphor. Experiments in sensory deprivation offer a taste of what happens to the brain when it is starved of experience. The effects go far beyond the spiritual moments described by Sargant. In sensory deprivation tests first performed in laboratories and, later, in personal growth experiments in the sixties, subjects were suspended in sightless, soundless tanks of water which produced an effect of weightlessness, the water warmed to body temperature to nullify all impressions of heat and cold. No physiological stress was applied (adequate oxygen was ensured), yet when all sources of experience were cut off, people's brains were totally disrupted. Disorientation resulted almost immediately. After about twenty minutes, the brain began trying to produce its own experiences! Visual and auditory hallucinations occurred first, followed by profound alterations of consciousness, ranging from high states of ecstasy and joy to deep realms of cosmic bliss and spiritual transcendence. After a point, however, prolonged periods of sensory deprivation may cause serious damage to the nervous system. Subjects in extended tests experienced episodes of insanity, violence and total withdrawal, not from chemical or physiological causes such as drugs or a lack of food or sleep, but from the simple lack of experience.

Apparently, the human hunger for experience is not merely a poetic notion but an explicit physical demand. Deprived of new information and experiences, the brain ceases functioning normally. Starved to extremes, it goes altogether haywire. Yet this life-giving information does not merely fuel the brain as gasoline fuels a precast auto engine. In human terms, experience plays a much more vital role in fundamental processes of brain growth and development. For all practical purposes, the size and structure of the human brain is genetically determined. The number of neurons in the brain is set at birth and does not increase appreciably from then on. However, the intricate synaptic connections between and among those neurons, the living information-processing pathways that determine how an individual's experience will, in fact, become ordered and interpreted, are only minimally organized at birth. The fundamental workings of the mind— the labyrinthine networks of synaptic connections that create the brain's higher communication capacities—are determined by experience.

In its first years, the infant brain establishes the basic information-processing pathways that govern its perceptions throughout life. What an individual sees, hears, senses, the manner in which he or she experiences the world, is determined by these first shaping experiences. Yet even as these basic faculties are developing, the child's awareness is also being shaped by his parents and others in the modes of perception of his culture. Different cultures perceive the world in different ways, seeing different forms, distinguishing different colors and ignoring different things as well; and a child's awareness can only expand within the social context of those first shared experiences and relationships. Later, more complex capacities evolve, such as thought, language and imagination, all of which grow and develop in response to further experience. And each capacity of mind appears to have its own specific "window" of development. If the mind's higher capacities are not tapped and nurtured in the child's early years, they will not develop on their own. If a child never uses his powers of imagination when he is young, when the brain is in its most ambitious period of organization and development, in all likelihood, the capacity will not be there when he grows older. In a complete reversal of earlier thinking on the subject, that prized quality called "genius" is now widely accepted to be primarily a product of experience, the result of active cultivation of an individual's higher powers of mind during the brain's most fertile and impressionable years.

This capacity for learning, for growth and development through experience, is unparalleled among other species. Experience literally *creates* the everyday workings of the mind, transforming the raw material of billions of loosely connected brain cells into a living triumph of communication. Experience also shapes the distinctive patterns of thought, feeling and self-expression that underlie that larger human form—personality.

Unlike that of animals, our genetic code contains almost no specific instructions for behavior, but rather an economical set of rules for developing individual patterns of response from our experiences. Long before the ability to communicate through language unfolds, these bedrock patterns of thought and feeling, the base on which personality rests, are forged in the intimate relationship between parent and child. A mother's touch, the sound of her voice, the warmth of her skin, provide the child's first experiences and shape feelings that will influence him throughout his life. As the child matures and ventures into the world, new experiences, modes of expression and relationships further shape his personality and inform his budding social nature.

All this information, virtually everything a person experiences, becomes a permanent part of the living structure of the brain, but the extent to which it shapes personality throughout life, or at any one moment, is not fixed or predetermined. Like human awareness itself, that elusive thing called personality is fluid and ever-changing, a mix of resonating bits of information and experience, past and present.

Our notion of a metabolism of experience offered new ways to think about the life of the mind in society. The metabolism process traveled back and forth, literally, from the world outside to the living world inside each human being. This idea that our experiences are metabolized organically and stored physically in living patterns of information distributed throughout the brain helped to explain the Freudian view of personality as the cumulative product of a child's early life experiences, as well as many aspects of behaviorist B.F. Skinner's developmental concepts of conditioning and environmental control.

More important, the metabolism concept accounted for the newly recognized processes of *adult* development. It placed the higher motivations of humanistic psychology, with its innate needs for personal growth and meaningful experience, on an equal footing with more basic biological responses, affirming the unflinching focus on experience that infused the human potential movement. It offered something more than the multitude of competing cognitive science theories and models, most of which continued to depict the mind as an assemblage of neural networks wired together in a more or less Darwinian fashion. In our view, the metabolism process more accurately described the multiple levels of biological, neurological and human communication actions that converge and cooperate throughout the brain to create the living whole of the mind.

And that process is ongoing. At any time in a person's life, new and intense experiences may leave lasting impressions on the mind and physically alter organic information-processing pathways deep in the brain. The process may spark all kinds of metabolic mixings and holographic convergences. Thoughts and feelings from past experiences may be regenerated by new experiences of a similar nature or frequency. Exotic smells may call up long-forgotten memories and their associated emotions. In one widely noted phenomenon, long after a person has reached adulthood, current pressures of a job or career may unleash feelings of anxiety and panic reminiscent of exam periods in high school or college—even triggering recurring nightmares of those bygone days. Marital or relationship problems may evoke feelings of insecurity and rejection that date back to earlier romances and long-gone love affairs. In later years, the aging process may let loose a flood of past impressions that mix with present-day thoughts and feelings; for although a person's memory of recent events usually deteriorates with age, his earliest experiences and the organic connections that embody them literally grow stronger and *more* salient over time. Finally, in a phenomenon that has been endlessly reported, with life's culminating experience of death the entire storehouse of the brain may be tapped and ignited simultaneously, causing the complete record of an individual's experience to flash before his eyes in a glow of light filled with beckoning images of beloved people and meaningful life events.

Yet, despite the mountains of scientific proof of this copious activity in the brain's lifelong metabolism of experience, the assumption still among scientists, psychologists and people generally is that the core components of each individual's awareness and personality—our everyday powers of thinking, feeling, perception, memory, imagination and conscious decision-making—are unfading flowers that grow out of childhood experiences, environmental conditioning and the rock-hard structure of the genetic code and that, once formed, they remain indelibly fixed, maintaining themselves effortlessly throughout life. The phenomenon of snapping makes clear beyond all doubt that this old assumption is invalid. In the course of human development, our early experiences do indeed shape our personalities and individual powers of mind. But we know now that this shaping process is organic, ongoing and in a state of constant change. An incessant flow of information and experience is needed to create and sustain our everyday powers of mind. And as our research reveals, that same shaping flow of experience can be used to alter, impair and even destroy those basic capacities as well.

This prospect was first suggested in the early fifties by a British engineer, W. Ross Ashby, a seminal figure in communication science who made the first comprehensive application of communication principles to the workings of the human brain. In two brilliant theoretical works published in the fifties, *An Introduction to Cybernetics* and *Design for a Brain,* Ashby showed how a sophisticated cybernetic device like the brain could organize itself from experience, and how new experience could alter that organization at its most basic organic levels.

Ashby made fundamental connections that linked the actions of complex technical communications systems to the behavior of simple organisms, to life processes in general, and to the workings of the human brain in particular. His core principles and processes described the universal laws that govern the day-to-day metabolism of human experience. He identified the innate communication imperative that drives human beings and all living things: their need for information and vital feedback from the world to sustain their basic biological functions and internal control operations. Ashby's "Law of Requisite Variety" made clear that it is not simply the amount of information a person takes in, but also the *kind* of information he experiences, that determines the health and balance of his mind and body. While overload researchers were pummeling human test subjects with massive quantities of information, Ashby demonstrated scientifically that, *to survive and adapt, human beings must have a steady flow of information that is rich and varied in both the kind and quality of its experiences.*

However, as every overloaded office worker and homemaker knows first-hand, to survive and flourish, human beings require more than endless amounts or even endless kinds of information. They require an organized process of growth and change through experience. This crucial organizing and adapting process was the focus of another law of communication first expressed by Ashby and named explicitly "The Law of Experience." Put simply, Ashby's Law of Experience states that *new information coming into a communication system tends to destroy and replace earlier information of a similar nature.*

We could observe countless instances of Ashby's laws at work in the everyday operations of the mind, brain and body. Among people generally, once a communication pattern has been ingrained organically, whether a pattern of speech, a bad habit or a widely accepted idea—the once universally held belief that the earth is flat, for example—that information, that way of experiencing the world, will prevail unless new information comes in to destroy and replace it. A pattern of speech may be consciously changed or corrected, a bad habit may be forcibly broken, or a new concept of the cosmos may gain popular acceptance. In each case, the newer, more intense and more meaningful experience supersedes the old.

Other everyday occurrences confirm the jurisdiction of Ashby's laws over all the mind's thinking and feeling powers. A traveler may have a mental image of a place in his mind, the French Riviera, for example, and specific emotions associated with it, such as fun, excitement, adventure and relaxation. However, that image and those feelings may be utterly shattered when he finally arrives and finds rundown hotels, polluted beaches, high prices and abominable weather. The combined impact will destroy and replace his previous impressions with new information that is a proper reflection of his experience. In another classic example, a rider who falls off a horse is traditionally instructed to get back on as soon as possible. His first feelings of mastery and safety have been destroyed and fresh, new, positive experience is prescribed immediately to erase the trauma of his fall.

These laws of experience are organic. In information terms, they are natural functions of our innate capacity for communication that work automatically and require no conscious attention. These basic communication principles apply to every aspect of human experience, establishing ongoing patterns of thought and feeling where none were before, yet always granting priority to newer, more intense and more meaningful experiences over older, more mundane ones.

Our research has benefited greatly from discoveries made since Ashby's day. A wealth of evidence has confirmed unequivocally that the laws of experience are enforced across the spectrum of the mind, from basic processes of perception to the whole of personality. In interviews with neuroscientists working on the forefronts of brain research, we learned about these exciting new discoveries that demonstrate the brain's lifelong response to experience and clearly describe the organic process of new information superseding old. In some cases, the latest research suggests, new and intense experiences may physically sever long-standing synaptic connections in the brain; in others, new information patterns may simply bypass or superimpose over earlier ones. Scientists have only begun to understand the dynamics of these minute yet immensely complex organic processes that may involve only the slightest shift in the electrical resistance of a tiny portion of a single neural cell, or change the most subtle chemical configurations at the terminals of a neuron's tentacle-like synapses. Yet most new neuroscientific findings uphold the spirit and letter of the law of experience. They confirm that the brain's living information networks are perpetually being shaped, changed, organized and *re*organized by both the kind and quality of each individual's day-to-day experiences.

Indeed, few actions in nature are as striking to behold as the interplay that takes place in this teeming inner world of communication. One of the most inspiring moments of our research, in fact, occurred when we were shown live-action pictures of brain cells, magnified many times, in which we could actually see the neurons waving their splayed synaptic fingers, reaching outward toward other neurons, apparently, making and breaking new synaptic connections with each moment's measure of information and experience.

We did not need a microscope to see Ashby's laws of experience in action. Many dramatic examples were visible in the new cults, sects and self-help therapies. Like a sudden trauma or electric shock, the new information stresses people were being subjected to in the intense physical, mental and emotional experiences of group rituals and therapeutic techniques were often powerful enough to destroy and replace lifelong patterns of mind and personality. They also appeared to alter and, in many cases, physically destroy long-standing information-processing pathways in people's brains and nervous systems. Our talk with Jean Turner revealed how the overwhelming experience of her marathon est encounter apparently destroyed patterns of emotion and sensation in her legs that had been sources of pain since childhood. Similarly, our interview with Lawrence and Cathy Gordon suggested that, in the course of their weekend retreat among the Moonies, the constant repetition of Unification Church doctrines effectively destroyed and replaced the couple's earlier spiritual beliefs. Presumably, the bombardment of new information and experiences they received in the sect's sermons, lectures, political discussion groups and personal confrontations, combined with the physical impact of the weekend, was powerful enough to bring about their rapid and complete conversion.

Yet these potent experiences, like all experiences, were holographic in nature and appeared to have deeper organic effects. Jean Turner's miracle cure was not simply a healing scalpel that excised the pain in her legs and left the rest of her mind and body unscathed. As she testified, her concentrated est encounter, in which group trainers tried to excavate a lifetime of shaping experiences and psychological traumas in two weekends, triggered a rippling physical, mental and emotional convulsion. She felt it in her legs, her wrists and throughout her body. During the second weekend of the training, it "came up like a ball," destabilizing the entire structure of her personality and leaving her in a state of disorientation and inner disarray. The Gordons, as well, underwent far more than a simple conversion of belief during their weekend among the Moonies. Their physical appearances changed noticeably—their eyes, their postures, their tones of voice. Indeed, they appeared to become different people altogether. Moreover, their sweeping inner changes also transformed the way the couple experienced the world around them. On their return, as Lawrence recalled, the everyday world seemed strangely alien and sinister. In the light of the new information and experience they had absorbed, the specter of Satan was omnipresent, even in the worried appearance and genuine concerns expressed by Lawrence's mother.

As these examples confirm, it is not possible to tamper with one element of an individual's awareness without endangering his personality as a whole. In many of the new groups, a sudden injection of experience may destroy some specific pattern of thought, feeling or belief, but it may also alter the entire field of consciousness, shifting the window of an individual's awareness—or changing the landscape altogether. In our research, we found good reasons to believe that these sudden stressful experiences may cause lasting changes in the physical organization of the brain. In their extremes, they may alter, impair and physically destroy organic pathways at the core of an individual's personality. Once these profound changes take place, as the new methods of deprogramming and rehabilitation make clear, the person's former sense of self can only be restored by cutting the connections to his new group identity, reestablishing communication with the deeper underlying personality, and then slowly, consciously reconnecting the individual with his past experiences, relationships and the wider world around him.

The laws of experience were cornerstones of our understanding of snapping, building blocks from communication, mathematics, biology, humanistic psychology and neuroscience which could be assembled to overcome the limitations of the robot model and other obsolete ways of thinking about the mind. With those new tools, we could explore more deeply how an individual's personality may be shaped and altered by specific information stresses and examine the effects of a variety of individual and group experiences on the brain's living information-processing powers. From this new perspective, we turn now to look directly at the moment of sudden personality change, at the abrupt snapping of human awareness from one frame of mind to another.

11 The Snapping Moment

In time to come it will often be difficult perhaps, to decide whether an advance in knowledge represents a step forward in physics, information theory or philosophy, whether physics is expanding into biology or whether biology is employing physical methods and approaches to an ever greater extent.

—*Werner Heisenberg,*
"The End of Physics?"

OUR FRAMEWORK COMPLETE, the separate pieces of our investigation came together to form a new picture of the phenomenon of snapping. All the predictable elements were there: intense physical experiences such as singing, dancing, jumping, drumming and other vigorous group activities, recognized physiological stresses such as lack of sleep and a poor diet, basic information stresses like noise, isolation, and other forms of sensory overload and deprivation.

In the right circumstances any of these experiences, alone or in combination, may produce an overwhelming peak moment, which may in turn be followed by a precipitous plunge into physical or emotional collapse. However, not even all of them in concert need set off the moment of snapping, which we have distinguished from a brief physical, emotional or spiritual high as the sudden drastic alteration of an individual's entire personality.

An altogether different kind of information is usually needed to trigger this extraordinary human response. It consists of the intense inner stresses generated by the potent tools of the technology of experience. These human tools may include specific rhetorical ploys, ritual practices, individual and group techniques, mass-marketing strategies and more subtle communication methods. They may include everything from fervid sermons and lectures to searing confessions, from casual conversations to aggressive confrontations to slickly packaged personal appeals, from repetitive prayers to prolonged practices of chanting and meditation, from passive indoctrination and small-group study sessions to active methods of role playing, psychodrama, guided fantasy and directed visualization. These powerful tools may be systematically orchestrated to engage the entire range of an individual's communication capacities, from the most rudimentary and automatic biological functions to the highest reaches of human awareness. The palpable information stresses they may produce can create profound mental and emotional conflicts: anxiety, confusion, disorientation, feelings of fear, guilt, hatred, anger, humiliation, embarrassment and alienation. They may prompt a person to seek release from a troubled past or from more immediate and pressing problems. Then, often in a sensuous, seductive or totally foreign environment, or immersed in an atmosphere of love, warmth, acceptance, sharing, openness, honesty and community, a person may yield to some call, either from without or within, to "surrender," to "let go," to "stop doubting" and "questioning," to "relinquish hold upon the will" or merely to "let things float." It is this invisible act of surrender, more than anything else, that sets off the inner explosion we call snapping.

In that moment, something quite remarkable may happen. With that flick of a switch, that change of heart and mind, an individual's personality may literally come apart, triggering an overwhelming, holographic crisis across the whole of the mind, brain and body.

The experience itself may give rise to a rush of physical sensation: a blinding light, a floating feeling, momentary paralysis, breathlessness, a flood of tears, a coursing of blood throughout the body, or a strong tingling that showers downward from the head with the surge of an electrical discharge. The immediate impact may be felt as awe, ecstasy, amazement, a quiet peace or complete collapse. In the aftermath of the moment, a person may feel a whole new sense of being, not one of enlightenment but of something on the far side of that spiritual crest. This is the moment when the individual falls off the precipice and crash lands with the distinct impression that somehow, somewhere, something has changed, either internally or in the outside world. Just what that change is usually remains a mystery at first, but the unmistakable sense is that whatever has happened is irreversible.

It is this sharp break in the continuity of awareness that the term snapping so vividly depicts. In the course of our travels and interviews, we were amazed to find that so many people were fully conscious of this exact moment when "something snapped." For some, it was as if the massive assault of new information blew out their existing personalities and unquestioned perception of the world around them. In many instances, this snapping moment took people by storm, creating a deluge of new sensations and dredging up a slurry of buried images and emotions from the past. Afterward, people were faced with more than a simple sensation of being "reborn." Many people we spoke with were indeed brought to a new and heightened state of awareness, but suddenly and inexplicably, in a manner that was jarring and led to panic and disorientation.

For the person who experiences it, the snapping moment may pose terrifying dilemmas. He may find it impossible to integrate the keen, clear presence of his new sense of being with some vague notion of his former self which he is no longer able to locate or define. In some instances, a person may feel catapulted across a one-way threshold that was more than he ever bargained for in his search for self or spirit. He may find himself completely severed from his past, thrown into a physical, mental and emotional tailspin.

In this condition, a person is dangerously vulnerable, for in the aftermath of this shattering break, the brain's information-processing capacities may become physically disorganized, not simply leaving the mind open to new ideas and information, but in fact rendering it re-ceptive to a whole new plan of organization. Someone whose sense of self has just been detonated in this way may seize upon the first avail-able interpretation or explanation of his experience. If he is told that his overwhelming ecstasy was the Holy Spirit visiting his mind and body, he will very likely believe it. If he is told that his feelings of detachment and depersonalization represent a state of "cosmic one-ness with the universe," in all probability he will find that not merely acceptable but absolute truth.

It is important to recognize that this state of near-total vulnerabil-ity to suggestion does not represent a physiological malfunction of the brain. In its holographic nature, the crisis the snapping moment evokes is purely one of information. As we learned in our talks with neurosci-entists, the brain's sturdy machinery is virtually indestructible except under the most extreme physical attack. Following the snapping mo-ment, it keeps on performing its natural functions, striving to make meaning and regain some semblance of inner organization. In fact, in this crucial state of searching and reorganization, the brain becomes capable of amazing feats of imagination. An individual may hop out of a water-filled "rebirthing" tank and begin barking like a seal, just as a person who surrenders his will to a stage hypnotist may become firmly convinced that he is a chicken! A mature adult may emerge from a marathon group training reconstructed in the image of his "inner child," or, in psychiatric terms, regressed to the emotional level of a selfish kid or rebellious adolescent. If he receives no help in dispelling such notions, that may in fact be the way his personality becomes reorganized from then on.

The resolution of this information crisis depends heavily on the course of action followed in its immediate aftermath. In keeping with the laws of experience, if the person returns to his former surroundings and actively restores his earlier relationships, the effects of the snapping moment may dissipate in a relatively short time. If, however, out of fear and panic he flees or withdraws into himself, he may linger in his precarious state of mind for months or even years, trapped in its mind-boggling aftereffects and extreme vulnerability to suggestion. If he remains in alien settings with little or no connection to his former life and relationships, his personality will almost certainly be refashioned in the image of his new surroundings, and his awareness will fall into line with that of the people around him.

So far in this book we have portrayed episodes of snapping in settings ranging from private, personal experiences to large public gatherings. In the examples that follow, we will look at some of the more unusual instances of the phenomenon that we came upon in our research. Our purpose: to demonstrate how, in certain circumstances, the buildup of external or internal information stresses may culminate in an intense snapping moment and the state of vulnerability that generally follows.

In our first cross-country research tour, the Hare Krishna sect emerged as one of the most practiced at inducing snapping moments that brought about striking changes in personality. Formally known as the International Society for Krishna Consciousness, this worldwide Hindu sect once boasted tens of thousands of full-time members in the United States alone. Then a series of bitter internal power struggles, the murders of several sect dissidents and defectors, and other alleged crimes diminished the appeal of this prototypical Eastern sect. Krishna members still are seen frequently, dressed in their bright orange devotional robes, chanting and singing on street corners in cities on every continent, but they also dress more conventionally to engage in fundraising activities, which may include the selling of incense and brightly illustrated copies of the *Bhagavad Gita*.

Some of the most bizarre tales we heard of the snapping phenomenon came from one-time Krishna members. In one of our earliest interviews, a former devotee described the ancient Hindu ritual the sect draws on in its devotions, which he experienced on his first visit to a Krishna temple in California.

"They have a ceremony called *arotika*," he told us, "where they offer a candle to their deities. They jump up and down and dance and sing. It was probably the most far-out feeling I'd ever had in my life. It was the first time I'd heard anybody chant like that, very loud, the *Hare-Krishna* mantra. Then they opened the doors and there were these deities, six of them. There was one deity in the middle which was supposed to be Krishna that I recognized from the literature I had been reading. It really came out at me. The statue was stark white and very colorfully attired. He was sort of in an s-shape, standing very casually playing the flute. That was when I had this incredibly bizarre experience. All at once, while we were dancing and chanting, there was something like a flash of light, except that it didn't really happen. It wasn't on a rational level at all. The deity seemed to move. I was dancing around and getting along in my chanting, and I focused my attention on this deity and it seemed to fill my mind completely. I stared at it for a minute, and it seemed to bore right through me. Physically, I felt separated from my body—it was really strange. I felt like I was completely there and my body had been washed away. There was just sort of a link-up between me and the statue, as if everything else had vanished."

For this devotee, the snapping moment came up fast and hit hard.

"The whole thing lasted maybe three seconds," he said. "I really have no idea because I lost all track of time. It was a new experience and I didn't know what to do with it. I didn't know if I wanted it or not. I was trying to resolve it, trying to analyze it and figure out why it happened, what it was."

Finally, he drew the same conclusion as those around him.

"The whole thing was very intense. I interpreted it as a powerful spiritual experience. It was the main reason I joined the temple."

Another Krishna devotee revealed the difference between a simple peak experience and the powerful *arotika* ritual. She described her ecstatic snapping moment in a ceremony at another Krishna temple.

"I was with these devotees who were all the way they get in the *arotika*," she said, "and I got all caught up in it just like everyone else. I was closing my eyes hard, trying to get that bliss and make it come; and it did, more or less. I felt like I saw a white light. I felt like I was going to explode. I guess you can relate it to a sexual thing, like a climax or something. Your mind has to be in a certain state of willingness to achieve it, then the chanting and the music and the incense and all those things just help to bring it on."

Looking back, this young woman told us how the entire *arotika* setting—the bright-colored statues, the incense, the chanting—put her mind in a state of readiness for her snapping experience. She reflected on the way sect leaders orchestrated and exploited the group frenzy.

"Right at the peak the person who was leading the ceremony blew the conch shell, then everyone fell to the floor and started reciting their little prayers. Afterwards, everyone was really high. Some people were in a trance state. Others became very quiet. Then we all sat down and received a lecture. When we were totally drained, they poured in all the indoctrination."

The comprehensive sensory assault that culminates in an ecstatic snapping moment is only one method used to bring about sudden conversions and transformations of personality. Other sects use less obvious methods to create a wholly different information environment, yet their impact may be equally bewildering and profound.

On a trip to the Pacific Northwest several years later, we met an ex-member of the Rajneesh sect that sparked controversy on four continents. In the eighties, the sect seized control of a rural Oregon town until the group's guru was deported for immigration fraud and other alleged criminal violations. This woman recalled her first snapping moment during a visit to the sect's ashram in India, where intense group techniques adapted from human potential movement practices shattered her awareness and opened her to deeper manipulations.

"When I arrived in Poona, there were seventy different groups all based on the newest human potential therapies. In the first group I attended, the leader took us through powerful deep breathing techniques. I remember, I was in the center of the group and everyone was walking around me and suddenly I just started screaming and yelling. Everything turned white. I was dizzy. I felt like I blacked out for hours, although it must have only been a few minutes. Then I started focusing in again and I was being held by everybody like I was a little baby. When I looked up, I saw these giant posters of Rajneesh all around the room and at that moment I was a goner. The leader pointed to the pictures and said: 'We owe it all to him. Give your life to him. Surrender yourself to Rajneesh and you will be enlightened forever.' "

An ex-member of the Divine Light Mission described a more subtle snapping moment. He explained how that Hindu-based sect combined fatigue, darkness and ancient scripture in its potent induction ritual.

"The initiation was held at three in the morning and none of us had had very much sleep going into it," he recalled. "The room was pitch black as the *mahatma* read from the scriptures of the Divine Light, emphasizing that the light referred to was not allegorical but real light and that all religions have been based on the same mystical experience. He told us to concentrate on a point in our foreheads where our third eye was located, and he would come and channel the divine energy into us. He came swishing through the darkness. I felt his fingers on my eyes, and I saw a light that seemed to stab down from the outer darkness. It came from somewhere behind me and created a figure eight of pure, white light. It lasted for a brief period of time and I was blown away by it."

Afterward, this new disciple experienced an eerie disorientation. Even as it was occurring, he sensed that something ominous had happened to his mind.

"After the initiation I went through a period of five or six hours in which I felt I was not really controlling what I was doing or saying," he remembered. "I felt like I was being spiritually controlled, like a marionette of some sort. It was very strange."

One of the most puzzling aspects of the snapping moment is that often it is not some overwhelming physical experience that sets it off but some subtle movement in the information dimension, some tiny thing, a seemingly irrelevant image or evanescent emotion that sparks a chain reaction in the mind. Countless group training veterans told us about some long-forgotten, otherwise inconsequential event that came stampeding into their awareness at the prompting of a group leader. Many said their snapping experience began with a whiff of incense or the moment they focused on a tension headache that developed during their group ordeal—a common self-help technique. Others, like Sally Kempton, told of a passing thought or phrase that set off a depth charge of emotional response.

There seems to be no limit to the kinds of settings in which the snapping moment may occur, from religious revivals to encounter groups, from public ordeals to private moments of relaxation and repose. We met a suburban housewife in her mid-thirties who described the disorientation she experienced in the privacy of her own home the first time she tried a meditation technique she read about in a book. Here, as in other cases, that curious white light switched on at the precise instant of snapping.

"This particular technique recommended that you go into a closet," she said. "I put a chair in there and I sat up straight, trying not to think about anything. The idea was that if a thought came into your mind, you should just watch it, just see it come and let it go out without fighting it. Soon I found that time had disappeared. I came out of the closet and saw that two hours had passed, and it really blew my mind. I had a feeling that I was something other than my body but other than my mind, too. I felt very light. I remember after that being in the kitchen and reaching for some equipment and it seemed as if a big light suddenly flashed on in front of me."

This sense of timelessness is another telling feature of the snapping moment—to us the flash of images and rush of sensations seemed clearly to describe a holographic information process occurring outside of normal time and space. Many people we met spoke of snapping moments that occurred in a burst of simultaneous experience. Others told of snapping experiences that were not instantaneous but drawn out. We heard from many people who, like Jean Turner after her second est weekend, came floating out of some sect or group on a magic carpet of bliss, only to experience a plunge into unhappiness and profound alienation after days or even months.

In the eighties, emerging new age therapies assembled more complex conglomerations of group rituals. The snapping moments they often produced could be quietly profound or devastatingly intense. On another trip to the Northwest, we met a devotee of new age guru J.Z. Knight who experienced a subtle snapping moment in a frenzied setting. The controversial Knight, who won a wide following through public lectures and videos in which she portrayed herself as a celestial "channeler" who yielded her body to the spirit of a 35,000-year-old Cro-Magnon prophet named Ramtha, cooked up a mixed brew of physical exertion, visualization and new age mysticism that brought this subject to her snapping point during a mass rite of "pagan dancing."

"We were in an arena filled with a thousand people. Everyone was blindfolded. The music was loud. It was hot and people were sweaty and we had been dancing for hours. J.Z. had us picture what we were dancing for, a tree or a bird or a body part you wanted to heal. We just danced free form and went through our own guided visualization. I visualized myself dressed in white flowing linens climbing a steep hill. The wind was blowing through my hair. I was climbing and climbing and I finally reached the top of this wonderful cliff. I was standing there overlooking this incredibly beautiful view and feeling this total sense of freedom, and I just got high and started smiling and laughing and was overwhelmed."

Freedom itself had become just another theme to exploit in many groups. Scads of seekers were drawn to the new cults and therapies in search of that quintessential quality they already possessed but now wanted to feel tangibly and experience in a whole new way. Ironically, in their quest, many unwittingly surrendered their freedom and years of their lives in the deal.

Peter M., a successful writer with a string of best-sellers on personal growth topics to his credit, experienced numerous snapping moments when he became immersed in Insight Seminars, the self-help arm of the Church of the Movement of Spiritual Inner Awareness. Insight/MSIA, a new age therapy *cum* religion founded in 1971 by a self-proclaimed "Mystical Traveler" named John-Roger, attracted thousands of eager searchers, overstressed professionals and corporate employees to mass trainings held in a dozen U.S. cities and countries as far afield as Australia. The group continued to draw new customers after its sometimes damaging practices, and John-Roger's own flagrant behavior, were exposed in the early nineties. Peter described two vivid snapping moments he experienced in Insight Seminars I and II that started him on a fifteen-year odyssey in Insight/MSIA. The first occurred in a group process in the initial Insight seminar in which participants were paired with a partner.

"I was doing a process called the 'What-Do-You-Want' process where you scream and yell and jump up and down," he told us. "You look into your partner's eyes and take turns screaming 'What do you want? What do you want?' People were screaming 'I want happiness,' 'I want God,' and their partners were screaming back 'Do you *really* want it?' I was screaming, 'I want to be free! I want to be free!' and suddenly I was knocked out, on my butt. It was like being hit with a bolt of lightning."

He lost consciousness momentarily, but his partner didn't even notice that he had attained the vaunted experience he had wished for.

"When I came to, the process was still going on. In fact, my partner was still yelling, 'What do you want? What do you want?' But I didn't want anything. I was absolutely ecstatic. It was the most wonderful let-go feeling. Afterwards, I was immediately surrounded by 'assistants' who put it in the context of the spirit moving and being hit by the 'mystical traveler consciousness.'"

His second snapping moment came late in Insight II during a group practice that has since become a pop culture cliche.

"It was called the 'Getting Your Affirmation' process," he went on. "We were there to get our affirmation, which is basically a statement about yourself that sums up all your positive qualities. The pressure was enormous because, if you didn't get your affirmation, you had to leave the training."

Insight leaders put tough constraints on the affirmation process.

"The problem was that you couldn't just get the proper words. You had to arrive at the proper *energy*. You could not just say, 'I'm a loving, caring being living my life totally free.' You had to *show* it to them."

The challenge pushed him to a snapping point.

"I was the thirty-ninth out of forty people to get my affirmation. Each time I stood up and said my affirmation, the trainers said, 'No, you don't have it yet. The energy's not right. Sit down.' I sat there watching people around me flipping out, having experiences of nirvana, and twenty hours later I still hadn't gotten my affirmation. Finally, I just lay on the floor and wallowed in my own negativity. I told myself how terrible I was because I couldn't get it, that I was an animal and not spiritual because everyone else was getting it and I wasn't. I said, 'I am such a miserable person, I'm hopeless, I'm too much in control,' all that stuff. Then something snapped and the pressure that had been on me so intensely was released and it just went *va-VOOM!*"

We asked him to share his hardwon affirmation.

"It's funny," he said, "I repeated those words for a day and a half, and now I cannot remember that affirmation. I don't have any memory of it at all, but that's the point when you're in that moment."

In that peak moment, Peter saw many trainees fall into an inchoate, convulsive state, a condition he witnessed repeatedly and experienced himself during his years in Insight/MSIA.

"Your hands curl up as if you are going to pick up a billiard ball or something. Then they start to shake and your fingers turn in toward your body. There was even a term for it in Insight—'lobster claws.' "

The primordial snapping response hit hardest at the extremities.

"When you reach that moment, your whole body starts taking energy away from parts that are not essential, like your hands. Your legs can become completely paralyzed and you fall on the floor, but in Insight that was something to be admired. It was a sign of spirit moving through you."

Many charismatic Christians experienced a similar response after intense episodes of speaking in tongues. Peter credited the convulsive state to hyperventilation, a simple mind-altering method instilled subtly in the rituals of Insight/MSIA, the Rajneeshees and other sects.

"At first it was taught as part of the technique," he recalled, looking back. "A process would start with 'take a deep breath, get some oxygen,' then it was always 'keep breathing, take another breath.' After a while, it became spontaneous. It was something we just did."

Many stopped short of that extreme peak, but he and other Insight/MSIA trainees found that the playfully named lobster claws experience caught them in a vise-like grip.

"When I reached it I felt so incredibly happy and euphoric. People said, 'This is what it feels like to be enlightened,' and immediately I wanted more. It was this incredible high, and the minute you start to slip out of the experience all you want to do is get it back."

Across the spectrum of personal growth and religious conversion, from ancient Hindu rituals, to Christian born-again and charismatic moments, to the potent peak experiences engineered by new age entrepreneurs, snapping may be an instant, conscious change. Or, as in groups like the Unification Church, a person may be slowly transformed over a weekend or three-week retreat without ever experiencing a sudden break in his awareness. Despite the differences, there are no contradictions among the various forms of snapping. Whether jolting and instantaneous or imperceptible and in slow motion, each indicates a similar surrender of thought, feeling and free will, and each follows its own characteristic course and consequences.

When we heard our first accounts of snapping, there was no systematic way to sort through the diverse personal experiences we were unearthing. No simple formula could explain how each infinitely complex convergence of physical, mental and emotional stresses could build up, crest in a holographic crisis in the brain, then resolve into a whole new organization of mind and personality. In our initial efforts to approach the problem scientifically, several scientists we spoke with pointed us in the direction of a promising new tool of mathematical interpretation. They suggested that it might help us to picture the dynamics of these varied leaps in awareness and assess their similarities and differences in relation to one another.

In the mid-seventies, this new mathematical perspective called "catastrophe theory" was introduced and debated across a broad spectrum of scientific disciplines. The new theory was concerned with events that take place abruptly—by fits, jumps and starts, as one advocate expressed it. Throughout nature such occurrences are abundant. The physical world offers many examples of sudden or discontinuous transformations: earthquakes, cloudbursts, waves breaking on a beach. The movements of humankind take place with equal outbreak and surprise: stock market crashes, prison riots and, of course, religious conversions. Each event represents an abrupt resolution of conflict between steadily interacting and opposing forces. In seeking to understand the dynamics of this type of discontinuous change, René Thom, a French mathematician, developed the math and logic of catastrophe theory.

The complex "topological" mathematics of catastrophe theory would be incomprehensible to most laymen. Thom's basic model, however, may be described, and even pictured, with little difficulty. (See Figure 1, a simplified depiction of the folding wave-shaped form, showing the curving surface smoothly continuous at the far side, then breaking in a wavelike manner on the near side; the breaking point or "catastrophe" is where the path plummets downward over the crest.) The im-

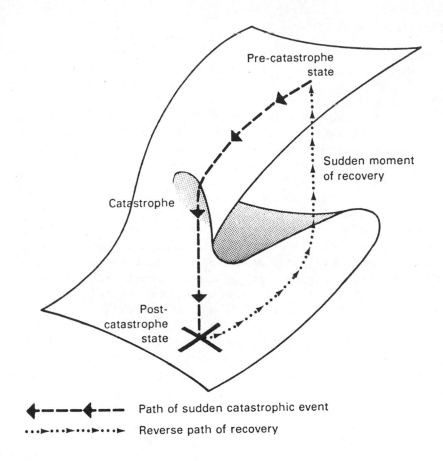

Figure 1: *Simplified version of Thom's elementary catastrophe curve*

ages of an earthquake or cresting wave are basic catastrophes of nature. They are products of dynamic forces—migrating land masses, flowing water—moving in direct opposition to each other. When the opposing forces meet and build up, on a beach, for instance, with water both flowing toward the land and slipping back into the sea, they converge, add, subtract and cancel each other out, until they cross a precise threshold of opposition and give way in the sudden breaking of a wave. On another scale, an earthquake too is the abrupt product of opposing forces, as the unseen stresses of moving and resisting land masses build to a cataclysmic breaking point. That breaking point, the final push, is no stronger than the forces that have gone before, but the change in activity, the earthquake, is sudden and discontinuous, wildly out of proportion to the tiny event that set it off.

Another example of this kind of sudden, discontinuous, catastrophic change would be the straw that broke the camel's back.

When it was introduced, the idea of a *theory* of catastrophes caught the fancy of the media and the public, many of whom hoped it would provide a method of predicting natural and economic disasters. In fact, Thom never intended catastrophe theory to be a tool of prediction, but rather a mathematical model and visual image that offered a way to understand the incalculable complexities of natural occurrences and living things—exactly what we were looking for in our attempt to grasp the complexity of snapping.

When we began to explore catastrophe theory, several scientists cautioned us that it was highly technical and controversial. However, as we spoke with other scientists and examined the underlying principles of Thom's work, we saw that catastrophe theory did indeed have valid and illuminating applications. One in particular convinced us that it could help us understand the complex dynamics of snapping.

Some of the first applications of catastrophe theory to human affairs were made by Professor E. Christopher Zeeman of the University of Warwick in England. In one model, Zeeman and British psychotherapist Dr. J. Hevesi offered a demonstration of the theory in action that was strikingly similar to the experience of snapping. Zeeman used Thom's catastrophe concept to study the then obscure affliction known as anorexia nervosa or obsessive fasting. The condition is now recognized as an emotional disorder found most often among adolescent girls struggling to reconcile conflicting personal needs, family problems and the normal social pressures of growing up. Anorexia usually begins as simple fasting, not extraordinary for a figure-conscious young woman. Unchecked, however, or taken to extremes, this harmless dieting strategy may cause a total degeneration of appetite, leading to profound emotional disturbance, starvation and, on rare occasions, death. Often anorexia also produces an extreme counterreaction in which the person will undergo episodes of bulimia or obsessive gorging.

Zeeman likened the experience to one of Thom's elementary catastrophes, plotting the progressive stages of the disorder on Thom's three-dimensional model. On the folding, wave-shaped form depicted in Figure 1, the appetite may be systematically plotted as the product of opposing forces of hunger and restraint. As these forces draw the anorexic toward the crest of the catastrophe wave, the appetite may jump from more or less normal to, paradoxically, practically nonexistent, to uncontrollable craving and compulsive gorging. Zeeman cited a sudden experience many anorexics call "the knockout," when feelings of exhaustion, disgust and humiliation sweep over them and cause them to crash abruptly from mounting hunger to no appetite at all.

In treating this disease, Dr. Hevesi developed a form of trance therapy in which he offered his patients reassurance, reduced their anxiety, and gradually brought their appetites back to normal. In an article in *Scientific American,* Zeeman described the observable moment of Dr. Hevesi's cure in terms that seemed to closely parallel the sudden snap of deprogramming (or in Figure 1, Sudden Moment of Recovery):

> After about two weeks of therapy and in about the seventh session of trance the patient's abnormal attitudes usually break down catastrophically and the personality is fused into a complete whole again. When the patient awakens from this trance, she may speak of it as a "moment of rebirth."

Catastrophe theory offered a surprisingly precise model of the anorexia experience: depicting the abrupt change from mere dieting to fasting, the contradictory jump from fasting to gorging, and the journey back from anorexia through a trance state to "rebirth." It also supplied a graphic image for the vivid terms like "knockout" and "let-go" in which anorexics described their experience. The correspondence was startling between the catastrophic jumps that occur in anorexia and the sudden personality changes that may take place in the new cults, sects and therapies. The abrupt changes in appearance and behavior, the instant transformation of lifelong patterns of thought, feeling and social relationship, all suggested the catastrophic resolution of opposing physical, mental and emotional stresses. Moreover, the folding, wave-shaped catastrophe curve seemed to offer a three-dimensional image of Ashby's laws of experience in action: charting the sudden, sweeping shift of the snapping moment when the flow of new information rises and crests, superseding the old. In the impending catastrophe, two natural and, usually, complementary processes of change and resistance are brought into direct opposition. In a stressful group encounter or personal confrontation with a skilled cult recruiter, the battle of advancing ideas and resisting emotions may crest in a sudden upheaval in the brain. In a ritual snapping moment, long-standing patterns of personality that have developed since childhood may give way to an entirely new personality formed from the mass of new information the person has absorbed. In the process, old pathways in the brain may be destabilized, physically disconnected and destroyed, and new pathways may be formed.

Soon after we became acquainted with catastrophe theory, we spoke with a young woman we will call Pam Mitchell who had spent more than a year in the Hare Krishna sect. As she described it, her experience in the cult and precarious re-emergence during deprogramming mapped onto Thom's model with near-perfect precision, describing two distinct yet fully interacting systems of personality.

Like most cult members, Pam Mitchell slipped gradually into her Krishna state of mind, just as most anorexics slip gradually into their state of uncontrollable fasting. Her boyfriend introduced her to the group and she grew familiar with the doctrines and rituals of Krishna life. She attended Sunday feasts at the Krishna temple and experienced repeated snapping moments during *arotika* ceremonies. Before long, she moved into the temple and became deeply involved in the daily life and practices of the group, sliding into a state of diminished awareness she referred to as being "dumbfounded." For months in that state of mind, she assumed the traditional Krishna woman's role of subservience, performing numerous menial chores. Through it all, she struggled to hold onto some thread of her former identity as she balanced the opposing forces of fear, guilt, confusion and exhaustion building within her. Her modern feminine consciousness opposed the Krishnas' lowly attitude toward women, her body reacted to the restricted diet and constant fatigue of cult life, her nervous system actively resisted the boredom and inactivity of hour upon hour of chanting. Finally, her strained emotions crested and gave way in a classic catastrophe.

"It slowly worked to the point where I was existing on such a low level that finally I cracked," she recalled. "I walked into the room and started laughing hysterically. Then I had a real breakdown. I just collapsed for about a day and a half.

"I guess you could say I snapped in a way," she said, without prompting. "I snapped to the point where I wasn't fighting anymore."

For the next three months, as she described it, her anxiety and frustration "went inside." The tensions she had been feeling disappeared, yet before long they began manifesting themselves in physical ways. Her hands and face broke out in eczema, and she gained weight dramatically. Concerned over her appearance, the temple president refused to let her go home to visit her family.

Then one day she experienced another catastrophic change.

"It was a snap thing," she said again. "I was just talking to another girl who was working in the kitchen with me and I went, *I've been brainwashed! What has happened to me?*"

In line with Thom's model, Pam's sudden moment of reawakening—

not a snapping into but, in this case, a snapping *out* of her cult state—was not the product of any intense or abrupt experience. Instead, it was a realization that happened in an instant, sparked by a passing impression that had been building up for some time. She remembered the dynamic nature of the experience.

"I felt alive again. I felt like I was thinking again. It was kind of gradual at first, like when you're slowly waking up and becoming conscious. I started to talk and become more and more excited, feeling, sensing more as I talked about what was happening to me. Then all of a sudden I looked at what I was doing and it hit me. It was like a connection."

Her description of the experience traced a precise path on the catastrophe curve.

"I felt like I had jumped off a cliff six months ago and I was just back up on the plateau I was on before," she said. "It was like I had gone backwards in my own development, but I knew myself again. It was me, not that other person. How can you explain how it feels to be alive?"

Soon after her awakening, Pam left the Krishna temple and returned to her hometown. But in a manner reminiscent of Kay Rambur's experience in the Children of God, her self-styled deprogramming was incomplete. For the next few weeks, she struggled in that peculiar limbo state known to ex-cultists as "floating."

"I was unable to relate to anybody," she recalled. "Within a week I was going back to the temple because I couldn't assimilate back here. Everyone else seemed crazy, and since nobody was aware of what had happened to me, I just couldn't make it by myself."

When Pam started revisiting the Krishna temple, her mother knew that her daughter was still in trouble. She made arrangements to have Pam deprogrammed properly.

"They told me I was going for a job interview," said Pam, recalling the irony of her floating state. "But as I was walking up to this house, I saw the deprogrammer standing in the doorway. Then I realized what was going on and I started to fight. Even though I had left the cult a week before of my own free will, I fought him. There was a big violent scene at the door, yelling and screaming. I started chanting *Hare Krishna* as loud as I could."

Paradoxical as it may seem, Pam Mitchell's peculiar reversion fit neatly into the catastrophe model, in the area of the fold in the middle of Thom's elementary catastrophe curve. In this limbo region, which could be depicted as relatively stable or highly unstable depending on the particular catastrophe equation, a cult member's awareness may lurch about at random. In the floating state, the cult member may go either way: toward full recovery or in the direction Ted Patrick called "backsliding," another term that aptly described a path on the catastrophe curve.

"I was crazy, going nuts," Pam continued. "I was at that insanity point people talk about when they know they're crazy but can't do anything about it. It was an uncontrollable thing. I couldn't make the transition back, even though I wanted to really bad."

But the deprogrammer brought her through the crisis. He talked to her about the sect's methods and played tapes of other ex-members describing similar experiences, until Pam finally experienced her own moment of reawakening.

"It was like a realization," she recalled, "and my old self fell right back into my body. I was totally exhausted, but the skeleton of my personality had come back."

Pam Mitchell's deprogramming was a complete success. Her final reawakening was another catastrophic jump. However, in contrast to the snapping moment of dissolution, this sudden transformation returned her to a healthy state of everyday awareness and conscious control over her own mind.

Did catastrophe theory offer a valid model of snapping? In the seventies, Thom's theory came under heavy fire in the scientific community. Prominent American scientists charged that proponents of catastrophe theory had rashly applied it to social phenomena that could not be verified by objective methods. Other critics claimed that perfectly fine mathematical formulas already existed for dealing with sudden change, albeit with far less glamorous names such as "bifurcation theory," "shock wave theory" and "thresholds," and still newer and more complex theories of abrupt, discontinuous and "chaotic" change were on the way.

To better determine whether our application of catastrophe theory to snapping was, as we believed, valuable and responsible, on our travels north from Stanford, we stopped to confer with Dr. Hans Bremermann, professor of mathematics and medical physics at the University of California at Berkeley. A respected figure in the world of science, Bremermann developed a fascinating concept in the physics of computation, referred to by many scientists (among them, W. Ross Ashby) as "Bremermann's Limit" on the amount of data, in strictly physical terms, any information-processing system is capable of handling. A brilliant and far-reaching scholar, Bremermann was one of the first American scientists to hail the arrival of catastrophe theory in his review of

Thom's book written for the journal *Science* in 1973.

We met in his office, overflowing with cartons of manuscripts and academic papers, and started by asking Bremermann if his enthusiasm for catastrophe theory had been dampened by the ongoing critical barrage. Speaking in a soft voice with a slight accent of his native Germany, he was quick to point out that despite the controversy surrounding catastrophe theory, no one had found fault with Thom's mathematics. It was in the application of the theory, Bremermann cautioned, that the disputes were arising. He believed the consensus in the mathematical community was that Zeeman and other propounders of catastrophe theory had been a bit *too* successful.

"I think some people are worried because the name, which really is a technical name, has such powerful associations," said Bremermann. "They fear it may be misunderstood in popular articles."

Since it first appeared, Bremermann said, he had felt, along with Thom himself, that catastrophe theory was not so much a scientific theory as a new mathematical *language*, a rich scientific metaphor. As such, he said, it offered ways to talk about complex natural phenomena that would not be possible using ordinary scientific language and concepts.

"A biological organism is a phenomenally complicated mathematical entity," he said, elaborating on the dilemma with an example from his own interdisciplinary field. "Look at a single bacterium. If you put it under a microscope, you can hardly see it. It's so small, only a few light waves in size. It's very close to the visible limits of light, and you can't see any of its rich structure. But there are thousands of genes in it. There are several thousand different kinds of molecules in it, plus intricate spatial structuring. This complexity is way beyond what any mathematician, even reinforced with a computer, can resolve, predict or compute."

At the human level, Bremermann went on, the enormous complexity of nature becomes more awesome—and incalculable.

"When you take human beings interacting and bringing about cultures, societies and civilizations, it's even more complex. You cannot look at the individual parts and try to figure out what the whole organism is going to do. You run into impenetrable physical barriers of computation. There are lots of things we simply cannot explore."

Catastrophe theory, said Bremermann, provided one way out of this labyrinth of complexity.

"Okay, in come Thom and Zeeman," he went on, "and they say that if we can't fully explore complex things, we can still look at them on another level. If you have a dynamic system, maybe you don't even need to know all the details. You can look at the states it settles down to and say something about the occasional and sudden transitions that it makes. That's what catastrophe theory is."

Like Pribram's holographic model, catastrophe theory offered a new way of picturing the world. To Bremermann, its promise lay in its power to use mathematics descriptively rather than deductively, as had been the custom in his field.

"The conceptual machinery that has served us more or less well for so long is breaking down," said Bremermann, speaking with the same urgency that characterized our talks with John Lyman and Karl Pribram. "It is not quite adequate to deal with the enormous phenomena we face in the world. Our poor brains can't follow the dynamics of modern society. The monster has developed, it's there, but we really don't understand it. The politicians don't know how to control it. Nobody has an intellectual penetration of the dynamics that are at work."

We asked Bremermann how well this new approach to complexity could be applied to our study of sudden personality change.

"Now we are talking about a very specific phenomenon," he said, "and I think we are on much firmer ground to try to fit it into the catastrophe framework than we are in simply discussing catastrophe theory in general."

As we laid out some of our findings, Bremermann was impressed by the similarities between snapping and other catastrophes, but he acknowledged the difficulty involved in applying the theory to human personality.

"In this situation there are lots of things which impinge upon the mind," he said. "To fit it into this folded surface and to single out specific control parameters would have to be carefully done. Instead of focusing on the mathematical theory, why not look at it simply as a model that allows us to see these different phenomena in the same frame of reference and draw comparisons? Here is a concrete problem. We have this phenomenon: on the one hand, the Moonies, say, or the Krishnas, on the other, what happened to Patty Hearst, for example. If enough people get hit by things like this in their homes, I think they will begin to understand that there are strange phenomena that require new concepts for understanding."

As we described some of the testimony we had gathered, Bremermann nodded.

"These deprogrammers have found something," he said. "These states of rapture and depression. It really fits the catastrophe model much better than I would have imagined, and one could draw comparisons with some other kinds of breakdowns, such as anorexia."

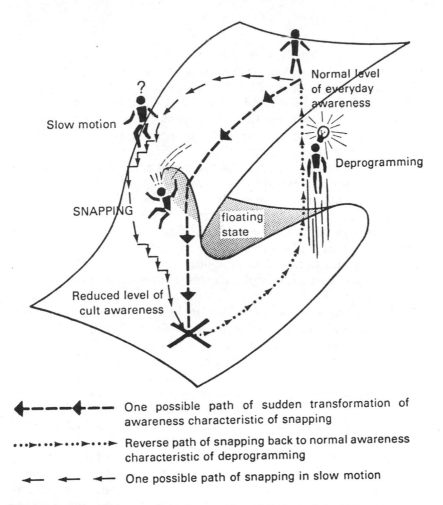

One possible path of sudden transformation of awareness characteristic of snapping

Reverse path of snapping back to normal awareness characteristic of deprogramming

One possible path of snapping in slow motion

Figure 2: Snapping as plotted on a simplified model of Thom's catastrophe curve

Toward the end of our discussion, we asked Bremermann about the numerous instances we had come across of snapping in slow motion. We told him that many people we had interviewed, in fact, talked of a gradual descent into their altered states of mind and personality. During deprogramming as well, some re-emerged in a smooth progression rather than a sudden snap. We asked if this more continuous experience invalidated our catastrophe model. On the contrary, he said, he found it perfectly in keeping with the finer points of Thom's work.

"Catastrophe is just a term that applies if you want to understand a dynamic phenomenon where something changes suddenly," he explained. "But mathematically all the ingredients *are* continuous. They're smooth and then, suddenly, something jumps, but you can move from one point to the other in slow motion, by a different path if you like.

"In other words, instead of falling down a cliff, you can walk down slowly, in a roundabout way, and reach the exact same point."

We came away from our talk with Hans Bremermann fully apprised of the pitfalls of proposing any real-world application of catastrophe theory, but more confident than ever that our use of the model was appropriate. As only one tool among many new scientific concepts we were drawing upon, catastrophe theory gave us a firm handle with which to grasp snapping in all its diverse forms, filling out and completing our initial picture of the phenomenon. Our first working diagram enabled us to trace any path of snapping and deprogramming on the simplified catastrophe curve shown in Figure 2. (In fact, a more detailed and accurate model of snapping could be drawn on one of Thom's more complex catastrophe curves, a slightly modified version of the wave shown here.)

We drove northward out of California, heading to the blustery Oregon coast for a few months of solitude in which to transcribe more interviews and review them in the light of our latest findings. Our growing understanding was rapidly drawing us toward a somber conclusion: that in some cases, although certainly not all, the clash of opposing information stresses that may result in the sudden catastrophe of snapping could lead to a frightening new form of mental disorder. Left unremedied, or reinforced over time, those sudden alterations of the mind may deteriorate into lasting afflictions of consciousness, *organic* impairments of awareness. With our new understanding of how information in the human form of experience is metabolized—broken up, distributed and reorganized—throughout the brain and nervous system, we could see clearly how this natural organic process also may become subject to disease, not in the usual medical sense, but an affliction nonetheless of the physical organization of a person's everyday powers of mind.

In the pages that follow, we will present in detail these diverse afflictions of mind we have found to plague participants in many of today's new cults, sects and self-help therapies. We now understand these afflictions to be ongoing, organic information stress responses, physical impairments of thought and feeling, and deeper alterations of mind and personality, that can be diagnosed in the strictest sense as varieties of *information disease*.

12 Varieties of Information Disease

Where is the Life we have lost in living?
Where is the wisdom we have lost in knowledge?
Where is the knowledge we have lost in information?

—T. S. Eliot,
"The Rock"

NOW THE FOCUS of our investigation shifts to the terrain beneath the precipice as we draw a distinction, for the first time, between snapping—a term that to this point we have used in a broad sense to indicate any sudden, drastic alteration of personality—and information disease, which we can now describe as any of several distinct, although often interrelated, states the mind may settle down to in the aftermath of the moment.

We define information disease as *an alteration through experience of a person's everyday information-processing capacities*—his everyday powers of thinking, feeling, perception, memory, imagination and conscious choice. When these vital capacities become altered or impaired, the resulting change is not simply one of behavior. When snapping turns to information disease, it marks a lasting change of awareness at the most fundamental level of personality. The disease is not physiological in origin; in most instances, it does not appear to damage or destroy the basic biological machinery of the brain. Nevertheless, as we have come to understand it, information disease represents an organic alteration of the brain's complex organization.

Information disease, the step beyond momentary episodes of snapping and information stress to *ongoing* impairments of mind, may lead to the physical breakdown of a person's entire ability to make sense of his experiences. It may come about suddenly, from some overwhelming mental or emotional experience or other intensely stressful or traumatic event, or gradually, from some cumulative information stress, overload or any other sustained assault on the mind's everyday thinking and feeling capacities. Either way, the impact appears to be the same: a marked alteration of awareness, diminished conscious control, and persisting impairments of an individual's everyday powers of mind.

The new cults, sects and self-help therapies offer an abundance of examples of information disease, individuals plagued by severe mental and emotional disturbances, states of altered and reduced awareness, delusions, hallucinations, detachment, withdrawal and, in the most extreme instances, violent and self-destructive tendencies. Undoubtedly, throughout history, similar afflictions of mind have occurred from natural stresses, physical pressures or at random. Now, however, they are becoming increasingly common consequences of modern culture's burgeoning information technologies and expanding human technology of experience.

Norbert Wiener first proposed that some mental disturbances could result from physical disorders of human information processing. In his groundbreaking book, *Cybernetics: Control and Communication in the Animal and the Machine,* Wiener discussed the information dimension of some traditional forms of mental illness. He wrote:

> Psychopathology has been rather a disappointment to the instinctive materialism of the doctors, who have taken the point of view that every disorder must be accompanied by material lesions of some specific tissue involved. . . . There is no way of identifying the brain of a schizophrenic . . . nor of a manic depressive patient, nor of a paranoiac. These disorders we call *functional,* and this distinction seems to contravene the dogma of modern materialism that every disorder in function has some physiological or anatomical basis in the tissues concerned.
>
> This distinction between functional and organic disorders receives a great deal of light from the consideration of the computing machine. As we have already seen, it is not the empty physical structure of the computing machine that corresponds to the brain—to the adult brain, at least—but the combination of this structure with the instructions given it at the beginning of a chain of operations and with all the additional information stored and gained from outside in the course of the chain. This information is stored in some physical form—in the form of memory.
>
> There is therefore nothing surprising in considering the functional mental disorders as fundamentally diseases of memory, of the circulating information kept by the brain in the active state,

and the long-time permeability of the synapses. . . . Even the grosser disorders . . . may produce a large part of their effects not so much by the destruction of tissue . . . as by the secondary disturbances of traffic.

Wiener's theory of "diseases of memory" and "circulating information" pertained primarily to psychopathology, and many of the fine points of his proposal have since been validated through medical research—for example, many instances of schizophrenia and manic depression have been shown to correspond to specific disturbances of traffic among chemical messengers circulating in the brain. In 1948, however, when Norbert Wiener wrote *Cybernetics,* the phenomenon of information stress had yet to be identified. The technology of experience was still confined to clinical settings and academic research laboratories. There was no such thing as a "consciousness movement," and the only cults in America were long-established sects that posed no glaring psychological, social or legal dilemmas. In his concern for what is human in human beings, Wiener foresaw the dangers of information overload, automation and runaway computer technologies, but it was only after his death in the early sixties that new forms of information, engineered experience and *human* communication control began to threaten people with startling new kinds of "functional" disorders.

Today information disease may result from a wide variety of experiences. Some may be strictly physical: as Wiener noted, fundamental changes in human information-processing capacities may result from injury to the brain or nervous system. Poor diet and prolonged lack of sleep, as well, may impair the brain's ability to perform vital information-processing functions. But information disease may also result from information alone, especially from intense experiences that abuse an individual's natural capacities for thought and feeling. The most dramatic examples of this type of information disorder, we believe, are resulting from the heedless experiments in thought, feeling, memory and imagination practiced by many modern cults, sects, self-help therapies and related enterprises, and from the abuse of popular techniques of mental and emotional control, group encounter, guided fantasy, meditation and other practices in widespread use today. These ritualized communication practices are as powerful as any physical force in their potential to disrupt and impair the brain's information-processing activities. By tampering with basic distinctions between reality and fantasy, right and wrong, past, present and future, or simply by stilling the workings of the mind over time, these intense communication practices may break down vital faculties of mind. There is also growing evidence that they may organically impair crucial working connections in the brain's underlying synaptic networks and neurochemical channels and, in their extremes, physically destroy long-standing information-processing pathways in the brain.

We can identify four distinct varieties of information disease, each of which may follow from a snapping moment or other intensely stressful experience, although none necessarily depends on the occurrence of a single episode of drastic change.

The most prevalent is the *ongoing altered state* of awareness. This altered state is not one of enlightenment or mind expansion. On the contrary, it is a state of narrowed or reduced awareness that people may experience both during and after their involvement in some cult or group, as it is often perceived as an unnerving, uncontrollable sensation of "floating."

A more extreme variety of information disease is marked by the lasting impairment of a vital capacity of the mind. This is the *delusional phase*. It may result in vivid delusions, hallucinations, and lead in its extremes to irrational, violent and self-destructive behavior. This variety, in our view, has been the cause of some of America's most shocking news events in recent years.

Two other varieties of information disease take the forms of *not thinking*, literally shutting off the mind, and *not feeling*, a parallel strain caused by actively suppressing one's emotional responses and which may ultimately numb a person's capacity for human feeling altogether. These advanced information disorders are reported frequently by practitioners of popular self-help therapies, members of cults, extreme fundamentalist sects and controlling ideological groups. In our view, they may be the most damaging forms of all and lead to the complete dissolution of personality.

Our research indicates that hundreds of thousands of people in America and many other cultures have been casualties of information disease in recent years—and that millions more may have experienced some of its symptoms. In the following examples, we will examine these four varieties of information disease one by one and present testimony that illustrates their intimate personal nature. With these examples in view, we hope that other individuals may come to understand how their own afflictions were brought about—and realize that they can happen to anyone.

Floating—The Ongoing Altered State. In the wake of a snapping experience, after an individual surrenders or lets go, whether in a sudden moment or gradually, he may slip into a level of reduced awareness in which the disorientation and confusion of the snapping moment become part of his everyday experience of the world. This trancelike floating state, in our view, marks the first stage in the change and reorganization of personality.

This is the state of mind that appears to have befallen so many modern cult members. In the ongoing altered state, an individual's basic abilities to think, question and act may be dramatically impaired. At the same time, he may become almost wholly vulnerable to suggestion and command, and so mentally and emotionally dependent on the group and its leaders that, for all practical purposes, the person can no longer be deemed responsible for either his actions or expressions.

Once a person's freedom of thought has been suspended in this manner, many groups then input a torrent of new information in the form of direct indoctrination. In protracted sermons, lectures, discussion groups, private study and personal confrontations, the new beliefs, values, doctrines and strict regulations of the group are inculcated.

An ex-Rajneeshee described the floating state he fell into in the sect that crippled his ability to function in the everyday world.

"I was in a state of complete disorientation," he told us. "I was so blurry, my mind was so narrowed, it was like being in a fog. There were physical things, I felt cold and clammy, in kind of a limbo state. Everything was dull. I couldn't hear sounds with any intensity or see sights or taste food. Mentally, I was in a state of total confusion. I couldn't talk in complete sentences or do any critical thinking of my own. I was floating in an altered state. I didn't know my own mind. I didn't know how I felt about anything."

One of the most potent communication factors in creating and maintaining an ongoing altered state is the severing of personal relationships outside the closed world of the group. By cutting off contact with parents, friends and other social connections, the group strips the new convert of those vital sources of self-reflection that anchor his awareness and personality in the everyday world. Once isolated in this way, an individual may then easily be remade in the group's own tightly controlled image.

Like induction into the military, cult induction often involves a change of physical appearance; the new devotee's head may be shaved and his clothes and money taken away. However, in contrast to military induction, the terms of which are well-known and vociferously set down, or even the hypnotic inductions of stage mesmerists and clinical hypnotherapists, the cult process is one we call *covert induction*—driven almost entirely by suggestions, codewords and other indirect commands.

An ex-Hare Krishna recalled how his altered state was induced and deepened through the use of these covert communication controls.

"The temple leaders talked in a soft voice, smiling, in a kind of I-don't-care tone," he said. "There was something strange about it, because I completely forgot about everything. I got the feeling I couldn't leave, like there was no way I could get out. I don't know what that was. I had the feeling that it was God calling me, and that the whole outside world had sort of vaporized."

Information, not any physical stress, is the engine of covert induction. It may be communicated nonverbally, as in the above instance, or verbally. Definitions of basic words such as "love" and "family" may be changed to promote the teachings of the group. In many groups, inductees receive new names as well, usually in a solemn ceremony. Parents and other family members often become "agents of Satan," their expressions of parental love and concern are redefined as attempts to "kill God." At the same time, sect leaders may recast themselves as the member's "true" father or mother, while biblical commandments and other scriptures may be reinterpreted to exclude from care and communication anyone who isn't a member of the group. These alterations of familiar markers from the outside world, each in itself a small or subtle change, all work to deepen and sustain the ongoing altered state, and may create high and impenetrable barriers between the sect member and his former identity.

One of the most subtle yet sweeping covert induction programs we came upon was carried out by the Love Israel cult of the Pacific Northwest, which was also called the Love Family by sect members. We met one young woman whose story typified the innocent way most people begin their descent into the ongoing altered state. While traveling through a small town in Washington, she told us, she sought overnight lodging in a safe Christian community. Directed to the Love Family house by local townspeople, she was immediately impressed.

"They had a sign on the door that said, *Anyone who wants to worship Jesus is welcome here,*" she recalled. "I was struck by how clean and orderly the house was. No two people ever talked at the same time, and everyone seemed so self-assured. They just had a certain air that they were important people."

At their invitation, this young woman stayed at the Love Family house for four days, she told us, growing increasingly attracted to their humble lifestyle and warm hospitality. Discipline was severe, but the family life appealed to her. Before long she made a decision to join the sect and "give up everything for God." At that point of surrender, the sect introduced her to their private world of thought and language.

"Everyone was given biblical names or virtue names," she said, "like Strength, Courage or Serendipity." (Or Logic—see chapter 6.) "When you joined the group, you were baptized into the Love Family, not the church or Christ. They used the word 'Christ' interchangeably with 'the Family.' They had different names for everything. The days of the week were named after the seven churches in the Book of Revelation; the months were named after the twelve tribes of Israel. Even their calendar was different: each month had thirty days, with extra days at the end for a Passover celebration. We also had different ages, which were computed according to the book of Matthew."

After she joined the Love Family and adopted their new vocabulary and schemes of mental organization, this young woman found that daily life in the group was not as wholesome as she had been led to believe. Members were never left alone. Elder males dominated an unyielding social and sexual hierarchy. Her physical environment was closed, controlled, distorted, and, before long, her inner world was too, as she slipped imperceptibly into an ongoing altered state.

"There was no possibility of seeing or understanding what was really happening," this young woman told us. "You knew who your boss was, you had your chores, and you were expected to be doing something at any given time. But there were always surprises. They changed the rules at random without warning. The propaganda was always being drummed into us. Their beliefs and information came at us from outside, and there was never any time to sift through it, never any time to step back and look at it and see if any of it fit together. The Family would always say, 'What's inside your mind is lies. We are your mind. The group is your mind.' "

Those phrases were vivid examples of covert hypnotic suggestions, and we found many more in every stage of the induction process. Before new cult members enter a larger environment, many are instilled with guilt and fear, to keep them from questioning their participation in the group and to negate the criticism of outsiders. Members of the Unification Church and many extreme Christian sects have the fear of Satan drummed into them. In the Hare Krishnas and other Eastern sects, members are told to shun outsiders, all of whom are reputed to be in a state of "maya" or alienation from God, a kind of spiritual contamination.

An ex-Krishna recalled his first excursions into the outside world.

"Everyone got dressed up in their robes and shaved heads and we'd go out chanting in public," he said. "We'd dance in the streets and hand out flyers and in general attract a lot of attention. All of a sudden, here we were in the middle of this bustling city, and we were the only people doing this stuff and everyone looked at us like we were crazy. You felt really solemnly religious, as if you were doing these people a fantastic favor because every time they heard the words *Hare Krishna* they were supposed to make tremendous spiritual advancement. There was a facelessness about the whole thing, though. We got used to feeling very foreign, and the more you got used to being there like that, the more accustomed you got to being in the cult."

For this young man, those journeys away from the temple only intensified his floating state and identification with the group.

"I had to put up a mental barrier shielding myself from the world," he admitted. "I'd have to hold everything out, because it was all hanging over me. The whole street atmosphere, the entire outside world was sitting there, just waiting to fall on me—and I used Krishna as a protection from the whole thing. I didn't realize I was doing it, but if I didn't do it I would have gone crazy for sure. I knew I'd left that world, and I really couldn't go back because it looked so terrifying."

In the eighties, new age guru J.Z. Knight's Ramtha School of Enlightenment in rural Washington state became a cauldron of experimentation with covert induction techniques. An ex-follower described the deep breathing rituals, similar to those of the Rajneeshees, Insight/MSIA and other new age groups, that started her slide into an ongoing floating state.

"The first class was called 'Beginning C&E'—consciousness and energy," she told us. "It began with this breathing technique of sitting with your legs crossed and your hands in front of your chest and deep-breathing from your diaphragm—hyperventilating really. At the first class there were maybe a thousand of us sitting on little mats, blindfolded. There was loud drumming and medieval music playing. You'd take this deep breath and then blow it out like *wwwwwhhhhhhhh*—we were told that by blowing all this air out you were actually forcing open the parts of your brain that you don't use—and it would make you high. It didn't take more than a few breaths and you'd start feeling really dizzy. Then she'd have you roll your eyes back into your head and, boy, you'd just feel like you were floating after a while."

From beginning C&E, followers progressed to advanced C&E methods that brought on more profound and enduring altered states.

"At first we spent ten or twelve hours doing this breathing and feeling this floaty, high feeling. Soon she had us breathing all day long. Then she incorporated a 'war cry' into the breathing. You would breath until the god within you told you to let out a big cry and scream.

Then she added this 'power breath' thing that blew your brains out even more. Finally, Ramtha incorporated the C&E into our daily lives. Even when we weren't at an event we were supposed to do it for forty-five minutes or an hour every day, preferably early in the morning."

Medical researchers have confirmed the physiological effects of hyperventilation. The rapid forcing of air through the lungs may lead quickly to a sharp drop in carbon dioxide levels in the brain, causing dizziness, a psychic high and, in extreme episodes, the convulsive clutching of the hands and limbs known in Insight/MSIA and other sects as "lobster claws." Other floating sensations were not so readily explainable. An ex-member of one Eastern sect noticed an eerie change in his perceptions as he slipped into his ongoing altered state.

"I got a distinct sense of things actually getting dark as I was going into this thing," he recalled. "It seemed like everything was getting a little bit darker, as if the weather had gotten really overcast, but this bleakness was only perceptual. At the same time, I started to notice more dark things around me, outside, in my room, sort of a heavy, gray mood."

Whether his darkening was actual or metaphorical is difficult to establish, although other researchers have found evidence of a reduction in the peripheral vision of cult members. This effect gives an inside view of an outward quality reported by many people who have had contact with cult members. As the person enters an ongoing altered state, the appearance of his eyes may undergo a dramatic change, taking on a glassy look, a cloudiness, giving the impression that the person is "not really looking back at you." This change in the eyes, more than any other outwardly observable effect, seems to us to indicate that some basic alteration has taken place in the person's inner capacities for receiving, processing and communicating information.

Other physical changes may be observed among cult members in ongoing altered states. Often their voices change. The pitch rises and the tone becomes more shrill, an alteration many cult observers believe to be another sign of fundamental change and mounting tensions within. Speech patterns may change dramatically. Posture and other nonverbal mannerisms may be transformed beyond recognition.

With each new day spent floating in the ongoing altered state, the cult member may drift further out of touch with his former thoughts, feelings and personality, while the cult environment pours in new information to destroy and replace the old. In this state, a person may be incapable of genuine communication or relationship. His speech may become a mindless parroting of cult doctrine, his thoughts never deviating from what he has been told by his superiors. As his alienation from the world and his former self reaches its maximum, his identification with the cult becomes all-encompassing and self-sustaining.

This state may persist for months, even years, and often endures through the entire time of the individual's involvement in the group. During this time, when long-standing information pathways in the brain are being continuously disassembled and reconstructed, it is usually still possible to deprogram a person and restore his freedom of thought and feeling. Past a point, however, as we saw among many long-term cult members, the individual's diminished awareness and impaired thought processes become less noticeable, and eventually the outward signs of his altered state may disappear. Then, his induction is complete, his transformation total. He is, to all but those who knew him before, quite undetectably a new person altogether.

The Delusional Phase. This second, more advanced form of information disease concerns reality and illusion and an individual's ability to distinguish between the two. For, along with the basic processes of perception that bring information to the brain, the human mind possesses the remarkable capacity to create information of its own. This capacity is generally referred to as *imagination.*

The power of imagination provides still more evidence of the mind's holographic nature. The fusion of apparently unrelated components into new images—dreams offer the most vivid example—suggests an obvious inner projection, or introjection, of information in the brain. But more important, imagination demonstrates the brain's innate ability to recombine the metabolized components of experience, to merge effortlessly people, places, objects, faces and meaning-filled symbols into striking new images and creative forms. The reach of imagination is limitless. Every physical sensation can be matched or superseded by an imagined one. Each image and idea can be instantly transformed into another. The human mind, aided by the brain's ingenious information-parsing powers and limitless storage capacities, its own incomparable powers of association and consummate playful nature, is capable of conjuring up all kinds of visions and sensations in superabundant detail.

For most people, the ability to distinguish between reality and imagination, between fact and fancy, is so basic that it can be taken for granted. At times, a person may be so awestruck by the sharpness or novelty of an experience he may question whether he is awake or dreaming, but on those rare occasions a quick pinch is usually enough to set matters straight. In fact, this elementary form of verification is the best of all possible arbiters, for the ability to distinguish between perception and imagination is inseparably connected to our ability to feel. Feeling, as we have come to understand it, is the ultimate human response, the champion of information-processing capacities, precisely because it is the most comprehensive activity human beings perform, one that requires the fullest integration of body, brain and mind.

Yet, powerful and primary as our capacity for feeling may be, it is a surprisingly simple and straightforward matter to weaken or destroy it. A direct attack on human feeling may leave a person stunned and numb, momentarily incapable of any emotion. A more concentrated, prolonged assault may bring about a lasting alteration of this capacity and, in doing so, break down the individual's fundamental ability to distinguish between reality and fantasy. This is the delusional phase of information disease and, from the evidence we have seen, it is a direct consequence of the impairment or destruction of human feeling.

It is also a common complaint of people who have participated in some of our era's most popular cults, sects and self-help therapies.

Scientology defines itself as "the study of knowledge in its fullest sense." The Church of Scientology, founded in the 1950s by a science-fiction writer named L. Ron Hubbard, consists of two major branches of activity: the "pandenominational religious philosophy" contained in Hubbard's books and the practices of the sect and the "applied philosophy," which the sect has defined as "methods which enable the individual to attain a higher state of existence through personal processing." Since its early days, Scientology has grown to include church organizations and processing centers on every continent. It has claimed to be the largest "self-betterment organization" in the world.

It may also be one of the most powerful religious cults in operation today. The tales that have come out of Scientology are nearly impossible to believe in relation to a new religious movement that gained worldwide credibility and clout in its first twenty-five years. By the nineties, it also claimed to have attracted six to eight million followers—although former high-ranking members say those figures are inflated. Nevertheless, in our research for nearly two decades, the reports we saw and heard in the media and in personal interviews with one-time Scientologists, including both rank-and-file members and sect higher-ups, were replete with allegations of psychological devastation, economic exploitation, and personal and legal harassment of ex-members, journalists and others who criticize the sect.

To most casual observers, however, Scientology is better known for its extensive advertising on television and in print of its late founder's books—the controversial Hubbard died in California in 1986—and for the group's intense efforts to recruit customers for its diversified self-betterment programs. The basic course, known as Dianetics, employs a technique called "auditing," ostensibly to raise an individual to higher levels of being. Halfway up the Scientology ladder, after the individual has passed through roughly eight levels of auditing, is the level of "clear," a state of existence in which the subject is supposedly capable of transcending all the quirks and pains of his past. At the top of the Scientology ladder, about eight levels above clear, are still higher levels of "O.T." or "Operating Thetan," which Hubbard defined as "The person himself—not his body or name, the physical universe, his mind, or anything else—that which is aware of being aware; the identity that IS the individual" (Hubbard's punctuation and emphasis).

Participants in Scientology's "pastoral counseling" programs pay for auditing by the hour. The cost of attaining the level of clear, which may require several hundred hours of auditing, has been known to run into tens of thousands of dollars. Some individual payments for Scientology techniques have been reported to exceed $100,000.

But for the beginning customer choosing among a vast assortment of currently available self-improvement techniques, the Scientology procedure is well-known, attractively packaged and relatively inexpensive to begin. The typical auditing process takes place in private sessions between subject and auditor, in which the subject's emotional responses are registered on a device called an E-meter, a kind of rudimentary lie detector. The subject grasp the two terminals of the E-meter, one in each hand, and the rise or fall of the needle on the meter, apparently caused by a change in electrical conductivity in response to pressure or perspiration emitted from the palms, is explained as a measure of emotional response to the auditor's course of questioning. The average response registers in the "normal" range on the meter, with abnormal indicating an overreaction, "uptightness," or sign of past trauma on the part of the subject.

The goal of auditing is to bring all the individual's responses within the range of "normal" on the E-meter. Using a technique that bears only superficial resemblance to the popular method known as biofeedback (a medically proven treatment for regulating basic biological functions such as heart rate and blood pressure), the sect auditor watches the E-meter as he leads the subject through intensive questioning on incidents spanning the range of his life experiences. The subject then follows instructions aimed at reducing his emotional response to experiences that may have been physically or psychologically painful. When the individual has mastered this ability, he becomes eligible for admission to the elite club of Scientology clears.

We met many Scientologists in our travels: students, housewives, professionals and even some respected scientists. Most fell into one of two categories: those who had just begun the auditing process or who were only occasional customers of Dianetics, and those who had become active members of the church or gone on to advanced levels of auditing. While visiting a large city on the West Coast, we were introduced to Karla Kraus (not her real name), a housewife in her late thirties whom we found to be an expressive representative of the novice Scientologists we interviewed. When we met, Karla Kraus had been undergoing Scientology's auditing process for almost a year. She understood it to be a concentrated course of study and one-to-one therapy. She was attending auditing sessions several times a week and looking forward to the higher levels of existence she saw before her.

As we sipped coffee in her living room, she explained to us the motivation behind her excursion into Dianetics.

"In Scientology you confront past experiences until there is no charge left on them," she said. "Then, once you get all the charge off that painful instance, it will never be a source of any aberrant type of behavior."

She spoke matter-of-factly, careful not to misrepresent the auditing process.

"I hope to become clear," she told us avidly, adding, "To the casual observer, this new terminology can sound almost like *1984,* but these are simply new terms that have not been identified before."

As Karla Kraus understood it, "Clear means that your active mind is clear of all aberrational behavior, and all psychosomatic illness disappears." After several hundred hours of auditing, she said, she hoped to reach a permanent level of clear existence. Already, after less than one hundred hours, she had glimpses of what that powerful state of being might be like. She recounted one of her most significant insights.

"I was returned to a prenatal experience," she said. "One time during auditing I heard my mother's voice just as clear as a bell. I've always had a vague feeling of not belonging, but I heard my mother say, 'I don't want babies.' I experienced pain and pressure, which my auditor told me was my mother sneezing or having intercourse or morning sickness. Through auditing they have determined that the fetus actually experiences and remembers these things."

Karla Kraus also revealed that her developing ability to control her emotional response to traumatic events in her earlier years was changing her ability to experience her present life in the everyday world. She viewed the change as positive.

"There are some residual effects to auditing," she told us. "Things get charged up while you're auditing which spill out onto your daily life. I can feel a change in my state of being, in my level of awareness. Where things used to cave me in, now there's nothing. Most disciplines give you ways to deal with negative emotions after they occur. This is something that I can go through which prevents those negative emotions from occurring in the first place."

She saw her potential for achievement in Scientology as infinite. She didn't know whether she would have the time or money to work her way up to the highest levels of Scientology awareness, but she looked with envy upon those who had the dedication to stick with it to the top. She offered us her perspective on life at those higher levels.

"It's really superpowerful stuff," she said. "For instance, individuals who are Operating Thetans are able to exteriorize at will. They can actually go into another person's body and find areas of disturbance and disease."

It was this level of O.T. to which many devout Scientologists aspired. "When you are O.T.," she said, "if you believe something and really *know* it to be so, it will be so! Scientology leads you to a level of consciousness that is beyond faith. These people are into certainty. They *know*."

In our opinion, however, Scientology did not lead people beyond faith to absolute certainty—it led them to levels of increasingly realistic hallucination. The crude technology of auditing, in our view, constituted a direct assault on human feeling and on the individual's ability to distinguish between what he is actually experiencing and what he is only imagining. The bizarre folklore of Scientology seemed to us a *tour de force* of science fiction. Many people at its highest levels reportedly claimed with confidence that trillions of years ago they knew each other on other planets, that they had the power to see at submicroscopic levels and leave their bodies at will. As we delved deeper into Scientology the evidence we gathered suggested to us that, more than anything else, this combination church and therapeutic service trained people in hallucination and delusion.

We gained an inside view of Scientology in a long telephone interview with a young man we will call Howard Davenport. During five and a half years as an active, dedicated Scientologist, he became a Dianetics auditor and moved freely within the highest levels of the organization.

Howard Davenport had been recruited by street encounter, the same manner of solicitation used by most cults and many new age therapies. At first, however, the Scientology appeal was neither religious nor psychological. Like so many groups that have turned to indirect recruitment methods, Scientology's come-on was casual and intimately personal. Davenport, then a shy young man in his mid-twenties, recalled the moment of initial contact.

"I was alone at the time and pretty depressed," he told us, "and a very good-looking girl gave me an address and said, 'Be there at seven thirty.' I asked her what was there and she said, 'Just a bunch of groovy people.' I envisioned this big party, but it turned out to be a Scientology meeting. We heard a lecture and saw the introductory movie, which was narrated by Stephen Boyd, the movie star. It started out in a planetarium and he was standing there as if Scientology had found the stars or something."

After the movie, Davenport continued, the Scientology leaders brought out an E-meter and demonstrated how it worked. The guests were given an opportunity to try it out, and the Scientologists interpreted their readings.

"They put me on the thing and I registered way off the dial," he said. "They told me it meant that I was in an extremely messed-up state of mind, and they convinced me to take a fifteen-dollar 'communication' course. This very good-looking girl took me into a little private room. She got up close to me and said she could see that I was depressed, that my life was in very bad shape, and that if I just took this course all my problems would be solved. I felt a great uplifting, like, *Wow, finally here's someone who can take care of my problems!*"

Soon afterward, Davenport began his journey into Scientology via a series of highly structured, pseudoscientific drills, trainings and processes. The first one, called TR-0 or Training Regimen Zero, was part of the basic communication course designed to develop the subject's ability to interact with others.

"They sat me down across from this other guy. They told us it wasn't staring, but it was simply staring at each other—two hours that first night. At first it was very uncomfortable. We sat with our knees touching and we weren't allowed to blink. We were told, 'You don't think, you don't move, you don't twitch, you don't giggle. Just be there with the other person.' "

Davenport recalled the confusion that resulted from his first session of "communication."

"I couldn't figure out what the purpose was. I thought it was to help you learn how to look somebody in the eye when you talk to them, but it took me a couple years in Scientology before I grasped the purpose of that drill. It was to teach you how to look really *high*."

From this initial course, Davenport went on to begin the auditing process.

"Each auditing session is run exactly like the last one," he said. "The auditor sits in a little room that is decorated so that they're all alike and interchangeable. Then he puts you on the E-meter and all you can do is look at each other, because there's not enough space in the room to look away. The auditor is not permitted to say anything except certain standard lines that are part of an exact script every time. You walk into the room and he says, 'Are you well-fed and rested?' and you say, 'Yes.' If he sees a reaction on the meter, he says, 'What did you think of there?' If there's no reaction on the meter, he says, 'Okay, that's good!' "

According to Davenport, the auditor asks a series of questions about the person's past and present and waits until the meter shows no sign of a reaction. Emerging from several hours of this intense process may be an exhilarating experience, in some instances even a snapping moment of sorts.

"That's when you feel the highest," Davenport explained, "when your thought processes finally break and you go, *Wow, I feel good!* There's a feeling of peacefulness about it."

Continued auditing may bring on a condition that resembles an ongoing altered state of awareness, complete with the accompanying changes in appearance and demeanor found in many cults. During Davenport's time in Scientology, however, there was a special technique that could disguise such changes.

"They have a drill to make your eyes look natural," he said. "You have someone sit three feet away from you. One person acts as a coach and the other as the student, and he'll say, 'Start!' and if you blink your eyes in an unnatural way, he'll say, 'Flunk! You blinked in an unnatural way. Start!' He coaches you for hours like that. He'll say, 'Flunk! You're starting to smile. Start!' Like robots."

Almost all Scientology drills consist of similar set patterns of commands and responses that may continue for hour upon hour. According to Davenport, other Scientology drills were practiced with less innocent objectives in mind. Number three, he claimed , taught the subject how to gain control over other people, a primary focus of many cult sales and recruitment techniques. The Scientology method, however, had no religious or spiritual pretensions.

"Training Drill Three is spelled out: its purpose is to get your question answered," said Davenport. "It teaches you the various things a person can do to avoid answering your question, and it gives you a technique which you later use in counseling other people. You can force them to talk about anything at all, even if they don't want to talk about it."

Looking back, Davenport recognized some of the practical value of these initial Scientology techniques. They gave him peaceful, relaxed feelings, he said, and they actually did improve his ability to communicate and assert himself socially. But he went on to explain what he considered the danger of the process.

"This is the thing," he stressed. "If people just took the communication course and then left Scientology for life, it would not be such a bad thing, because the beginning course does help you out. But then the technique itself sucks you into further and further courses. The counseling never ends."

As Davenport became more deeply involved in the auditing process, he also grew more dependent on the organization. Unlike many other cults, Scientology does not require its members to live in communal settings, but as people become more involved, they often tend naturally to associate mainly with other Scientologists. Davenport recalled one interaction that drew him further into the organization.

"When I first got in, I was with a friend whom I met in the course; we were talking to one of the guys who was way up in the organization. My friend asked him, 'Is it anything like drugs at those higher levels?' and he said, 'It's just like acid, man. I see colors all around just like particles flowing across the room.' "

Before long, Davenport began to experience those higher levels for himself, as he progressed to drills designed to teach him how to leave his body and travel through space. Looking back, he observed that in all likelihood the events never took place as described.

"They have drills that create images of things in your mind that do not exist," he said, "and they have drills that even change your image of what does exist. For instance, if I see this door that I'm looking at as being the way it is, Scientology would talk about it in such a way that I would see it in another light, *their* light."

This transformation of awareness seemed to be accomplished by a specific, highly refined Scientology technique.

"It happens in degrees," he said, "and it may take years to achieve, although some people can do it in a matter of weeks. First you start just looking at something the way it is. Then they tell you that you can actually see all the molecules flowing through it—that's just one example of something they would tell you that you should see. So you start looking for the molecules, and you try all these different ways to imagine it. At first you know that you're just trying to imagine it, but then suddenly you'll have this experience. You'll be sitting there and one day you'll look over at the door and you'll just see the molecules. It's a hallucination, but you actually see them, and the leaders of Scientology say, 'How do you know it's just a hallucination?' And they have a point."

The point is that by that time it may no longer be possible for the individual to distinguish what is real. Once this barrier is broken through, a person's sense of reality may seem wholly arbitrary. His daily life may become intermixed with vivid hallucinations. Davenport experienced this state of mind as well.

"One day I was walking around convinced that I was controlling the weather," he said. "I was out selling burglar alarms door to door to make money to pay Scientology so I could buy their higher levels. It looked like it was going to rain all day long, and I felt I was using my own thought to hold the rain back. Another time, as I was going to bed, I wanted to talk to a friend, so I thought to myself, *I'll go exterior,* and I started getting into these things about leaving my body and visiting people. The next day if they didn't say anything to me about it I would say that they weren't aware enough to have seen it."

Davenport told us that he was reluctant to call all his strange experiences hallucinations, especially in the light of so much popular testimony about astral travel and telepathy. What he denied, however, was the validity of Scientology's fantastic world view and cosmology, despite the fact that many "Thetans" he worked with in the organization were devout believers in Hubbard's sci-fi philosophy.

"People would remember experiences on other planets or marriages from three or four lifetimes ago," he recalled. "They'd talk about people from Xerkeson who flew down to Earth in doll-bodies and drove around in long black limousines observing the people on our planet. When you use the techniques, finally you start seeing these things, too. And you say, 'Yeah, he's right. How come we were never aware enough to see them before?' "

Most Scientology programs and practices, including the initial free personality test, starting communication course and training regimens described above, were still current and reportedly unchanged in the nineties, and, apparently, many more elaborate, and more expensive, higher-level courses had been added. By that time, the sect was reportedly bringing in hundreds of millions of dollars annually from counseling fees, book sales, investments and other sources. According to *Time* magazine, in a court filing in the late 1980s only one of more than a hundred incorporated Scientology entities listed over $500 million in annual income. The price for some church services had risen as high as $800 per hour; the cost of becoming clear, for some, as much as $400,000. The sect's methods also were being applied in many other domains unrelated to religion or self-help therapy, including education, corporate consulting and professional services management.

In our opinion, Scientology has refined the most reliable methods for bringing about the delusional phase of information disease. But the same condition can be found across the spectrum of new spiritual and personal growth practices. Similar techniques are employed in fundamentalist and charismatic Christian sects, new age therapies, group training enterprises and clinical psychotherapy. The method called guided fantasy is a recognized therapeutic technique that uses the power of imagination to bring about changes in consciousness and personality. Another method, called psychodrama, is one of the most potent tools of modern psychiatry. Psychodrama takes the imagination one step further than fantasy, engaging the individual in a physical dramatization of his past traumas and psychological problems, and in active role-playing of desired outcomes. Its power lies in the converging patterns of information—mental, emotional and physical—the method may give rise to in the context of an intense group interaction.

We spoke with many people who reported experiencing overwhelming discomfort, anxiety and even intense snapping moments during guided fantasy, psychodrama and role-playing sessions. The experience left some in states of disorientation that lasted for months, during which they found themselves constantly struggling to test the reality of their perceptions. Only with the passage of time and the support of people close to them were they able once again to discern the boundaries between what was genuine and certain and what was not.

Spirit "channeler" J.Z. Knight seemed a mistress of delusion. The larger cultural trend she was part of, the new age movement, made valiant efforts to take forward the sixties' human potential discoveries and shape them into sound personal growth methods and alternative medical practices. The free-spirited movement attracted millions to its eclectic mix of self-help, holistic healing, relaxing music, aromas and other playful paraphernalia. At its fringes, however, gimmicky gurus like Knight and her 35,000-year-old inner warrior Ramtha embodied the movement's penchant for self-promoting seers and ascendant masters who, it seemed, rarely rose above the level of mountebanks.

Like other new age gurus, Knight conjured illusions among her followers using powerful visualization techniques. In the eighties, these basic tools from the technology of experience won wide respect for their demonstrated curative powers and were broadly deployed in religion, therapy, medicine, business training and other public domains. The tools are simple to operate but easy to abuse. A former devotee recalled the guided fantasies and more extreme delusions she experienced during her seven years at Knight's Ramtha School of Enlightenment.

"She would guide us down spirals and through doorways," she told us. "She said she was trying to guide us into different dimensions of consciousness. I remember, in one, she said that we each knew inside of us how we were going to die and she had us visualize the circumstance of our death. Then as we were doing that we were to visualize changing that circumstance—she was leading us to believe that we could change the future."

This former Ramtha follower traced her descent into a maelstrom of primitive myths, space-age fantasies and doom-filled "days to come" prophecies.

"In the beginning I was attracted to the peacefulness and beautifulness of the teaching," she said, "the idea that God was not outside of you but within you. Then, around '85, the teaching changed. Ramtha began warning about terrible things that were coming, planetary changes, earthquakes, floods. He said we had to put food away, get land, drill wells. J.Z. began advising people to move to the Northwest, because that was going to be the safest place."

Ramtha's revelations bore strong resemblances to the militant "survivalist" ideology that bloomed in the Northwest and scattered widely across late-twentieth-century America. The millennial survivalist mentality crossed the spectrum from new age adherents to devout fundamentalist Christians to an ardent and, in many places, heavily-armed extremist fringe. Although less militant than most, Knight's survivalism showed a similar paranoid-delusional style.

"First came the earth catastrophes, then came the government thing," this ex-follower recalled. "Ramtha said there was a government conspiracy to enslave us all and create this Soviet-like America. We were told to get out of the system and become sovereign. You had to dig an underground shelter and store food. It was constantly hung over your head that time was running out."

As the sect's paranoia intensified, the fantasies became even more bizarre.

"Next came the alien invasion. Ramtha said the god Jehovah was in cahoots with a race of extraterrestrials who were going to come and take control of the earth. So now you had the earth changes plus the government conspiracy *plus* the aliens trying to enslave us. Ramtha said it, so by God it was true! He knew because, after he ascended from earth, he hung out in the Pleiades."

California guru John-Roger also seemed to be a prolific producer of delusions. His hybrid Insight Seminars self-help therapy and new age religion, the Movement of Spiritual Inner Awareness, were presented to newcomers as "practical personal growth for everyday life," but they redirected many trainees to impractical places. Group leaders created experiences of "astral initiation," "aura balancing" and "soul transcendence" using every tool in the technology of experience: chanting, marathon encounter, guided fantasy, rebirthing, water baptism, and a raft of brand-name processes with names like "The Cocktail Party," "I've Got A Secret," "Innerphasings" and the holy grail of "Getting Your Affirmation."

However, the sect's more egregious delusions seemed to spin around the personality of John-Roger himself. The sect leader promoted himself as the "physical embodiment of the Mystical Traveler Consciousness," allegedly a cosmic being—like Hubbard's Thetans and Knight's Ramtha—who comes to earth only once every 25,000 years. In his winding "discourses" and promotional materials, he claimed to be a higher figure than Jesus, Buddha and Moses, the "direct line of authority into God." And thousands of MSIA members believed him.

Former Insight trainer and MSIA minister Peter M. described how he and many other intelligent people passed through Insight's commercial gateway into the insular world of the MSIA religion, where virtually every spiritual exercise revolved around the personality of John-Roger.

"They start by giving you these nice euphoric experiences and they put it all in terms of 'spirit,' and then somewhere along the line spirit is inevitably connected to John-Roger," he told us. "When you get into the main stream of the cult, you start chanting the 'divine names' and he gives you those names. We were told, 'You can chant the names of God, Jesus, the Holy Spirit, John-Roger'—he just kind of throws it in there. Then we were given visual exercises. You were supposed to imagine all this loving energy coming from this spiritual being. We were told, 'You could imagine Jesus, a white light, John-Roger.' We were encouraged to buy pictures of him and put them in a frame next to where we did the exercises. They said, 'You can open your eyes and you look into his eyes and through the pictures you will get *darshan*— the divine look of the master.'"

Like many worldly professionals, Peter M. was at first highly skeptical of John-Roger's claims to divinity, but powerful MSIA rituals turned him around 180-degrees.

"When I started Insight I couldn't stand the guy," he recalled. "To me he was just this guy in a Hawaiian shirt. But the Insight processes were so effective that, in time, I became convinced it was my own limitations that were preventing me from seeing the divine in him."

He described the process that helped him make the mental switch.

"I started doing an Insight visualization technique known as 'Calling in the Light.' You sit and ask the 'light' to surround you, I did it and it felt nice and gradually I started to believe that it came from him, it was *his* light. Soon I was spending two hours a day sitting in the light, and it was *his* light. I was saying the names of god, and they were *his* name. I was constantly thinking about this person I loved most in the world and who loved me unconditionally—and he was the one who filled the bill."

He bought the delusion wholeheartedly. For the next ten years, he abandoned his other personal and professional interests and devoted his energies to Insight/MSIA. He wrote two bestselling books that introduced millions to John-Roger's teachings, to which he granted John-Roger co-authorship and turned over nearly all the books' earnings. His contributions to John-Roger and Insight/MSIA topped $1 million.

But those were only the material costs of his devotion to John-Roger. He revealed a more profound number his guru put on him during his protracted delusional phase.

"The real rape was when he got me to believe that I was dying from AIDS and tuberculosis and that he was the one keeping me alive," said Peter M. "He told me I had only nine months to live and that those months were going to be pretty terrible. Then he said, 'I'll handle it and keep it from you as long as you do these things'—which, coincidentally, greatly increased his power and money. I believed that for six years, and all the while I was working with him I was so grateful he was allowing me this simple opportunity to save my life."

The delusional phase of information disease was widespread in the seventies, and it grew rampant in the years that followed. In the eighties, the media were inundated with testimony from people who had suddenly uncovered astounding incidents from past lives, mystical life-after-death experiences, and alleged "recovered memories" of childhood sexual abuse, satanic rituals and abductions by extraterrestrials. Some of these recovered memories were endorsed by mental health professionals and law enforcement officials as genuine accounts of repressed experiences that returned to consciousness spontaneously, and, indeed, in most instances where real abuses had occurred, those memories usually returned without prompting or any evidence of outside influence. Other vivid tales, however, appeared to have little grounding in reality. Many were recounted by individuals who had been associated with controversial cults, sects and therapies. Others emerged in clinical sessions among patients of professional therapists who, skeptics claimed, were sometimes deeply deluded themselves. The acrid debate cut to the heart of the therapeutic process. Prominent practitioners actively promoted the new methods of recovered memory and past life "regression therapy." Their critics cited subtle suggestions and explicit coaching by some therapists that appeared to induce the "recovered" traumas. Other mental health professionals sought to have the whole business of recovered memory condemned as an industry of induced delusion, and to have the new traumas that were being inflicted on innocent individuals and families recognized as a distinct and potentially damaging "false memory syndrome."

Not Thinking—Mind Control. But a far more frightening threat to personality posed by the new technology of experience is the impairment of a more fundamental capacity of mind: quite simply, an individual's ability to think, not just for himself, but to think at all.

Almost every major cult and cult-like group we came upon teaches some form of not thinking or "mind control" as part of its regular program of activity. The process may take the form of repetitive prayer, chanting, speaking in tongues, self-hypnosis or diverse methods of meditation. As countless studies have shown, such techniques, when practiced in moderation, may yield real physical and mental health benefits, feelings of inner peace, relaxation and a calming of nervous tension. Extended practice may bring on euphoric transcendent states: emotional highs, feelings of bliss, and a pleasing lightness of mind and body. In such states, a person may have sensations of being in intangible realms or alternate realities. He may see divine visions, receive spiritual communications, or experience breakthrough moments of revelation or enlightenment.

Prolonged stilling of the mind, however, may wear on the brain physically until it readjusts, suddenly and sharply, to its new condition of not thinking. When that happens, we have found, the brain's information-processing capacities may be disrupted or enter a state of complete suspension, producing states of mind that incorporate many other symptoms of information stress and disease: disorientation, detachment, ongoing altered states, hallucinations, delusions and, in extreme instances, total withdrawal.

In the United States and many countries today, aware, intelligent individuals of all ages are being persuaded to stop thinking voluntarily. Millions are doing so in their escape from the real world through mystical belief systems and extravagant psychological fantasies. Many more are being covertly induced to stop thinking by misleading, often blatantly deceptive authoritarian cult religions. Still more stop thinking with no immediate spiritual or psychological goal in mind. Their intentions are, instead, quite down to earth and practical as they pursue training in simple techniques for reducing brain activity that, they hope, will produce desired and immediately beneficial effects.

What they do not realize is how the brain responds organically to the experience of not thinking: as we have seen, positively at first, but over time those benefits may vanish as the brain readjusts in a catastrophic manner. When that happens, not thinking becomes the norm, and with it may come a dramatic reduction of awareness. Moreover, once a person's brain enters this state, the individual may be physically incapable of coming out of it on his own.

This can be one cumulative effect on personality of the experience known generally today as meditation.

To gain a close-up view of meditation's well-known benefits and lesser-known dangers, we turned to a veteran—and an insider. A man we call Barry Robertson practiced Transcendental Meditation for four and a half years. For nearly half that time he earned his living as a beginning instructor in the popular technique. In the seventies, the "TM" trademark surpassed all competitors and became the largest and most successful self-help therapy in America. Transported from the Himalayas to the West in the late fifties by its developer, Maharishi Mahesh Yogi, TM was hailed in the United States, Europe and elsewhere as an instant, nonchemical tranquilizer for the relief of nervous tension. The basic meditation technique cost $125 to learn, and, in 1977, the TM organization reported that in the United States alone 30,000 new meditators were signing up for the introductory course each month. A Gallup poll taken then found that 4 percent of Americans—nearly ten million people—had become involved in Transcendental Meditation.

At the beginning of our talk, Barry Robertson cautioned us that his experiences in TM would come as a shock to most casual practitioners of the technique. This was because, according to him, most Western meditators never succeeded in actually *transcending*. Most, he said, only use their twice-daily meditation sessions for simple rest and relaxation. Robertson, an energetic and resolute young man in his late twenties, slim, fair-haired and eager to be heard, explained why he believed the transcendental form represented a particularly hazardous method among many varieties of meditation.

"There are four basic types of meditation," he began, "and there is a major difference between TM and the others. First, there's *contemplation*, in which you take a sentence or a parable and you think about it. You just go into your mind and close out the outside world and you think. A good example which I find very funny is one the Zen Buddhists use: 'What is the sound of one hand clapping?' They think about it, they meditate on it for hours, and they come out with nothing. That's contemplation.

"Contemplation is similar to another type of meditation that I would classify as *Christian meditation,*" he continued. "This consists of studying the scriptures and pondering God and thinking about how you can use that scripture to give meaning to your life. The third type of meditation is simply *concentration,* where you concentrate on one spot on the wall or on your navel or on a spot in the middle of your forehead. You concentrate on one thing and you try to get the ability to hold your thoughts there. If you find yourself wandering off into other things, you bring your mind right back to that one point."

As Robertson saw it, however, Transcendental Meditation was none of the above.

"In TM you *empty* your mind," he stressed. "TM is switching your mind into neutral. You have no control over it; you try not to have control over it. You try to let your mind just go flat, with no thoughts whatsoever. When you concentrate on anything, you have at least one thought. TM attempts to go beyond that."

According to Robertson, to achieve this emptying of the mind, each TM student is given what is said to be his own custom-tailored mantra, a Sanskrit word which the Maharishi had defined as a meaningless sound with a "vibratory effect" that helps the mind reach a quiet state. According to the TM organization, the various sound qualities of particular mantras have been known for over five thousand years.

"To do TM," Robertson told us, "you repeat the mantra over and over in your mind, and as with anything, if you hear a steady noise over and over again, eventually your ears won't hear that noise anymore. For instance, I live by a railroad track, and when I first moved there the noise was terrible. Now I don't even know when the trains go by. My ears have been turned off to that sound."

Unlike a passing train, Robertson said, TM mantras are pleasant sounds with no harsh vibrations or side effects. As the mind becomes accustomed to a particular one, the meditator's awareness begins to change.

"You start the mantra in your mind, saying it over and over," he explained. "Then all of a sudden it gets quieter. At first it's a voice in your head, you're subvocalizing it in your mind. Then your mind just kind of floats on this nice sensation."

As Robertson described it, the first effect of TM is a soothing emotional high brought on by the brain's response to repetition. Then, slowly, as the mind adjusts to the repetition, the sound of the individual's "inner voice" diminishes. At this level of relaxation, the technique can be beneficial, a kind of tranquilizer, relieving stress and providing the "restful alertness" TM claims to offer.

"A lot of people do experience these positive effects for a long time," said Robertson. "A certain amount of relaxation and clarity of mind results when you reach this mental state."

Robertson noted, however, that for some reason, after about six months at this level of achievement, almost half of all Transcendental Meditators stopped practicing the technique. Despite its immediate benefits, the initial high wears off quickly and, for many, the twice-daily, twenty-minute meditation periods become a chore.

"People stop because they find it boring," he said. "Those who go into TM because they're uptight can't stick with the technique, and those who become involved in it for spiritual reasons usually drop it for something else."

According to Robertson, those who stay with this form of meditation for any length of time become vulnerable to its long-range impact. He described his impression of the cumulative effects of TM in startling terms.

"To say that TM is a technique of rest is like saying that shooting off a forty-four magnum is just exercise for the forefinger," he said. At first the new student has to work very hard at meditating, but eventually the mantra will just take over the mind. As you get better at it, your mantra is just there all the time. It gets to be like an impulse, something very subtle happening in your mind. It's not even a sound, it's just a kind of rhythm. Then it gets to a place where it's very, very still and then, finally, nothing."

Robertson traced TM's roots in Hinduism and Tantra Yoga. Then he explained why he believed that among Western meditators mantras may have a particularly destructive effect.

"Soon your mind gets to a place where it no longer associates meaning to anything," he said. "You just have this sound going on in your mind, and you get to a place where there's no longer concrete meaning. You're just abstractly experiencing nothing. You'd think a person would become afraid in this emptiness or vacuum, but this happens to your feelings, too. You reach a state where you're not feeling anything either. By the way, this is the state the Maharishi calls *bliss.*"

As Robertson described it, the TM state of bliss was not a state of profound pleasure. It was a level of awareness devoid not only of all thought but of all feeling and, by default, of all pain.

"At first you don't even know you're experiencing this transcendental consciousness," he said. "You can't remember it, you can't grasp it. But as you do more meditating, you become aware that you are aware of nothing. You are able to experience that nothingness, that emptiness. You can peer down into it."

This level of awareness is what TM called Cosmic Consciousness. In this state, according to Robertson, the individual experiences the world around him from a peculiar orientation.

"You can experience everything around you in Cosmic Consciousness," he said, "but you're totally detached from the world. It's like being at a movie theater when you're watching a boring movie. You're not really part of it. What you are doing, your personality, your emotions, your thoughts are no longer important to you. You can watch yourself do things, you can even watch yourself sleep! You actually— it's hard to explain—dissolve would be a good word."

After he had been a casual meditator for a couple of years, Robertson said, he traveled to Spain to enroll in the Maharishi's training course for beginning TM instructors. There he found the course of instruction to be rigorous and methodical, consisting of lectures which had to be memorized word for word, individual training, class-time practice, and meditation for periods of up to ten hours a day. During that official instruction period, Robertson first experienced the TM state of Cosmic Consciousness.

"I only had glimpses of it," he admitted. "I never had a steady flow. I'd be driving a car and all of a sudden my arms would be holding onto the steering wheel and I'd be sitting back watching it happen. My body seemed more like part of the car than part of me. But again, there were no feelings involved with it. There was no fear, no joy. It was neutral, just happening."

When Robertson returned to the United States and began to pursue his new career as a TM teacher, his ongoing state of bliss and Cosmic Consciousness made life in the everyday world a bit bizarre.

"I was sensing all kinds of telepathic things," he remembered. "I would see energy surrounding people, little thin auras of different pastel colors, and bigger egg-shaped ones made out of huge spirals. It was weird, trying to associate in the ordinary world when you're seeing all these things happening around people."

During this time, as Robertson described it, he became trapped in his state of Cosmic Consciousness. Yet, while he continued to teach

TM and advance the cause of the Maharishi, he was beginning to grow disenchanted with the organization.

"I was sold on it," he said. "I honestly believed that the Maharishi was the world's spiritual leader and that TM was going to usher in a new era of mankind. But the constant hassling for customers got to me eventually, and some of the Maharishi's teachings started rubbing me the wrong way. Deep down, I knew I was lying to the public. I was lying when I said that TM wasn't a religion. I was lying about the mantras—they weren't meaningless sounds, they were actually the names of Hindu demigods—and about how many different ones there were—we had sixteen to give out to our students. I felt the Maharishi's goal was to bring about his particular bent of religious belief and get everybody into it, but I objected to the way he was going about it. He gives them a little tidbit and they have a certain experience. Then he gives them a little more, until they're lured into it and caught. When I say caught, I mean that a person's brain reaches this place where it's humanly impossible to come out of it."

In the beginning of our investigation, we had looked kindly on TM. Among many mass-marketed self-help therapies, it was the only one that seemed to be completely beneficial, having amassed a wealth of medical and scientific support which had been widely circulated and the subject of several best-selling books. After our talk with Robertson and other TM instructors, however, we went back and examined the scientific data that had been amassed. We were surprised to discover the amount of questionable research that had been reported as fact and published by the TM organization, and the extent to which TM made unsubstantiated claims from biology and quantum physics to build its argument for "inner energy" and "creative intelligence. More disturbing was the way TM invoked alleged scientific facts to prove that only its own secret mantras would produce the beneficial effects of meditation. TM promoters had claimed that, unless meditators took TM's brand-name course and purchased their custom-tailored mantra, they would be vulnerable to "severely deleterious effects."

The seventies were a heyday for TM. With the end of the "Me" Decade's self-help boom, the commercial enterprise faded from the media spotlight, but unlike other nascent new age ventures, TM kept up its aggressive promotion and impressive growth worldwide. Sect promoters introduced an expensive new "levitation" program that, they claimed, could enable advanced meditators to fly, but the technique, a kind of cross-legged hopping, caused the sect's credibility to plummet. In the eighties, TM repackaged its basic meditation program as a healthful method of "stress reduction." Sect marketers sought lucrative group training grants from the U.S. military and other government agencies, claiming that TM offered windfall benefits for peace-making and measurable crime reduction on a nationwide and even global scale—the so-called "Maharishi Effect." Anticipating major breakthroughs, sect leaders formed a TM "World Government for the Age of Enlightenment" and "Natural Law" political party. They launched ambitious "Heaven on Earth" commercial developments around the world, equipped with TM-based teaching centers, health education facilities and stress management clinics. Other popularizers of TM built their own medical and financial empires promoting the Maharishi's teachings, the benefits of meditation generally and its alleged "quantum healing" effects.

But enlightenment proved elusive to many TM adherents. In 1987, a group of former TM trainers and practitioners formed TM-EX, an information and support group for those who claimed to have been harmed personally or financially by Transcendental Meditation. By 1995, inquiries to TM-EX numbered in the hundreds, but by then TM was only one brand name among many popular mind-stilling methods.

Meditation had long since gone generic. The practice was now widely recognized in mainstream medical circles as a proven palliative for the mind and the body, a simple non-prescription method for treating heart disease and high blood pressure, reducing stress and alleviating many psychological complaints. Its power appeared indisputable. Its potential health benefits, cost savings and value over more invasive chemical and surgical procedures were impressive, but the technique still lacked professional protocols and basic guidelines for the throngs of health-seeking meditators and more ambitious spiritual explorers.

Largely overlooked in the enthusiasm was the parallel stream of reports of adverse reactions to this ritualized process of not thinking. Dozens of scientific studies confirmed the potential negative effects of prolonged or even short-term meditation, including instances where meditation was upsetting, inappropriate or medically ill-advised. Like any medication or treatment protocol, meditation was not for every personality. Researchers logged countless reports of "relaxation-induced anxiety," panic, confusion, depression, agitation, uncontrollable floating sensations, hallucinations, sweating, trembling, shivering and, in extreme instances, schizophrenic breakdowns and suicidal tendencies. In one study, sixty-three percent of meditators reported experiencing one or more of those adverse effects—some after as few as fifteen minutes of mind-stilling. And, as we heard in our interviews, those effects increased markedly as people spent more time in meditation.

TM was not the only organization in America that appeared to abuse the practice of meditation. Nearly every cult, pop therapy and similar group we investigated employed some version of the practice in ways that often seemed to impair their members' thinking abilities.

A former Hare Krishna devotee told us how the Krishna ritual of chanting the familiar *Hare Krishna* mantra—in his case 1,700 times each day—maintained and deepened his ongoing altered state.

"The chanting puts your mind on hold," he said. "You totally concentrate on the words and listen to them and say them and don't try to think about anything else. It's difficult at first, because your mind has a much higher capacity than just chanting for hours on end. Of course, we aren't told at the time that we're putting our minds on hold. It's just part of the program of activity, and it does reduce our anxieties because we aren't thinking about things while we're chanting."

For this new devotee, chanting was the principal activity of Krishna life, in our view a way to kill not only time but thought itself. Members were constantly being sold on the value of the activity.

"They always tell you that chanting is the answer to everything," he said. "I remember one Krishna leader saying, 'I know the cure for cancer.' And I said, 'You know the cure for cancer! What is it?' And he said, 'Chant *Hare Krishna.*'"

The Divine Light Mission was even more direct in its abuses of meditation. In contrast to the emptying of the mind that was characteristic of TM, the DLM style of meditation was what Barry Robertson called concentration. As one ex-member explained the differences to us, the similarities also became apparent.

"The meditation Maharaj Ji was teaching involved intensity, not depth. The intensity was the concentration with which you focused on, say, the sound of your own breathing. As such, it was simply a technique for jamming the mind. It gave me a certain absence of feeling. It reached a point where, when I had doubts, guilt or other uncomfortable emotions, I would react by meditating. After a while, any significant thought I might have was immediately obliterated by meditating."

When he was finally deprogrammed, he found himself unable to refrain from meditating.

"After my deprogramming, it took several weeks before I was able to maintain a train of thought and make two sentences go together without having the whole thing erased. Meditation had become a conditioned response. My mind just kept doing it automatically."

It took this former Divine Light Missionary months to rebuild his capacities of thought.

"After I finally broke the reflex of meditating, I found I was going through another stage where my thoughts were like a very weak telephone signal," he said. "Normally, when you're thinking, you're with your thoughts; they're right where you're talking from. In this case, my thoughts were like way off over there, way out yonder, very faint. I really had to pay attention to them to hear them at all."

Eastern religious cults were not the only ones that put the mind on hold. The fundamentalist Christian cult called The Way International, one of the largest cults in America from the seventies to the mid-eighties, used the charismatic practice of speaking in tongues to still the mind over time. A young woman who spent several years in The Way explained the sect's systematic method of teaching its members this ritual mind-stilling technique designed to bring about the "infilling" of the holy spirit.

"The first class is twelve sessions long," she said. "It's a whole buildup to get you to the point where you believe you'll be speaking in tongues. You go to their fellowships and they call on people to speak in tongues and then interpret and prophesy. It's like kindergarten. When you hear it enough, you learn how to do it. When I finally started to do it, there were no ecstatic moments. It was no bolt of lightning. I could control it. I could start it and stop it. It's kind of funny, now that I think back on it."

Her instruction in tongues appeared to be a more methodical version of the informal learning process Marjoe described to us.

"We were told to do it 'much,' " she recalled. " 'Speak in tongues *much'* was the phrase, and that meant as much as you could, whenever you weren't talking or reading the Bible. It wasn't out loud, it was in the mind. It was no more than a silent chant, like the Krishna mantras, only we were just babbling in tongues. Toward the end of my involvement with The Way, I was doing it all the time without being aware of it. It's weird. It's something that gets out of control."

After her deprogramming, this former Way member still experienced difficulty breaking the tongues habit.

"When I got out of the group it was still going on in my mind. When I tried to stop myself from speaking in tongues and couldn't, I knew I was in trouble. Finally, I developed my own way of breaking it. When I listened to someone talk, I formed their words in my mind. I'd concentrate on every word that came out. I'd make mental images and spell their words out to keep from straying. It took me a good six months before it was completely gone."

The Unification Church developed its own form of meditation called "centering," a process that corresponded closely to Robertson's category of Christian meditation. A former Moonie described for us how centering focused on the specific teachings of the Moon church to the exclusion of all other thoughts and feelings.

"Centering is centering yourself on Moon's definition of God as the church gives it to you," he said. "You're instructed to concentrate on the thinkings of the church at all times and take the upper hand in any threatening situation. You are to assume dominion over the people you're around, because you're the enlightened one."

Instead of jamming the mind by endlessly repeating mantras and chants or focusing on their breathing or heartbeat, Moonies appear to control their thought processes at a higher level of mental activity. Every person who is not a fellow member, and every social, religious and political institution that lies outside the sect's domain, is portrayed as a representative of Satan's world. In our research, we found that Moonies and members of many Christian sects with similar religious and political doctrines often focus on such beliefs to the exclusion of all other thought. In this way, centering and Christian meditation may achieve two purposes at once: they may neatly prevent the individual from thinking independently and, at the same time, add larger elements of social and political control to an already airtight web of intellectual domination.

Like its many imitators, Erhard Seminars Training, the prototypical self-help therapy, attacked the process of thinking head-on. In the original est training, group leaders commonly focused on thinking as the cause of their trainees' problems. Group lectures and processes provided trainees with alternatives to thinking as it was customarily defined, using basic techniques of meditation and visualization that effectively stilled the activity of their minds. Throughout the training, est kept up its own form of indoctrination, urging trainees to refrain from the activity that was causing all their problems and, instead, to simply "experience" life itself.

We spoke with one est graduate about this curious distinction between "experience" and thinking.

"Thinking is the enemy," he said flatly. "Thinking is absolutely the enemy to me because it is a barrier to experience. Thoughts are not based on truth; they're based on tapes, things from the past. People are such machines, they let their thoughts run their lives rather than their experiences."

As this man, a professional in his late thirties, explained it to us,

est appeared to view the process of thinking essentially as tape recording. It declared the mind a storage vault of troublesome tapes that clog
the essence of pure experience. In the seventies, Erhard's pop philosophy worked like a charm for individuals fleeing their pasts and other
troubling life choices, and its successor, The Forum, found equally fervid audiences in the eighties and nineties.

Erhard's philosophy of pure experience brought us full circle in
our understanding of the new mind control methods, through the techniques of chanting and meditation in religion and therapy back to the
starting point of experience itself. By most standards, est and The
Forum were not cults, but, amid the proliferation of commercial self-
help enterprises in the nineties, they were among the best examples of
the spreading influence of the technology of experience. By slickly pack-
aging concepts and techniques that had been roaming loose in popular
culture since the sixties, they offered their participants a fully rationalized, socially legitimized self-defense for shutting off the mind.

Mind control—the nebulous term became clearer now as we dis-
tilled the specific techniques of covert control, or more specifically,
covert *communication* control, that pervaded the ritual practices of
new cults, sects and therapies: subtle codewords and nonverbal cues
that triggered the onset of ongoing trancelike states of detachment
from the world and near-total vulnerability to suggestion. For most
the control process was far from passive. Eastern sect members labored arduously to control their minds from within. Many fundamentalist Christians achieved the same state through "tongues" or, more
simply, by intensive repetition of Scriptures. For the individuals we
interviewed, these simple, self-absorbing rituals accomplished a number of seemingly desirable ends. As promised, they relieved much of
the inner stress people were feeling by stilling the mind's natural flow
of worries, doubts, questions and other disquieting thoughts. In many
cases, they also suppressed people's concerns for their families, friends,
loved ones and everyone else in the outside world, for their personal
goals and ambitions and, often, for their own health and physical survival. In the process, the new techniques produced a kind of "ecstasy
by default," a blissful, detached high that many interpreted as the
attainment of the higher spiritual realm they were seeking. However,
the new methods led others into frightening states from which they
were unable to emerge.

What are the long-term effects of this widespread process of not
thinking? Toward the end of our first cross-country research tour, we
interviewed a former Hare Krishna *brahmin,* a temple executive. He
gave us his view of how, by the late seventies, the once peaceful, as-

cetic International Society for Krishna Consciousness had turned into an aggressive full-time religious tract and book distribution operation, while more spurious activities were going on behind the scenes. Experienced salesmen traveled to Krishna temples instructing devotees in the techniques of salesmanship. According to him, in their unthinking state, the devotees remained perfectly willing to solicit sales and donations up to twenty hours a day. But some, over time, were no longer able to do so.

As our contact described it:

"There were two vegetables at our temple, people who were really bad off from chanting. We'd have to spend about two hours a day chanting our rounds to Krishna, but they would take four or five hours to get through them. There's not a whole lot of work to do around the temple, so we would just let them chant all day. Eventually these people deteriorated to the point where they couldn't get their chanting done. They would become slower and we couldn't get them to work or do anything. They were basket cases."

"There were a couple of nuts in our temple," another ex-Krishna we interviewed during that period recalled. "We had a crazy girl there who would go nuts occasionally and start throwing knives at people. Some people would have attacks and become very violent. Others would suddenly just turn on you and scream and yell. After a while you just accept it. You accept insanity as a matter of course."

Amid the spreading epidemic we were chronicling, those early reports of mental deterioration, derangement and violent acts were among our first intimations of serious long-term effects of snapping—and of more tragic cult cataclysms to come.

Not Feeling—Emotional Control. Mind control was only half the story of the new covert control. As our inquiry expanded, we uncovered a second control pattern pervading the inner lives of millions of spiritual seekers, a pattern not of mind control but of *emotional* control. In contrast to identifiable techniques that stilled the mind's critical thinking and decision-making capacities, these more subtle methods of emotional control targeted a deeper domain of human information processes: people's inner feelings of fear, guilt, love, hate, anger and other universal emotions.

For a decade, we watched the pattern spread through the new fundamentalism sweeping strife-torn societies and world religions. Then it moved with fervor into mainstream religions in the United States and broadly across the American heartland. There, we found, leaders of the new strain of fundamentalist Christian sects were recasting their

faith's timeless messages and devotional rituals into systematic programs of control and manipulation. Using vivid words and images from
the Bible, they commanded unwavering belief in their followers, stirred
primal fears, induced fervent born-again moments and other overwhelming emotional experiences.

In California's central valley, we met a member of a small-town
fundamentalist sect that dominated the life of the town. He described
the mix of emotionally charged words, images and social pressures
that drew him into an intense born-again conversion ritual.

"When I first moved to town I was rejected by everybody. People
said I wasn't *in* because I wasn't 'born again.' When I went to church,
people looked at me funny because I didn't go up to the altar. They
kept saying, 'If you aren't saved, you'll be damned to hell.' Then one
Sunday I went up and kneeled down before the preacher. It was very
heady, very emotional. There were people crying all around. The
preacher laid his hands on me and told me to think of Jesus and I
closed my eyes and tried hard to picture him. Then I got this strange
feeling. I got chills in my body and started to shake all over. Suddenly,
I could actually see him there with his arms open wide. I could see the
spirit swooping. I heard the wind blowing. I could just feel myself getting righteous and having this new power. The people were jumping
up and down in a frenzy and shouting, '*Hallelujah! Oh, hallelujah!*'
Then I went back to my chair and everyone said, 'Oh, we're so proud of
you,' and I felt, well, accepted."

His experience was a far cry from Helen Spates' natural rebirth
experience in childhood. From that moment on, he told us, his church
elders deployed an arsenal of graphic symbols, images and biblical
figures to enforce obedience among church members. The storm of emotions pervaded his inner life.

"They were preaching that the 'Devil' was everywhere in the world,
everything was 'satanic,' and it was 'evil' to do this and 'evil' to do that.
At first I thought it was funny, but soon I actually found myself lying
awake at night scared. I'd hear a noise outside and think, *that's him,
it's the Devil, it's Armageddon starting.* Before long I started to feel
guilty, afraid, really *bound*, like there was nowhere I could go, nothing
I could do that wasn't part of the evil. Every second that fear would
control you. I'd lie in bed at night and say to myself, *This doesn't feel
right.* I had all these questions inside, but when I went to the pastor,
he told me the doubt I felt was Satan whispering in my ear."

Some fundamentalist groups strived to suppress people's feelings
altogether, as the new cults sought to suppress people's thoughts. In
our travels, we were surprised to learn that respected fundamentalist

missionary organizations active on college campuses, in local churches, public schools, professional sports, politics and the military taught systematic practices that continually stilled their followers' feelings. Tracts published by the Navigators military ministry planted the suggestion in subtle ways: "Alas, it is this that deceives you, for your heart is the worst part." Campus Crusade for Christ's "Four Spiritual Laws" proselytizing pamphlet was more direct. It closed with the explicit command: "DO NOT DEPEND ON FEELINGS!" The message was reinforced with a drawing of a toy train with "Fact (the Bible)" as the engine, "Faith" as the tender and "Feeling" as the lowly caboose. "The train will run with or without the caboose," the pamphlet said. "In the same way, we as Christians do not depend on feelings or emotions, but we place our faith (trust) in God and the promises of His Word."

For those who wavered, some fundamentalist groups taught explicit thought-stopping techniques that stilled any remaining doubts or fears. One method called "spiritual breathing," described in a Campus Crusade magazine, bore striking resemblance to the meditation rituals practiced by many cults: "If you retake the throne of your life through sin—a definite act of disobedience—breathe spiritually . . . Exhale—confess your sin. . . . Inhale—surrender control of your life to Christ." The article suggested that, done properly, spiritual breathing might submerge to unconscious levels. "At first, [it] may seem a bit mechanical. . . . you feel a bit frustrated, and you are conscious of every move that you make. . . . However, after a while. . . . You find yourself, without any conscious effort, exhaling and inhaling. You even forget the whole concept of spiritual breathing because it becomes so automatic."

Mind control. Emotional control. In practice, many cults, self-help therapies and fundamentalist sects alike used mixed methods of mind control and emotional control in their daily rituals and regimens. The babble of tongues was, for many Christians, a mantra that blocked their doubting thoughts and impious feelings. Scientology's auditing technique, according to dozens of Scientologists we interviewed, appeared to control their minds and emotions simultaneously. Across the board, the combined methods induced all manner of ecstatic highs, blissful states and mystical sensations. They also left members of many groups in ongoing states of floating, delusion, emotional numbing, and suffering other information disease symptoms.

A former Scientologist who spent nearly two decades in the sect recalled the cumulative impact of that group's practices on his emotions, and his intense reaction afterwards.

"In Scientology you have what we called a 'somatic shutoff.' A somatic shutoff is basically where you stop feeling. Your emotions are being subverted but you *think* they're coming out. In fact, you think it's wonderful. It wasn't until I left the group that I realized what had happened, and then I began to tap into my emotions for real. I found myself almost like a small child. I would feel something and say 'What is this emotion?' and then I would just break down. It was like suddenly there were all these raw areas of my life, things that had been bandaged up, hidden away, renamed, and I didn't know what to do with them. It was like opening a time capsule and all these emotions from twenty years before came flooding to the surface."

New age "channeler" J.Z. Knight developed her own imaginative emotional control methods. In Knight's Ramtha theme world, vivid guided fantasies evoked fear-filled emotions that seemed to deepen Knight's control over many of her adherents. An ex-follower recalled one Ramtha vision that turned the popular idea of life-after-death experience into a hellride with predatory demons.

"One time Ramtha did this teaching on what he called the 'light beings.' He said that when you die you don't want to go to the light. You want to go to the void, the darkness, because if you go to the light there are entities that live there that have never incarnated in human form. They live in this light spectrum but they want to evolve, so when you die they suck the experience from your spirit and that's how you are reincarnated and come back with no memory of your last life."

For this devotee, already steeped in Knight's endtimes prophecies and scary tales of government conspirators in cahoots with aliens, Ramtha's light beings were the last straw that tipped her tenuous emotional balance.

"My emotions had become so twisted, and now here was this whole new fear factor. Even in death there was no escape from the fear."

She described Ramtha's insidious covert messages that snared her in a mental and emotional double bind.

"He warned of all these terrible things that were going to happen. I was in total fear but I would not admit it because Ramtha taught that whatever we fear we draw to us, so eventually I became afraid of my own thoughts. Some little scenario would pop into my mind and it would send fear down my whole being that if I even thought of something I was going to create it."

She recalled the range of fearful beliefs along those lines that pervaded her life as a Ramtha disciple.

"The teaching was that if you bought life insurance you would surely die, because you had embraced that thought. If you put on a seat belt you would surely have a car accident. I worked nights and I remember when I drove home from work I would pick up every hitch-hiker, because *not* to pick them up would have meant that I was afraid, and that meant that eventually he or someone like him would get me. Even sex was a source of fear. Ramtha said that each orgasm brought you closer to death, so you became afraid of sexual pleasure. There's not even words to describe the torment that I lived in trying to suppress all this fear that I could not even admit to."

Back in New York, we met a young professional woman whose spiritual odyssey had taken her across four continents and deep into an Eastern sect called Sant Mat or "The Path of the Saints." The obscure sect was led by a "spiritual master" who taught a powerful form of meditation derived from the Hindu Radhasoami tradition. (Similar Radhasoami teachings and practices were reportedly drawn on by founders of the American sect Eckankar and, via Eckankar, by John-Roger's Insight/MSIA.)

After serving a stint as an overseas reporter for a national magazine, this young woman embraced Sant Mat's teachings and began practicing its intensive meditation rituals. The experience consumed her mind and body and left her in a state of physical and emotional numbness that she was still grappling with long after she returned to the United States. Her story, in many ways a bookend on journalist Sally Kempton's experience two decades earlier, confirmed the dangers of emotional control and the tenacity of this new information disease symptom of numbing that was becoming pervasive in the nineties.

She recalled the covert commands that instilled the emotional control process and the effects that set in soon after.

"In Sant Mat we were told that feelings were just a stage you had to pass through, and that the only feelings you were allowed were devotion to the master," she told us. "We weren't *supposed* to feel. They said, 'Channel your emotion to devotion.' Feelings for anyone in the outside world were 'attachments' that would only spoil your chance for 'god realization.' So when I had those natural emotions, I would feel guilty for having them and that would lead to the numbness."

Her numbing was not metaphorical.

"I couldn't feel my senses literally, sound, touch, smell," she told us. "I felt numb physically, deadened, like my head and neck were cut off from the rest of my body, but I was *taught* to be that way. We meditated six hours a day. You had to sit there and make sure no thoughts or feelings came in. Then one night I was lying in my bed and I felt my whole body going numb. I had this sinking feeling, like my emotions and my entire identity were swimming away from me and I was becoming unconscious, falling into this dark state. I called my friend and said, 'What is this? I think I'm going numb and it really scares me.' He said, 'Oh, that feeling is the master within you.' "

Her effort to grasp what was happening to her led her to the sect's main ashram, where she encountered other devotees in a similar condition. "When I went to India, I was desperate. I kept going to people and telling them how numb I felt and asking, 'Is this part of the process?' They all said the same thing, 'There gets to be a time when you're completely numb and that's a good sign. It means you're making spiritual progress.' I think they had been in that state for years. There were people zombied out all around me saying, 'Oh, isn't it wonderful. You can meditate and have such inner peace.' But I didn't feel any inner peace. I felt like I was going crazy."

Finally, after two years spent traveling with sect members through Europe, India and Asia, she left the group and returned to the U.S.

"When I got back I was numb and, at the same time, incredibly tense. I sat in my room for three days and nights and said to myself, *I just want to feel, I just want to feel.* I shut my eyes and did my mantra and tried to feel something within me, but I couldn't feel anything. There was this frustration, like I was holding back everything I wasn't supposed to feel. It was like holding your breath and holding your breath—"

She stopped. "You know what this numbing thing is like? Dante's inferno," she said, suddenly making an inner connection. "It's like someone putting fire all around you. Here's everything you love in this world all around you, but you're not allowed to see it, not allowed to feel it. Your whole body feels like it's on fire and they're saying to you, 'You're not allowed to feel, you're not allowed to feel.' "

Three years later, she was still mired in her own private inferno.

"I still have that numb feeling for weeks at a time," she said, contemplating her predicament. "I start withdrawing because I can't feel my body, then I get scared and the fear triggers more numbness and it becomes a vicious cycle. Everything seems dreamlike and I get spacey. I feel cut off from the world, like the information isn't coming in. I get a headache, my feet get tingly and I feel claustrophobic, like I want some feeling but can't reach that part of me. I play-act to get by, as though I'm participating in the world, but it's all very mechanical. I don't know what it's all about, this numbing. A lot of it is blocked up emotions, I think."

With the spread of the technology of experience into religion, therapy and wider everyday domains, millions no doubt had achieved impressive personal breakthroughs and spiritual awakenings, yet we saw little recognition of the perils inherent in the new technology and the intense experiences it evoked. These new practices that had proved beneficial in many contexts were not supernatural powers or pinpoint engineering tools but living information and communication processes that reached to bedrock levels of the mind and body. When used manipulatively or covertly, they could be turned into paralyzing instruments of human control. When practiced recklessly or to excess, they spawned debilitating mental, emotional and physical effects.

As we came to better understand these new covert control processes, we saw how millions of Americans and people worldwide had advanced in their personal searches for meaning and spiritual experience to unquestioning acceptance of fanatical belief systems, bizarre pseudo-psychologies and absolutist ideologies. For those swept up in the new groups, their daily lives became, not unfettered exercises of individual freedom, but ongoing, inner distortions of the experience of freedom itself!

And waiting at the end of their spiritual quests was the ultimate test of their experience. It was the same test spelled out a century ago by the founding father of American psychology, William James, in his classic study *The Varieties of Religious Experience*: the "fruits for life" of those experiences for individuals and others in the world around them. For so many modern searchers, those fruits were overripe with the new human disorders we called information disease. As our research went forward, we probed deeper into those new disorders and their lasting effects on the mind, brain and body.

13 Follow Up: PISCES, PTSD and Other Projects

Bent as we are on studying religion's existential conditions, we cannot possibly ignore these pathological aspects of the subject. We must describe and name them just as if they occurred in non-religious men.

—*William James*
The Varieties of Religious Experience

INFORMATION DISEASE WAS NOT some hype phrase or scare word. The term described precisely the organic alterations of mind and body people told us they experienced both during and after their involvement in manipulative cults, sects and self-help therapies. These new disorders were caused, not by germs, drugs, poisons, physical injury or any commonly recognized force or substance, but, we found, by information itself: by the new information and experiences people consumed and metabolized over weeks, months and years spent in various spiritual, personal growth and group indoctrination practices.

From the start of our research, we counted more than twenty clinically recognized signs of disorder, including physical illness, exhaustion, depression, withdrawal, overwhelming feelings of fear, guilt, hostility, violent outbursts, and suicidal or self-destructive tendencies. However, the most startling effects fell into a new and different category: lasting disturbances of awareness, perception, memory, imagination and other everyday human information-processing capacities. These symptoms included ongoing problems of confusion, disorientation and dissociation, recurring nightmares, daytime "flashbacks," hallucinations and delusions, periods of uncontrollable "floating" in and out of altered states, reported instances of bewildering "psychic" phenomena, and a frustrating inability to break persisting mental rhythms, images, voices and other repetitive thought patterns.

When we first discerned this new category of effects, we sensed we had uncovered something important from a mental health standpoint and, potentially, of greater significance for a new information age understanding of the mind. We also knew that substantive follow-up research was needed and that such research would be controversial. To learn more, in the fall of 1980, we met with senior editors of *Science Digest* magazine and, with their support, launched a major research project: a nationwide survey of the cult experience and its long-term effects. With help from leading deprogrammers, ex-member support groups, Cult Awareness Network affiliates, independent counseling centers, mental health professionals and a dozen other sources, we distributed more than 1000 confidential questionnaires to people throughout the United States and Canada. We got back over 400 replies from former members of forty-eight cults, sects and therapies.

The first report on our findings, published in *Science Digest* in 1982, attracted national media attention and won a National Mental Health Association media award. The report sparked predictable protests from prominent cults, but our study, funded by a popular science magazine and not subjected to the scholarly process of peer review, also spurred academic debates and numerous calls for release of the full survey data—to that time the largest body of raw data gathered on the cult phenomenon. The pull of contending interests persuaded us not to release the full study until the entire data sample could be thoroughly analyzed, critiqued and prepared for more formal presentation.

The PISCES Project. In the spring of 1984, scholars at the University of Oregon invited us to their Center for Communication Research. There our raw data became the subject of a year-long data analysis conducted jointly by the two of us and researchers with the center's newly formed Project on Information and Social Change—to which we assigned the convenient acronym and computer password PISCES. The project's expanded findings were presented at the International Communication Association meeting in Honolulu, Hawaii, in May 1985 and reprinted in summary form in *Update*, a journal of new religious movements published by the Dialog Center in Aarhus, Denmark.

The completed study was rich with insights into snapping and information disease.*

Our survey sample was sweeping. We solicited ninety-eight de-

---

* see Appendix for the PISCES study statistical profile.

tailed answers and four open-ended responses to questions covering every stage of the cult experience: from recruitment to daily life in the group, to separation, deprogramming and long-term effects. Our questionnaire drew responses from thirty-nine American states and four Canadian provinces and spanned the range of spiritual and personal growth enterprises active in North America and worldwide. Our respondents included ex-members of the largest international religious cults of the seventies and eighties—the Unification Church, Church of Scientology, International Society for Krishna Consciousness, Divine Light Mission and The Way International—smaller cults such as the Children of God and followers of Eastern guru Bhagwan Shree Rajneesh, participants in self-help therapies such as est and a similar training called Lifespring, and ex-members of several dozen Christian Bible cults and extreme fundamentalist sects.

Our respondents varied widely in age, from mid-teens to mid-fifties, and in the time they spent in their groups—from three days to twelve years. They divided almost evenly by sex, broadly by religious background, and they were recruited in a variety of ways and places. Significantly, few people said they joined their groups because of overt pressure from group members, a leader's "charisma," or even the group's advertised rituals, expressed beliefs or avowed social-political goals. Most people were drawn to their groups by a more subtle communication factor: the pull of positive emotions, especially the feelings of love, happiness, acceptance and seeming spiritual fulfillment communicated by group recruiters in their first contacts and personal encounters. (See Appendix, Table I.)

Once in the group, however, those happy qualities gave way to grimmer realities. Most cult members spent their days in perpetual motion, pursuing prescribed programs of chores and menial labor, work in sect-owned businesses, required fund raising, street proselytizing and social-political crusades. Throughout, their time was suffused with group rituals, therapeutic practices and private devotional activities. Exhaustion was widespread but, surprisingly, basic physical deprivations turned out to be minimal. In contrast to earlier studies of cult life, which cited poor diet and lack of sleep as primary factors in the cult control process, most people we surveyed reported eating normal, balanced meals or vegetarian but not unhealthy diets and sleeping an average of almost six hours per night—a low but by no means inadequate amount. (Appendix, Table II.)

Among the shuffled priorities of most cults, sexual relations ranked low. Celibacy predominated, although roughly one-quarter of our sample reported having sexual relations at least occasionally while in the group.

Sexual exploitation of these sect members was minimal—only one in twenty reported having sex with leaders of their group. One notable exception here was the Children of God, whose female members were commanded in the seventies by the cult's founder to become "fishers of men" and "happy hookers for Jesus." Sixty percent of COG members reported having sexual relations with group leaders.

And the groups we surveyed asked for more than spiritual or even sexual dues paying. Our modest sample donated more than $1.3 million of their personal savings and possessions to their groups. Nearly half worked on fund-raising drives, in sect businesses or at outside jobs that brought in another $5.7 million over their time in the group.

But, as we suspected, the most compelling acts of cult life were the intense ritual and therapeutic practices required by virtually every

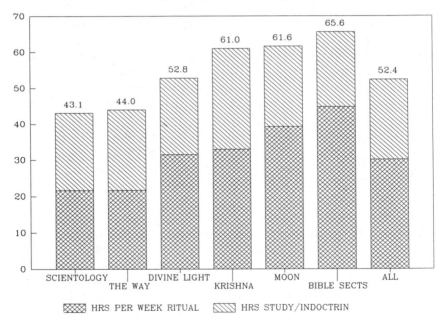

Graph 1: Ritual & study time/indoctrination (hours per week)

group in our survey. Practices varied widely from group to group: from chanting and meditation in Eastern sects like the Hare Krishna and Divine Light Mission, to the Moonies' act of "centering" the mind on the teachings of Moon, to Scientology's auditing and training regimens, to the extended ritual of speaking in tongues in The Way and other charismatic sects, to fervent scripture recitation and repetitive prayer in extreme fundamentalist sects. Our respondents spent from *three to*

seven hours per day in ritual mind-stilling and related group communication practices, including marathon encounters, sensitivity sessions,
psychodramas, role-playing games, guided fantasies and emotion-filled
confessional activities. Moreover, nearly all spent an additional *twenty
to thirty hours per week* studying sect books, tracts and scriptures,
attending required sermons, lectures, seminars and self-help work-
shops, listening to pre-recorded tapes, or in other classic indoctrination practices.

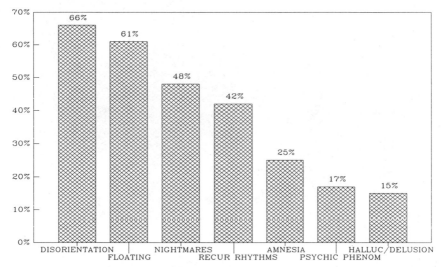

Graph 2: Cognitive effects—all groups (% reporting)

This grueling schedule of activities added up to a numbing *forty to
eighty hours per week* spent in mind-altering rituals, required study,
indoctrination, and other individual and group communication practices. (See Graph 1.)

The impact was imperceptible to most people while they were in
their groups, but it surfaced with a vengeance afterwards. One in five
of our survey respondents experienced some physical health problem.
Two-thirds experienced lasting emotional difficulties. And almost everyone reported one or more of the information disease symptoms we
had catalogued. Two-thirds reported periods of disorientation, dissociation or uncontrollable floating in and out of altered states. Half
reported recurring nightmares. More than a third were unable to break
persisting mental rhythms of chanting, meditation or speaking in
tongues. One in four experienced some memory loss. One in six reported hallucinations or delusions for up to *twelve years* after leaving
their groups! (See Graph 2; Appendix, Table III.)

As important as the numbers were the written comments people sent in with their questionnaires. Many claimed they had become *unable* to think, incapable of making even the simplest choices about what to eat, what clothes to wear, how to get through the easiest day. Some couldn't focus or concentrate for months, couldn't read a news-

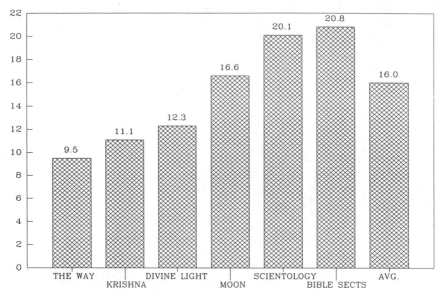

Graph 3: Rehabilitation time—all groups (months)

paper or write basic sentences. Others told of experiencing physical pain while attempting to make reasoned, independent decisions for the first time in years.

"It hurts to think, physically aches," wrote a former member of the Divine Light Mission. "I went through intense pain, like my insides were exploding," a young woman recalled in words reminiscent of Jean Turner's snapping experience in est. Many were plagued by recurring rhythms and intrusive images of their time in the group and by uncontrollable floating episodes afterwards. "In times of stress, I still find myself meditating without having decided to do so," wrote an ex-member of another Eastern sect. A woman emerged from the Church of Scientology with near-total amnesia: "I woke up in horror and realized that I had been shut off, sleeping mentally, for six and a half years, since the first day of doing the cult exercises."

For many, the process of leaving their groups and re-entering society proved to be the most stressful ordeal of all. It took most people six months to two years—on average sixteen months—before they felt fully recovered from their information disease symptoms. (See Graph 3.) During that crucial period, a third reported having suicidal thoughts or self-destructive tendencies, two-thirds sought professional counseling, while others labored in vain to deny the disturbing symptoms they were experiencing.

"My life was blown to bits by the experience," said an ex-member of an Eastern meditation sect. "I never knew such bewilderment, pain and feeling on the brink of insanity," wrote an ex-Moonie. "I cried all the time. I experienced more fear and terror than I imagined existed," said another. Another raged: "I'm really mad! My body is damaged from poor nutrition and years of fear and guilt and pressure on my nerves."

For others the trauma was ongoing. Many people felt that their unwanted changes were permanent. "The cult has limited my imaginative and creative abilities in ways that may be irreparable," one ex-fundamentalist said. An ex-Moonie wrote in clipped phrases: "Can't function properly in society due to instability...still suffering from amnesia and sexual dysfunction, among other things...totally different person...the world looks flat...without initiative...can't feel or find myself."

Did these first-hand reports of traumatic effects prove that the new spiritual and personal growth practices were the indisputable *cause* of people's information disease symptoms? Not by themselves, of course. But before we could begin to consider the sticky scientific question of "causation," we needed to test for "correlation." We ran the numbers—first on hand-held calculators, then on the University of Oregon's mainframe computers—and found strong evidence of a relationship between two crucial information factors. The full computer analysis confirmed a connection the two of us had suspected from early in our research between the time people spent in mind-altering ritual and therapeutic practices and their reported difficulties afterwards. The numbers showed *a direct relationship between ritual time and effects.* The more time people spent per week in sect rituals and self-help techniques, the greater was the extent of their later information disease symptoms. They also showed *a direct relationship between ritual time and rehabilitation time.* The more time people spent in mind-altering practices, the longer it took for them to recover from their symptoms and feel completely rehabilitated.

Put simply: our findings appeared to confirm that *the psychological trauma the new sects and therapies may inflict on their members is directly proportional to the amount of time people spend in mind-alter-*

ing rituals and self-help practices. (See Graphs 4 and 5.) In more than one hundred statistical tests, the PISCES team found statistically significant correlations in two-thirds of the test runs. The tests spanned

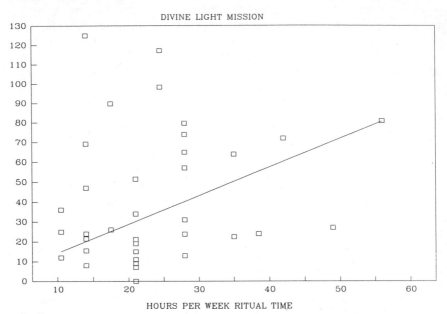

Graph 4: Ritual time vs. months of effects—Hindu sect

more than a dozen information disease symptoms and included tests of all former members and separate breakdowns for the four largest groups in our sample. (Appendix, Table IV.)

Two groups in particular appeared to have the most severe impact on their members: the Church of Scientology and extreme Christian fundamentalist sects. The rituals of the Church of Scientology bore little resemblance to those of other groups. With its extensive program of training regimens and "auditing" counseling, the sect operated successfully as both a religion and a mass-marketed therapy. However, according to those who responded to our questionnaire, the sect's rituals appeared to be the most debilitating of any cult or therapy we surveyed. One-time Scientologists told us that it took them, on average, nearly two years (20 months) before they felt fully rehabilitated—twice the time of those from other major cult groups. Moreover, former Scientologists claimed the highest rates of persisting fear (76%), sleeplessness (52%), suicidal or self-destructive tendencies (51%), violent outbursts (27%), hallucinations and delusions (24%), and sexual dysfunction (24%, tied with The Way). On average, former Scientologists surveyed reported nearly *twice* the combined negative effects of all other cults and therapies we studied (total: 139 months) and *triple* those of some other major cult groups.

Ironically, although they claimed the most severe long-term effects, the former Scientologists we surveyed reported the *lowest* total of hours per week spent in sect rituals and indoctrination. This appar-

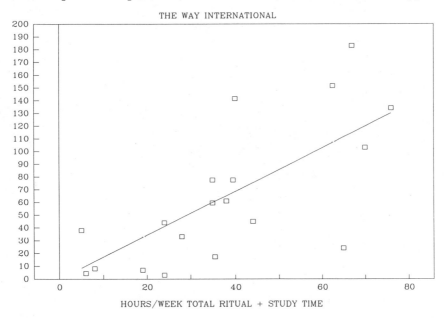

THE WAY INTERNATIONAL

HOURS/WEEK TOTAL RITUAL + STUDY TIME

Graph 5: Ritual & study time vs. effects—Bible sect

ent discrepancy supported opinions we had expressed earlier that, in combination, Scientology's intense training regimens and auditing sessions—the latter augmented by the sect's electrical E-meter counseling aid—may have compounding effects on the nervous system that go beyond those of other spiritual and personal growth practices. Overall, our survey indicated that, *hour for hour, Scientology's techniques may be more than twice as damaging as those of other cults and self-help therapies, and up to four times as damaging per hour as the rituals of some other major cult groups!* Later, when we double-checked those correlations and plotted our findings using more precise statistical curve-fitting methods, the trend line for former Scientologists appeared, not as a straight-line, linear relationship of reported effects per reported hour of group ritual, but as an upward sweeping curve that seemed to suggest a more swiftly rising, *geometric* relationship between that sect's rituals and their reported effects. (See Graph 6.)

"The overall impact? Devastating!" wrote one ex-member. "I still tend to view the world in Scientological terms: 'Truth is only an illusion.' 'People are robots.' 'People are basically insane and dangerous.'"

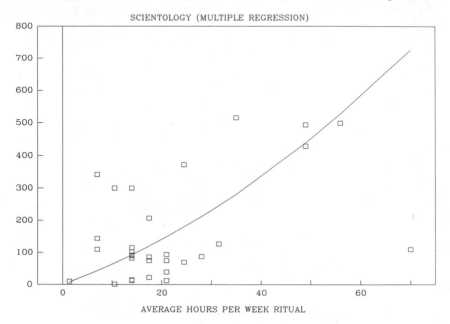

SCIENTOLOGY (MULTIPLE REGRESSION)

AVERAGE HOURS PER WEEK RITUAL

Graph 6: Ritual time vs. months of effects—religion/self-help therapy

Another was more bitter: "The only thing I got out of this scam was deep suicidal depression coinciding with the fear of death within five years after separation. We were told that ninety percent of all 'refund cases' eventually commit suicide."

Equally surprising were our survey findings concerning the burgeoning numbers of Bible cults and extreme fundamentalist sects. As it turned out, the majority of sects named by our survey respondents were not classic cults with bizarre beliefs and self-proclaimed gods and gurus but, rather, extreme charismatic and fundamentalist Christian sects employing sophisticated mental and emotional control methods. Thirty of the forty-eight groups in our survey emerged out of this traditional branch of Christianity. Taken together, they reported the highest average hours per week spent in ritual and indoctrination. They also rated higher than all cults in rehabilitation time (21 months) and higher than all except Scientology in combined months of long-term effects (113 months).

Our last block of findings concerned the controversial issue of deprogramming. The numbers confirmed that deprogramming was indeed a vital first step on the road back from cult control. Nearly three-quarters (73%) of the people in our survey were deprogrammed, about half voluntarily and half involuntarily. As a group, they reported a third less, and in many cases only half as many, post-cult effects than those who weren't deprogrammed. Average rehabilitation time was one-third longer—more than a year and a half—for those who weren't deprogrammed compared to just over a year for those who were. Overall, deprogrammees reported a third fewer months of depression, forty percent less disorientation, half as many sleepless nights—clearly, something in the process worked! (Appendix, Tables V, VI.)

The numbers were consistent. The sixty-three significant correlations (in the conventions of statistics judged to be 95% certain, with many correlations coming in at 99.99% or better) convinced the communication scholars on the PISCES team that our information disease hypothesis had scientific merit. In his report to the International Communication Association, PISCES Project Director Carl W. Carmichael, Ph.D., a respected scholar and authority in the field of persuasion, described information disease as "a new communication paradigm and mental health phenomenon in which both causes and effects are information-related." In his summary of data findings, Dr. Carmichael wrote, "The strength of Conway and Siegelman's assumptions about the relationships between ritualized communication activities and such effects is confirmed in the extent of these correlations."

But the PISCES team was not looking merely to bedazzle with numbers. Integral to the project was a rigorous peer review of our methods and findings. In his portion of the ICA report, research associate John C. Coggins, chief statistician for the project, critiqued our questionnaire and evaluated the validity of our sample. Coggins scoured our survey sample for signs of both balance and bias. "The distributions of the few demographic variables available suggest that the sample differs little from the general population," he found. The sample divided evenly between male and female and the range of replies was "weighted. . . as the distribution of sects appears to be weighted." "In these ways," wrote Coggins, "the study can be said to have the best sample available on this specialized population."

Coggins' second concern, a possible negative bias among our respondents, prompted him to define more precisely the subpopulation of sect members our survey represented. "Doing so would characterize the respondents here as 'casualties' of the new religious sect movement, rather than simply 'ex-members,' " he wrote. "With that stipulated, the sample becomes well-taken."

A fifth member of the PISCES team was not affiliated with the University of Oregon. Gary Cronkhite, Ph.D., then Professor of Communication at Cleveland State University and, later, Professor of Communication Studies, Semiotic Studies and Cognitive Science at Indiana University, was widely regarded as one of the foremost research methodologists in the field of persuasion. Cronkhite's ICA report sought to locate our information disease concept within the larger body of theory and research on social change. His paper offered a sweeping review of a half century of social scientific literature on persuasion, religious conversion, attitude change and other methods of social influence.

Cronkhite questioned the value of earlier social science theories and research for understanding new communication-based phenomena such as snapping and information disease. Conventional theories of social change through "reasoned action" offered only limited insight, he said, because "it is specifically 'reasoned action' of which those suffering from information disease appear to be incapable." Research on "opinion change" seemed "surprisingly irrelevant" because it concentrated mainly on "single-issue appeals" and tacitly assumed that such messages operated at relatively high levels of listener awareness. Most studies of "subliminal persuasion," on the other hand, were focused even more narrowly on specific consumer-product advertising appeals. Theories of "brainwashing" and "coercive persuasion" came closer but, as we knew too, they involved techniques "that could never be practiced in an open society" or applied "in a non-totalitarian context."

Those and other social science approaches, like our statistical sampling itself, were at best "correlational," said Cronkhite. The real challenge was to seek the verifiable cause-and-effect relationships that underlay our new communication phenomena; however, that scientific task, he said, posed "very serious practical and ethical problems."

"The hypothesis is that cult indoctrination techniques produce deficits in information processing that should be identifiable at both cognitive and neurophysiological levels," wrote Cronkhite. Referring to our survey findings, he noted, "The consistency in those reports from one interviewee to another... constitutes powerful evidence that former cult members at least believe they have suffered cognitive and neurophysiological damage. Still, we need more objective measures."

He proposed specific methods for detecting neurophysiological changes, and he had his own suspicions where evidence of information disease might appear in the brain, but for Cronkhite measurement was not the greatest impediment. Writing in 1985, seven years after the massacre at Jonestown that catapulted the cult phenomenon to world attention, and blind to events to come, he closed his review on a prescient note: "These are not *theoretical* methodological problems, they are *practical* ones. That is, the hypothesis makes unambiguous, testable claims regarding measurable events. The problem is that the manipulations and measurements necessary to its testing are fraught with social and economic impediments....Let us hope that another Jonestown mass suicide/massacre is not required to overcome the social and economic impediments to the testing of the hypothesis central to the concept of information disease."

Three later studies upheld our findings.

A study of sixty-six former Moonies, published in the *American Journal of Psychiatry* in 1983, found that more than a third (36%) reported serious emotional problems after leaving the group, one in four (24%) sought professional help, and nearly two-thirds (61%) felt that group leaders had "negatively impacted" on sect members.

A 1986 study of fifty-eight former members of a West Coast psychotherapy cult found that half suffered extreme emotional effects and information-processing problems, including anxiety (52%), depression (48%), difficulty making decisions (48%), confusion (41%) and disorientation (40%).

A second, large-scale study of 308 former members of 101 groups, reported in 1992 in *Cultic Studies Journal*, a publication of the American Family Foundation, closely paralleled our findings. The AFF researchers found widespread problems among people leaving cults a decade after we took our national sampling. Their team found similar measures of emotional disorders, including depression (67% vs. our 75%), guilt (56% vs. 59%), fear of physical harm by the group (38% vs. 40%) and despair and hopelessness (61% vs. 59%), and worse measures of anger toward group leaders (76% vs. 68%), anxiety and fear (83% vs. 40%), low self-confidence (72% vs. 19%) and severe anxiety attacks (34%). They found comparable levels of floating (55% vs. 61%) and other information-processing disorders, including difficulty concentrating (67%), flashbacks (71%), dissociated feelings of living in an "unreal world" (51%), and a higher number who sought professional counseling (70% vs. 59%).

The massing numbers challenged claims made by many groups that they had moderated their methods in response to reported excesses and public criticism. They also suggested that, after more than a decade of efforts by cult awareness organizations, the media, mainline religions, educators and mental health professionals, the damage being done by new cults, sects and therapies was increasing, not diminishing. The new studies found similar patterns of disorder, yet they consistently overlooked crucial communication factors that had yielded some of our most important findings: none of the new studies tested for correlation between the mind-altering rituals and indoctrination methods people were subjected to in their groups and the extent of their problems afterwards.

On that count, a parallel body of scientific data was emerging.

Post-Traumatic Stress Disorder. In the eighties, striking similarities appeared between two huge and highly unlikely cohort populations: casualties of contemporary cults and American Vietnam war veterans suffering debilitating aftereffects of their country's longest and most divisive foreign war. In 1980, the American Psychiatric Association recognized a new disorder Vietnam veterans had been suffering in the shadows for years. The clinical syndrome called Post-Traumatic Stress Disorder, or PTSD, described the baffling state of mind that came to afflict many "Nam" vets when they came home from the war. Hundreds of thousands of vets—by some estimates up to sixty percent of those who served in Vietnam—were plagued by debilitating delayed responses to the war's fierce guerrilla combat and other events they witnessed or actively took part in.

In the formal diagnosis of post-traumatic stress, a person palpably "re-experiences" elements of an earlier trauma in disturbing nightmares, daytime images, lifelike flashbacks, hallucinations, and other dissociated or altered states. At the same time, he may also feel numb to his emotions and deny, or attempt to deny, the syndrome altogether. Waves of vivid recurring images alternate with cycles of numbing and denial as individuals gripped by PTSD may experience more than a dozen paradoxical effects: anger, depression, terror, guilt, passivity, violent outbursts, nightmares, insomnia, intrusive memories, sounds and images, and amnesia. The syndrome's social repercussions show up in patterns of avoidance, withdrawal, suspicion, grand delusions, and a marked inability among those suffering from PTSD to hold jobs and maintain intimate relationships.

In the mid-eighties, the two of us began to explore this new stress syndrome with Vietnam vets across the country. As in our earlier research, we found PTSD to be a hybrid medical-psychiatric diagnosis in which, ironically, the usual physical and mental health factors appeared to be almost incidental. Many Vietnam vets beset by post-traumatic stress were in good health physically and never injured in the war. Most showed no other signs of mental illness except for their eerie post-traumatic stress symptoms. In fact, the most pronounced symptoms of PTSD were virtually identical to the information disease symptoms we had catalogued in our earlier inquiries. Although the syndrome's origins in guerrilla warfare had almost nothing in common with the quixotic quests of those in the new cults, sects and self-help therapies, the persisting effects described by people in both groups matched almost perfectly!

In our own quest for understanding, we took part in informal "rap sessions" with a cross-section of Vietnam-era vets. The effects they described were real and chillingly familiar. Like many cult casualties we had interviewed, Nam vets in those rap groups told us that, throughout their time in Vietnam, they were unaware of the changes taking place within them. In most cases, the sense of alteration struck home only after they returned from their grueling wartime experiences.

"I never felt it over there," one vet told us of his recurring flashbacks and ongoing emotional numbing, "that was all afterwards." Another described a strange dissociation and basic alteration in the way his mind processed information after Vietnam. "When I came home, I remember feeling like the world around me was a motion picture slowed down maybe two-speeds from normal," he said. Another vet experienced the opposite effect. "When I got back, everything was going on superspeed all around me. Everyday life seemed abruptly fast and *I* was slow for some reason." Another described his PTSD symptoms in terms almost identical to the dissociated floating state we had heard about from hundreds of former sect members. "I know inside when I'm slipping back into the stress. It's an altered state, like walking around in a fog, and it may last weeks until I can pull myself out of it. Sometimes it catches me by surprise. One time, I didn't even know I was in it for a couple of months."

When it first appeared in the mid-seventies, the perplexing phenomenon initially dubbed Post-Vietnam Delayed Stress Syndrome defied every medical and mental health explanation. Then gradually researchers began to investigate the new syndrome on its own terms. One of the earliest formal studies of returning Vietnam veterans, the Forgotten Warrior Project initiated in 1976 by John P. Wilson, Ph.D, a psychologist at Cleveland State University, produced a sampling of 400 Vietnam-era veterans, including combatants and noncombatants from every branch of the military, and was presented in testimony before the U.S. Senate. Those findings led to a comprehensive Vietnam Era Stress Inventory conducted jointly by Wilson and Gus Krauss, director of a Cleveland Vietnam Veterans Outreach Center.

In that PTSD study, Wilson and Krauss tested for correlation. Their findings mapped onto those from our PISCES data analysis almost exactly.

As in our study of the cult experience and its effects, Wilson and Krauss were looking for the relationships, if any, between the specific stresses that made up the engulfing Vietnam experience and the ongoing stress symptoms so many vets reported afterwards. Surprisingly, the most traumatic stress turned out to be, not the palpable experi-

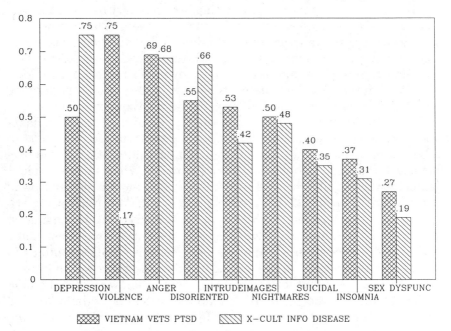

Graph 7: *PTSD vs. Information Disease Symptoms*
(loading factors vs. percent reporting)

ences of physical injury or intense pain endured by many soldiers in Vietnam, but the less tangible information stress of "repeated exposure to injury and death." That traumatizing information might be derived from direct combat experiences, as it no doubt was for many American troops, or indirectly, as we heard many times, from the passive viewing of dead Vietnamese and American soldiers, civilian casualties and victims of the war's atrocities on both sides.

In this stress category, Wilson and Krauss found *a direct relation-*

ship between the intensity and frequency of such "exposure experiences" and the extent of post-Vietnam stress symptoms. The finding paralleled our correlation between the amount of time sect members spent in intense rituals and group experiences and their reported aftereffects. The Wilson-Krauss study showed other parallels to our findings, including high scores for nineteen PTSD stress symptoms that compared closely to our twenty indicators of information disease, including depression, anger, violent outbursts, insomnia, nightmares, memory loss, suicidal tendencies, sexual dysfunction, disorientation, problems of concentration, and repetitive and intrusive thought patterns. (See Graph 7.) More alarming were later findings by Wilson, Krauss and others that incidents of post-Vietnam stress were *increasing,* not diminishing, with time. By the mid-eighties, a decade after the last American troops pulled out of Vietnam, the number of newly reported cases of PTSD was still rising and had yet to peak.

Later researchers found more parallels to our information disease concept. A 1992 study of forty Vietnam veterans with PTSD found the same strong correlations between the stressful information of the war's experiences and their post-traumatic stress responses. That study linked both the *amount* and *kind* of information to the severity of later PTSD symptoms.

The expanding stress inventory fleshed out the syndrome in clinical terms. Like many former sect members after years in the encapsulated worlds they stumbled into in their personal searches, many Nam vets we met seemed literally to have blown their minds in the otherworldly information environment of the Vietnam war. Some appeared hopelessly confounded by a national mission that went tragically astray. For many, the war and their personal roles in it only seemed to become more senseless the longer they thought about it. For others, coming home to a divided society that seemed unable or unwilling to understand them only compounded their confusion, stress and anger.

A Nam vet we met in one of our rap sessions, who had been grappling with PTSD for more than a decade, summed up his experience in terms that echoed our perspective's deeper organic implications. "So I walk in one day and they end up giving me this stuff about 'post-traumatic stress.' I mean, what it all boils down to is bad nerves—that may not be a bull's eye, but I know goddamn well I'm hitting the target. I mean, common sense will tell you a human being can only take so much, whether it's a war, a job, a marriage or anything in life, and their nerves are going to crack. People expect them to get better one day. They never get better. The cut has gone so long and festered so long that the disease is all through your body."

In our travels to these remote outposts on the human information frontier, we found in two widely divergent experiences a series of striking parallels: parallel stresses and pressures, parallel short-term responses and long-term changes, with origins and effects that could be linked organically to identifiable information and communication factors. Obviously, there were striking differences between the two experiences as well, but the Nam vets' struggle gave us important insights into snapping and information disease.

Later PTSD studies confirmed the role of experience in a wide new category of information age disorders. Similar stress patterns were found to afflict survivors of the Nazi Holocaust and the atomic bombs dropped on Japan, casualties of horrific airplane crashes, natural disasters, victims of terrorism, rape, inner city violence, and the soldiers and civilian rescue crews who cared for them. Children were especially vulnerable to the new disorders. No culture was exempt; symptoms were diagnosed among traumatized populations from Armenia to Northern Ireland. In many instances, follow-up studies uncovered the same direct link between the intensity of people's experiences and the extent of their stress symptoms afterwards.

These diverse ordeals confirmed that, not only for blithe-spirited sect members and struggling Vietnam veterans but for individuals in every walk of modern life, the worst stresses impinging on people everywhere were not physical in the usual sense but information stresses affecting their minds, brains and bodies.

Dissociative Disorders. The patterns of a second new mental health syndrome made other intriguing connections. In 1980, along with PTSD, a new category of "dissociative disorders" appeared in *DSM-III*, the revised diagnostic and statistical manual of the American Psychiatric Association. The concept of dissociation, introduced into psychology in the late nineteenth century, described literally a lack of connection between one piece of consciousness and another. The phenomenon was recast in information terms in 1967 by UCLA psychiatrist Dr. Louis Jolyon West. West defined the dissociative reaction as a "state of experience or behavior" that produces "a discernible alteration in a person's thoughts, feelings or actions, so that for a period of time certain information is not associated or integrated with other information as it normally or logically would be."

The new dissociative disorders bore many resemblances to snapping and information disease. Symptoms included: disturbances of memory, awareness and identity, "depersonalization" (feeling estranged from one's personality or physically separated from one's body), "derealization" (feelings of detachment from reality or sensations that the world itself is unreal) and various hypnosis-like trance states. In one dissociative disorder, termed a "fugue" state, a person temporarily loses memory of his whereabouts and identity. In another, called "splitting" or "multiple personality disorder," one individual personality divides into two or more separate personalities, a phenomenon found most frequently among children who have been physically or sexually abused, but which may occur at any age.

Other dissociative disorders included "brief reactive dissociative disorder," a clinical cousin to the experience we called snapping, and "atypical" dissociative disorders, such as the estranged states many anorexics fall into during their catastrophic swings of purging and binging. Another clinical disorder identified in 1992 by West, who was also a member of the American Family Foundation and a respected figure in cult studies, described a dissociative experience in which a person adopts an entire secondary personality or "pseudo-identity," an apt description of the new identities many cult members assumed.

The new syndromes marked a major advance over earlier mental health diagnoses, yet the advance of knowledge and clinical treatment of these new disorders was itself becoming a casualty of widening culture wars, religious-political controversies, and the growing influence of new spiritual and self-help enterprises in established medical arenas. By 1994, the long-awaited *DSM-IV*, the definitive fourth edition of the psychiatric manual, revealed the extent to which sacrosanct domains of medical and scientific research had become part of the wider cultural battleground. The new guidelines for diagnosing mental health disorders, like people themselves, had become fragmented, scattered, and in many ways compromised, lost in a welter of qualifications and religious-political concerns that had little to do with the scientific method. The main criterion of PTSD was eliminated. The original definition, which had linked the onset of post-traumatic stress to any "psychologically distressing event that is outside the range of usual human experience," was replaced by purely physical markers limited to a person's directly experiencing or witnessing "an event that involves actual or threatened death or serious injury, or other threat to one's physical integrity." Casualties of less disfiguring experiences were relegated to a new category of short-lived "adjustment disorders" or rediagnosed as having general "anxiety disorders."

The catch-all category of "Dissociative Disorders Not Otherwise Specified"—which in the previous edition had included people subjected to "prolonged or intense coercive persuasion (e.g., brainwashing, thought reform or indoctrination while the captive of terrorist or cultists)"— was revised to eliminate any mention of cult-related casualties and limited only to experiences "while captive." A cultural note was added to Depersonalization Disorder to explicitly exclude experiences resulting from "meditative and trance practices that are prevalent in many religions and cultures."

Several promising new clinical categories were proposed for further study, including a specific "Dissociative Trance Disorder"; however, the new category exempted all religious experiences and episodes of spirit possession entered "voluntarily and without distress or impairment in the context of cultural and religious practices." Another new category was expressly banned from diagnosis as a psychiatric disorder. The new non-disorder termed "Religious or Spiritual Problem" included "distressing experiences that involve loss or questioning of faith," unspecified "problems associated with conversion" and other problems "that may not necessarily be related to an organized church or religious institution."

The recognition of cultural considerations was welcome and long overdue. Yet, by restricting virtually all categories of post-traumatic stress and dissociative disorder to impairments resulting from material traumas or physical coercion, the mental health establishment seemed to be bending over backwards to exclude from their helping profession the growing numbers struggling, for the most part alone and with inadequate professional help, to recover from traumas caused by engineered spiritual and personal growth experiences. Nowhere in the new psychiatric manual—the last word on the subject, no doubt, before the onrushing millennium—did we see even one acknowledgment of these ongoing stress responses and real-world problems of mind that people were describing to us by the hundreds and thousands.

Four Possible Pathways of Information Disease. In contrast to the official disorders the mental health profession was leaving to clinicians, clergy and unnamed cultural arbiters to discern, the new information age disorders we were tracking were immediately palpable to people. They were at once conscious, ongoing, uncontrollable and, from all appearances, organic in nature. From the start of our research, we had speculated that, over time, the distorted information communicated in those abusive spiritual and personal growth experiences would come home to roost at the neurophysiological level—in lasting changes in the living workings of the human brain and nervous system. It took more than a decade before neuroscientists were able to produce empirical evidence of those changes, but now many of them were being illuminated brilliantly by other researchers on the cutting edge of information age science.

In the eighties, a rolling revolution in neuroscience unearthed stunning discoveries about the brain's lifelong responses to new information and experiences of every kind. This new research gave hard scientific support to the concepts of snapping and information disease. It provided further proof of Ross Ashby's laws of experience and Karl Pribram's holistic principles of brain function. It revealed the precise neurological and neurochemical pathways by which lasting changes may take place in the brain's living networks of communicating synapses in response to each moment's flow of information and experience. It even showed how a rush of new and intense experience could cause a sudden snapping of synaptic connections throughout the brain.

Laboratory experiments dating back to the late sixties confirmed that new synaptic connections sprout in the brain in direct response to the flow of information and experience. Later experiments found that new synapses may form from intense experiences in as few as ten seconds, or even less, and that opposite processes may destroy older synapses, whole brain cells and the experiences they encode at an equally swift pace.

Other evidence could be found at deeper neurochemical levels. Medical researchers studying Vietnam veterans with PTSD discovered that their stressful experiences caused lasting changes in the flow of essential chemical messengers in their brains. Veterans of Vietnam's high-intensity warfare were found to have permanently elevated brain levels of adrenalin, an elementary neurotransmitter involved in brain processes of arousal and the body's physical responses to danger. The neurochemical change correlated with their PTSD symptoms of hypervigilance and hair-trigger emotional responses. Other vets showed elevated levels of endorphins, the newly discovered brain messenger that mimics the narcotic effects of morphine. That change was believed by some neuroscientists to explain the persistent emotional numbing many American soldiers experienced in Vietnam and for years afterwards.

Similar changes were detected in the brains of people subjected to very different experiences. A 1993 study of twenty-seven anorexics and bulimics found measurable surges of arousing adrenalins and numbing endorphins during the most acute phases of their uncontrollable eating disorders. Studies of long-distance runners found elevated endorphin levels that correlated with the legendary euphoria known to athletes in many sports as a "runner's high." These new neuroscientific findings made concrete connections to several broad categories of information disease symptoms. They pointed us to four possible pathways of organic change that might underlie the new disorders and their effects on people's minds, emotions and the whole of their personalities.

PATHWAY #1: NUMBING. Among Vietnam veterans whose sensitivity to pain and emotion was overwhelmed and devastated by the war, as for sect members and self-help participants who were systematically trained to suppress their feelings, we traced a common pathway of numbing in the action of the brain's opiate-like endorphins. Hundreds of experiments confirmed that endorphins help the human system to cope with pain and other negative emotions. In times of stress, streams of endorphins flood the brain's feeling networks, dampening the conscious experience of pain and other distressing emotions until those unwanted sensations subside. The same studies also suggested that, when a person is continually exposed to high levels of physical and emotional stress, broad regions of the brain and the body as well may become physically addicted to those powerful natural narcotics.

Once it has become established, the numbing response may be elicited purely by information. In one experiment, researchers studying Vietnam veterans with PTSD measured a rush of endorphins through their nervous systems after they watched graphically violent scenes from the Oscar-winning Vietnam movie "Platoon." The research team speculated that the endorphin flood the vets experienced while watching film scenes reminiscent of their Vietnam experiences, and the marked decrease in their pain thresholds that accompanied it, reflected a "learned response" that had persisted for years after the war.

In the same way, it seemed to us, former sect and self-help participants subjected to prolonged mind and emotion-stilling practices could develop similar learned responses that might permanently affect their capacities for feeling and emotion. Such responses could account for other information disease symptoms: in several studies, excesses of the same endorphin messengers had been shown to promote amnesia as well as numbing.

PATHWAY #2: FLOATING. A second pathway pertained to the "blissed-out" highs many people experienced while in their groups, and to the periods of uncontrollable floating in and out of altered states that may keep up for months and years afterwards. The new research implicated a distinct chemical messenger in this category of information disease symptoms. The chemical, another natural brain opiate discovered in the mid-1970s, was named by its discoverers enkephalin—Greek for "in the head." The messenger's chemical structure was similar to that of the emotion-numbing endorphins; however, there were major differences between the two neurotransmitters and where they were dispersed in the brain. As might be expected, the numbing endorphins cluster in deep brain regions that govern basic pain and emotional responses. Enkephalins saturate higher brain regions involved in cognitive processes of perception, awareness and imagination.

Laboratory studies confirmed that enkephalins are released in the brain during uniquely human communication activities such as hypnosis and meditation. The chemical rush appears to evoke the physical high those activities can produce. When practiced in moderation, such activities may bring on blissful states with real physical and mental health benefits. However, the new research also suggested that, when those same experiences become the consuming activity in people's daily lives, the potent neurochemicals they let loose, like any other stimulating or narcotizing substance, may cause lasting changes in the chemical balance of enkephalin-rich brain networks and trigger ongoing floating symptoms and other uncontrollable dissociated states.

PATHWAY #3: THE DELUSIONAL PHASE. A third pathway linked the wild hallucinations and delusions reported by ex-cult members, Vietnam veterans and others to decreased levels of serotonin, another basic neurotransmitter that helps to regulate the mind's sensory perceptions. In the seventies, researchers learned that serotonin is similar in structure to the celebrated psychedelic LSD. Studies showed that LSD produced its bizarre perceptual distortions and dream-like hallucinatory effects by plugging into the brain's serotonin receptor sites and blocking the natural brain messenger from performing its appointed regulating and stabilizing functions. Later findings indicated that the same mind-bending distortions might result from meditation and other mind-stilling practices that suppress activity in brain regions where the organ's essential serotonin supplies are produced in the first place.

The resulting serotonin shortfall could prompt vital brain networks to go temporarily or even continually haywire, triggering bizarre hallucinations, delusions and—like psychedelics and every form of hypnosis—making people highly receptive to all manner of odd beliefs, perceptions and suggestions.

PATHWAY #4: SNAPPING. Those possible pathways of information disease explained how many kinds of information, intense experiences, ritual practices and even subtle suggestions might cause lasting changes in the balance of brain messengers that mediate basic processes of thinking and feeling. The brain's fleet-footed neurotransmitters carry information from neuron to neuron, leaping the synapses and flooding the inner space between, but they were not the only agents of information disease. As we pressed deeper into the labyrinths of the brain's living information environment, we learned that other brain messengers could cause even more profound organic changes. One neurochemical in particular traced a fourth pathway that brought us full circle in our scientific journey: back to the sudden, sweeping change of mind and awareness we first heard described as an all-engulfing experience of "snapping."

This palpable experience could be triggered by any number of real-life causes: by a single, hard-hitting trauma, a more gradual buildup of stresses, or some packaged concoction of communication techniques that delivers a systematically engineered snapping moment. In the new neuroscientific research, we found an extraordinary organic action that seemed to explain this walloping snapping experience and the far-reaching changes it could unleash. The action originated in a revolutionary theory of learning and memory first proposed in the mid-eighties by neurobiologist Gary Lynch at the University of California at Irvine.

Lynch's theory focused on an obscure brain chemical called "calpain" which, he claimed, was present in the synaptic terminals of many, if not all, the brain's branching neurons. According to Lynch, during any new experience, these idle calpain enyzmes are literally switched on by a sudden influx of electrically charged calcium ions that stream into the cell from the brain's bathing chemical fluids. The energized calpain enzymes then quickly eat away the surrounding layers of brain matter that make up the inner scaffolding of the neuron.

This rapid enzyme action may cause the cell's outer walls to collapse almost instantly, prompting synaptic nerve endings to break suddenly from their neighboring connections and, thereby, destroy that working synapse. The disintegrating calpain blitz may also spur an equally sudden sprouting of new synapses and the formation of whole new networks of working connections in those brain regions.

The supercharged calpain hypothesis was devised by Lynch to explain how memories of specific experiences might be formed instantly in the brain, as they seem to be in real life, not through the gradual accretion of neurological patterns described in conventional memory models, but in one fell neurochemical swoop. Lynch's theory also struck us as a plausible explanation for far greater sudden changes of awareness and the whole of personality described to us by people who had experienced such changes first-hand. The link to calcium was crucial—it was one of the most basic and prolific chemicals in the brain's information metabolism. The driving engines of the reaction, electrically charged calcium ions, acted globally and could easily account for holographic shifts of awareness and comprehensive processes of personality change.

And, apparently, we weren't the only people who thought so. By the end of the eighties, Lynch's daring calpain hypothesis was widely accepted. Our computer searches of the neuroscience literature turned up hundreds of scientific studies of the minuscule molecule, which was now being parsed into a multitude of subtypes and embraced by researchers worldwide as a primary agent of sudden change within the brain.

The evidence was growing that many kinds of experiences could cause a sudden snapping of synaptic connections and lasting neurochemical changes in brain regions where the mind's everyday powers of thinking, feeling, awareness, imagination and long-term memory are concentrated. Within those sprawling brain regions, information coming in from every organ of perception mixes with all the brain's entwined synapses, meandering messengers and higher holographic communication processes. We could easily envision how some sudden, traumatic experience, the buildup of lesser stresses, or an invisible act of mind as simple as heeding a quiet call to surrender could instantly break and reform incalculable numbers of working brain connections.

The experience could let loose a chain reaction of inner responses and all the swift, surprising, often devastating effects we had seen in so many real-life snapping experiences: instant religious conversions, skyrocketing peak experiences, abrupt shatterings of awareness and more bizarre personality changes. In their minds' scrambling efforts to make sense of the experience, people might become convinced that they had gone crazy or, as we heard frequently, literally "blown their minds." The experience could make people blindly accepting of the suggestions and commands of others or prompt some visibly to regress to helpless childlike states. In such instances, people might remain dissociated and diffused for months in their struggle to reform severed threads of mind and strands of personality that may have been physically obliterated.

These four information disease pathways came to life before our eyes in talks with former sect members, Vietnam veterans and others who had been through some of modern life's most extraordinary, most exotic—and most appalling—experiences. But they also illuminated serious incidents of snapping that were being reported in a growing number of everyday life situations. In America and many places, the news was crackling with reports of people who "just snapped" and then did something deplorable. Celebrated crimes and court cases for three decades testified to the human consequences of the phenomenon and its real-world repercussions.

Our perspective offered one alternate way to understand how and why so many were responding in desperate ways to the stress of life in an information age.

PART THREE
Social Implications

14 Snapping and Punishment

A population subjected to drastic change is a population of misfits—unbalanced, explosive, and hungry for action.

—*Eric Hoffer,*
The Ordeal of Change

WHO, THEN, IS RESPONSIBLE for the actions of people who have been pushed to the breaking point and beyond, for those who may have snapped and become entrapped in a less than fully human state? The individuals themselves? Their leaders? Society in general? And who is to be punished when those actions are serious crimes, violent deeds— even murder?

Since the end of the sixties, a number of those horrifying crimes have been committed in America and elsewhere by young men and women who were wholly unlikely candidates for the crimes with which they were charged. In none of these cases, however, was the individual proven to have a classic Jekyll-Hyde split personality. Rather, all had, in the period preceding the commission of their criminal acts, undergone drastic transformations of their minds and personalities, if not in a sudden moment, at least over a relatively short, identifiable span of time.

Three notorious cases continue to stir heated debates: the Tate-LaBianca murders committed by the young members of the Manson Family in Los Angeles, California in 1969, the armed bank robbery and other acts committed by millionaire heiress Patricia Hearst following her kidnapping in Berkeley, California by the Symbionese Liberation Army in 1974, and the series of random street murders in New York City in the late seventies for which a young postal worker named David Berkowitz was apprehended and, soon after, convicted as the .44-caliber killer who called himself the "Son of Sam." Years later, each case in its own way still confounds traditional psychological and legal interpretation.

Our inquiry into snapping has provided us with a new vantage point from which to view and analyze these spectacular crimes. We examined the public record of each event and gathered new material in private interviews and confidential communications. It seemed worthwhile and potentially important to see if these cases and the questions they raised could be further illuminated by our new understanding of snapping and information disease.

Without exception, we found that they could. The sudden changes in personality common to the people who were recruited by Charles Manson into his Family, to Patty Hearst and to David Berkowitz as well, were all traceable to specific experiences, manipulative techniques, mental and emotional stresses, or extreme and prolonged changes in the individual's surrounding information environment. The result was a dramatic personality shift from the individuals they were before to the individuals they were at the time they allegedly committed their crimes. In our view, the diverse psychological and legal explanations of these historic examples of sudden personality change have proved to be of limited value in informing courts, juries and the public of the deeper meaning and larger social implications of these unprecedented modern tragedies. As an alternative, we offer the following interpretation from a human communication perspective on the information dimension of these historic events.

The Manson Murders. Although it is public knowledge that Charles Manson was deeply interested in Scientology before he formed his Family, even though he never joined the sect, the possible resemblance between some Scientological practices and Manson's methods of controlling his band has not been fully explored. We do not believe or intend to imply that there was any formal or informal connection between the Church of Scientology and the now legendary murders of actress Sharon Tate and her houseguests and another couple, Leno and Rosemary LaBianca. We are, however, suggesting a similarity between some techniques used and taught by Scientology and the manner in which Charles Manson manipulated the members of his Family.

Vincent Bugliosi, prosecuting attorney in the Manson trial, made frequent mention of Scientology and one-time Scientologists with reference to Manson's life and career in his best-selling account of the case, *Helter Skelter: The True Story of the Manson Murders*, published in 1974. Bugliosi served up all the details of Manson's drifting, troubled youth—an illegitimate child, he bounced from town to town, engaging in a haphazard string of petty crimes and larcenous acts. Seventeen of

Manson's first thirty-two years were spent in jails and prisons, yet, Bugliosi noted, Manson's criminal record to that time showed no sustained history of violence.

"Burglar, car thief, forger, pimp," he wrote, "was this the portrait of a mass murderer?"

It was in prison, apparently, that Manson became interested in Scientology. According to *Helter Skelter,* in the early sixties, Manson's tutor in Scientology was another convict, Lanier Rayner, and under his direction Manson claimed to have achieved Scientology's highest level, which he described as "Theta clear." Bugliosi wrote that Manson, whose career goal was to gain recognition as a rock musician, remained interested in Scientology longer than in any other subject except music. A prison progress report written during that period asserted that Manson "appears to have developed a certain amount of insight into his problems through his study of this discipline."

There is no way to determine whether Charles Manson actually experienced becoming a Scientology clear. It is known that not long afterward, upon his release from prison in 1967, Manson began to formulate his grand delusionary and messianic schemes. It was also during this period that he began to demonstrate an uncanny ability to exert influence and control over other people.

There were many influences during those years, psychedelic drugs being the most prominent, along with the culture-wide impact of the San Francisco scene to which Manson gravitated during the Haight-Ashbury's famous Summer of Love. Another powerful element in that roiling information environment was the music of the Beatles, who wrote "Helter Skelter" and many other songs that Manson took to be personal communications from cosmic forces. A greater influence was the biblical Book of Revelation which, like suggestible sect leaders before and since, Manson interpreted as an explicit battle plan for the coming apocalypse. He read into its prophecies hidden meanings that licensed him to initiate his campaign of mass murder. Manson's interest in Revelation may have been derived in part from a second cult. Through the spring and summer of 1967, when Manson was recruiting members from the hippies, drifters and runaway flower children of the Haight, his fledgling Family had frequent interaction with an ominous tribe that lived just two blocks away. This was the archetypal sixties-era religious cult called the Process, or the Church of the Final Judgment, a group whose members walked the streets in long black robes, preaching the imminent arrival of a violent Armageddon as presaged in the Book of Revelation. According to Bugliosi, the Process was founded by a former disciple of L. Ron Hubbard himself who broke with Scientology to form his own group after attaining an important position in Scientology's London headquarters. Bugliosi cited numerous elements in Manson's worldview he believed were borrowed from the Process: distorted attitudes toward life and death, the worshipping of fear and violence, and a variety of satanic delusions and black revolutionary schemes.

Manson's activities as a pimp and forger and his years in prison certainly schooled him in the basic skills of an expert con man. But it may have been his experiences with Rayner that provided him with some of the communication tools he used to manipulate the minds of his young followers. "Undoubtedly," wrote Bugliosi, "he picked up from his 'auditing' sessions in prison some knowledge of mind control, as well as some techniques which he later put to use in programming his followers."

Bugliosi identified these influences in his attempt to explain how Charles Manson formed his philosophy and recruited the Family. However, he declined to make any connection between Manson's background, with his protracted exposure to rudimentary techniques of controlling others, and the almost unbelievably twisted states of mind of his followers, in particular, the three women who were convicted along with Manson for the Tate-LaBianca murders: Susan Atkins, Patricia Krenwinkel and Leslie Van Houten.

No one knows how Manson worked each individual conversion, but as we came to understand it, his technique was classic—and potent. In the Haight's atmosphere of psychedelics and free love, and later while recruiting young runaways on the Sunset Strip in Los Angeles, Manson approached prospective Family members, most of them young women, using two of the most common and effective cult recruiting ploys: affection and acceptance. More important, he relied on specific covert suggestions to stop thinking and questioning that, if heeded, might in themselves evoke the powerful snapping moment and condition of extreme vulnerability that follows.

Susan Atkins, in a book about her experiences in the Family, described what went on "in the storm of my mind" when she first met Manson. During a typical Haight scene of loud rock music and easy encounters, Manson came up behind her and began dancing with her, putting his hands on her hips and guiding her body in rhythmic, sensual movements. As she remembered the scene, he also planted powerful suggestions that opened her to his advances—both psychological and sexual.

"He whispered into my left ear," wrote Atkins, "'That's right. That's good. . . . In reality . . . there's no repetition. No two moves, no two actions are the same. Everything is new. Let it be new.' "

It appears that, in this fleeting moment of physical contact, Manson managed to induce a profound snapping experience in Susan Atkins.

"Suddenly I experienced a moment unlike any other," she wrote. "This stranger and I dancing, passed through one another. It was as though my body moved closer and closer to him and actually passed through him. I thought for a second that I would collapse. What had happened? Was I crazy? It was beyond human reality."

In the days that followed, Manson moved in on Susan Atkins in a total sexual and psychological assault. In their first sexual encounter, he took full advantage of the experience to bring her under his direct control. "You must break free from the past," Manson told her. "You must live now. There is no past. The past is gone. There's no tomorrow." That sentiment was commonplace in the sixties, a touch of Eastern philosophy and a touch of Western existentialism. Taken literally, however, in the Family's world of frequent sexual and psychedelic orgies, Manson's followers slid into suspended states of consciousness. They totally identified with his prophecies, including his claim to be Christ or the Messiah, and with his plan to set off a worldwide revolution through a series of random ritual murders.

In the aftermath of the Tate-LaBianca killings, the trial of the four accused murderers turned into a ghastly public spectacle, complete with garrulous courtroom outbursts by the defendants and a noisy sideshow outside the L.A. courthouse orchestrated by other Manson Family members. At the time, in the thick of the pandemonium, no one in the courts, the press or the public asked the very serious question of what in the world had happened to "Charlie's girls."

Least of all Bugliosi. Riding a tidal wave of public outrage, Bugliosi, District Attorney of Los Angeles, pressed hard for the swift conviction and execution of the defendants. Calling a succession of psychiatrists as expert witnesses, Bugliosi shot down every plausible contention of the defense concerning Manson's conversion tactics, the role of LSD and other psychedelic drugs, and the psychological histories of the defendants, asserting that each defendant was mentally competent and a willing participant in the Tate-LaBianca murders. During the penalty trial to determine the sentences of the convicted murderers, Bugliosi contended that each of the accused Family members possessed some kind of "inner flaw" that would have prompted her to kill—even without Manson's orders and influence. Bugliosi called upon the jury to "have the fortitude" to return verdicts of death for all four defendants.

"These defendants are not human beings, ladies and gentlemen," said Bugliosi in his final statement to the jury. "Human beings have a heart and a soul. No one with a heart and a soul could have done what these defendants did to these seven victims.

"These defendants are human monsters, human mutations."

The jury in the Manson trial did return verdicts of death for Manson and the three women. In 1972, however, before the executions could be carried out, the California State Supreme Court abolished the state's death penalty on the grounds that it constituted cruel and unusual punishment. The sentences of all four were commuted to life imprisonment, and through the seventies, Manson, Atkins, Krenwinkel and Van Houten remained in prison, first on death row, then in isolation.

During our initial research tour through California, we tried to arrange interviews with members of the Manson Family to determine whether their transformations could be understood from our perspective. We quickly discovered that there would be little to gain from conversations with three of the four.

Manson himself turned out to be the most unreachable and unlikely prospect. "Charlie?" one official at the California State Prison at Vacaville told us, "Charlie is anyone he wants to be these days." From all reports, Manson had not changed noticeably in prison. He was said to be still shuffling his con man roles, at times appearing to play the part of a model prisoner yet showing little sign of genuine rehabilitation.

Patricia Krenwinkel, we were advised by those following her activities at the California Institute for Women at Frontera, was still struggling to find her identity.

Susan Atkins, on the other hand, had become an ardent born-again Christian after being baptized in a water tank in her prison yard in early 1975. From accounts we gathered, it appeared that, like many other people we interviewed during that time, she had found her private answer to an irresolvable emotional crisis in America's most widely accepted form of personal and spiritual renewal.

Of the four, a decade after the Manson murders, Leslie Van Houten was the only one who appeared to have fully emerged from her cult state of mind.

By every measure, Leslie Van Houten was the most unlikely of the accused Manson Family members. A one-time high school homecoming princess, she grew up in an active, concerned home where her childhood was shared with an older brother and two younger adopted children. When she was fourteen, however, her parents separated and divorced, and Leslie was profoundly affected by the breakup. During that turbulent era in Southern California, Leslie began taking LSD fairly regularly with a young man with whom she had fallen deeply in love. In time, the young couple drifted apart and Leslie, barely eighteen, dropped out, fell into the Haight-Ashbury scene and ultimately found her way to Manson and his Family at Spahn Movie Ranch, an isolated, dilapidated Western movie set at the mouth of the San Fernando Valley.

Unlike Manson, Atkins and Krenwinkel, Leslie Van Houten had no part in the murder of Sharon Tate and her houseguests. She was tried and convicted along with the others of the gruesome murder of Rosemary LaBianca, but the case against her was sufficiently cloudy to justify a second trial, separate from the confusion and media circus of the first proceedings. Late in the course of that chaotic trial, Leslie's attorney disappeared mysteriously while on a weekend camping trip. (He was later found dead in what some have speculated to have been the first of the Manson Family's "retaliation murders.") In his absence, another lawyer, Maxwell Keith, a prominent and highly respected Los Angeles attorney, took over Leslie's defense. It was largely through Keith's efforts that the courts granted Leslie a retrial in 1977.

In February, 1977, a month before the scheduled retrial, not yet attuned to any of the details of the case, we contacted Maxwell Keith in his Los Angeles office, telling him a little about our backgrounds and our project and expressing our interest in speaking with Leslie. At first, Keith was leery of us, but he admitted that he was still in the process of formulating his defense and that he was interested in hearing our thinking and our findings. Making no promises, he invited us to have lunch and a talk.

At lunch, Keith told us of his conviction that his client was now a totally different person. Leslie, he explained, had completely come out from under Manson's spell. "You wouldn't recognize her," he said, contrasting her to the fanatic individual last seen publicly in 1971 with a cross cut into her forehead. In the intervening years on death row and then in isolation, Keith said, while many women members of the Family had remained unswervingly loyal to Manson, Leslie was talking with prison psychiatrists, other prisoners, her family and loyal friends who had stood by her through the years, in an attempt to understand the transformation that had come over her. This personality change, one of her early lawyers once pleaded to a California judge, had made her "insane, in a way that is almost science fiction."

She was back to normal now, he assured us, returned to a stable, healthy state of mind. Though we were impressed by Keith's sincerity, at the time, we were skeptical about Leslie's transformation. By now we were completely willing to admit that a person could snap out of that kind of mental state. But, according to Keith, Leslie hadn't emerged in a sudden moment of renewed awareness. The change had taken place slowly, he observed, over a period of years. From his description, it seemed likely that, not having been formally deprogrammed, she could still be in some confused, floating state beyond the detection of prison officials and psychiatrists. On the other hand, we knew that if Keith's report of Leslie's re-emergence was accurate, it could confirm our thesis of snapping and expand it in a way we had not anticipated. Above all, it would demonstrate that even the most extreme forms of information disease could be cured. We also knew that, if Keith was right, as her lawyer he would face a new and almost unfathomably complex legal challenge. Not only were there no precedents in defense of this kind of sudden personality change among traditional insanity contentions, there were no established criteria whatsoever for a jury to use to reach a judicious verdict. Before we could begin to offer any interpretation, we told Keith, we would have to see and hear for ourselves how Leslie experienced her re-emergence.

The next day Keith accompanied us to L.A.'s Sybil Brand Women's Jail, where Leslie was being held while awaiting her retrial. By agreement with Keith, for legal reasons, we promised to refrain from discussing the killings or the events immediately surrounding them.

It took us two hours to get through Sybil Brand's rigorous security procedures. Finally, after each of us had passed a computerized identity check and personal inspection that included fingerprinting, mug shots, frisking and electronic weapons detection, we were allowed to pass through a series of iron gates, clanging doors and bulletproof partitions into a hot visiting room just large enough to contain a wooden table and four chairs. Moments later, a prison guard escorted Leslie Van Houten into the room.

She was wearing a floppy, navy blue sweater over her dark gray prison dress. Her long brown hair was neat and shiny, with bangs curving down covering her forehead to her eyebrows. Although slightly pallid from her years in prison, she looked almost wholesomely attractive. And there were tears in her eyes. She greeted Keith warmly, telling him that she had been taken from her cell into a dim holding room and given no information about why she was being detained. For the two hours we were being checked, she had sat in this small, barren room. It was, she explained, typical of the impersonal treatment she had come to expect, yet she couldn't help crying once in a while, she said, over the boredom, isolation and daily humiliations of prison life.

Keith offered her a cigarette and lit it for her, giving her a moment to relax before our talk began. He updated Leslie on the latest developments in her case; then he introduced the two of us and told her a little about our project and our lunchtime conversation the day before. Leslie seemed to grasp our mission immediately. She turned toward us openly. When we told her that we wanted to focus on her transformation of personality, she said that she would be very interested in talking about it and happy to cooperate in any way she could.

It was difficult to match this woman we were observing with the headlines' cold "thrill killer" of nineteen who, when asked at the trial if she were sorry for what she had done, replied blankly, "Sorry is only a five-letter word." At twenty-seven, Leslie seemed sober and thoughtful, in sharp contrast to her sensationalized media image. Her eyes were soft and alive, her smile relaxed, her posture altogether natural. It seemed to us very possible that she had indeed broken free of Manson's spell. For the next two hours she talked easily, with full awareness and composure, commenting on the significance or irrelevance to her plight of various experiences from her childhood and high school years. She described her close relationships with her family, especially her mother who had visited her every Sunday since her conviction. She recalled with great clarity the paths by which she went into and came out of her nightmare existence in the Manson Family. As we addressed the question of her initial transformation, Leslie reflected on the naïveté with which she first became involved with Manson. We found this part of her story extremely familiar.

"I didn't know Charlie had studied Scientology," she said. "I never realized how he manipulated our minds with all his Eastern philosophy about getting us out of the ego and not thinking."

According to Leslie, "the way Charlie did it" was through strict isolation and unrelenting intimidation. "The isolation was the major factor," she said. "We completely severed ourselves from the rest of the world." Then she went on to describe Manson's manner of capitalizing on each Family member's personal weaknesses and needs.

"I was always frightened of not being accepted," she admitted, "even when I was in school, but Charlie played on that. He saw a danger in my humor and outgoingness. He put me down all the time and I went into a shell. The whole thing just was not me. He'd try to make me feel I was missing something. He said I didn't know what was happening and that I was really stupid."

Leslie confirmed our suspicions about the role of LSD in the Manson murders. The drug issue had never been completely settled in the case. During the original trial, attorneys and expert witnesses on both sides seemed unable to determine whether the Family's frequent use of potent psychedelics could be blamed for transforming innocent teenagers into a gang of crazed, unfeeling murderers. A decade after the murders, the mind-altering power of LSD still awaited full medical interpretation. Use of the drug, which researchers were only then learning blocked the action of the brain chemical serotonin, an essential neurotransmitter involved in the regular of perception, had been widely linked to hallucinations and delusions, and there was ample evidence that young people on LSD and similar psychedelics may become extremely vulnerable to suggestion. Yet, despite the drug's observed chemical actions and psychological effects, most researchers at the time agreed that if LSD had any inherent impact on behavior, it was not to make the user crazed and murderous but generally passive and nonviolent.

Leslie didn't discount the importance of LSD in the rituals of the Family, but she stressed that like most Family members she had had extensive experience with the drug before she met Manson. She took many "really mellow trips" during her high school years, she said, and none ever led to violent acts or even violent impulses. A child of California in the sixties, when psychedelics were commonplace in the cultural environment, Leslie knew what to expect from the drug.

She did not know what to expect from Manson.

"I felt an immediate affinity with the Family," she said, recalling her attitude in the beginning. "They lived that 'acid reality' everyone was looking for at the time. It wasn't until the last four months that things started getting really weird. Then, out at Spahn's ranch, instead of coming back down after each LSD trip, Charlie would reinforce everything that was going on in the Family. He would make gestures that would take root in our minds. One time he acted out the entire crucifixion, going through contortions of pain and making really ugly faces. Then he would play card tricks, and because he was quick with his hands, we would all think we had seen a miracle performed by a very special person. But he was always so unpredictable. He would play Beatle records over and over, saying to us, 'Can you hear it? They're talking to me!' Then he would read from the Book of Revelation and say that it was calling for us to find a hole in the desert and stay there until the race war was over. To this day, I don't know if he really believed what he was saying, or if everything he did was just to get even with the world."

Listening to Leslie, we begin to see how Manson had manipulated his followers during their frequent group LSD trips by leading intense role-playing sessions and fantasy games for up to eight hours at a time which, as Leslie said, "took root" in their minds. Under Charlie's direction, they played pirates and maidens, cowboys and Indians, devils and witches, in scenes replete with violent and sadistic imagery. When it came time to play Helter Skelter, life in the Family had become a game with no borders on fantasy and reality, an extended "trip" that kept up long after any chemical effects had worn off. Using the same kinds of covert communication techniques employed in many cults, Manson guided and badgered his followers into lasting states of confusion and not thinking that laid them open to every further suggestion and command he gave. At all times, especially during the Family's psychedelic episodes, Charlie's adept wordplay hammered home the final spikes of snapping.

"Being around Charlie during that time was like playing a game of Scrabble," Leslie told us, aptly characterizing Manson's method. "He never labeled anything as exactly like it was. He'd say, 'The question is in the answer,' and 'No sense makes sense'—things that would make your mind stop functioning. Then it wasn't a matter of questioning when things began to get bad. We'd stopped questioning *months* before."

Skipping over the period of the killings, we asked Leslie when she first started to feel herself coming out from under Manson's spell.

She thought about it for a moment. "When we were in court, I was still feeling like I was with him," she said slowly, "but toward the end of the trial he started to mess with me. He was playing his same old games, but I was starting to break away. If he said to do something, I'd do it. But my heart wasn't in it anymore."

Her description of the trial suggested to us that, had the proceedings been conducted differently and the defendants been separated from one another, she might have broken free of Manson sooner.

"I really didn't know I was under his control," she said. "In the courtroom I was only starting to hesitate and feel stupid, but just being locked up in this place was not enough to free me."

Leslie looked back on that first trial with some bitterness. "I know I was on trial for something horrible," she acknowledged, but she seemed to resent the attitude of Bugliosi and others who displayed little interest in finding out what had happened to her mind.

"Bugliosi was always saying it was 'bad blood,' " she told us, "but he never asked us any questions. One second we were Charlie's robots; the next we were completely responsible for what we did. He never looked for answers. He only looked for the conviction."

With so many factors working against her, Leslie's real "coming to," as she called it, didn't begin until after the trial, when the clamor had subsided and she, along with other Family members, was awaiting her execution.

"When they left us on death row, we were in complete isolation," she recalled. "For almost three years, I was only in touch with my parents and family. At first, when I realized how much my family loved me, I felt guilty, terribly guilty, for having hurt my mother. But I hadn't even started thinking about the crime itself. I was still thinking about the revolution that would come."

We asked if during those years she ever felt herself awaken from her cult state of mind in what other former cult members had described to us as a sudden *"Aha!"* experience.

"Sometimes," she said, "I could feel myself on the verge of that kind of experience. But I always ran from those moments because, at the time, my mind really fought that more than anything."

It was during her years on death row, however, that Leslie did in fact snap out of her altered state, not in one overwhelming moment but, apparently, in a series of partial deprogrammings effected inadvertently by a prison psychiatrist and another condemned prisoner. Neither of them possessed any intimate knowledge of deprogramming. Both simply talked straight to Leslie, showing their genuine care and concern and, in the process, helping her to start thinking for herself.

"Slowly," said Leslie, "without realizing it, the prison psychiatrist got me to start questioning things in myself again. Another woman on death row helped me even more. I'd be talking to her, and she would say, 'That doesn't make any sense. Explain yourself.' And I knew I couldn't. I thought, *If I'm not making any sense, then maybe there's something wrong with what I'm saying.*"

Through these informal confrontations, Leslie actually pulled herself up by her own mental bootstraps, yet she recalled the real pain she experienced trying to free her mind in this manner. As we listened and watched, we were struck by the resemblance between Leslie's plight and that of many other cult members we had interviewed.

"When I'd be questioned and not have any answers," she said, "I'd go blank and become frustrated, like when a machine jams and just sits there making noise. In my head, nothing was functioning. More than anything, I was trying to understand, breaking down stiff little slogans that had been drilled into me every day for months."

Eventually, the breakthrough came, and the spark that set it off was California's abolishment of the death penalty. For Leslie, the hope of leaving prison alive spurred her on to active thought.

"When they abolished the death penalty, the director of corrections brought the three of us together and said it was up to us to prove we could handle it," she said. "For me, that made all the difference in the world, when I saw that they were going to give me the responsibility for my future."

With the specter of death row out of the picture for them, although it would later return to haunt others, the three Manson women were held in a special security unit constructed for them at the prison. It was during this time, isolated from the other prisoners, Leslie said, that she regained full control over her thought processes.

"In the long run I'm glad I spent so much time in isolation," she said, "because it gave me a chance to get to know myself again. I continued to receive letters from other women in the Family, but when it came time to write and talk to them, I realized that there was no relating at all. I was seeing them in their absurdity."

Like other newly deprogrammed individuals, Leslie had the most trouble confronting her fellow Family members, who were not making the same progress she was. Now back in Sybil Brand while her former sisters remained at Frontera, Leslie admitted to being proud of the progress she had made in that first decade after the Manson crimes.

"I don't mean to be bragging," she said, "but out of everyone, I'm probably the only one who has done well."

Since her re-emergence she had become an active participant in prison life, serving as editor of the prison newspaper and devoting much of her time to reading and writing in an effort to prepare herself for eventual release or parole.

"I hope that after I'm out for a while," she said, trying not to sound overconfident, "once I'm used to being out there again, I can do something, not as a big cause but just to bring to light some of the things that can happen to young people. That's one thing that never came out in the trial."

Hearing her speak, we tended to agree with Keith that Leslie's newfound stability appeared to be genuine. But was it really? Could it be, as a future jury or parole board might suspect, that she was simply pulling a clever con to win sympathy and approval? We weighed the evidence before us and, after our many interviews with other former cult members, felt confident that Leslie displayed the vital signs of full recovery. We noted her poised, natural appearance, her interest and attention as we spoke, her clarity of expression and understanding of her thoughts, feelings and experiences. As our interview ended and the guard came to escort her back to her cell, Leslie's departing words confirmed for us that she had not only regained control of her mind but that, despite her awful experience and role in a heinous crime, she was already embarked on a road that might lead to a new and meaningful life.

"My coming to was slow," she emphasized, "but I've made every step on my own and I'll never lose it. I have a complete drive to make it. I'm going to make sense out of it all, and I know I'm going to be heard."

In August 1977, a California Superior Court judge declared a mistrial in Leslie's second murder trial when the jury reported that it was hopelessly deadlocked after twenty-five days of deliberation. In her third trial, she was convicted again. Despite repeated efforts by her lawyers and loyal friends to win her parole, two decades after the Tate-LaBianca killings, Leslie Van Houten remained in prison, granted no more distinctions or dispensations by society than Atkins, Krenwinkel or Manson himself.

It took another seventeen years after our interview, and a string of eleven rejected parole requests, before the public heard from her in any meaningful way again. In 1994, on the twenty-fifth anniversary of the Manson killings, Leslie gave two national media interviews and relived her experience publicly for the first time since the trial. Calmly, and making no excuses, she described to new generations the controls she fell victim to which had led her, in turn, to victimize others. It was also reported that, during those years of her continuing confinement, she had completed her college degree and become a role model for other women in prison.

Patty Hearst. In the years between Leslie's first and second trials, the world and another American jury were confronted with what seemed to be an even more startling example of the sudden transformation of a young woman into a hardened criminal. On February 4, 1974, nineteen-year-old Patricia Campbell Hearst, granddaughter of legendary publisher William Randolph Hearst, was kidnapped at gunpoint from her apartment near the University of California at Berkeley and taken captive by a group of revolutionaries who identified themselves as members of the Symbionese Liberation Army. The SLA was a political cult, not a religious one, yet its leader, a charismatic figure named Donald DeFreeze who called himself Field Marshal Cinque, was regarded as a prophet by his followers and commanded total reverence and obedience.

The exact methods by which DeFreeze recruited and organized his small band of loyal followers were never established, yet DeFreeze's extensive criminal record and revolutionary goals bore surprising similarity to both the background and visions of Charles Manson. Many of his techniques—including intimidation, isolation, and the use of intimate sexual experiences for purposes of psychological control—showed other strange resemblances to Manson's. DeFreeze's motivation was also similar to Manson's: through a campaign of carefully targeted violent acts, he hoped to set off an uprising of the underprivileged. And like Manson's igniting string of ritual murders, DeFreeze's plot to kidnap Patty Hearst misfired from the start.

Patty's father, Randolph Hearst, in his earnest response to SLA ransom demands, hurried the distribution of several million dollars' worth of food to California's poor, setting off riotous outbreaks and a backlash of black resentment of the SLA. In those first weeks after the kidnapping, DeFreeze also failed to exploit Patty for the purpose of freeing several other SLA members imprisoned on earlier charges. Before long DeFreeze enacted an even more daring plan for capitalizing on his newly acquired asset, as he put the finishing touches on a scheme that may or may not have been his intention all along: that of making Patty Hearst a highly visible and seemingly willing member of the SLA.

His methods in this effort are now on the public record: the conversion was accomplished by means of classic brainwashing techniques—and much more. For the first two months of her captivity, Patty Hearst was kept blindfolded on the floor of a cramped closet in the SLA's headquarters, repeatedly abused physically and sexually by DeFreeze and other members of the group, further traumatized by constant threats of death if she did not cooperate with their instructions, and told that she had been abandoned by both her parents and society. In April 1974, Patty re-emerged from this onslaught as "Tania," brandishing a submachine gun during an SLA bank robbery in San Francisco. For more than a year she kept up a fugitive existence, after the lies she had accepted seemed to be confirmed when her six captors burned to death in a police raid on their Los Angeles hideout. Then, in September 1975, she was apprehended by the FBI.

The trial that followed, on federal charges of bank robbery, still stands two decades later as one of the more contestable proceedings in American legal history. In what many charged at the time to be an attempt to court the overwhelming consensus of public opinion against Patty and her family's wealth and social position, the U.S. Attorney who prosecuted the case called as his expert witness Dr. Joel Fort, described in the *New York Times* as a "maverick," neither a psychiatrist nor a psychologist, who had testified in over 260 criminal cases, including the original Manson trial. Fort, whose professional practices had raised numerous questions of propriety, argued that Patty was a "willing participant" in the bank robbery, that her personal history clearly established her as a "rebel looking for a cause," and that she was not raped by SLA members but surrendered willingly—if not happily.

The defense contended that Patty had been a "brutally victimized prisoner of war." But the three expert witnesses called by celebrated defense attorney F. Lee Bailey—among them brainwashing expert Robert Jay Lifton—repeatedly contradicted one another's testimony, arguing in favor of both conversion and coercion, and were so strongly opposed in their views that, as prosecutors told the jury, "they wash each other out." Lifton's analysis was thorough and well-grounded, comparing point by point the SLA's tactics to those of the Chinese thought reformers he studied in the fifties. But he and Bailey's other experts were unable to give the jury any insight into Patty's plight as something altogether new on the American social, political and psychological scenes. To add to the jury's bewilderment, attorneys for both sides engaged in endless rounds of courtroom bickering. Bailey's attempt to bring Fort's questionable medical background to the jury's attention was denied, while one assistant prosecutor succeeded in suggesting to jury members that Lifton had a vested interest in finding a clear-cut case of "domestic" brainwashing.

The result was that no one, neither the jury nor the public, ever got a comprehensive, and comprehendible, explanation of what happened to Patty Hearst. The significance of her ordeal in the SLA closet got lost, along with the demonstrated effects of the SLA's program of alternating brutality and sympathy toward Patty. The outcome of the trial was a verdict of guilty for Patty Hearst, similar convictions in a second trial on eleven related counts of kidnapping, armed robbery and assault, and a seven-year prison sentence.

What about Patty? From most accounts, following her capture she became a legal fiction herself, playing whatever role her lawyers or psychiatrists deemed most advantageous at the time. For seven months following her initial conviction she remained in jail pending appeal, and then was reported to have suffered a severe emotional breakdown. In the wake of that incident, Randolph Hearst posted the $1.5 million bail that freed his daughter, only for her to become a prisoner again, this time in her family's lavish Bay Area surroundings, guarded around the clock until her legal fate was resolved.

During that time, we attempted to contact Patty Hearst. While on the West Coast, we wrote to her father, exchanged telephone messages with his secretary and, finally, wrote to Patty herself. All our efforts proved futile. We did talk with several people who had spoken with Patty or the Hearsts, among them, Ted Patrick, who discussed with her parents the possibility of deprogramming Patty on her release from prison, but that plan was tabled when Patrick's own legal problems landed him in jail at the opposite end of the state.

From those conversations and the small amount of information that was made public concerning Patty's state of health and mind, it seemed clear to us that the destruction of her personality, so methodically carried out, had left her in a state that fit our picture of snapping at its most extreme. When we first considered her condition, more than a year after her trial and all the psychiatric care and treatment money could buy, Patty Hearst still seemed to be a troubled young woman, still wondering what had happened to her mind.

The most visible proof of her distress surfaced in Patty's own words. In a network television interview granted shortly after her release from jail, she spoke with surprising lucidity about some of her experiences in the SLA. When it came to her participation in the bank robbery, however, and the trauma of personality change she had undergone, she showed noticeable confusion.

"I remember so little," said Patty of her performance during the robbery. "I remember what happened inside the bank up to—well, up to where their man was shot, and then it just all goes blank and I don't remember getting outside, getting in the car, any of it."

She did remember the SLA's death threats if she did not cooperate, and her own feelings when she watched SLA members burn to death on television. It was then, she said, when she concluded that everything her captors had been telling her was true, that her parents had abandoned her and that the FBI was out to kill her along with the rest of the SLA—a common claim of cult leaders preparing their followers for armed confrontations with authorities, and one that, too often, has become a self-fulfilling prophecy.

Despite Patty's explanations, like her original jury and so many other Americans, her media interviewer still sought an answer to the question of why Patty did not call home during her desperate year on the run. Her reply further revealed her own profound confusion and the degree to which she continued to be misunderstood. It reminded us of the frustration Leslie Van Houten experienced in her struggle to come to grips with her own thoughts while in prison.

"Well, you know," Patty told her nationwide audience, "I've tried to explain about the not calling home, or going home, the best I can. And I know it's really hard to understand, because it's really hard for me now to try to think of what was really in my mi—you know, how I could have thought that way, because it's crazy. It doesn't make any sense at all, and it's something that I'm still working on myself, trying to understand how I could get so twisted around in my own head."

During that interview, three years after her kidnapping, Patty Hearst displayed all the characteristics of a cult casualty who had not been properly deprogrammed. She laughed uneasily and cried sporadically in her muddled attempt to make her case to the public. The impression she left, however, was that she was at best uncertain and at worst attempting to cover up her guilt. The one point Patty did not address in her interview, which from all reports her family was bent on pushing into the shadows, was what happened to her in that closet during the first two months of her captivity. In our view, it was that prolonged, comprehensive assault on her mind and body which annihilated the foundations of Patty Hearst's personality, making her every subsequent action problematical from any recognized psychiatric view and moot with respect to charges of criminal intent.

In his testimony, Dr. Martin Orne, an expert witness for the defense, stated that in his interviews with Patty before her trial, whenever he asked her about her time in the closet, "You would see an immediate collapse. A totally helpless person would appear at that time." Others who talked with Patty after her apprehension reported similar reactions whenever they brought up the subject.

Another picture, drawn by *New York Times* reporter Lacey Fosburgh, provided further insight into the lasting effects of the SLA's assault on Patty Hearst's mind. From her own observations and those of others close to Patty at the time, Fosburgh determined that Patty was in an unstable and paradoxical condition, one that suggested to us the post-cult floating state—a warp of conflicting thoughts and emotions. Friends described Patty as a "chameleon" capable of assuming a wide variety of personalities, from dutiful daughter to flirting coquette to angry, bitter, spoiled child. A year and a half after her life in the SLA ended, Patty reportedly was still in a state of physical, mental and emotional upheaval: menstruating nonstop for months at a time, her moods alternately anxious, giddy or withdrawn, and manifesting other signs of distress characteristic of someone who has suffered a severe traumatic experience. At the time, however, there was no such diagnosis as Post-Traumatic Stress Disorder, and we were only beginning to formulate our concept of information disease.

Fosburgh's description of Patty's appearance completed our sense of this misjudged young woman. She pictured Patty as perpetually tentative, her voice a dull monotone, still tending to lapse into long and frequent periods of silence. "Her eyes are as large as plates," wrote Fosburgh, "and they are as sad as the history of the world."

Through the final rounds of her legal battles, and for all that she was known to have been through, many in the legal community and the public continued to view her as a criminal. Despite her sworn contention that she was kidnapped, blindfolded, locked in a closet, assaulted, raped, threatened with death, and cruelly remolded in her captors' image, most Americans seemed to agree with the man in the street whose opinion was printed shortly after the jury delivered its initial guilty verdict, that "brainwashing can only be done by experts, not by kooks."

As we considered those harsh judgments, both official and unofficial, in the light of everything we had discovered about snapping, it struck us both how desperately most people still wanted to believe that the human mind is invincible, and that their personalities, still widely considered to be shaped once and for all in childhood, were not subject to any form of covert control or manipulation. For us, that pervasive denial only underscored our larger concern, shared by the many learned minds we had interviewed, that the compounding complexities of modern life had created an urgent need for new ways of looking at these extraordinary new human phenomena emerging in the day-to-day world, and for new ways to understand and help the casualties mounting on all sides.

Patty Hearst served nearly two years in prison before President Jimmy Carter commuted her sentence in 1979. After her release, she married her former bodyguard and moved to the opposite end of the country, settling into a quiet life in suburban Connecticut and eventually giving birth to two daughters of her own. Ten more years passed, but the mood of the country never softened. In January 1989, outgoing President Ronald Reagan, who had urged executive clemency for her when he was governor of California, denied her request for a presidential pardon for her actions in the events she was a part of so many years ago.

Son of Sam. Soon after we returned to New York from our first research tour on the West Coast, another shocking series of crimes stole the headlines. On August 10, 1977, New York City police arrested twenty-four-year-old David Berkowitz in connection with a year-long killing spree in the New York area which left six persons dead and seven wounded. The assailant wielded a .44-caliber handgun and identified himself as the "Son of Sam."

This awkward, chubby postal worker bore no resemblance to the bloodlusting, psychopathic figure conjured up by the media prior to the arrest. Neighbors and co-workers described Berkowitz as "quiet," "subdued" and "a loner." No one could imagine what would prompt this meek, clean-shaven, well-fed young man—if, in fact, he was the murderer—to prowl the lovers' lanes around New York seeking out young couples parked in cars, shoot them in the head at close range and then flee.

Upon his capture, after what was hailed as the longest and most extensive manhunt in New York City's history, Berkowitz was said to have shown "no remorse." Throughout his arrest and interrogation, he remained placid and uninvolved, a bemused smile on his face at all times. People who saw the suspect remarked, "That couldn't be him. No way. He doesn't look mean enough. He looks so soft." A police investigator who talked with Berkowitz said that he couldn't even feel anger toward the man.

The story grew stranger. Under questioning, Berkowitz talked easily about his neighbor, Sam Carr, the real "Sam" whose barking dog reportedly tormented Berkowitz and, as he later declared, instructed him to begin his campaign of terror. Throughout that year, in a series of letters to local newsmen, Berkowitz had spoken of himself as "Sam's creation," in cryptic references to the owner of the howling black Labrador retriever which Berkowitz once wounded in the leg with his famous .44 handgun, and which later became the focus of his hallucinations and delusions.

The more facts that emerged, the more clouded the picture became. Berkowitz in custody did not conform to anyone's image of a psychopath or mass murderer. In their initial examinations, court-appointed psychiatrists beat the traditional diagnostic bushes in their efforts to determine whether Berkowitz was certifiably schizophrenic or psychotic in a way that might be linked to some disruption of normal neurological activity. After a battery of medical tests, including a brain scan, doctors ruled out the possibility that Berkowitz had any known neurochemical imbalance, tumor or other form of physical brain damage recognized at the time. Further psychiatric examinations and psychological tests also failed to establish the form of functional disorder from which some observers believed him to be suffering.

As we followed the unfolding mystery of David Berkowitz, noting the doctors' exasperated findings that the machinery of his brain appeared to be thoroughly intact, we began to suspect that Berkowitz's condition might be better understood from our perspective as a severe form of information disease. Studying all the available testimony and waiting each day for the latest reports, we were convinced within weeks of his capture that Berkowitz was the first clear-cut case of snapping in its most destructive form that we had uncovered outside the context of the new cults and therapies. As more on his background came to light from published interviews with former friends and letters written by Berkowitz himself, we formed our own provisional understanding of how he had reached his state of delusion and emotional detachment. Berkowitz had snapped, we concluded, not from any known cult ritual or therapeutic technique but from some other, as yet obscure, sequence of stressful experiences in his recent past.

We learned later that those experiences in fact had direct connections both to the backwaters of American born-again Christianity and to its dark, devil-worshipping counterforce, a veiled network of teen "dabblers," serious Satanists and death-dealing occult practitioners.

Unlike Charles Manson or Donald DeFreeze, David Berkowitz was not the typical product of a broken home, misspent youth or mile-long criminal record. Although adopted, he was raised by responsible, loving parents in a middle-class Bronx family. He grew up in the youth culture and strife-torn social environment of the late sixties and early seventies. However, it was not in a cult or counterculture but in the United States Army that Berkowitz began the stepwise shift of personality. In the army, through the course of his three-year enlistment, Berkowitz set off on a winding road of religion, occult practices and frequent drug use that left him, in the words of one psychiatrist who examined him, "emotionally dead"—a macabre but precise description of our numbed and delusional strains of information disease.

Until he joined the army, Berkowitz had led a relatively normal, if somewhat disaffected youth. Although chided in school for being a "fat little Jewish boy," he had many close friends, both male and female. In 1971 at the age of eighteen, he found himself with a high school degree, little money and few desirable alternatives for the future. So during that time of political protest and social upheaval, Berkowitz, by all accounts a straight, conservative, retiring youth, enlisted in the army and was shipped off to basic training.

Like any rigidly structured organization with a restricted philosophy, clear-cut objectives, and its own alien, harsh environment, the U.S. armed forces long have been known to produce dramatic changes in personality. In World War II, back when the word "War!" commanded unwavering national support, every branch of service turned out its instant warriors and "90-Day Wonders." When their tours of duty ended, most soldiers had ample sources of help for confronting the emotional difficulties that often accompanied the mustering-out process. Specific service programs focused on reintegrating soldiers with society. The GI Bill offered generous benefits for higher education; and a grateful public heaped on its homecoming soldiers the added rewards of a hero's welcome. Only in the seventies, amid the quickening pace of American life and the bitter controversy that surrounded the latter years of the

Vietnam war, did American troops in large numbers begin to face personal battles more intense than their military conflicts. And only afterwards did many learn that making the transition back into civilian life could be a lonely, painful and frighteningly difficult ordeal.

In many ways, David Berkowitz seemed to us to be among the first soldiers of his generation to snap under those converging pressures, even though he never saw combat or Vietnam. In basic training, Berkowitz performed admirably and he was shipped out to South Korea, where, in a clerk-typist position with official responsibilities, he displayed fast thinking, a good appearance and natural ability. However, few Americans who had not been there could appreciate the hidden hazards of the limbo state American troops encountered in Korea for decades after a cease-fire halted that undeclared war. In that environment lurked psychological dangers comparable to those of combat itself.

During his years in that remote culture, Berkowitz was pummeled by alien ideas and experiences, tossed back and forth in a sealed environment until the unique configuration of strengths and vulnerabilities that comprised his personality was shaken apart. In a series of handwritten letters to a former girlfriend sent from various army posts in Korea, Berkowitz described how easy it was to "get hooked" on the LSD and morphine that were easily available to bored American soldiers in every theater of action.

In that macho world of enduring army traditions, Berkowitz, until then a gentle young man and a vocal pacifist, was court-martialed over a confrontation in a chow line with a superior officer who demanded to know why he wasn't wearing a gun.

"I said I didn't bring it to the field and I refuse to bring it to the field," Berkowitz wrote at the time. "Well all hell broke out after that. They just can't tell me when to carry a gun. I explained it to them but it didn't do much good."

From the concern expressed frequently in his letters, it seemed that the gun incident set off a crisis of both conscience and consciousness in Berkowitz. After that, he became heavily involved in the drug scene within the military and immersed himself in the peace, love and rock music culture that, at the time, was as popular among American soldiers in Southeast Asia as it was among young people in the United States. Like Charles Manson and millions more of his generation, David Berkowitz had his rock interests and satanic influences, and it was speculated that in a suggestible psychedelic state he read apocalyptic meaning into the lyrics of an album by the popular "heavy metal" band Black Sabbath.

His army buddies were the first to detect Berkowitz's transformation. "There seemed to be a personality change," a soldier who knew Berkowitz in Korea reported. "He tried talking to me about it. He used to say, 'If it makes you feel good, do what you want to do. Don't ask me to accept you. Do what makes you feel good.'" His letters changed, too. He began writing about lurking colors, dark red and purple hues, and "things" coming at him from mists. In phrases familiar to us, he described the same feelings of dissociation and detachment that characterized many victims of snapping and information disease.

"When I look in the mirror all I see is one green soldier staring at me," he wrote his girl friend. "I feel like a robot being told when and where I can do things."

However, those sentiments and others expressed in Berkowitz's letters suggested to us that, as with Leslie Van Houten, drug use was at most only an indirect cause of his later violent acts, just one factor among many new experiences and building inner stresses that made him vulnerable to a wide range of distorted ideas and delusions, both paranoid and messianic. In fact, Berkowitz himself declared that drugs provided him, not with violent urges, but with a rare source of release from the quiet tortures of military life in Korea. Either way, there is little doubt that drugs contributed to the free-for-all of reality and fantasy taking shape in Berkowitz's mind. His letters of that time, rampant with misspellings and bad grammar, demonstrate the extent of his confusion.

"I must truly admitt [sic] to myself that unless I don't manage somehow to find a way to temporarily escape this lousy life, I will become really insane. So it doesn't hurt to escape [on drugs] once and awhile or often, to straighten out my distorted messed up mind.... Why dope you ask.' Because it is to damn boring here. Where all a bunch of humanoid robots, so we feel."

After all that transpired during his two years in Korea, like many victims of snapping, Berkowitz was fully aware that he had undergone a drastic change of personality. The change frightened him, as did the prospect of returning to his former life in the United States. He expressed those fears in another letter to his girl friend.

"I hope they let me go home in July. You know something, I'm really scared to go. I think the freedom will get to me. . . . Do you know something Iris. I have really changed. To much I think. I don't understand what its all about. . . ."

Berkowitz's letters from Korea recorded his protracted snapping experience, but that was only the beginning of what soon grew into an even more tortuous and bizarre inner odyssey. When he returned to the U.S., Berkowitz was as unstable as a former prisoner of war and as desperate to find an identity as someone who had quit a cult without being deprogrammed. After Korea, Berkowitz was assigned to another clerical position with a combat brigade stationed at Fort Knox, Kentucky, where he spent a year trying to accustom himself to his new personality and to a new and equally foreign domestic environment. There, like many of his fellow soldiers who may have been no more sure of their identities than Berkowitz, he settled on a highly popular but, for him, highly unlikely new course of action: he converted to evangelical Christianity.

"I just asked him to go to church with me one day," said Jim Almond, the fellow soldier who introduced Berkowitz to that old-time religion. "He said, 'I'm a Jew.'" Almond told a reporter, "and I told him I didn't care what he was, did he want to go to church?" Berkowitz accepted Christ on his first visit to the Beth Haven Baptist Church. "Well, we went and he really enjoyed it," said Almond. "He went forward at the invitation. . . And after the service, he came up to me grinning and laughing and saying, 'Man, I'm saved.' Then we came back that same day for the evening service and he went forward again at the invitation. He told me afterward that he just wanted to make sure it took."

For a while, his renewal appeared to be successful. Berkowitz spent the next year fervently attending three church services a week and reading Bible stories to little children. Fellow church members described him as "a really fantastic guy with a great personality" and "a great soul-winner" who brought a number of GIs from the base into the born-again fold. However, after a year of Christian life, Almond noted, Berkowitz began "backsliding"—a term used as frequently among born-again Christians as among cult deprogrammers. Berkowitz's parents were greatly dismayed when they found out that he had become a Christian. During this time, we can imagine, Berkowitz anticipating his discharge began to seek a new anchor for his personality that would serve him when he returned to his former life in New York.

But he never found it. It seemed as though Berkowitz returned to New York in 1974 in that peculiar twilight zone of floating, poised for the catastrophe that lay ahead. Upon his return, he drifted through a series of low-level jobs and assumed a nondescript life in the New York suburb of Yonkers. The first press reports described the nagging sound of a neighbor's barking dog as the last small push that sent him over the edge. Having run the gamut of alternatives, from drugs to Jesus, it seemed, he slipped fully into the fantasy world with which his mind had long before become acquainted. He began hearing voices, receiving messages from God and, reportedly, commands from a black Labrador retriever who ordered him to launch a reign of terror on New York as a warning to the world from the demons he perceived.

Later reports, and a controversial 1993 television interview filmed with Berkowitz in prison, traced his spiraling descent into a murderous satanic cult. Breaking his silence after sixteen years, Berkowitz then claimed he had indeed been a member of a Yonkers coven that practiced demonic chanting, animal sacrifice and ritual murder. He insisted that, although he was present at each shooting scene, he personally killed only three of the six victims, and that at least three other sect members, including one woman, committed the other Son of Sam murders. He described his initiation into the satanic sect in terms that paralleled countless conversions and cult inductions we had documented: "I was chanting the name of Lucifer over and over. And I was calling out to him, 'Son of the morning and prince, my Lord, come into me right now, take control, I give myself into your hands.' People were around me chanting very low, in unison....I felt like I was being emptied of my personality and that something else, somehow, was coming in."

On camera, Berkowitz presented an altogether different visage from his earlier trance-like demeanor that a police detective once likened to "talking to a zucchini." He apologized tearfully to his victims' families and joyously introduced the prison evangelist who, he claimed, had brought him fully to Jesus in the late eighties after his mere flirtation years earlier. It was this preacher, Berkowitz said, who had urged a full confession of his and his co-conspirators' killing spree, although Berkowitz refused to name some names, he claimed, out of continuing fears for his own life and the safety of his family members.

New York police adamantly rejected Berkowitz's jailhouse repentance and stuck to their winning case that Berkowitz had acted alone. Serious questions remained about the scope and reach of Berkowitz's devil-worshipping sect, whether it was part of a nationwide network of avenging Satanists or a local case of young devil dabblers going beyond all documented extremes. But, to our ears, Berkowitz's new testimony, in its rich detail and coherence, fit the patterns of cult control and their proven potential for death and destruction.

Whether he acted alone or in concert with satanic cultists, it seemed to us, David Berkowitz was only one in a long line of Sons of Sam still on the loose and in the making, as Berkowitz himself once tried to explain. In America today, there are growing numbers of frustrated, confused, disconnected individuals, young and old, who have searched in vain through fields of drugs, religion, pop therapy, Satanism and a mushrooming undergrowth of ideological sects preaching violence and vengeful criminal acts. Many are searching for meaning and direction for their lives, looking for themselves and some route to other people. Others are angry at the government, the military, corporations or the media. Still others are feeling powerless and betrayed by society generally.

Since the sixties, when this latest wave of social change and reaction began, America's mental health professions have demonstrated how little they understand about the tragic transformations of Leslie Van Houten, Patty Hearst, David Berkowitz and others who have trudged in their footsteps. America's justice system, too, has shown its inability to judge and rehabilitate such people in accordance with the conventional codes of criminal law and modern penal systems. No social purpose is served by subjecting them to public pillorying and tabloid media morality plays. No greater good is derived from merely imprisoning them for life or sentencing them to death.

In our view, Leslie Van Houten, Patty Hearst, David Berkowitz and those like them are not "common criminals," nor can they be dismissed as "human monsters, human mutations." If anything, their tragedies underscore the urgent need to acknowledge that snapping is something new and threatening to America and every civilized society. Until we in America take steps to find out what has really happened to these individuals, and to those who have come after in so many celebrated and unsung cases, our society will remain vulnerable to the blows of those who suffer similar fates.

For these criminals are victims, too, victims of something no one in this new era fully understands yet. And we have a lot to learn from them.

15 Jonestown: End of Innocence

> *They lying long shall not die windily;*
> *Twisting on racks when sinews give way,*
> *Strapped to a wheel, yet they shall not break;*
> *Faith in their hands shall snap in two,*
> *And the unicorn evils run them through;*
> *Split all ends up they shan't crack;*
> *And death shall have no dominion.*
>
> —*Dylan Thomas*
> *"And Death Shall Have No Dominion"*

IN THE FALL of 1978, the phenomenon of "the cults," still considered by many to be a fad of little or no social consequence, exploded before the public eye with a fury that shocked America and the world. The epic tragedy of Jonestown transformed the curious cult phenomenon into what many journalists soon recognized as "the story of the decade." Having struggled with the complexities of that story throughout the seventies, we had long been convinced of its significance, but the events that took place in the remote South American jungle unveiled new pieces of the puzzle, sharp fragments of a picture we perceived to be not just one of the decade that had nearly passed but of the nearing future as well.

The facts quickly became legend: On November 18, 1978, a U.S. Congressman and three journalists were shot and killed while on a fact-finding mission to investigate charges that American citizens were being held against their will, beaten, and subjected to other physical and emotional abuses at the commune of an American religious sect, the Peoples Temple, in Jonestown, Guyana. The victims, among them Rep. Leo J. Ryan of California, NBC News correspondent Don Harris, NBC cameraman Bob Brown and *San Francisco Examiner* photographer Greg Robinson, had uncovered evidence confirming many of the charges made by a group of concerned relatives and had agreed to take with them more than a dozen temple members who had requested safe passage from the isolated jungle compound back to the United States. At the grassy airstrip in nearby Port Kaituma, as Ryan's party was boarding two chartered planes, a red tractor and trailer from the Peoples Temple pulled up to the runway. Three or four men jumped off and opened fire on the group. As the wounded fell to the ground, the attackers strode forward and shot them in the head at point-blank range.

At the same time in Jonestown, Peoples Temple founder and leader Rev. Jim Jones signaled his followers to enact the final scene in what turned out to be a well-rehearsed tragedy. Jones' lieutenants gathered at the commune's main pavilion, their automatic rifles ready. Then Jones called together the population of Jonestown. He informed them that the congressman and the journalists were dead and, in the familiar refrain, that Guyanese defense forces were on their way to Jonestown to torture and kill the commune residents. "It is time to die with dignity," said Jones, reiterating for the last time his repeated vow that he would lead his followers in a "mass suicide for the glory of socialism." Next, at Jones' command, the temple doctor and his medical team brought forth a battered washtub of strawberry Flavour-aide laced with heavy doses of cyanide, tranquilizers and painkillers. Jones told the assembly that "the time has come to meet in another place." "Bring the babies first," he ordered, and his nurses shot the poison down their throats with syringes. Then the rest came forward, including whole families, each member drinking a cupful of poison and being led away by temple guards and told to lie face down with others in rows. Within minutes, people began to gasp for air, blood flowing from their mouths and noses before the final convulsions set in. According to one witness who managed to escape, the entire ritual lasted almost five hours. All the while, they said, Jim Jones sat on his raised chair in the pavilion repeating, "I tried. I tried. I tried." Then, "Mother. Mother. Mother. Mother." When it was over, Jones lay toppled on the podium with a bullet in his head. And 912 people were dead.

The massacre and mass suicide in Guyana left the entire world stunned and groping for answers. Who was Rev. Jim Jones? What manner of religious sect was the Peoples Temple? What was the chain of events that led to what the *New York Times* termed "one of the most shocking and extensive losses of U.S. lives outside of wartime"? Even before the final body count was completed, the real story of what happened in Jonestown began to emerge.

As it turned out, Peoples Temple was not a temple at all, but a scheme devised by Jim Jones to create a socialist utopian community in the guise of fundamentalist Christianity. Although he was an avid churchgoer from an early age, by the time he reached adolescence James Warren Jones no longer believed in religion. At eighteen, Mao Zedong was his hero, yet he continued to espouse his Christian faith—believing religion to be the ideal tool with which to build a Marxist social group in the United States. In 1956, he formed the first Peoples Temple in Indianapolis, and in 1965, fearing racial bigotry and anti-Communist persecution, Jones and one hundred of his most devout followers moved to Redwood Valley, California.

Jones' temple flourished in California, attracting thousands and establishing centers in San Francisco and Los Angeles. But it soon became apparent that life inside the Peoples Temple fell far short of the utopia Jones depicted. Jones began making stringent demands on his followers, commanding them to make a total commitment to the sect, instructing them to break off relationships with family members outside, and urging them to donate all their money and possessions and sign over their homes and real estate to the temple treasury. Reports of beatings, violence, bizarre sexual practices, criminal activities, and death threats to former members and potential defectors led to a series of exposés in California newspapers and magazines. In August 1977, Jones quickly removed his flock to Guyana, where he had leased 27,000 acres of land from the Guyanese government for the establishment of an "agricultural mission."

At the jungle site, its climate almost unbearably hot and steamy and its living conditions primitive, Jones managed to cut off the entire populace from the outside world. A few rare visitors and defectors brought back information on worsening deprivations and physical abuses inflicted on temple members, along with reports of Jones' own progressive mental deterioration. There were also rumors that millions of dollars were being cached in secret temple bank accounts in Switzerland and Panama, and that Jones was planning a mass migration to Cuba or the Soviet Union. Those reports and the desperate pleas of a newly established Concerned Relatives Committee prompted Congressman Ryan's mission. When Ryan's authority to conduct such an investigation was challenged by sect lawyers, and information was received that any intruders might be met by heavily armed defenders, Ryan permitted television and newspaper journalists to accompany him, convinced that full media coverage would be his best protection. The journalists, on the other hand, felt that the presence of a U.S. Congressman was theirs.

These sad details surfaced in the first media inquiries. Additional information emerged in later criminal investigations and government inquests into the events that transpired. Names of individuals who committed specific acts, exact balances of the temple's foreign bank accounts, and a fuller picture of Jones' political aims added new dimensions to a tragedy already rich in grotesque subplots. However, from our vantage point, the key factor in the equation was never adequately explored: the state of mind of Jim Jones and his followers at the time of the debacle in Guyana. In its aftermath, the world's print media and airwaves overflowed with speculation, but as the public thirst for information waned, serious questions remained unaddressed that, we felt, merited further inquiry out of respect for the dead and responsibility to the living. Was Jim Jones from the beginning a sadistic, calculating megalomaniac, or did he begin with a sincere dream of an interracial socialist utopia that went awry? What factors led to his final blaze of infamy, and what manipulations did he employ that led nine hundred people to take their lives at his command? Indeed, in view of the particulars of life in Jonestown—especially the presence of arms and many reports of beatings and other acts of coercion—could what finally happened truly be called suicide, or was it more properly to be labeled mass murder?

We undertook our own inquiry into life and death in the Peoples Temple. For two months we researched Jim Jones and his organization and interviewed individuals with personal experience in the group. We spoke to former members of the sect, to people who lost family members in Guyana, to representatives of the Concerned Relatives Committee who had tried to bring the threat of mass violence to public and government attention, and to staff members of the Human Freedom Center, the Berkeley, California halfway house established by former temple members to help others make the difficult transition back into the larger society. Most people we interviewed requested anonymity, but two former members of Jones' executive Planning Commission, Jeannie Mills and Grace Stoen, permitted us to use their names and quote liberally from our conversations. Like ours, their concern at the time was that the tragedy of Peoples Temple be given a full public airing, so the lessons that might be derived from it could be applied responsibly to any similar cult threat that might arise in the future.

Our findings made deep impressions on both of us. From the outset, we were struck by Jones' crude, almost primitive manner of manipulation. Repeatedly we had to ask ourselves if his method even warranted the label of mind control. Certainly, Jones achieved that alteration of belief and behavior among his followers described classically as "brainwashing." And we could see that, by his strong-arm intimidation tactics, to a certain extent he even gained control over his followers' minds. But we were hard-pressed to find among the sect's few survivors the kind of bedrock alterations of personality we termed *information disease*. For unlike other cult methods we had studied, Jones had no specific ritual or communication technique that appeared, over time, to alter or impair the mind's underlying information-processing pathways.

In fact, Jones' method seemed to tamper only superficially with the deeper structures of mind and personality we were exploring. Jones used many elements of physical, mental and emotional control—isolation, deception, indoctrination, exhaustion, poor diet and an instilled fear of the outside world—and together these techniques managed to suppress, if not overwhelm, his followers' freedom of thought. But the very fact that Jones resorted to blatant physical coercion, frequent beatings, punishments, sexual abuse and, eventually, the forced use of psychoactive drugs on temple rebels and dissidents suggested the profound ineffectiveness, and the ultimate failure, of Jones' attempt to gain mastery over the minds of his followers.

A Radical Departure. As we delved deeper, we found sharp points of departure from other religious cults in the radically different nature of the Peoples Temple experience. Where most religious cults attract converts with the promise of life-changing spiritual experiences— moments of rebirth, revelation, enlightenment, ecstasy or bliss—from the beginning, Jim Jones' approach was, for most temple members, more social and political than spiritual. It could even be argued, ostensibly, that the main attraction of the Peoples Temple was a legitimate social objective: the establishment of an experimental interracial community based on principles of shared labor and equitable distribution of wealth. This often-expressed goal was down-to-earth and genuinely attractive to the underprivileged blacks who comprised the great majority of temple members. It also had great appeal to those white fundamentalist Christians who were drawn to Jones' plan from the first days of his ministry in the Midwest, and to the middle- and upper-middle-class white liberals and intellectuals who, in the heyday of sixties' political activism in California, saw Jones as an effective organizer and dynamic agent of social change.

But where Jones' initial social intentions may have had admirable aspects, his methods were questionable from the outset. From his earliest preaching days, he proved to be an expert manipulator, combining the wealth of knowledge he had gleaned on the Holy Roller circuit with the force of his own charisma to tailor-make a personal pitch to every potential convert. When courting black recruits, he made moving appeals to their deep desire for a better life, both materially and spiritually. He spoke of their longing for racial harmony and sympathized with their historical plight dating back to the roots of slavery in America.

"You know, black people have suffered all down through history," a black woman who belonged to the temple for five years told us, "and he used to tell us about the slave ships and the suffering. The man laid it on heavy, I'm not lying. He knew how to talk to you. He knew how to make you feel good."

Jones' overtures to blacks were not without their spiritual elements, at least in the initial stages. He was well-acquainted with the central role of religion in their lives, and in his weekly religious services he employed techniques that wooed their belief in his supernatural and divine powers. His miraculous healings and psychic "readings" helped to build his illustrious reputation among blacks in California. A woman who lost five relatives in Jonestown told us how she and her family were recruited into the temple:

"I went to the beauty shop and my operator told me about this Jim Jones, that he could heal people. That's the way he drew his crowds, telling people that he healed cancer. So my momma and I decided to go and check it out, just for kicks, one Sunday morning. The place was packed. They had singing and dancing and people meeting other people for two or three hours before Jim Jones came out. Finally, he appeared to preach or whatever he called it. He picked out one person and told him that he had cancer and said that he was going to heal him. Then a nurse ran back to this person with a cup and told him to spit the cancer in the cup, and the person started gagging and spat this cancer into the cup—it was supposed to have been cancer, but I heard it was rotten chicken liver. They put it on a piece of gauze and passed it all through the church and it smelled up the whole place. Everybody jumped up and down and clapped their hands and shouted and carried on. I was hard to convince, but of course my momma believed it. She joined the temple, then she got my sister to go. Then she joined and convinced her daughter to join. Then her daughter brought in her husband and several of their friends."

Jones' trick of extracting "tumorous masses" in his healings was a classic ploy of faith healers, voodoo priests and "psychic surgeons" around the world. His famed psychic "readings" were carried out with similar flourish and showmanship. "He used to 'call people out,' " another ex-member told us, "and when he called out a person's name that person would stand up and the usher would go up to him with a mike. Jim would ask him, 'Have you ever seen me before?' And he'd say no. 'Have I ever been in your house before?' No. 'Well, you live in such and such a place, your phone number is such and such, and in your living room you've got this, that and the other, and on your sofa you've got such and such a pillow . . . Now do you remember me ever being in your house?' "

Grace Stoen, one of Jones' closest aides for many years before she quit the temple in 1976, explained Jones' elaborate system for gathering information that he used in these "readings."

"It wasn't until I left the church that I found out how he did it," Stoen told us. "He had a whole staff of people, about six women, and when you entered the church you had to give them your name, address and phone number. Then, once the services began, before Jim came out the staff would go and call up the numbers and say, 'Hi, we're doing a survey and we would like to ask you some questions.' That's how they got the information, then he had it all handy when he called people out during the service."

Grace Stoen recalled the breadth of Jones' preaching expertise. "He was good-looking and he had charisma," she said. "He would rush onto the stage and everyone would clap. Then in the course of the meeting he would do a little religious stuff for the religious people, a little political stuff for the political people, for the real intellectuals he would become intellectual—at my first meeting, instead of reading the gospel he read the San Francisco newspaper—and for the common people without much education, he would make a very emotional appeal. Jim Jones had the ability to speak to a thousand people and 999 would get something out of it."

At the Peoples Temple commune in Redwood Valley, Jones' fervid preaching and other spiritual pyrotechnics took a back seat to his interracial agricultural community. It was there, at the Ukiah commune in the late sixties and early seventies, that Jones had little trouble converting many of the middle-class members who were to become his top temple executives.

"My husband had always been into social work and working with the underprivileged, and we had five kids of our own who we were concerned about," said Jeannie Mills who, with her husband, Al, served on the Peoples Temple Planning Commission. "So we went up to Redwood Valley to see this man who, we had been told, was helping young people get off drugs. We found a group of caring, loving, friendly, warm people who immediately accepted us just exactly as we were. These people didn't care what I had. They were more concerned with who I was. My children had instant acceptance. The other kids came over to them and were surprisingly friendly. My kids loved it and my husband

and I were really impressed with the social structure of the group, so we joined to be a part of a cause that was doing good."

Once they joined the temple, most of the people we interviewed told us, their first two or three months of communal life were rich with emotional rewards and inspiration. By the mid-seventies, however, members began to notice gradual changes in temple life and the conduct of temple affairs. In the first of many moves to isolate temple members and consolidate his control, Jones began to separate sect members from their families.

Jeannie Mills explained to us how Jones dissolved family bonds. "He did it slowly. He would say, 'You should always spend Thanksgiving and Christmas with me.' Eventually we had to clear any visits to our relatives. Soon he started saying, 'Your relatives don't care for you. We're the only ones who care for you.' Then he would say, 'If you have to go see them, just ask them for money'—but that would cause them to cut *you* off! Eventually, he denounced the whole world outside Peoples Temple as unenlightened and uninformed. 'The only real caring people are in the group,' he said. 'If you really cared about society, you'd be in Peoples Temple.'"

In the same way, Jones' financial requests of his members increased in stages. Until the early seventies, the temple had a policy of not exacting forced offerings from its members. Then, citing the practices of other churches, Jones inaugurated a tithing policy of 10 percent, which soon grew to 25 percent of each member's income. Finally, Jones ordered members to turn over everything they owned as a measure of loyalty and devotion to the temple. Also during this time, individual work loads were increased to the point of exhaustion. Great physical stress was placed on each member in the name of greater service to the church and its urgent mission. Members were sent on frequent church campaigns throughout the state and across the country and regularly subjected to marathon sermons that kept up for six hours or more. The hard work, arduous travel and Jones' lengthening indoctrination sessions monopolized members' energy and attention, leaving them little opportunity to stray or even doubt. As temple life became more demanding, each member's capacity to choose or reject it became more clouded.

"Nothing was ever done drastically," recalled Grace Stoen, "that's how Jim Jones got away with so much. You slowly gave up things and slowly had to put up with more, but it was always done very gradually. It was amazing, because you would sit up sometimes and say, *Wow, I really have given up a lot. I really am putting up with a lot.* But he did it so slowly that you figured, *I've made it this far, what the hell is the difference?"*

A revealing example of Jones' gradual manipulation could be seen in his attitude toward the Bible. From the beginning, in typical cult style, he relied on subtle scriptural distortions to soften and remold his converts' beliefs. Jeannie Mills recalled how this technique made her a firm believer in Jones.

"For the first four months we heard the same sermon about errors in the Bible," she said. "He cited Matthew 1:16 and Luke 3:23, which gave two different genealogies of Jesus. Then he handed out this whole long list of errors, and I went home and checked them out and it was just incredible. God wasn't the sweet, loving God I had always thought him to be. Here I saw he was murdering and commanding people to murder and to take young women for handmaidens and do other atrocious things. I was really disillusioned. When he destroyed my Bible, it was as if he had just pulled the rug out from under me. There I was with everything I had believed for thirty years gone. So I figured, *Yeah, he must be right.* And I saw that he was doing all these very humanitarian, loving things, and I thought, *Well, by their fruits ye shall know them.*"

In 1976, as Jones' attacks on the Bible grew more vicious, he prompted one woman to quit the temple. "I left when he denied God," she said. "At first he preached Christ just like anybody else would, but then he cursed God and called Mary a whore and he threw the Bible across the church. He said he was going to destroy the Bible, that it was nothing but a paper idol. Until then I had really believed in him. I thought he was a prophet come from God."

While his temple was expanding rapidly, accumulating wealth, membership and political power, Jones gorged on his own positive feedback, and his declarations and behavior grew more extreme. Like endtimes prophets historically and the budding survivalists of the late seventies, he began preaching about imminent earthquakes, nuclear holocausts and—in echoes of Manson's "Helter-Skelter" scheme, Commander Cinque's creed, and the visions of so many religious and political extremists—of a coming race war between blacks and whites.

During that period, Jones established a "relationship committee" to preside over his methodical splitting up of marriages and families and, while he declared sex evil, he solicited temple members to have sex with him as a sign of their loyalty. He carried on impulsive affairs with female members of his inner circle and pursued illicit relationships with other members, both men and women, and with people outside the sect as well. Yet, despite his own sexual profligacy, at one point Jones directed temple members to swear off all sexual relations, even with their own spouses.

According to Jeannie Mills, Jones' call for abstention was based on ideological, not spiritual grounds.

"He considered sex to be counterrevolutionary," she told us. "He justified it by saying that when Mao Zedong went on his Long March all of his soldiers gave up sex because you just can't have a revolution when your heads are filled with sexual desires. He said, 'We're in the middle of a revolution, and you should all be willing to put aside sex until we're able to live in our beautiful utopia.' "

Jones' prohibition against sex was heeded by much of the sect's membership, but like so many arbitrary rules, it also spurred frequent transgressions and other disobedient acts. Jones was deeply disturbed by any violation of his edicts, however minor. In the early years, in Redwood Valley, discipline was mild and evenly meted out. Mischievous children were spanked, goldbricking members were chastised verbally. But in the mid-seventies, Jones' punishments became less evenhanded and progressively more severe to the point of brutality. A young child who had stolen a cookie or two teenagers caught holding hands were beaten repeatedly with a heavy wooden paddle known as the "Board of Education." Older members deemed slack in their duties were compelled to fight in "boxing matches," sometimes for several hours, with up to three or four bigger, stronger opponents. Others, particularly the children, were subjected to the "blue-eyed monster"— a secret disciplinary weapon said to be an electric cattle prod that sent a severe shock through the child's body. Jones rarely administered these punishments himself. He required members of his choosing to carry out the beatings.

In addition to physical correction, Jones had other ways of keeping people in line. In Planning Commission meetings, he asked members to sign "loyalty oaths," in which they confessed to having committed criminal acts or to being homosexuals or lesbians. He made them sign statements swearing that they were willing to kill enemies of the temple and then commit suicide, and he instructed members that if they should ever leave the temple and attempt to expose him, he would release the documents to discredit them.

And always, from the beginning, Jones threatened the lives of potential defectors. "You know, after '73 we didn't stay in because we loved the group," said Jeannie Mills. "We stayed in because we knew we would be killed if we left. Jones had told us hundreds of times, privately, publicly, in Planning Commission meetings—it was common knowledge—that if you left the church you'd be killed."

Several years later, when the Millses finally did leave the church,

Jones' henchmen seemed bent on carrying out his orders. "We lived in cold terror for a year," said Jeannie Mills. "They put harassing letters on our porch. They called us in the middle of the night. We had cars tailing us. Jones used any tactic he could think of, figuring that if he could keep us scared, we would be quiet. And in most cases it worked. People who left him twenty years ago in Indianapolis are still afraid to speak out."

These acts of physical punishment, coercion and repeated threats of murder underscore the failure of Jones' haphazard attempts at mind control. For the most part his methods were randomly selected and crude. Because he had no systematic technique for controlling his members' thought processes from within, Jones was constantly forced to control them physically from without.

"What was amazing was that he would beat these people, and it would hurt, really hurt," remembered Grace Stoen, "but they would still go ahead and disobey his rules. Then, as each form of punishment would lose its effect, he would introduce a new one that was more drastic. This really bothered Jim Jones, the fact that he could not obtain that control."

Ironically, Jones was losing control over his own members as he appeared to be gaining influence in the outside world. In 1975, Jones mobilized his followers to deliver a bloc of votes that helped liberal Democrat George Moscone become mayor of San Francisco, a favor that was returned when Jones was appointed chairman of the San Francisco Housing Authority. Flexing his newfound political muscle, in the following years Jones used his position to make other contacts. Like the growing throngs of cult leaders worldwide, he collected a file of signed photographs and letters from public figures and political luminaries, among them, First Lady Rosalynn Carter, Vice President Walter Mondale, and U.S. Senators Hubert Humphrey and Henry Jackson, which he then used as letters of endorsement and entrée to Guyana and elsewhere, although some of those letters later were found to have been forged.

And with each social and political gain, the focus of Jones' attention shifted further away from his people and his temple. Like other cult leaders, Jones became obsessed with himself, playing his role of "Dad" and "Father" to the point of irrationality. Eventually, he not only claimed to be God but, at various times, the reincarnation of Christ and Lenin, and he came to demand his followers' total embrace of his mushrooming self-image. "No matter what you did as an individual," recalled Grace Stoen, "everything had to be credited to Jim Jones. We had to constantly say that the only reason we were in the temple was because of Jim Jones, that the only reason we did something was because of Jim Jones. If you didn't, you got confronted for not giving him credit. He was a megalomaniac. He was determined to go down in history."

If he was concerned with his place in history, Jones was also obsessed with his personal welfare and physical safety. He endeavored to make "Father's" safety a universal concern.

"He would say to people in meetings, 'What are we going to do if anyone ever tries to get Jim Jones?' And everyone would scream, 'Kill! Kill!' " recalled Grace Stoen. "A thousand people with their fists in the air screaming, 'Kill! Kill!' That was heavy."

In time, someone did try to get Jim Jones, not to harm him physically but to expose him. As early as 1972, the *San Francisco Examiner's* religion writer attacked Jones in print for his claim to have brought more than forty persons back from the dead, also for his habit of surrounding himself with aides armed with pistols and guns. Jones was outraged. According to Grace Stoen, it was this first media criticism that confirmed his worst fears.

"The bad press totally blew him apart," said Stoen. "That's when he began to believe there was a conspiracy out to get us."

Jones sustained other crushing blows. During that period, the temple had its first large-scale defection. Eight young members of Jones' "revolutionary guard" quit in response to Jones' growing extremism. According to Jeannie Mills, this defection, coming on the heels of the *Examiner* article, pushed Jones to the edge.

"Those eight young people were a revolutionary group within the temple," she said. "They'd been hyped up with stories of Che Guevara and they had been doing some practice with weapons, and when they left, Jones got scared. He really thought they were going to come after him. Actually, all they wanted to do was get out of the temple so they could live their own lives. It was at that point that Jones started taking ridiculous precautions to save his life, like instituting the guards and having us sign incriminating letters for his protection. That was also when he issued the order that if anything ever happened to him, every person who had ever left the temple was to be killed."

Jones' fear of defection was apparently linked to his fear of betrayal and exposure, and he soon introduced a new practice that would turn out to be his final solution to the problem. Two years before events played out in Guyana, Jones tested his first suicide drill on Planning Commission members in California. He explained afterward that the drill was designed to test their loyalty. Grace Stoen recalled:

"Jim Jones said, 'Just to show you how much I love you, I'm going to give all of you some wine.' We couldn't drink or smoke so everybody was excited about this treat. We all drank it and Jim Jones asked, 'Is everybody finished?' And we said yes. Then he said, 'Okay, you've all just been poisoned and you have one hour to live.' When I first heard that I said no, I don't believe it; but Jones went so far as to have some people fake that they had dropped dead. Others pretended to be freaking out to encourage anybody on the borderline to do the same. When the hour was up, Jim Jones said, 'Well, that was just a test. You did well.' "

The frequent temple-wide suicide drills that followed were the most dramatic of many indignities Jones forced on his flock, and a steady trickle of defectors—including, to Jones' great dismay, Grace Stoen—caused a mounting wave of rumors and horror stories to begin cresting around the Peoples Temple. In early 1977, when Jones received word that a devastating exposé based on interviews with ten defectors was being prepared for publication in *New West* magazine, he did everything in his power to prevent its appearance, including eliciting prepublication protests from the magazine's advertisers and representatives of the American Civil Liberties Union. Jones' move to censor *New West* failed, however, and as the publication date neared he began his crash move to Guyana.

Passage to Guyana. Jones used multiple ploys to induce temple members to accompany him on his journey. Many have since become common levers, in theme and variation, among cult leaders and political extremists. He told black followers that if they stayed in America they would be put in concentration camps. He warned white members that they were already on government enemies lists. As always, potential defectors were threatened with blackmail and death. From the outset, Jones spoke of the life they would find in Guyana in only the most glowing terms: everyone would live and work together in tropical splendor and interracial harmony, Only temple executives knew Jones' real intention.

"I remember once in San Francisco, Jim Jones said to me, 'Boy, when we get people down to Guyana we can do anything we want to them,' " said Grace Stoen.

When *New West* hit the stands, the word was out. There were more defections of temple members who hadn't yet gone to Guyana, and the temple's San Francisco headquarters became primarily a supply and communications base for operations in Jones' southern command. A shortwave radio link was set up between the two points as

Jones proceeded to conduct his distant forces and his attending throng in the creation of his earthly paradise.

Life in Jonestown, however, resembled not so much a paradise as a prison. According to survivors' reports, Jones' commune became the real concentration camp he had warned of. Residents were required to work eleven-hour days in 120° heat with only a ten-minute break, constructing camp facilities and attempting to cultivate the land they had cleared of jungle growth. But farming proved to be a futile undertaking. Dense weeds would grow back and choke the crops within twenty-four hours. Before long, the commune's residents, who once had visions of sharing their harvests with the Guyanese people, were themselves reduced to living on a diet of boiled rice with gravy.

On the surface Jones did manage to build an impressive jungle community, complete with living quarters, a central meeting place, a school, and one of the best-equipped medical facilities in Guyana. But as his agricultural experiment foundered, Jones sank deeper into madness and despair. He ordered disciplinary measures more harsh and punishments more brutal than those he practiced in California. Members cited for infractions were sentenced to "the box"—a kind of isolation and sensory deprivation cell. Young children were tied up and lowered down a well until they screamed for mercy. In nightly "business meetings" that often lasted until 3 A.M., which all commune members were required to attend, women who violated Jones' moral code were forced to have sex publicly with sect members selected at random by Jones. Those found guilty of other crimes were called on the floor before the assembly, then stripped naked and whipped, beaten unconscious by security guards, or pummeled bloody in boxing matches against opponents wearing weighted gloves.

For the boldest dissidents or those who could not be dissuaded from wanting to leave, Jones established a special "extended-care unit" of the Jonestown medical facility. There runaways and other unruly members were confined and given massive doses of mood-altering drugs. Later reports confirmed that huge supplies of psychoactive drugs were smuggled into Jonestown by temple officials, including Quaaludes, Demerol, Valium, morphine and 11,000 doses of Thorazine, a powerful tranquilizer. After a few days in "extended care, "several sect survivors reported, people seemed to lose any desire they might have had to leave Jonestown or disobey Jones. "When they came out a week later, they were changed," one observer remembered. "They couldn't talk to you and they walked around with empty faces."

There seemed to be no end to the inhumanity at Jonestown. Mail to residents from relatives in the United States was never delivered, but those whose families expressed concern were forced to write letters home dictated by temple officials in which they would describe the idyllic lives they had found, express their unqualified joy and reaffirm their commitment to make Jonestown their permanent home. Around the clock, Jones kept up his feverish ranting. In nightly meetings and for up to six hours each day, loudspeakers broadcast to the farthest reaches of the Jonestown clearing. At night, after the exhausted, overloaded and battered workers were finally permitted to go to sleep, Jones would turn on his loudspeakers again, screaming "Alert, alert, alert! Everyone to the pavilion!" and begin to rave anew about imminent attacks by the U.S. Army or CIA guerrillas. In these frequent "White Night" ceremonies, Jones would order commune members to drink from a fifty-gallon vat a fruit drink that was said to contain lethal poisons. He declared that the commune was on the verge of being destroyed and that the only remaining course of action was "mass suicide for the glory of socialism." Afterward, when those who had fainted with fright or keeled over from suggestion alone had been revived, Jones announced that he had only been putting them through a loyalty test and now they could go back to sleep.

These tales of life in Jonestown first came to public attention in the spring of 1978, when Deborah Layton Blakey, once Jones' trusted aide and financial secretary of the Peoples Temple, escaped from Guyana and returned to the United States intent on notifying the media and authorities of the abuses taking place, and of the prospect of mass suicide as she witnessed it in Jones' White Night rehearsals. She submitted a detailed affidavit to the press, local officials and the U.S. Justice Department; but even after her sworn testimony was printed in the *San Francisco Chronicle,* there was little public outcry and no widespread call for an investigation. When official inquiries were made, Jones responded with legal challenges and menacing warnings. In a letter Jones reportedly sent to all U.S. Senators and Congressmen when he heard of a possible government investigation, he spoke of his readiness to sacrifice himself and the members of his temple. "I can say without hesitation," stated Jones, "that we are devoted to a decision that it is better even to die than to be constantly harassed from one continent to the next."

When Representative Leo Ryan left for Guyana with the media and representatives of the Concerned Relatives group, there had been ample warning and demonstrated cause for concern, not only from sworn testimony and Jones' own mass suicide threats, but from reports that originated in San Francisco of illegal shipments of arms and ammunition to Guyana.

From the testimony of former members, we came to understand many aspects of the Peoples Temple experience, but, as we had suspected, they provided few hard clues to the states of mind of the nine hundred who died. The few survivors who returned to tell their stories proved to be rare exceptions: an elderly woman who slept through the entire ritual, a young man who had an opportunity to escape when a nurse sent him to get a stethoscope. These individuals could not tell us what went through the others' minds when they sipped the poison, but from their accounts, as well as those of other defectors, ex-members and relatives, we were able to draw some preliminary conclusions about the degree to which Peoples Temple members were under mind control.

Former temple members confirmed for us that Jones did impair his followers' ability to question and make choices, not through some covert induction or protracted mind-stilling ritual but in a direct and straightforward manner. "When he would ask people to do something," one elderly woman told us, "he would say to them, 'Now don't ask me why, just do it.' He never gave anyone a reason." Jeannie Mills recalled how Jones justified his call for unquestioning obedience. "He told us that he was set up in a position of leadership and that in order to be an effective agent for change he had to have full power and we had to protect the office—which is what he called himself. He said that meant we could never criticize him or question him because to do so would be to weaken the effectiveness of the group."

Jones also relied on unrelenting group pressure to keep people from questioning and objecting. "I always had a nagging doubt in the back of my mind about whether or not his healings were for real," one woman recalled. "But I couldn't just say to someone, hey, that looks phony. You just didn't talk like that about Jim Jones. No one else was questioning. It seemed to me that I was the only person in the whole group questioning, so eventually I stopped questioning."

And, like every cult leader, Jones used his finely honed rhetorical skills to dissect his members' minds. "He would talk for hours and hours about slavery and Fascists and Hitler killing the Jews," said another ex-member. "It would be like a bell ringing in your ears all the time. Then you would get to where you didn't listen to anything else. Your mind didn't have time to create anything on its own, and that was all you'd know."

Overwhelmed and exhausted, as in other cults, at some point many of Jones' followers simply switched off their own thought processes. Jeannie Mills told us that after she and her husband had quit the church, only to be coaxed back several months later by their children, they made a conscious decision to close their minds to the contradictions and "strange things" they had observed. She recalled how she, and no doubt many others, surrendered her will to Jim Jones. "You voluntarily chose not to question. You voluntarily chose to allow someone else to make your decisions. Then you kind of turned off this logical portion of your mind which people use to make everyday decisions. You stopped using it. And eventually you lost the capability of making decisions."

By the end of our interviews, among relatives and other close observers of temple members, we found a virtual unanimity of opinion on our question of mind control. One elderly ex-member expressed the reigning view in less than clinical terms. "Toward the end, they looked like they were under some sort of spell. It seemed like they were helpless under him. They looked weary and worried and depressed, very depressed."

However, the strongest evidence of mind control was provided by those who left the Peoples Temple. They reported the same aftereffects that commonly follow a cult experience, including the persisting disturbances of thought and feeling that suggested to us that deeper organic alterations had in fact occurred. "After I left, it took me five months to a year to come around," said Grace Stoen. "I moved as far away from the temple as I could, I got a job, but all I wanted to do was sleep. I would just sleep and sleep and sleep. I was very confused and mixed up and crying a lot. I couldn't talk to anyone because people couldn't relate to what I had to tell them. It was just too bizarre. I was very depressed, and I was having bad dreams. At one point, I said, I'm going back, I'm already a ruined person and I can't make it out here. And one of the people who had left earlier said not to worry, that I needed more time, that time alone would heal it. I said, yes, but what's wrong with me? She said, 'I don't know, but I went through the same thing.' "

Massacre or mass suicide? There was ample evidence, plus the weight of official opinion, to support the contention that the dead took their lives of their own free will. It was equally possible to argue that Jim Jones was a mad, sadistic figure who presided over the execution of nine hundred helpless people—nearly three hundred of them children. For many, the public debate dissolved largely into a rhetorical one, but much more was at stake than mere semantics.

From our perspective, the tragedy could best be judged a *mass murder-suicide under cult control*. The Jonestown commune was a living hell. The people there were subjected to extreme physical, mental and emotional duress, willfully deceived and confused beyond the point of self-responsibility. But, to us, there was a terrible irony in the Jonestown tragedy that made the deaths so much sadder and more foreboding. With his wealth and power, Jones was free to pursue any course of action he desired. But his followers had no alternatives. They had indeed been charmed, coerced, controlled and expatriated under false pretenses, then, for many, physically imprisoned. Yet, despite the lies Jones told them, their twisted perceptions probably found their way to the truth: following the airport killings, there was no escape—not to freedom nor from the inevitability of Jones' wrath.

Few who died in Guyana knew how correct they were in that final belief that they had no other way out. They presumed all defectors had already been murdered. Those who even knew of the existence of the Concerned Relatives Committee and the Human Freedom Center knew only the truth: that all their missions to Guyana had ended in failure. And beyond that, most members had no idea that, with one exception, every government agency that had been asked to investigate the Peoples Temple had refused. The Treasury Department had been informed of illegal arms shipments to Guyana eighteen months earlier. The Federal Communications Commission had declined to press charges against the Peoples Temple for violations of shortwave radio broadcast regulations. Twice in the preceding year, the Social Security Administration had attempted to determine whether cult members were being forced to sign over to the temple more than $40,000 in government payments every month, only to be told by the State Department that they found no evidence that members had been forced to sign away their benefits. The Justice Department, after receiving hundreds of reports alleging brainwashing, coercion and criminal activities in connection with the Peoples Temple and many other religious cults, had repeatedly refused to investigate such groups on the grounds that any investigation would violate the groups' constitutional guarantees of freedom of religion.

Even lacking that knowledge, in all likelihood the residents of Jonestown were overcome that afternoon by a profound sense of hopelessness. For the majority of them, born black and poor, life had always been an uphill struggle against insurmountable odds. For the rest, the young white college graduates and the earnest middle Americans, their ideals and values shaken by the cultural upheavals of the sixties and seventies, Jonestown may have simply been the last letdown in a long series of disillusionments. For a time, unlike other cults we had studied, the Peoples Temple offered them a real course of action for social change. "It was like you died and went to heaven and it was beautiful," said Jeannie Mills, "then suddenly God went crazy and everything went sour."

And, almost unbelievably, it seemed, Jim Jones continued to command his surviving followers from the grave. In March 1980, more than 15 months after the Jonestown massacre, after hundreds of media interviews and their tireless efforts to help casualties of the Peoples Temple and other cults, Jeannie and Al Mills were found shot to death in their Berkeley, California home. Their sixteen-year-old daughter Daphene was critically wounded and died two days later. Their home was not burglarized and there was no sign of forced entry or even a struggle. The killings remain unsolved.

Jonestown was the end of innocence and America's blissful ignorance of the cult phenomenon. The events in its aftermath brought to light still greater outrages and set precedents for more sadness to come. Two government inquests probed the tragedy and its implications. The main congressional inquiry, conducted by the House Foreign Affairs Committee in early 1979, found that the State Department had buried numerous warnings of Jones' mass suicide plan in bureaucracy and official reluctance to interfere. The committee concluded that one of the State Department's worst errors was to take no action on the written warnings cult defectors had delivered six months before the massacre. The U.S. Ambassador to Guyana claimed that his own warnings sent back to Washington were "cautiously worded" from fear of future embarrassing disclosures under the Freedom of Information Act, but that defense may have been a ruse. Later FOIA inquiries revealed that the CIA was using the U.S. embassy in Guyana as a base for operations aimed at destabilizing the country's socialist government and, although intelligence officials swore that Jim Jones' jungle outpost played no part in their plan, there appeared to be a clear hands-off policy toward Jones' activities in Guyana.

Among the few positive recommendations that came out of the House committee report was for the government to undertake "a concentrated program of research and training on cults."

The second inquiry, lasting one day, was conducted in February 1979, by an ad hoc committee of House and Senate members. The "Information Meeting on the Cult Phenomenon in the United States," chaired by Republican Senator Robert Dole of Kansas, was a response to the pleas of thousands of families across the country and the concerns expressed by congressional leaders. Researchers, including the two of us, lawyers, deprogrammers and mental health professionals knowledgeable on the subject called for government action on the complex issues of personal freedom and public safety that surrounded the cult phenomenon. Spokespersons for major cult groups were also invited to address the proceedings. The chorus of catcalls from cult members in the Senate hearing room and protests from allied civil libertarians decrying government intrusion into forbidden religious arenas were only first tastes of the intimidation and public confusion that would foreclose any hope of meaningful action in the years that followed.

During those years, the problem was denied, the congressional findings ignored, the official recommendations quietly buried beneath the heavings of politics and bureaucracy. In the capital and across the heartland a new ideology took hold, filled with talk of God and the Bible, and with it came a new awe and fear of religion in politics, government and American society generally.

The changing religious-political climate only fed into the problems posed by the new cults and sects, and those problems were not going away.

16 Chaos at Waco: The Death Spiral

Turning and turning in the widening gyre
The falcon cannot hear the falconer;
Things fall apart; the centre cannot hold;
Mere anarchy is loosed upon the world,
The blood-dimmed tide is loosed, and everywhere
The ceremony of innocence is drowned....

—W.B. Yeats
"The Second Coming"

IN THE EIGHTIES, shades of Jonestown fell on American soil, as we watched a new pattern unfold within the wider cult phenomenon, one of escalating confrontations between groups across the religious-political spectrum and their surrounding societies. The new pattern, most visible in conflicts involving armed apocalyptic cults, murderous satanic sects, radical political groups and paramilitary survivalist sects, broke out repeatedly in violent shootouts and flame-filled cataclysms:

In 1983, two federal marshals were killed in North Dakota while attempting to arrest fugitive tax-protester Gordon Kahl, an adherent of the ultrafundamentalist, anti-government Posse Comitatus movement. Kahl and a local sheriff died later in a gunfight at an Arkansas farmhouse.

In 1985, weapons belonging to leaders of the paramilitary sect the Order, a breakaway group from the Idaho-based neo-Nazi Church of the Aryan Nations, were linked to the machine-gun assassination a year earlier of a Denver radio talk-show host. Federal agents cornered suspects in the killing at a sect compound on an island northwest of Seattle. The sect's co-founder died in a 35-hour gun battle that ended in a fiery explosion.

In Philadelphia, the same year, authorities surrounded the inner city headquarters of the radical back-to-nature sect MOVE, whose members had been involved in a fatal shootout with police and firemen several years earlier. After a protracted siege and standoff, police helicopters bombed the building. Six adults and five children died in the blaze that followed, which destroyed sixty neighboring houses.

Sometimes the pattern of conflict stopped short of tragedy. In the early eighties, devotees of red-robed Indian guru Bhagwan Shree Rajneesh purchased a 62,000-acre ranch and took domain over the rural community of Antelope in north central Oregon. Thousands of disciples converged on the commune from around the world, voted themselves into power and renamed the town Rajneeshpuram. A series of legal challenges and angry clashes with neighbors followed, and a siege mentality set in. Sect leaders amassed a cache of assault weapons and, according to local authorities, "enough ammo to supply a battalion for a year." The conflict came to a head in 1985, when reports surfaced of a sect plot to assassinate government officials investigating the group, but the crisis was defused. Three sect members were arrested and charged with conspiracy to commit murder. Rajneesh and seven sect lieutenants were charged with federal immigration law violations. The guru pleaded guilty, was deported to India, and the commune rapidly disbanded.

However, many other actions took the lives of sect members and their opponents. Dissident cultists died in rural Nebraska and Ohio, at Hare Krishna temples in West Virginia, and in a devil-worshipping cult ritual on the Texas-Mexico border. Armed insurgencies were mounted by followers of the anti-abortion Army of God, the paramilitary the Covenant, the Sword and the Arm of the Lord sect, and the White Aryan Resistance. Other violent acts were committed by members of white racist Identity Christian sects, Posse Comitatus militias, and extremist Ku Klux Klan, neo-Nazi and "skinhead" hate groups active in forty states.

In 1992, the next escalation took place, when a showdown between Randall Weaver, a white separatist Identity Christian, and federal officers who had come to arrest him for firearms violations triggered an exchange of gunfire at Weaver's mountain home in Idaho. A decorated federal marshal and Weaver's 14-year-old son were killed. A massive deployment followed. Four hundred federal agents, including the FBI's elite Hostage Rescue Team, converged on the scene. The next day, sharpshooters acting under loosened law enforcement rules that permitted them to shoot, not only in self-defense but at any armed person in sight, purportedly fired at Weaver as he ran for cover and accidently shot and killed Weaver's wife as she stood holding her infant child behind a door. The siege ended ten days later when Weaver surrendered. In the tumultuous trial that followed, Weaver was acquitted of murder by jury members appalled by the government's aggressive actions. Three years later, the case was still generating criticism of federal officials and bitter charges from the growing numbers of armed separatist sects and anti-government extremists.

On the surface, these escalating conflicts, ostensibly, over guns, land and crimes of the most brutal physical nature, seemed to have little to do with life in America's advancing information society. However, their driving forces in almost every instance could be located squarely in the information dimension: in the domain of beliefs, emotions, ideologies and other messages passing among people, in the new realm of human communication and control, and in the effects of religious conversions and political convictions held by individuals in states of mind that eluded, and often completely defied, established psychological, social and legal conventions.

These vastly different confrontations could not be simply equated, but their emerging pattern gave shape to a recurring image in our minds. The image was a spiral turning in a widening gyre. The winding spiral shape seemed to us to depict the almost unstoppable momentum that seemed to gather in public confrontations with cults and cult-like groups: the swirl of information, events, and predictable actions and reactions that seemed to build to inevitable conclusions in such conflicts. Repeatedly, we watched the same spiral dynamic draw everything in its path—individuals, families, communities, the media, law enforcement and higher government officials—into a vortex that exploded in fury and left a trail of death and destruction in its wake.

We mapped our prototype "death spiral," as we began to refer to it, retrospectively at Jonestown and tracked it from one cult confrontation to the next. The pattern was consistent: the controlling individual and group dynamics, the obsessed sect leader, the gathering of followers in an isolated location, the progressive personal abuses and criminal allegations. Invariably, as news of those destructive dynamics reached the world, the spiral began to turn: concerned relatives and defectors spurred media investigations and government inquiries. Those external pressures, in turn, fed each group's building internal combustion, collective paranoia and bunker mentality eager for confrontation.

Obviously, every conflict was not identical—the death spiral was as impulsive as the new sects themselves—but the pattern repeated itself in theme and variation. Sometimes tiny pivot points of belief or ideology marked the difference between loving faith and warring fanaticism. In armed showdowns, the slightest miscalculations in police tactics or timing could spin a peaceful surrender into a fatal shootout or blazing inferno. Often fierce confrontations erupted in a sudden runup of events no one foresaw or ever would have predicted. By their nature, in fact, most cult conflicts grew out of odd convergences of unruly forces and turned on seemingly insignificant factors that only became obvious in hindsight. But not once, in the cases we examined, was the pattern wholly random or totally unpredictable.

The death spiral, as we began to discern it, was *a fatal pattern of response that may arise in the life of cults, sects and social organizations of every kind.* Our spiral image was not arbitrary. It came from communication theory, which used the spiral shape to depict the real-world dynamics of complex human communication systems as they unfold over time. The spiral dynamic, an advance over earlier group dynamics models, was introduced in the sixties by Francis E. X. Dance, Ph.D., of the University of Wisconsin, a respected figure in human communication theory. His model added the all-important element of *feedback* to the communication life of groups as they change and evolve in response to feedback generated from within the group and, inevitably, from without, in the group's interactions with society. More complex systems, Dance noted, might be depicted by two or more spirals "interacting and intertwining." In particular, wrote Dance, the spiral form "presents a rather fascinating variety of possibilities for representing pathologies of communication."

Pathologies of communication—that seemed to describe the fatal group responses we were observing. As Dance had predicted, these deadly spirals appeared to be composed of, not one, but two intertwining feedback loops, one positive, one negative, winding outward and inward from the centerpoint of the group. In healthy groups, the communication process was ongoing and richly interactive in both directions, from the group to society and vice versa. In the death spiral, that healthy process turned pathological. Instead of reaching outward and remaining open to information from the world, the group became closed, folded in on itself and, slowly or with frightening speed, turned destructive to individuals, to the group and to the surrounding society. This sudden change in the life of the group, which we watched in a dozen confrontations from the seventies to the nineties, seemed to describe a *collective* snapping experience that was fast-breeding, self-propelling, often catastrophic—and sometimes utterly chaotic.

Strange Attractors. As we wrestled with these emerging dynamics of the death spiral, we explored a wide range of innovative models that might help us to understand the whirlwind events we were chronicling. The most promising came from the enticing new science of "chaos theory" that burst on the scene in the eighties. Chaos theory offered new ways to understand sudden, seemingly inexplicable changes in complex, often highly unstable systems. Of particular interest to us, it showed mathematically how a pattern of small errors and uncertainties in a volatile environment could multiply many fold and trigger a tumultuous chain of events with catastrophic consequences.

The new science went beyond the dynamics of sudden change we had found a decade earlier in René Thom's catastrophe theory. Chaos theory unveiled a vast universe of dynamic changes of which Thom's folding catastrophe waves were only one part. Its new mathematics generated spellbinding images of orderly phenomena emerging from seemingly random and hopelessly complex processes in nature. One set of chaos curves mapped diverging patterns of branching or "bifurcation" in nature's ebbs and flows: in the meanderings of mighty rivers across lowland contours and wind-whipped terrain, in the growth of plants and trees as their trunks strained skyward and branched in armloads of festooned flowers and fork-tipped leaves. Another depicted intriguing patterns of "attraction" or recurring behavior converging around alluring focal points or gravitating toward odd-shaped, often highly unstable "strange attractors." The first recognized strange attractor, derived from the maddeningly imprecise science of meteorology, was named the "butterfly effect." Its swooping curves, depicting tiny movements that may cause sudden cataclysmic events, explained, in theory at least, how "a butterfly flapping its wings in Brazil can set off a tornado in Texas."

And the chaos was not just material. We found chaos everywhere in the information dimension. Chaotic patterns appeared often in the flow of technical and human communication: in the chaotic bursts of electrical noise that disrupted the transmission of voices and data over long-distance telephone lines, in the chaotic communication patterns of people in small groups, large families and poorly-managed corporations, in the neurological lightning storms that disrupted the brains of epileptics and the neurochemical surges that swept over schizophrenics, manic-depressives and people with clinical personality disorders.

In fact, some chaos theorists asserted that, at bottom, the new science was not about matter and energy at all. It was about information itself! And, like so many information age insights, some of chaos theory's first breakthroughs were made years ago by founding figures in the field of communication.

In the 1920s, Norbert Wiener was among the first mathematicians to analyze the curious property of "attraction" that emerged spontaneously in dynamic systems. Two decades later, in *Cybernetics*, he explained how some communication systems, when subjected to uncontrolled positive feedback, "will go into unrestrained and increasing oscillation" and "certainly produce something catastrophic." To illustrate, he traced a simple graph depicting the rudimentary, bare buttocks-shaped curve that re-emerged thirty years later as a dominant feature of the famed "Mandelbrot set" of chaos equations.

The new equations were based on Wiener's universal principle of feedback: they used the outcome of each successive calculation as a

Figure 3: Double-spiral chaos curve from the Mandelbrot set

new input to create a series of fast-breeding "iterations." Those simple feedback equations, reiterated millions of times over on high-capacity computers, traced richly articulated images that bore striking resemblance to familiar shapes in nature: crystalline snowflakes, branching trees, leafy ferns.

One of the most common chaotic shapes, appearing ubiquitously in the Mandelbrot set and other reiterating feedback equations, was a breathtaking double spiral that curled back on itself and vanished into its own gyrating tail. (See Figure 3.)

The blooming, buzzing science of chaos offered valuable insights for our widening inquiry into snapping. It enabled us to model whole new dimensions of communication complexity, to go beyond the simpler leaps and slides of snapping in individual cases of sudden personality change and parse the dynamics of more complex *social* transformations. The new chaos pictures gave substance to the invisible streams of information and experience that pass among people daily. They generated tangible images of the communication forces that flow and change continuously, and often discontinuously, in the lives of individuals, groups and societies.

Indeed, the new science seemed custom-made for the complex group dynamics we were tracking. Chaos theory aptly described the "strange attractors" who changed by degrees from charismatic figures into controlling cult leaders, the "fractal branching" of breakaway sects from the trunks of more mainstream religious denominations, political movements and other social organizations, the "phase shift" when seemingly benign or merely threatening groups turned into deadly destructive cults, and the fateful "butterfly effect"—the flashpoint where some small or seemingly insignificant event caused the system to heave wildly and break out in the turbulence of a Jonestown or other chaotic confrontation.

Our working model drawn, appropriately enough, from the fringes of the vast virtual landscape of the Mandelbrot set, portrayed the complex sect-society dynamic as two converging streams of information moving in opposite directions. (See Figure 4, a computer projection of the Mandelbrot spiral onto a three-dimensional plane.) At the center of the action was the strange attractor, the group leader whose personal charisma and alluring beliefs draw intrigued searchers into his expanding orbit of influence. In true chaos form, the group's actions generate positive and negative feedback that both attract and repel outsiders and people inside the group as well. Fractious sects spawn their own internal factions and spinoff groups of disillusioned members. The flashpoint of conflict occurs along the boundary where sect meets society in mounting friction between the group and its neighbors, or between sect leaders and secular authorities.

The turning points in the chaos cycle, the pivotal events that set the death spiral in motion, were marked consistently by three critical communication thresholds which we termed *closure, control* and *confrontation.* The first threshold and most tangible danger sign, *closure,* was that point where an otherwise open, beneficial group, for whatever reasons, turns inward and becomes sealed off from the larger society in its mindset or physical location. With that crucial turn, we found, cults and groups of every kind begin quickly to feed on themselves.

The second threshold, *control,* was the driving force of the dynamic. In our model, it marked the turn where an esoteric but otherwise benign group crosses the line from sect to cult. The changeover may begin imperceptibly with a subtle shift in focus from the group to its

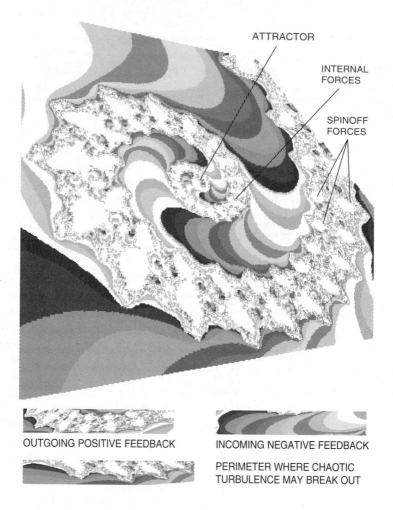

ATTRACTOR

INTERNAL
FORCES

SPINOFF
FORCES

OUTGOING POSITIVE FEEDBACK

INCOMING NEGATIVE FEEDBACK

PERIMETER WHERE CHAOTIC
TURBULENCE MAY BREAK OUT

Figure 4: A computer projection of the Mandelbrot double spiral onto a three-dimensional plane

leader—in chaos terms, a phase shift from the "fixed" attractor of the group's guiding beliefs, message or mission to the strange attractor of a self-centered, erratic and often dangerously unstable leader. More important, from our perspective, that turn also marked a shift from beneficial group practices to identifiable mind control methods that make members vulnerable to manipulation and more serious abuses.

The turn to control often proves equally damaging to group leaders. Within their closed information environments, personality weaknesses may snowball into certifiable psychopathologies. Leaders may become distorted in their identities, paranoid in their worldviews, and veer off on dangerous paths of *confrontation*. As the spiral accelerates in its turns, propelled by unchecked positive feedback from an unquestioning population within and a buildup of negativity from without—from defectors, families, investigating media, local law enforcement and higher government agencies—sect leaders commonly step up their hostile preachings and abusive practices.

The final threshold is crossed when words turn to actions, when group leaders no longer simply preach doom and holy warfare but begin to acquire arms, train their members for violence or self-destruction, and in the pattern first witnessed at Jonestown, even stage elaborate dress rehearsals. At that point, as we watched repeatedly, it took only some tiny triggering event, from within or without, to throw the entire system into chaos and violently destroy group leaders, members, journalists, lawmen and anyone else in the path of the vortex.

The death spiral fit the pattern of cult tragedies with chilling congruity. The run of recent confrontations conformed, more or less precisely, to our model.

Then, one deceptively quiet Sunday morning in late February 1993, true to every turn of chaos theory, a canvas tarpaulin fluttered in the warming breeze and set off a tornado in Texas.

The Branch Davidians were a fractal branch of the 1.5 million-member Seventh Day Adventist church. They believed literally that the long-prophesied Second Coming of Christ and its consequence, the end of the world, were close at hand.

Their leader, David Koresh, was a voice in the whirlwind and a vortex in the classical sense, a spinning tower of overheated air that grew larger as it consumed the cooler air around it. From the beginning, Koresh was a strange attractor, a one-man energy center fixed in space and biblical time who both charmed and repelled those who came near him, but his roiling persona soon underwent a radical shift of phase from sect leader to cult commander. Koresh sealed off the Branch Davidians from the larger society. He controlled and overwhelmed them with interminable preachings and sexual domination. He took up arms against his opponents and amassed an arsenal of combat-grade weapons. In the name of discipline, he beat his followers, starved their children, and abused them physically and sexually. He foretold a coming holy war with the society around him and threatened violence on an epic scale. He vowed never to be taken alive and trained his flock for mass suicide. His outrageous behavior, apocalyptic preachings and greed for guns surpassed the safety limits society could tolerate—and broke the laws of that society as well.

Then the beast in Koresh's eschatology, the United States Government, came round on cue.

On Sunday, February 28, 1993, after months of investigation, surveillance and logistical planning, seventy-five armed agents of the Bureau of Alcohol, Tobacco and Firearms, a division of the U.S. Treasury Department, converged on the Branch Davidians' 77-acre compound at Mount Carmel outside Waco. Their mission was to arrest Koresh and search for a cache of illegal automatic weapons and other arms reportedly amassed by the sect leader and his lieutenants. Like growing numbers of religious and political extremists across the country, Koresh and his crew were venturing into the arms trade and, according to multiple sources, making plans for armed insurrection as well. They had reportedly spent more than $200,000 buying guns, grenades and other explosive devices, including assault rifles, shotguns, pistols, legal semiautomatic rifles and parts to convert them into illegal automatic firearms, an armor-piercing .50-caliber machine gun and four tons of ammunition.

The events that followed swiftly escalated into one of the most bizarre and tragic chapters in American law enforcement history.

The ATF assault conformed generally with accepted procedures for raiding fortified premises and apprehending heavily armed suspects, only this raid was staged on the scale of a military operation, perhaps to avoid a replay of the killing of a U.S. marshal in the Weaver raid in Idaho months earlier—or, as raid planners feared, an orchestrated assault on federal officers. After receiving training in communications, tactics and emergency medical procedures from Army Special Forces instructors at nearby Fort Hood, Texas (a consultation that was later questioned but found to be entirely legal under such circumstances), agents equipped with assault gear, bulletproof vests and riot control devices rolled toward the Branch Davidian farmhouse in two cattlewagons covered by tarpaulins. Texas National Guard helicopters provided reconnaissance and standby air cover.

When the wagons reached their objective, the Trojan cattle deployed, but the Davidians were waiting. A butterfly in the vortex, a local TV cameraman who had learned of the raid from a co-worker's girlfriend, an emergency medical technician hired to support the federal effort, stopped to ask a postman for directions and told him the ATF was coming. The postman was Koresh's brother-in-law, and he promptly passed word to Koresh that the long-expected raid was under way. As the agents approached the compound, Koresh was standing at the front door. When they identified themselves, he stepped back inside and a massive firefight broke out through every wall and window. Media observers confirmed government claims that the Davidians fired first. When the smoke cleared after forty-five minutes of battle, four ATF agents lay dead; sixteen more were wounded from gunfire and grenades hurled at government forces. Inside, Koresh himself was wounded, five sect members were dead and a sixth died several hours later.

The standoff that followed lasted an excruciating fifty-one days. During that time, the 400 special agents of the FBI who took over the Waco operation, an occupying army of national and global media, and a transfixed world learned more than they ever cared to know about David Koresh and his Branch Davidians. Koresh, 33, a.k.a. Vernon Wayne Howell, a gangly kid with wavy hair and wire-framed glasses, was no Jim Jones. He was more like a "Generation X" Charles Manson, an aspiring rock musician who lured his followers with a piper's charms and who later, like Manson, declared himself to be God.

In 1984, young Vernon Howell joined the straggling Branch Davidian sect and promptly began wrestling for control over the group. After a brief apprenticeship under sect leader Lois Roden, the widow of the sect's founder Ben Roden, Howell proclaimed himself to be the Davidians' new prophet, rallied older members around him, and began recruiting new followers from across the U.S., Great Britain and Australia. In 1987, he led a shootout against a rival sect leader and emerged the victor after a local jury deadlocked in his trial for attempted murder. Soon after, he claimed divine visions of a coming apocalypse and removed his flock to the sect's secluded compound on the central Texas plains.

There he proceeded to spin out of control by degrees. He systematically separated husbands from wives and children from parents. He took nineteen "wives" for himself, including girls ten, twelve, fourteen, another seventeen and, later, her fifty-year-old mother. In 1990, Howell changed his name legally to David Koresh—Hebrew for Cyrus, after the benevolent king of Persia who welcomed the wandering tribes of David back to Israel in the sixth century B.C.—and began predicting that the Battle of Armageddon would now commence in Texas. In Koresh's scenario, the American army would attack his new Israelites and ignite a conflagration that would bring on the end of the world. In preparation, he ordered the sect's male adherents, who included a core group of zealous lieutenants schooled in paramilitary tactics and retooling automatic weapons, to arm and fortify the Waco compound and make ready for the Final Battle. He buried a bus beneath the compound and stocked it with food for a year. Sect members practiced daily military drills and were put on a rationed vegetarian diet. Children and adults were instructed in the surest way to commit suicide with a gun.

For sect members inside the besieged compound, the ATF raid proved Koresh's *bona fides* as a prophet of God. For lawmen outside the cult enclave, Koresh proved to be a devil of an adversary. Veteran FBI negotiators set up shop in a trailer near the compound. The Bureau's crack-shot Hostage Rescue Team was airlifted to the scene. Early on, Koresh cleaned house, releasing six adult Davidians he considered potentially disloyal and twenty-three children of sect members. Then he dug in for the long haul, keeping fifty adult followers and twenty-five children he claimed as his own.

Days stretched into weeks of frustrating, infuriating negotiations. Koresh made and broke repeated promises to come out with his flock. In rambling phone conversations and cryptic messages relayed by his lawyers, he applied to federal agents the same mind-numbing methods and manipulative ploys he plied among his followers. Negotiations were stymied by days of biblical exegesis and entire weeks during which Koresh claimed he was awaiting "further instruction from God." FBI negotiators talked tough, then conciliatory, then tough again. Ground commanders ringed the compound with razor wire, surrounded it with tanks and bathed it in white light through the night. Koresh gave back more Bible verses.

After a month, the FBI stepped up the psychological warfare. Loudspeakers were set up in an effort to communicate directly with sect members. Tapes were played of those who had left attesting to their good treatment by authorities. At one point, the loudspeakers blared at the compound—Tibetan chants, trumpets blowing reveille, screams of dying rabbits, Christmas carol sing-alongs—in a bizarre attempt to beat Koresh at his own mind-scrambling game. In reply, Koresh fired back a request for quiet through the Davidians' Passover celebration and promised once again to come out, this time, as soon as he had completed writing his interpretation of the Seven Seals in the Bible's final Book of Revelation. His lieutenant said that might take "six months or six years."

On day fifty-one, the FBI took command of the situation. Before dawn on April 19, military assault vehicles closed on the compound, led by a Bradley tank equipped with a long battering ram. Holes were punched in the wood frame walls and a non-lethal tear gas was pumped in, as the loudspeakers informed the Davidians that the game was over. FBI tacticians were confident that the stinging tear gas would persuade Koresh and his weary Davidians to come streaming out and surrender. At the very least, anxious government officials in Washington were assured, the devoted mothers inside Mt. Carmel would not let their children suffer the sickening but otherwise harmless fumes.

They were wrong.

The Davidians opened fired. A sect lieutenant threw the negotiating phone out the window. The tear gas flow increased but no one emerged. At noon, Koresh and his followers made their own exit. As the tanks continued to pummel the sect's living quarters, flames broke out in the second floor of the building. Whipped by gale-force winds blowing across the prairie, the compound became an inferno in seconds. Exploding ammunition stockpiles spewed debris and flaming mushroom clouds hundreds of feet into the sky. First reports said a tank had knocked over a kerosene lamp in an upstairs storeroom, but FBI surveillance tapes and aerial photographs released later confirmed that fires were set in at least three separate sites throughout the compound by the Davidians themselves.

At least seventy-five people died that day, including seventeen children ages ten or younger. Combined with the sect's earlier casualties and the government's own dead and wounded, the deadliest operation in federal law enforcement history now also ranked as one of the longest, costliest and most destructive police actions on American soil.

Pathologies of Communication. The story of Waco grew larger than the legend that played out on television. For years afterward, the case smouldered and caught fire anew in the public mind. Investigators in government and the media probed and reprobed unanswered questions. Religious and political groups made *"Waco!"* the rallying cry for their private agendas. But, amid the recurring fact-finding inquiries and search for scapegoats by special interests, it seemed to us, no one was really addressing the deeper human dimensions of the case.

We spent months exploring the tragedy from our perspective, talking to people who participated up front and behind the scenes at each stage of the action. From our vantage point as communication researchers, the tragedy was a stunning real-life exercise in the chaotic dynamics of the death spiral, and one in which pathological communication responses by both parties to the conflict—the cult and the government—contributed materially to the disaster. For a view from inside the spiral, we spoke first with several former Branch Davidians.

David Bunds became a Branch Davidian in childhood, when his father brought their family into the group in 1970. In an extended interview that paced through the group's history and horrific end, he described the Davidians' transition by degrees from a small religious sect like countless others on America's spiritual landscape into a militant apocalyptic cult.

"I was five when our family became Branch Davidians," Bunds began. "They were not a very strange group at the time. People led normal lives in different cities around the country and the world. Some people lived at the headquarters in Waco and every now and then you would go visit, but there was nothing extreme or unusual going on."

He recalled his religious upbringing as a young Branch Davidian.

"It was standard stuff. We prayed like anyone else. We met locally in California at places we would rent. We got together on holidays. There were studies where we would read the Bible for an hour together. As a child, I was required to sit in the studies but I didn't really understand what they were about. They were kind of boring."

A child of any faith might have said as much and, for the next ten years, the Bunds family led a normal life in Southern California. Bunds' father worked in a "regular" job. His mother tended to her family. David and his younger sister Robyn enrolled in public schools. There was just one point of departure.

"The only thing different about my life was that we would go to these meetings and talk about the end of the world."

Years before David Koresh came on the scene, the Branch Davidians were already preoccupied with death and the fiery end of the world foretold in the Book of Revelation. In the new terms of chaos science, the sect's endtimes prophecy was itself a strange attractor—a predetermined point, fixed in history but forever receding in time—around which the minds of sect members had revolved since the first Davidians branched off from the Adventist church in the 1930s. Surprisingly, this youth was untroubled by the thought of the world's end or his own imminent death. In fact, he and other Branch Davidians welcomed it.

"I wasn't afraid of it. In a way, I was looking forward to it," said Bunds. "It sounded kind of neat. There was going to be this beautiful kingdom and we were going to live there, and all the other nations of the world were going to be envious of this beautiful kingdom, just like the prophecy in Isaiah. I was just sort of floating along waiting for it all to happen. I figured my parents knew what they were doing."

In 1980, the Bunds family moved to Texas to be close to the Davidian headquarters in Waco. The next year, Vernon Howell came to the group. Bunds recalled his first encounter with Howell in the summer of 1981, when Bunds was sixteen and Howell a stripling of twenty-two.

"He was just like anybody else," said Bunds. "He came looking for truth. I didn't think much about him. He talked a lot. He would get up at the meetings and cry sometimes because of different problems he was having. I thought he was weird."

Despite its endtimes beliefs, the sect was no haven for fanatics, Bunds said. Vernon Howell's personality stood out in sharp contrast to the tenor of the sect from its inception, and he quickly became a destabilizing factor in the spiritual scene at Waco.

"We were a very reserved, very conservative group. There were no emotional displays. Then along came Vernon Howell. I remember my father said one day, 'Well, that guy sounds like he's going to end up saying he's a prophet the way he's acting.'"

The next year, the elder Bunds became disillusioned with the sect and its new rising star and the family moved back to California. Then, in late 1983, word came down from Waco that Howell had gained ascendancy over the group. Suddenly the sect's message and traditional center of attraction began to change.

"I remember getting Vernon's new message in the mail," said Bunds. "I read the letters and put them away. They didn't make any sense to me. They did not clearly state what the message was, which was typical of Vernon. He liked to be cryptic and mysterious."

Early in 1984, an enterprising Howell came to Southern California to convince Branch Davidians in the area that he had the truth.

"He called us up," Bunds recalled. "My father said, 'You go meet him,' so I went by myself. He presented his message and various biblical proofs that he was the true prophet. He used charts. One had a little beast from Revelation on it with seven heads. He said that meant his was the seventh angel's message—in Adventist teaching, seven is a very biblical number. I remember thinking, *Wow, the seventh angel's message. This is the one we've been waiting for!*"

Subtly, Howell made himself one with the sect's main attractor, the Bible. Before his eyes, Bunds watched the weird, not very likeable youth metamorphose into a persuasive presenter of the Scriptures who weaved circles around his prey with his encyclopedic knowledge of the good book. Then slowly, outside the awareness of everyone, perhaps even including himself, Howell began to shift the center of attraction from the sect's biblical theology to its brash new leader. Bunds felt the power in that initial encounter as, one-on-one, Howell raised him to a spiritual high and convinced him that he was in fact the Davidians' seventh and, as the sacred seals foretold, final prophet.

"That first meeting lasted six hours," Bunds recalled. "I went in skeptical but open-minded. I was just going to listen, and by the time I left I had made a 180-degree turnaround. I went home and I was going crazy. My parents kept saying, 'You can't decide that in just a few hours.' And I said, 'You guys, I *know* it's true.' I was gung-ho."

That spring, Howell decreed another change in doctrine that would have far-reaching impact on the lives of Branch Davidians: he called for the ingathering of all sect members. Bunds thought he knew why.

"He said all Branch Davidians were required to come to Mt. Carmel for Passover that year. That was something I learned about Vernon. He did not like to communicate through the mail or over the phone. He wanted to have people right there in front of him so he could read their emotions and act accordingly. Other Davidian leaders were content to send out mailings and collect tithes from followers across the country. Vernon wanted to be in personal contact with the group. He wanted to have everybody under one roof."

In 1984, Bunds persuaded his family to move to Waco where, along with others from the Davidian diaspora, they fell under Howell's growing influence and personal power. It was a turning point for the group as it crossed the threshold of closure that would seal off the sect and its members from the surrounding society. There Howell completed the shift from sect to cult, as he commanded his followers to attend protracted sermons and Bible study sessions that were a far cry from the staid Davidian prayer meetings of old.

"Vernon's meetings would go on for hours," Bunds recalled. "I would walk in and sit down and start listening to him and I was just mesmerized. He was very powerful."

As his power grew, Howell's urge to control intensified. The Davidians' twice-daily Bible study sessions became grueling marathons steaming with hellfire and images of the Apocalypse to come.

"He said the time was short and he had a lot of Bible teachings to go through. We were told by 1989 it would all be over with," said Bunds, recalling Howell's first prophesied date of the world's end. "The morning meeting would go until lunchtime. The evening meeting would start at three and last until seven at night."

During those months, Howell consolidated his hold over the group. He defeated his main rival in the group's first armed confrontation and crowned himself Koresh, King Cyrus of the Davidians, his new Israelites. Reeling with unchecked power, his own personality began to change. Bunds traced Koresh's trail around a quickening curve of extremist belief and behavior that would bring him into open conflict with the surrounding society.

"In '86 he got a revelation that he should marry another girl. That's when he started to get really radical. Rachel, his first wife, had a younger sister. He took her when she was twelve. He made his case from the Bible. He said, 'David had a lot of wives, Solomon had a lot of wives,' so we accepted it, but then he had to have *more* women."

That year, Bunds' younger sister Robyn, then seventeen, came to live at Waco. She, too, was claimed by Koresh and bore him a son. A year later, Koresh took Bunds' mother Jeannine, then fifty, for a bride. His "wives" reached double digits, including a dozen underage girls. Most were children of Davidian members who were willingly surrendered by their parents and later bore children of their own with Koresh. Then, in 1989, Koresh extended his divine profligacy. He claimed he had been commanded by God to take as many wives as he wanted and, in the same breath, he annulled every other marriage at Mt. Carmel. The move prompted the first mass defection of alienated Davidians, but by then Koresh had already started on his final trajectory.

"The weapons were the next phase," said Bunds. "By '89, Koresh wanted to get every weapon he could get his hands on, and he knew instinctively that when you do that you're going to get into trouble."

Koresh primed his followers.

"He said we were going to have a confrontation with the authorities. He said the United States government was going to come and get us because they were enemies of the truth."

As the group grew more extreme, Bunds began to seriously question his participation, as many cult members do sooner or later. "I was getting doubts, but at first I would just shelve them, store them away," he said. He recalled Koresh's method of emotional control.

"He had this ability to appeal to people's base emotions and deepest feelings, and that's what Vernon did for me initially. He controlled you through fear, hope, love, want, desire." Like other cult leaders, Koresh intuitively employed a mix of positive and negative controls, but to keep his followers in line, negative emotions were his instruments of choice. "The fear was dominant," said Bunds. "He was always putting things in the negative, always threatening. He would describe hell and start screaming in the most horrible way to show people what it was like to burn in hell."

Like Charles Manson, Koresh acted out his threats. "He used very graphic descriptions," said Bunds. "He would portray all kinds of things and people were scared. Sometimes he would be all upbeat and describe all the good things we would get when we got our reward, but most of the time he was negative, beating on people's heads, trying to whip them into shape."

And like Jim Jones, Koresh reinforced his mental and emotional controls with physical punishment. Children were the first targets, beginning at the age of eight months. Sect members were given wooden

paddles and told to whack their children's bare behinds for any disobedience. Some children were beaten bloody, others were deprived of
food, others confined in dark spaces. Koresh and his henchmen got
violent with adult Davidians as well, assaulting some with their bare
fists and others with a large boat oar. Bunds witnessed several incidents during his waning months in the sect.

"Those last ten months were the worst time I'd ever had. He was
really cracking down, putting the screws on the group. He would not
tolerate any disagreement, and the threat of being beaten was there."

Several times, Bunds challenged Koresh's twisted interpretations
of Scriptures. Against Koresh's wishes, he courted and married a young
woman in the sect, and when Koresh announced his sexual *Anschluss*
on the Davidian women, Bunds' wife rejected his propositions. Through
it all, however, the couple made no effort to leave. Ultimately, it wasn't
Bunds who forced the break but Koresh himself.

"He had to kick me out. I didn't leave on my own. He kicked my
wife and me and my child out and left us with nothing. He was just
tired of our rebellious attitude. We were breaking his rules."

Marc Breault followed a different path in, and out of, the Branch
Davidian fold. Breault joined the group in the mid-eighties, at the age
of twenty-two, and became a ranking member of the cult leader's inner
circle until he parted company with Koresh and led the first mass
defection of Davidians in 1989. In contrast to David Bund's view from
the sect's bottom ranks up, Breault gave us a rare look into the Davidian
death spiral from the top down.

Breault, who is legally blind but not sightless, had himself trained
to be a Seventh Day Adventist minister but was passed over. "I was
told there was no need for a blind person to be a minister," he said. He
recalled his recruitment soon after by long-time Davidian Perry Jones,
the sect's vice president and the father of two of Koresh's teen brides,
in a Southern California town with a large Adventist population.

"I met Perry Jones in a supermarket in Loma Linda. I was wearing a Dallas Cowboys T-shirt, so he thought I was from Texas, and
that's how he started making conversation. He said he was a religious
journalist. He said he believed in the gift of prophecy, what he called
'inspiration.' That made sense to me. The Bible was full of prophets.
Then he said he believed his son-in-law was inspired by God. He never
used the word 'prophet,' because he knew how I would react to it, but
that's what he was saying. I figured, okay, I'll give this guy a hearing."

Several days later, Breault met Vernon Howell.

"I met Vernon in January 1986 in Loma Linda. He was wearing

faded trousers, a blue shirt, unkempt hair. He seemed very down to earth. He offered to give me a Bible study. He claimed he would show me more in three hours than I had learned in four years of college. That struck me as something a prophet would say—prophets in the Bible were never known for their tact."

Breault recalled Koresh's mastery of the Bible and sheer physical endurance that attracted him to the Davidian message.

"That session lasted three hours. He went through the books of Daniel and Revelation. I had always been interested in both books and this guy was putting them together for me in a way that I thought, *yeah, this might be prophecy.*"

The two hit it off and, within months, Breault became an eager recruiter himself. That spring, Breault went to Hawaii, where he had grown up and still maintained many close friendships, to start a new Davidian branch. "No one thought anything would come of it, including myself, but I recruited quite a few people and everybody was stunned. I would go in and establish a small group, the same way Vernon did. I would go somewhere for a week and just watch people and say, who is most likely to be receptive?"

While in the sect, Breault helped to enlist many of the young die-hard disciples who formed a firewall around Koresh at Waco. Among his first recruits was an old friend, Steve Schneider, who became one Koresh's most militant and loyal lieutenants.

"Steve was in a similar situation to mine," said Breault. "He had studied to be a pastor but he was passed up. The Adventist church is not a church for rebels and Steve was very independent. He didn't just accept things."

Breault described what both men, in their separate spiritual quests, found in the Davidians. For starters, Koresh brought a youthful new outlook and iconoclastic spirit to their established Adventist faith.

"A good example was the music," said Breault. "Vernon was a musician and we wanted good music in the church. We had nothing against 'Rock of Ages,' but we were tired of it. We wanted to bring guitars and amplifiers and keyboards into the church."

Koresh also brought new energy to the ritual practices of the staid sect. However, in the Davidians, as in other Bible cults, the traditional practice of reading the Bible grew pathological in the hands of the group's new prophet. Breault recalled how Koresh turned the sect's biblical "message" into a consuming mind control process that dominated every thought, belief and daily activity in the sect.

"When I joined the group, I was very enthusiastic about Vernon's Bible studies. They went on for two hours in the early days and just got longer and longer. Eventually, your whole life revolved around the Bible. When you talked to people, you shared the message. When you met people, your whole aim was to introduce them to the message. Even when you ate, you studied the message—we had strict dietary laws so you would always have the Bible in mind."

In addition to Koresh's marathon sermons and group Bible studies, sect members spent hours each day in intensive individual prayer. Amid the many deprivations Branch Davidians endured, that arduous ritual practice, which emerged in our studies as a core component of cult mind control, was almost universally overlooked by investigators.

"The prayer thing was very intense, I realize now," Breault said. "Vernon spent a lot of time praying, a couple hours a day, and others did, mostly those of us who were newcomers to the group."

During one of those intense rituals, soon after he joined the sect, Breault had the first of many snapping experiences which he, like Koresh, called "visions." One vision, born of hours of immersion in Koresh's apocalyptic theology and anti-governmental preaching, was thick with images of a fiery end.

"We were in Jerusalem, the whole group, and there were American troops all over the place. The city was in ruins. There was obviously some sort of war going on, which we believed would be the case from Daniel, and we were in hiding. Then we heard a sound like thunder in the distance coming closer and the earth began to shake and everyone was scared. We went out and saw this huge, I suppose 'chariot' sounds a little too biblical, whatever you want to call it, and it was surrounded by white lights and energy. It was huge, like the throne of God described in Ezekiel, and as this thing came toward us it shook and trembled and mountains were leveled and this voice said to 'Come hither' and this cloud came down and surrounded us. Then I just relaxed and reached up and got sucked up into this cloud and rose above the earth. As we were going up, there was this huge wind. We saw the whole earth shaking off its axis and graves were opening up and the dead were coming up from hell."

His waking dream bore chilling resemblances to the nightmare sect members would live out seven years later. Breault explained how such images flowed naturally from life in the group and the drumbeat of Koresh's daily teachings.

"Other people experienced these things, I was by no means the only one. Your whole life revolved around these teachings to the point where they became a fixation."

As Koresh's controls intensified and Koresh himself grew more grandiose, Breault, like Bunds, watched the group's focus of attraction shift from the Bible to Koresh's increasingly strange persona.

"About 1987, things began to go downhill. We had worked together as a team but then Vernon needed to be in total control. I noticed in his Bible studies that everything he was saying about the Bible was centering around him. Before it was centered around God, God's word and God's mission. Now it was, 'Look at *me*. The Bible says *I'm* this, *I'm* that, this is going to happen to *me*'. We believed he was a prophet, even in the early days, but that was never the big thing; then it gradually became the whole purpose of the Bible to talk about Vernon."

Breault's words mapped verbatim onto our chaos model. Like a storm in the making, as Koresh's power increased, he began to swell. As the group grew more insulated, the sect began to feed on itself and the turbulence within accelerated. Like Jim Jones at his Ukiah commune and later in the Guyana jungle, Koresh developed a thundering paranoia atop his apocalyptic mindset. Breault tracked the storm front gathering over Waco.

"At first it was a slow progression. Vernon was off in California or South Carolina, traveling all over the place, so he wasn't as isolated. Then, when everyone moved to Mt. Carmel, things really started going bad. At Mt. Carmel, he was king of this little kingdom. He made all the rules. There was no external check or balance, and there was no police force to make sure everyone was okay."

As Koresh got crazier, Breault's own inner alarms began sounding, but like others in the sect, he was helpless to act on his feelings.

"Vernon would give Bible study after Bible study, for thirteen, sixteen hours, and I wrestled and wrestled with the doctrines he was teaching. I knew I did not like who Vernon was becoming, but I couldn't separate myself from the group."

Koresh went too far when he announced his new teaching that he "owned" all the women in the sect. Breault's wife Elizabeth, also a Davidian, was visiting family in Australia at the time, but the new doctrine threw Breault into a crisis.

"The problem was forcing my inner turmoil to calm so I could think logically," he remembered. Eventually, he managed to assemble two mutually exclusive, although not entirely logical, alternatives.

"I thought to myself, *maybe Vernon is right. This new talk of violence and Vernon having all the women is what God really wants and, therefore, I should hang in there and endure until paradise.* But then I thought, *if this is what God wants, that God isn't worth worshipping.* My only other option was that Vernon was wrong and that I should take steps to leave the group."

He recalled the moment several months later when he made the connection in a sudden awakening we had come to recognize as a reverse "snapping out" process—a true enlightenment experience.

"I'll never forget that moment. I felt as if a great weight was lifted off me. I felt lighter. But most of all I felt free, like I was my own master again after so many years of being controlled. It was as if I had been another person less than a second before, then I reached this conclusion and the change was almost instantaneous. I was a different person and I felt better than I had in years."

Breault shared his new awareness with his wife when she returned. The pair confronted Koresh and, soon after, walked away from the sect. They relocated in Australia and later helped more than thirty Davidians to leave Koresh's degenerating New Jerusalem. Others snapped out of it as he did, Breault told us—providing ample proof that Branch Davidians at Waco were subject to debilitating mind control practices that impaired and physically diminished their capacities to think, feel and chose.

"One woman said it was like 'a controlling spirit' had left her," Breault reported. "She said she felt as if she had been hypnotized, and the instant she concluded that Vernon was wrong, she woke up."

Many suffered great guilt after leaving the group. Others left filled with fear from Koresh's preaching that apostates were destined for unending torment and divine punishment. Amid reports that Koresh kept a hit list of defectors targeted for death by his loyal corps of "Mighty Men," some who left went into hiding, like those who left the Peoples Temple, and remained hidden after Waco's demise.

Marc Breault and David Bunds walked us through the confrontation. In 1990, Breault, his wife and their group of mostly Australian ex-members brought their concerns to the attention of U.S. government authorities. Two years and many futile efforts later, out of frustration and growing fear for those still in the sect, like the concerned relatives group whose warnings to public officials fell on deaf ears before the Jonestown disaster, they turned to the media. An Australian TV crew was the first to discern that the once-docile Davidians had become a dangerous armed cult. Worried relatives and child welfare agencies crowded in. The death dance began—two accelerating spirals of building energy and information turning in steadily opposing directions. Soon turbulence began to appear at the perimeter. Armed guards circled the encampment around the clock. Neighbors alarmed by sounds of gunfire complained to local authorities. A shipment of grenade casings split open en route to Waco and started an investigation by local lawmen, who soon appealed to federal firearms officials for assistance.

Late in 1992, in another pattern with parallels to Jonestown, the *Waco Tribune-Herald* started work on a multi-part series about the sect. As the publication date neared, Breault and other ex-members were contacted by ATF investigators. Breault cautioned the agency against adding heat to the reaction.

"The ATF agents I spoke with were quite good," he recalled. "They said they wanted to get Vernon on his own, to lure him away from Mt. Carmel and arrest him. Their other scenario was a raid on Mt. Carmel. I said if they were going to do a raid they had better have the element of surprise or they would end up with an armed confrontation."

Within hours of the raid, Breault received a call in Australia from FBI agents on the scene who had moved in to manage the crisis.

"It was pretty chaotic. I talked with an FBI negotiator for half an hour. He asked what I thought Koresh would do. I said I thought it would end in massive death, a mass suicide. I explained Vernon's belief about the fifth seal of Revelations, which said there had to be a certain number of martyrs before the end could come."

But that knowledgeable warning and others like it went unheeded.

Like Breault, David Bunds watched in horror as the events unfolded. Prior to the raid, he, too, had been interviewed at length by ATF agents planning the government's action.

"I said, 'Don't go in there with your guns. It won't work,' " he recalled. "And they said, 'Oh, we're not going to do that.' "

When the siege began, FBI field agents pumped Bunds for information but never asked for his advice. When the end came, Bunds was at a loss to understand the government's reasoning and how things had gone so tragically wrong.

"Here we are in the 1990s," he said. "We have all this information on cults and the way they work, yet the FBI didn't have a clue. They thought they could pressure them into surrendering. I knew like my own self that wasn't going to work."

He laid out the fatal theology outsiders were not privy to, the pathological thought process at the center of the Branch Davidian cult that government tacticians obviously had failed to take seriously enough.

"Koresh taught them that when they started to burn they would be glorified. They would be transformed into radiant beings and ascend into heaven. In their minds they believed they weren't really going to die. They were going to be transformed. They were going to get their reward. Then they would come back and take over the world."

Bund's sister Robyn and her four-year-old son fathered by Koresh left the sect in 1990. His mother left a year later. His father, the first to join and to criticize Koresh, stayed. On the morning of the ATF raid, he went into Waco and was taken into custody by the ATF when he returned. The fate of the others is public record. Perry Jones, the Davidian elder who recruited Marc Breault, was killed in the ATF raid. Jones' daughters Rachel and Michelle, Koresh's first wives, along with Breault's friend Steve Schneider, Schneider's wife Judy, her two-year-old child with Koresh and seventy more perished in the flames.

Post-mortem. The official post-mortems fleshed out the chaos at Waco. Autopsies revealed that at least twenty-seven Davidians had died of bullet wounds. Seven were shot in the forehead at close range, including Koresh himself. Children took special abuse: a three-year-old was stabbed in the chest, three children were shot in the head, others appeared to have been beaten to death. Yet investigators could not say whether those killings were part of a planned mass suicide, whether some sect members were killed while trying to escape by Koresh's lieutenants, or whether some killed themselves and their children to escape the horror of death by fire.

Government sources provided other information. In the first public testimony, ATF agents wounded in the initial raid claimed their superiors knew in advance that the critical element of surprise was blown but sent their team into a near-certain ambush anyway. At the ATF and FBI, evidence emerged of attempted cover-ups and official misrepresentations all along the chain of command. Only U.S. Attorney General Janet Reno, who came to her post halfway through the FBI siege, publicly accepted responsibility for the disaster.

And everyone swore there was no evidence to support the possibility of a Jonestown-style mass suicide occurring at Waco.

Two executive branch inquests, six congressional hearings, and our own follow-up inquiries under the Freedom of Information Act painted a very different picture. Along with the sworn testimony of public officials and the documented chronology of events, our inquiries revealed how little homework the government had done in response to Congress' call after Jonestown for a concentrated program of research and training on cults. Our FOIA searches confirmed that, throughout the Waco standoff, the entire FBI knowledge base on cults, cult mind control and related subjects consisted of a lone twelve-page white paper titled "Cults." The paper, a superficial summary of identifying characteristics of cult leaders and methods, was all cribbed from one obscure academic work on the subject. We learned later that it was not even prepared until weeks after the ATF raid and the start of the FBI siege.

The official inquests, conducted in-house by the ATF's and FBI's parents, the U.S. Treasury and Justice Departments, produced two final reports totalling nearly 800 pages and released within days of each other in late 1993. The Treasury report was excoriating and self-reprimanding. "The decision to proceed was tragically wrong," it concluded. The report acknowledged that senior ATF officials made misleading statements to Congress and doctored official records relating to the planning and execution of the operation. The ATF director resigned, his two deputies and the bureau's intelligence chief were forcibly retired, and the two senior agents who led the raid were fired.

The Department of Justice inquest was more problematical. DOJ investigators chronicled a long list of judgment errors and tactical mistakes. Their review found widespread confusion, disagreement and breakdowns in communication among FBI personnel involved in the Waco operation, but reviewers refused to assign blame or responsibility. No heads rolled. No ranking FBI or Justice Department official was even reprimanded.

The *New York Times* and other critics dismissed the report as a "whitewash," however, the DOJ report contained many revealing insights. Significantly, the report illuminated the role of the FBI's discreet Behavioral Science subunit, headquartered in Quantico, Virginia, in the play of events on the Texas plain. During the first weeks of the siege, two behavioral science experts prepared a series of memoranda recommending specific strategies for the government to follow in the standoff. Special agents Peter Smerick and Mark Young called for a de-escalation of "tactical pressure," and for patient negotiations aimed at facilitating a peaceful surrender. They warned that "a strong show of force" could "draw David Koresh and his followers closer together in the 'bunker mentality,' and they would rather die than surrender."

In contrast to the FBI's earlier representations, the bureau's own experts had in fact warned explicitly, more than a month before the final conflagration, that "mass suicide ordered by Koresh cannot be discounted." From the outset, Smerick and Young cautioned against high-pressure tactical options that, they believed, might result in "Davidians fighting to the death and tremendous loss of life." However, those views were rejected by FBI commanders on the scene.

As the standoff wore on, outside experts from the FBI's approved roster of contract consultants were called in to advise the ground tacticians. The FBI's high-profile Hostage Rescue Team carried more clout and ultimately carried the day. The outcome could hardly have been worse, but it was by no means unforeseen. By the end, in addition to the bureau's in-house advisers, four of six FBI consultants in psychiatry and psychology, along with Marc Breault and others with first-hand knowledge of the sect, had warned that, a group suicide was not only possible but probable—despite Koresh's solemn assurances to negotiators that suicide was against his religion. The last signals came only a month before the final assault, when the Houston psychiatrist who interviewed the children freed early in the siege reported that several had drawn pictures of the compound being consumed by flames. Others told him that "everyone is going to die," that sect leaders were planning "to blow you all up" and that, as they left the compound, their parents had promised to "see them in heaven."

Public sensitivities were shocked by the bungled ATF raid and the FBI's military-style aggressions. Despite overwhelming evidence of the Davidians' illegal arms and documented abuses, including Koresh's own acts that constituted statutory rape, a felony in Texas, many Americans were sympathetic toward Koresh and even defended the sect's violent actions. On the far right, a cottage industry sprang up among anti-government ideologues, conspiracy theorists and propagandists promulgating heinous claims and some patently false reports. Among their many assertions defied by the facts: that the Davidians had no illegal arms, that the ATF agents were killed by their own teammates, and that government commandos in flameproof suits secretly murdered the sect members, shot, stabbed and clubbed the children, and lit the fires that consumed the compound.

In the trial that followed, sect survivors charged the government with persecuting them for their unorthodox religious beliefs and for exercising their constitutional right to bear arms. As in the Weaver trial, all eleven Davidian survivors were acquitted of murder charges, although nine were convicted on lesser counts and sentenced to prison terms up to forty years. In other actions, the two fired ATF agents sued the government and were reinstated to civilian jobs in the agency. Civil suits were filed against those who managed the Waco action, including a $500 million wrongful death suit against Attorney General Reno and twenty-five other federal officials. A 1995 congressional hearing, packed with witnesses, consultants and peripheral figures allied with the powerful national gun lobby, tried hard to turn the tragedy into a political triumph for the far right, but by all accounts the effort backfired and, in many ways, affirmed the government's actions.

Lost in all the legalizing was a clear view of how the U.S. government became the other arm of the twister that tore through Texas. In late 1994, before the tragedy turned into a political football, we interviewed officials who participated in the action and others who later investigated it. They described first-hand how the conflict was apprehended, and misapprehended, by government officials who were legitimately focused on serious law enforcements matters but, at the same time, blind to the perils of their own questionable law enforcement strategies. We also learned how well-meaning civil servants concerned for the safety of American citizens, and the lives of federal officers as well, were sucked into the vortex by their own institutional pathologies of communication—or, as they were frequently described by government evaluators, "communication breakdowns." These included: the tough-cop culture of law-enforcement entrenched in both the ATF and the FBI, which fed both bureaus' reactions to Koresh's defiance and manipulations; official ignorance and erroneous assumptions about the new phenomenon of cult control, which government agencies had denied for decades and which affected every aspect of the government's actions; and, behind the scenes, misplaced concerns for religious-political sensitivities among the public and powerful special interests, which hounded the government throughout the Waco operation and long afterwards.

These patterns and others created their own forms of closure, control and confrontation that probably cost some lives needlessly and, no doubt, changed many more forever.

We spoke first with former Deputy Attorney General Philip B. Heymann, who headed the Justice Department's inquiry into FBI operations in Waco. Like other DOJ officials, Heymann entered the picture late in the action. He arrived at Justice the day the fire broke out in Waco and, a month later, he was asked to manage the DOJ review. In our talk after the report was completed and he had returned to teaching at Harvard, Heymann acknowledged that the FBI went into Waco unprepared for a major cult confrontation.

"The FBI was trained to deal with terrorists," said Heymann, "but it wasn't trained to deal with a religious group with a messianic leader. There was no precedent of the FBI's handling such a situation and there had been no planning for one."

From the outset, Heymann said, he wanted to make the government inquest, not an exercise in blame-placing, but a constructive review with an eye toward any future eventualities that might arise on the domestic scene. He had in mind, not only cult showdowns like Waco, but more ominous acts of religious-political terror like the World Trade Center bombing that took place just two days before the ATF raid on the Branch Davidian compound.

"I wanted to see that we were organized and managed in such a way that, if this situation came up again in any form, including an extreme Islamic fundamentalist group, we could understand how to think about them, how to talk to them, when to put pressure on and when not to put pressure on, all the things that go into negotiations."

We told Heymann that we detected much ambivalence in the government on the issue of cults. He acknowledged that, from the outset, there was reluctance among officials to confront the cult aspects of the Waco standoff, to engage the concept of cult mind control, or even to use the word "cult" in the government's investigation.

"You're absolutely right. I hesitated to use any of those terms," he admitted. "We tried to avoid labeling the group as a 'cult,' suggesting crazies. There was a purposeful attempt to not give the group one label or another. The general understanding was that we were dealing with a, you know, a group that had passionate beliefs, that was extremely suspicious of the government—"

Was his hesitation caused by concerns of legal terminology or religious sensitivity?

"It was in relation to religious sensitivities," Heymann said candidly. "We wanted to avoid having to dispute the people who, on the one side, treat groups like this as just another fundamentalist religion and, on the other, regard them as a dangerous form of mind control. I did not want to come down on one side or the other of that debate."

His explanation sounded reasonable enough but bespoke deeper political considerations. In our view, the official silence from beginning to end on the mind control factor in the conflict, and the government's persisting avoidance of the entire subject of cult control, were two critical breakdowns in the communication process that contributed significantly to the chaos at Waco and the public confusion that abounded in its aftermath.

A related concern to us were numerous factual errors that were disseminated in the official record of events at Waco. We cited several errors we had documented in the DOJ report that seriously misrepresented the extent of FBI contacts with cult experts and former Branch Davidians. Those errors were relevant, we said, because of persisting questions about the nature of Koresh's control over his followers and the many warning flags raised by ex-members, and by experts within and without the FBI, about the cult's potential for mass suicide. Apparently, concerns over the politically sensitive cult issue caused some to ignore those warnings and even deny receiving them. Heymann did not defend the government's sources.

"I think you have to assume that any organization after a result like this is going to try to play down their responsibility, but we ought to have picked that up in our report and I'm disappointed if we weren't skeptical enough."

Another part of the report dismissed the entire body of scientific knowledge on the nature and effects of cult control. One outside expert Heymann had selected to aid in the DOJ review asserted that "the notion of 'cult brainwashing' has been thoroughly discredited in the academic community" and castigated federal agents for "failing to recognize the free choice those people had made in following Koresh." We suggested to Heymann that the work of respected social scientists and mental health professionals—knowledge and clinical expertise that could have been of practical value to negotiators and for future contingency planning—had been disparaged, while cult propaganda that had been exposed long ago was disseminated with the government's imprimatur. Heymann was silent for some time before speaking.

"Yes, I understand what you're saying," he told us. "We wanted each expert to say what he or she thought. We certainly didn't want to censor or edit them in any way, but we weren't embracing all their views."

Heymann assured us that the government had learned important lessons from Waco and would be better prepared to deal with future contingencies on the fractious boundary between law and religion. However, his closing comments made clear to us that, when it came to the legal dilemmas of cult control and other issues in the sensitive, and increasingly political, arena of religion, understanding was still lacking and the government's position was far from resolved.

"I think we're going to be prepared to confront any obvious illegality done in the name of religion," said Heymann. "If someone commits a serious crime, like killing government agents, there's no doubt that the government will be prepared to use force to make an arrest. But if they haven't, if it's a question of whether people have been brainwashed, I think you'll continue to see the same history we've had for the last twenty or thirty years. We don't really have any way of deciding whether brainwashing is holding someone against one's will or not, or what to do about it."

Heymann directed us to other officials still in the Justice Department. Richard Scruggs, Assistant to the Attorney General, assembled the official chronology of events for the DOJ review. He recalled the mood at the Justice Department when he came to work at the midpoint of the Waco standoff.

"The AG started here two weeks into the siege. I arrived two weeks later and, by that time, planning was already well underway to get the people out of the compound. After the fire, I was called in to try to figure out what the hell had happened. We did a thousand interviews. We got every piece of the story from everyone's perspective."

We asked Scruggs a key question: had the Attorney General been given the full range of evidence and opinion on the chances of mass suicide by the sect before she approved the final assault? He described the process by which this crucial information was relayed up the chain of command from bureau resources and senior FBI officials.

"The whole issue of suicide and the psychological makeup of Koresh and his followers was obviously something we looked into," said Scruggs. "The bureau sought dozens of expert opinions and many more were offered. There were literally hundreds of people calling in with advice, not just people off the street but people from recognized institutes and universities. The result was that FBI commanders, both in Waco and in Washington, had so many opinions, ranging from 'they'll commit suicide as soon as you make any move at all' to 'they'll never commit suicide,' that it really allowed them to pick whichever experts confirmed their own point of view. The experts FBI officials judged to be the most accurate were those who said suicide was unlikely, which turned out to be wrong."

How much of that range of opinion did the Attorney General receive? Scruggs confirmed our suspicion.

"She only got the no-suicide opinion."

He insisted that the Attorney General was indeed aware of the cult's suicide potential, but that FBI officials only cited the "no-suicide opinion" in their final briefing. Scruggs offered two explanations for the lapse, one more sinister, one more benign.

"My first impression was that someone made a conscious decision to keep this information away from the AG. It certainly looked that way. On the other hand, sometimes these things just happen, one decision leads to another, and nobody really thinks things through. I think the people who were putting together the material truly believed there was a low chance of suicide and then simply picked the materials that confirmed what they wanted to believe."

No doubt government officials preferred that more benign explanation, although serious questions remained about exactly what information FBI officials provided to the Attorney General. Either way, we recognized two more major breakdowns in the government's patterns of communication. One, commonly referred to as "groupthink," was the familiar phenomenon by which conformity is maximized and dissension minimized among people in organizations. Another, known as "dissonance reduction," part of the classic communication theory of "cognitive dissonance," described the internal process by which people unconsciously rationalize ill-fated actions and decisions after they have made them. In the process of dissonance reduction, new information that threatens accepted ideas and structures of understanding, information that causes "psychological discomfort," in our colleague Dr. Gary Cronkhite's terms, or in our perspective information stress, is systematically eliminated from the pool of plausible options.

Similar stress reduction strategies apparently were employed by people all along the chain of command in the Waco operation. The same communication processes lower down in the FBI command chain caused Waco field officers to reject the suicide warnings of their own in-house behavioral experts Peter Smerick and Mark Young.

"Oh yes, absolutely," Scruggs agreed. "Smerick and Young got wiped out by the on-site commander, who wanted a combination of negotiation and increasing pressure on the compound, the so-called 'carrot-and-stick' approach."

Scruggs attributed those tragic errors of judgment and tactics, along with many other snafus at Waco, to a plague of "information overload" that reportedly descended on stressed-out FBI commanders, negotiators and agents in the field.

"There was the most massive flood of information coming in that you could imagine," he went on. "Did a lot of stuff get filtered out as it went up the line? The answer is yes. But I think it's more reflective of the way every bureaucratic initiative goes through. The bureaucracy scrubs out dissent. I think what happened was more of a bureaucratic scrub, if you will."

We asked Scruggs if a similar "bureaucratic scrub" might have caused government decision makers to ignore the crucial mind control factor, and the discomforting issues it raised legally and politically, in their strategic thinking and contingency planning for resolving the Waco crisis.

"Oh, no. The bureau believes strongly in mind control, believe me," said Scruggs, "oh, absolutely." His statement struck us as a minor revelation after decades of categorical denials by government officials. He pulled back the curtain on the FBI's internal assumptions that reigned throughout the standoff. "There was a great debate going on in the bureau whether Koresh was a con man or whether he really thought he was some kind of messiah, but whichever he was there was no doubt that he was effectively controlling the rest of the people. Everybody assumed that."

Yet apparently that assumption was not for public consumption. "Everybody believed he did it through some kind of brainwashing or mind control. We scrubbed the report of words like that, but the bureau used them. They fully understood that."

Scruggs said that understanding extended to FBI commanders in the field and to the bureau's elite Hostage Rescue Team. He cited it as a rationale for the use of the loudspeakers and the psywar tactics.

"Most people in the bureau believed Koresh and his core supporters would never come out. But even up to the tear gas insertion on the last day, they had hopes that, by making it very uncomfortable, they could overcome the control Koresh exercised over the rest and get out a large number of the women and children. They even used the phrase 'the motherhood instinct.'"

It was a plausible theory but a poor place to test it, and it made us wonder even more what government officials meant when they alternately denied, then acknowledged, the reality of cult control. In this instance, the FBI's actions seemed only to prove how powerful such control was that it could overwhelm the most basic human instincts.

"Yes," Scruggs acknowledged, "in that case it may have."

By that point, however, the other options available to FBI commanders were even less attractive. Scruggs gave a glimpse of some alternatives government officials considered, then quickly dismissed.

"The options were minimal. They could have killed Koresh—the Israelis couldn't understand why we didn't do that. The HRT had Koresh in their sights fifty times. They could have killed him and all his leaders and that would have been the end of it, but that was not an option. They looked into all kinds of other things. One official had heard rumors that the government had a secret weapon, like a laser weapon or sound weapon, that could vibrate people in some nonlethal way and get them out of there. We didn't. We found out later there was a microwave weapon, but they couldn't use it because it affected people differently based on their body size and weight. It didn't do much to big people but it tended to cook little people."

The anecdote showed the depth of the government's frustration and its powerlessness to counter the new mind control methods by conventional matter-and-energy means. During those tense weeks, and in public debates for years afterwards, everyone and his brother seemed to have a sure-fire strategy that would have saved the day, but for Scruggs and other officials we spoke with, Waco was a no-win situation. He summed up the damnable dilemma of the Waco debacle as he saw it.

"I'm not saying that mistakes weren't made, because they were, but I became firmly convinced in my own mind, after looking at this sixteen hours a day for six months, that it was Koresh's game. He was, in effect, controlling us no less than he was controlling his own people."

The death spiral cut both ways. Its chaotic dynamics consumed the sect members at its center and pulled public officials from the top of the system downward into the vortex. Our last interview took us into the other eye of the storm. Carl Stern, Director of Public Affairs for the Department of Justice, was present at those crucial decision-making sessions held in the office of Attorney General Janet Reno in which the FBI presented its tear gas assault plan for her approval. He recalled his personal predicament, shared by all the new administration appointees in Washington, of coming cold to events in progress, and the tumult of meetings and decisions during that final weekend before the culminating events of Monday, April 19.

"I arrived here on Thursday and had my first meeting on Waco fifteen minutes after I walked in the door," Stern told us. "Two people from the criminal division were advocating the tear gas plan. I took the other position and we argued it in front of the Attorney General. The next day I attended a meeting where I really felt the idea had been turned off. I was confident that nothing was going forward. Then on Saturday it got turned around 180 degrees."

How did that happen?

"I'm not certain," Stern said, truly puzzled. He was called late to the Saturday meeting of senior Justice and FBI officials, and by the time he arrived the assault plan seemed to have gained a new and unstoppable momentum.

"The AG was there with her deputies, the FBI Director was there with his deputies, and they were going through the whole thing all over again."

Stern summarized the long list of official priorities that weighed in favor of the action.

"The FBI was concerned about deteriorating health conditions in the compound. There were dead bodies on the premises. The building had no indoor plumbing. People were defecating in buckets and dumping it in a pit out back and, after fifty days, there was real concern that there would be a massive disease outbreak and the first ones to get sick and die would be the kids. They were concerned that the perimeter of the compound was highly unstable. It was a large perimeter. There had been several breaches of it. There were rumors that armed pro-Koresh groups might come from Houston or California or elsewhere to put an end to the siege. Finally, the Hostage Rescue Team had been there for forty-nine days at that point—the longest they had ever gone before was four days. They were in sniper positions around the clock. They were losing their edge, not training, sitting out there in mudholes, and they were afraid if something went wrong in the rest of the country they would not be able to respond."

Stern talked down reports that false claims of new child abuses by Koresh were the determining factor in the decision to attack.

"The AG asked a number of questions and this became the legend of what she was concerned about. She asked first about sanitary conditions. She asked next about sexual assault and child abuse. The FBI replied that if Koresh was still doing what he had been doing prior to the raid he was legally committing statutory rape. Third, the question of beatings came up. As recently as March 21, youngsters had been released who described having been beaten. The consensus was that, at a minimum, the government was not adequately protecting these children, but all that got distorted later."

We asked about discussion of the risks associated with the tear gas assault, particularly the threat of suicide by Koresh and other Davidians. Stern confirmed that the prospect was firmly dismissed by FBI officials and played no role in the final decision-making process. Was the AG told about the many expert assessments to the contrary? He replied as a witness to history and official government spokesman.

"What the Attorney General heard was the assessment that he was not suicidal."

He offered other insights into traditional law enforcement thinking and the historical tough-cop culture of the FBI, which later evaluators cited as central factors in the proposal by bureau commanders to attack the compound with tear gas.

"Remember, four officers had been killed, the FBI had never waited so long in a hostage situation, and from their perspective, it was really untenable that people who had killed federal officers were going on week after week thumbing their noses at law enforcement."

However, Stern also acknowledged that the assault plan which was presented and approved was at odds with the operation as it was executed.

"Please keep in mind that there was no plan to demolish the compound. As we said at the time, it was not D-Day. The original plan was a two-day plan for gradual insertion of gas to progressively shrink the usable space and continually encourage people to come out."

Instead, when the Davidians met the tanks with hundreds of rounds of automatic weapons fire, ground commanders responded by stepping up their timetable and increasing the flow of tear gas into more areas of the compound—all, apparently, to no avail. Stern claimed that unforeseen factors, the inevitable precursors to chaos, played havoc with events that day.

"No one anticipated the wind," he said. "The tanks were not supposed to strike the building, but because of the wind, the gas wasn't getting in and they had to get closer and finally insert the booms through the window millwork. In the course of doing so, they struck the walls and the roof."

By that time, no one was anticipating David Koresh either. Stern recalled the scene at the FBI command center in Washington when the standoff spiraled into its death throes.

"I was in the SIOC [Strategic Intervention Operations Center] when the fire broke out. At first, Floyd Clarke, the FBI's Deputy Director, thought an engine had blown on one of the vehicles they had rented from the Army. They didn't realize what had happened. Then, when it became clear that it was a fire, they all sat there waiting for the people to come out. They were saying, 'Come on baby, come on out, come on out.' They were expecting people to come flooding out and there were no people coming out and they were absolutely incredulous. Even when it was over, they were still assuming they would find the kids in the bus they had buried underground."

That assumption, too, proved tragically wrong. Stern made no excuses for the FBI's failure to take the suicide threat seriously.

"All I can tell you is that, given the atmosphere at the time, it was a surprise the suicide occurred. Remember, by then, most of the children in the compound were Koresh's own. The thought that he would permit his own children to be harmed was inconceivable."

For us, that assumption, and many others that were perhaps justifiable in dealings with more conventional criminal minds, showed up the fatal flaw in the FBI's thinking—and the overriding problem with the government's approach to the social problems posed by cult control groups. Reading between Stern's carefully metered lines and those of other officials, our gut feelings told us that ranking FBI officers, tired of being manipulated by Koresh and, no doubt, genuinely concerned for the precedents they were setting for future confrontations, may have misguided the Attorney General into giving ground commanders too much leeway in the execution of the final assault plan—leeway that, as the tank and tear gas assault progressed, unleashed the full destructive potential of Koresh and the people under his control. However, in our view, that gaping hole in the government's strategy was not wrought by any battering ram or armored vehicle. Amid the push and pull of the government's internal debate, the failure of FBI officials in Washington and Waco to heed warning after warning that the cult's destructive urges would ignite under pressure hastened the demise of the doom-bent Davidians.

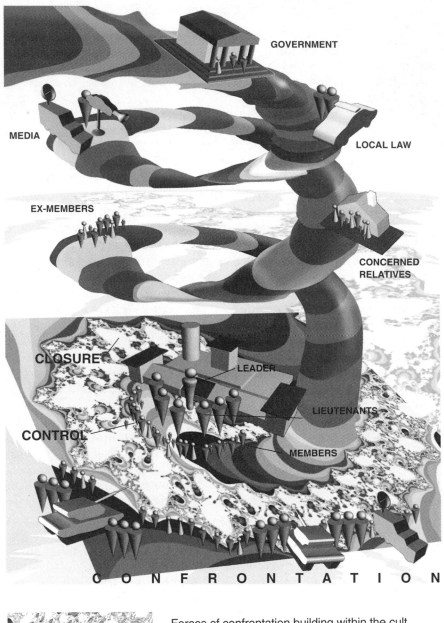

GOVERNMENT

MEDIA

LOCAL LAW

EX-MEMBERS

CONCERNED RELATIVES

CLOSURE

LEADER

CONTROL

LIEUTENANTS

MEMBERS

C O N F R O N T A T I O N

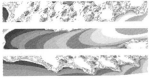 Forces of confrontation building within the cult

Incoming negative feedback from society

Boundary where chaotic actions & reactions occurred

Figure 5: The Waco conflict modeled on the dynamics of chaos theory

Stern offered his own closing argument in an effort to, if not excuse, at least account for the trust in government that, for many Americans, went up in flames at Waco.

"The Attorney General had only been on the job five weeks," Stern reminded us. "She didn't even have her own staff yet. She was really flying solo. She had to rely on somebody, so she relied on the FBI and their vaunted Hostage Rescue Team. Those of us who have been around town a little longer know that, while there's much to admire about the FBI, it does not have an unblemished record. There are times when they have been mistaken. They're not perfect. In the world of cats and dogs, sometimes they're closer to dogs than cats. If she had been Attorney General for two years and had more experience dealing with the bureau, she might have solicited more information."

The lessons of Waco cannot be simply drawn, but some conclusions can be made from the evidence and supporting testimony: the actions of David Koresh and his followers placed the government in a position where some intervention was called for to apprehend a suspected lawbreaker with a history and declared plan of violence who posed a danger to those around him and, potentially, to a much wider population. However, the challenge of defusing a delusional cult leader with scores of armed followers under his control was never fully comprehended or accurately informed and, as a result, it led to the exact outcome it had sought to avoid.

We mapped the incident at Waco onto our computer-generated chaos curve extracted from the Mandelbrot set. (See Figure 5). From the start, the conflict was grimly deterministic. Its path was charted, not by any logical progression of real-world facts and events, but by a prophesied event in biblical time as foretold in a tale scripted by a madman. The two spirals paced through their turns with a seemingly unstoppable momentum. The sect's leaders, lieutenants and followers progressed predictably from closure to control to confrontation. The ATF raid was a ceremony in chaos, a monument to that tell-tale quality and certain recipe for disaster chaos theorists call "sensitive dependence on initial conditions." A series of seemingly small errors in the government's calculations about a highly sensitive situation—the assumption by raid planners that they were dealing with conventional criminal minds; the butterfly in the breeze, the leak to local TV crews; the belief of raid commanders that their plan could still succeed once the element of surprise was lost—produced an enormous consequence.

The same chaotic volatility ruled throughout the FBI siege. Strategic errors considered of negligible concern to negotiators had major ramifications. The assumption that sect members were merely "hostages" allowed the crucial question of cult control to be altogether ignored. The erroneous "mother instinct" assumption proved fatal to mothers and their children. The FBI's tactical teams, ground commanders and field negotiators, many of whom were themselves physically exhausted, mentally overloaded and utterly frustrated by Koresh, dismissed the warnings of ex-members, independent witnesses and their own experts and played a longshot in the no-win game they had inherited. In the process, the entire command chain gave way to its own set of chaotic dynamics: to closed institutional thinking, subtle internecine struggles, serious errors in judgment and—not to forget—genuine differences of opinion among people acting in good faith and with the best intentions.

In the end, both parties to the action were consumed by their respective internal communication pathologies. Both fell victim to their own runaway positive feedback within that carried a lethal negative charge to the tensions massing along their shared perimeter—and to Koresh's endgame of duel-to-the-death. In the aftermath, by skirting the entire issue of cult control, then systematically scrubbing any mention of the problem from the government's internal reviews and public accountings, government officials virtually insured that the same gross communication breakdowns and chaotic dynamics would be passed down to the next cult crisis, terrorist threat and religious-political challenge waiting in the wings.

The lessons of Jonestown and Waco need to be grasped sooner rather than later, for those conflicts were microcosms auguring larger conflicts that have already begun to turn in pre-chaotic patterns. Our chaos model offered one tool for mapping the communication dynamics of social confrontations with cults and other ideologically controlled groups, for determining when critical thresholds were being approached and crossed, and when crucial windows were opening and closing for appropriate interventions by law enforcement, social services and mental health professionals. However, in our view, the greater lesson for people in America and elsewhere was this: without new understanding of the vulnerabilities of the mind and new legal protections for the basic human freedom that must come before any other in an information age—freedom of thought—freedom itself becomes just another strange attractor in the hands of artful manipulators drawing individuals and societies downward to destruction.

17 Snapping in Everyday Life

Consciousness is a social product.

—B. F. Skinner,
Beyond Freedom and Dignity

AND WHAT ABOUT the rest of us—those of us who have not even remotely considered participating in a mind-altering cult, pop therapy or apocalyptic sect and, in all likelihood, never will? Why should we be concerned about snapping?

The answer is, because it's all around us. The threat of snapping extends far beyond cults and cult-like groups, beyond their controlling rituals and engineered experiences, to the constant stresses and shared traumas of daily life at the end of the twentieth century. Just as moving land masses may shift gradually and imperceptibly and then give way in a massive earthquake, so, too, the cumulative forces of our stress-filled technological society have brought unprecedented changes to individuals and cultures: masses of information, mountains of technology and an explosion of new experiences, increased pressures on our minds and bodies, new strains of illness, spreading social turmoil, and the breakdown of basic human bonds and supporting social structures . These changes are making people anxious and confused, feeling overwhelmed and overloaded, more vulnerable to manipulation, and ultimately less capable of thinking and acting as fully human beings.

Social scientists have studied the effects of these new pressures on work and family life in today's post-industrial, high-technological society. Culture watchers have described the effects of "future shock" and other ills caused by unrelenting change, and the many forms of backlash and reaction those changes may evoke socially, politically and spiritually. Since the sixties, people in cultures worldwide have been warned about these spreading threats to their health, happiness and prosperity. They have been offered countless strategies for coping, recipes for living, exercises for relaxation, and no shortage of self-proclaimed saviors. Yet, for many, as those looming threats become realities, the barrage of urgent warnings and offered cures has become just another part of the onslaught, more information for their brains to metabolize and attempt to make into something meaningful. This mounting information assault on the modern mind is leading many people to a form of snapping that is more subtle yet clearly observable in America and many cultures today—the form we call snapping in everyday life.

In this chapter, we offer a few scenarios from this spreading epidemic as we have been tracking it in wider real-world arenas.

Information Stress Revisited. Like snapping in cults, like human consciousness itself, snapping in everyday life is a product of information and communication. Volumes have been written about the information revolution in the half century since it began, about the impact of computers, automation and global telecommunications on our industries, economies and lifestyles. However, the media and our social institutions have barely begun to address the physical effects of the information revolution on our minds, brains and bodies, and its impact on our meanings and identities as human beings.

The evidence is everywhere that the massive amounts of information each individual is called upon to take in and process daily are pressing people to the limits of their endurance and adaptability. Yet most people remain only dimly aware of their own palpable responses to this new stress caused, not by any material force or substance, but by information: by the press of each day's news, facts, numbers, thoughts, feelings, beliefs, opinions, decisions, social demands and other information human beings need just to survive today. We saw that stress first-hand in every domain of work and daily life we looked into. People of all ages and occupations are being subjected to crushing information stresses. They are being overwhelmed by the accelerating pace of daily life and the snowballing complexity of technology, by endless demands on their awareness and countless interests competing for their attention, by all the details they must remember and decisions they must make each day, and by deeper inner stresses many feel but can barely begin to express.

Near our home base in New York City, we talked with a vice-president at one of the nation's largest communications corporations. He vividly described the information stresses he and his colleagues endured each day as they created and disseminated the mass-produced messages that were themselves a source of stress for millions.

"Working in this office day-to-day is, and I can't emphasize this enough, an extremely stressful experience," he told us. "At any given instant, you're working on ten different things, the phone is ringing constantly, you're due at three meetings at once, you've got a stack of paper on your desk two feet high, secretaries are nailing notes to your door, and people are crowding into your office talking at you at the top of their lungs. You wade through all this madness and sometimes you just want to say, 'Enough, already! Wait a minute!' But you can't stop. You've got to deal with it all."

Those suffering even worse stresses are people toiling in the human fields: in medicine, mental health, social work and other helping professions. On a trip through the Southwest, we met a physical therapist in her late thirties who described the creeping "burnout" for which her field was notorious and her chronic feelings of inner "acceleration."

"I burned out completely in my last job," she said, still smarting from the experience. "I was working at one of the best clinics around, and then everything fell through in me. They wanted us to treat twenty patients a day. I tell you *nobody* can treat twenty patients a day. I treat twelve and I am beat. I had to work in a very small space. There was music pounding away nonstop. The whole environment was just bombarding me from every direction and I couldn't handle it. My mind took on a running pace. I felt like I was running a hundred miles an hour all the time and I couldn't slow down."

She strained to describe the intangible stresses that pushed her to a physical and emotional edge.

"It built in me," she said. "It wasn't just one thing, this or that, but a lot of things, this, this, this, this, *this*, and that, that, that, that, *that*. Everything was just assaulting me from everywhere, inside, outside, until I couldn't absorb any more. Sometimes I'd come home at night and just cry and cry and cry from the pain of trying to deal with it all."

Everyone today is susceptible to the pressures of snapping in everyday life. The pace of modern life alone is enough to do the job. In addition, many of the same information stresses which have been identified as potent tools of control and manipulation in cults are so much a part of life in the nineties that their impact on all our abilities to think and feel may be easily overlooked.

Like the professionals we met, people in every job are being subjected to overwhelming pressure to work harder, think faster, respond quicker, contain more complexity, juggle more diverse tasks, absorb more passing insults, and improve both the quantity and quality of the goods they make and the services they perform. In their personal lives as well, they are finding little reprieve from the demands of children and family, social relationships, money problems, health concerns, fears about the food they eat, the air they breathe, the safety of their homes and communities, the state of their country, and other matters that leave the mind scant time for rest or self-reflection.

Through it all, people are being pushed, prodded and propelled, from without and within, by the expanding technology of experience. At work, millions immerse themselves daily in factory and office environments that have been scientifically engineered to maximize their feelings of employee motivation and satisfaction. In the marketplace, consumers conditioned over years to respond to simple, behavior-oriented advertising appeals are now being retrained to think and feel in the new language of "experiential" marketing, an idiom that speaks to select target audiences of potential buyers in terms formed from sophisticated computer profiles of their shared beliefs, values, lifestyles, goals and other intimate inner responses. In forums of politics and public debate, people are being appealed to increasingly by professionally coached communicators, "spin doctors" and media image-makers, all armed with the same polling analyses, "psychographic breakdowns," "sound bites" and "talking points" custom-tailored for each citizen according to his or her personal attributes, ethnic origin, sexual orientation and religious affiliation.

Those who simply consume this loaded diet of information uncritically, like junk food or candy, may become inattentive and passively receptive to the engineered messages that come at them daily, messages urging them to surrender to the impulses of mass society, to the routine manipulation of their opinions, beliefs and emotions, and to contrived self-images, social roles, political solutions and spiritual rewards that make promises their messengers cannot and, often, do not intend to keep.

The impact of information stress is well-known: the more complex information and experience a person consumes, the more suggestible he may become. Cults and many other groups exploit this principle. They concoct exotic information environments and ritual practices that confuse and covertly control people's awareness. The same principle can be seen at work in countless everyday communications: in the deluge of commercial messages, phone solicitations, catalogs and junk mail pouring into people's homes, in the use of dazzling images and surreptitious "product placement" in popular films and electronic entertainments, in the psychological design of enchanting children's stores, theme parks, resorts, restaurants and other modern consumer environments. Each engineered experience is devised in its own way to manipulate and covertly influence the buyer's desires, bombard the shopper's senses, challenge the customer's self-image, create confusion among competing brands of virtually identical products and, as Sargant noted, construct "emotionally charged mental conflicts needing urgent resolution."

These subtle everyday life experiences are only a few of the ways in which each individual's awareness is divided and conquered daily.

Crises of Identity. The profusion of engineered images, experiences and environments has made information stress a fact of life for Americans and many others, but information stress alone does not tell the whole story of snapping in everyday life. Beyond the boom in cults, sects and self-help therapies, the new awareness that came out of the sixties set off a culture-wide consciousness explosion. It also set off a collective identity crisis that has been rolling through America and other cultures for three decades.

Almost everyone today is capable of imagining a deeper and richer personal life. People have been given new visions of awareness, wholeness, spiritual fulfillment and the realization of their human potential. The consciousness explosion, which has been both widely defamed and cynically exploited, may seem like ancient history to younger generations and to many who lived through that era, yet it left its mark on every aspect of contemporary society. Even among those who were not touched directly by the sixties' cultural changes, by the human potential movement, the civil rights movement, the antiwar movement and their offspring, the women's movement, gay liberation, the environmental movement and the new age movement at its best (as opposed to its extremes), all of us are heirs to the new awareness.

Each day, through mass media and the global communications revolution, more people in more cultures become aware of their expanding opportunities for enriching personal, social and spiritual experiences. At the same time, many of the older institutions that once gave support and stability to people's lives are cracking under the strain of that new awareness. The revered institutions of the nuclear family, work, government and organized religion historically served as culture-wide modes of shared experience and communal information processing. They gave people a sense of identity and belonging. They set patterns of thinking, feeling and everyday living that reduced potential chaos for millions to personal and social order. As these institutions regrouped in the seventies in the name of social justice, economic equality, the environment and other long-overdue reforms, the resulting changes brought new upheavals, reactions and widespread personal confusion.

Those years left many people feeling frustrated and angry. Others felt left out and wronged in return. In the eighties, much of that new consciousness imploded, triggering a collective personality change that tore through America and other places. The implosion let loose a new wave of anti-intellectualism, an orgy of self-interest, and socially approved states of numbed "compassion fatigue." In many camps, the sixties' legacy became, not a search for personal fulfillment and a shared sense of community, but a reaction of individuals, organized interest groups and more extreme forces seeking to impose their beliefs on others.

Through it all, millions were being buffeted by another wave of change that was breeding its own new forms of snapping in everyday life.

Post-Industrial Stress. The late seventies marked the start of this next turn of awareness and shared crisis of identity. In that period, while new cults and therapies were attracting idealistic youths and upscale searchers in record numbers, a burst of technical innovation and economic competition threw the rest of American society into turmoil. Emerging nations were building their young economies from the ground up, taking advantage of new automated technologies and populations eager to work for wages a fraction of those of American workers to enhance their edge in the global marketplace.

Suddenly, after generations of progress and decades of postwar prosperity, American businesses and industries began scrambling for their lives, retrenching, retooling, tightening up and paring down every aspect of their enterprises. For workers in those enterprises, the change was shocking and often traumatic. People with steady incomes, stable lives and respected places in their communities were abruptly stripped of their livelihoods and identities. Entire populations were cut loose from their moorings, shorn of the time-tested social and cultural traditions that gave meaning to people's lives. In their absence, old animosities, new fears and long-suppressed angers began to surface.

For decades, social theorists had been warning of just such deep, structural changes coming worldwide with the spread of economic development, computers, automation and global telecommunications. Yet few took those warnings seriously until the specter of technological society began to reduce whole communities and cultures to menial labor and subsistence living. In the eighties, that specter began to stalk towns across America. In the nineties, it invaded every domain of daily life, as growing numbers experienced first-hand the rolling traumas of the global information age transition.

In a once-great industrial town in the Midwest, we met a former steelworker and his wife whose way of life was swept away in the post-industrial tide. He could barely express the pain and personal disloca-tion that overtook him when their town's aging steel mills were shut down *en masse*. She described the shock wave that hit her family when the last blast furnace went off.

"See, it happened so fast," she told us in a group discussion at a local career counseling center. "It was nothing you could plan for. At first you don't understand, then you find out your whole life has changed and you aren't prepared for it."

Six years later, this proud husband and this gentle homemaker, along with thousands of men and women like them in their town and communities across the American heartland, were still traumatized from their collective experience of sudden change. Many remained lit-erally immobilized, unable to act to find new work or move to a more promising location. Others were plagued by denial and vain delusions that their demolished mills would miraculously reopen and revive their devastated towns. Some lived in ongoing states of post-traumatic stress that affected their emotions and the everyday workings of their minds.

"I think about it all the time. I can't get it off my mind," she said, describing her intrusive thoughts and feelings in words like those we had heard from ex-sect members, Vietnam veterans and casualties of other traumatic experiences. However, her stress symptoms were not mystical delusions or combat flashbacks but real-life effects on her mind as she searched furiously for workable solutions to her family's plight. With each attempt to find viable alternatives, new dilemmas seemed to spring up one after another until they formed a hopeless maze in her head.

"You try to solve one problem and you hit a wall," she said. "You think, I'll sell the house and move to a different state. Then you think, no, I can't sell the house and, even if I could, we might move to a different state and still have nothing. You hit more walls. Our daugh-ter needs money for college, but we don't have enough money for food and the washer's about to break down. You try to solve things one way, you hit a wall, you try to solve things another way, you hit an-other wall, until you just keep hitting so many walls that you don't know what to do."

Across the table sat an unemployed college professor, unable to find work in his field because of cutbacks at local colleges. Out of desperation, he took a job at a machine tool plant until it, too, shut down for lack of business. He recalled his ongoing stress responses that struck hard at his self-confidence, identity and everyday powers of mind.

"At first, when I was laid off, I was happy, really. I had been working hard and needed a break, but as the months dragged on, the stress began to show. I had all the time in the world but I stopped reading. I couldn't concentrate. When I sat down to write, the words would not come. I would sit at the table and, three hours later, I would still be in the same place. I was aware of myself sitting there, but my mind was just blank."

He traced the path of his slow descent into a dazed state of everyday awareness. Like other casualties of snapping we had met, he was conscious of his altered state but at a loss to understand or control it. Worse still, over time, his stress was deepening and more debilitating losses were beginning to appear.

"I don't know what it is, really," he said. "Things don't stick in my mind the way they used to and, besides, now I've stopped looking for work. I have all this time on my hands and I can't deal with it. I sit and stare. I put things off."

Technostress. As we looked closer at the problems of snapping in everyday life, and at our growing list of information stress responses, we found that other researchers were drawing parallel lists of information stress disorders rising among people in very different occupations and everyday life situations.

Another major category was surfacing among the information elite of the new technological era: skilled computer engineers, software programmers and other high-tech workers. A study published in the *Harvard Medical School Health Bulletin* found that, among the millions of technicians and office workers who interact daily with computers and related high-tech devices, three-quarters reported some psychological stress response or stress-related physical ailment. A study by the National Institute for Occupational Safety and Health found simple clerical work with computers to be among the most stressful of all occupations, surpassing even the sky-high stress levels reported by air traffic controllers.

Other researchers identified the problem specifically as a new form of "information sickness." In California's fabled Silicon Valley and its East Coast counterpart, Cambridge, Massachusetts, two epicenters of the information explosion, stress management consultants were observing dramatic personality changes among people in high-technology occupations: changes in workers' personal hygiene, habits, physical appearance, and other responses which prompted two researchers to conclude that "a distinct type of individual has begun to emerge in high-tech environments." Drs. Paul Greenfield and Larry Raskin described the new personalities as "bright, analytic and driven. . . emotionally rigid or flat, out of touch with their feelings and withdrawn from family, friends and co-workers."

Berkeley, California, psychotherapist Craig Brod, in his groundbreaking 1984 book *Technostress: The Human Cost of the Computer Revolution,* described dozens of stress responses he observed in therapy sessions with high-tech workers and their families. His list of technostress responses bore striking resemblances to our catalog of information disease symptoms, and to John Wilson and Gus Krauss' inventory of PTSD symptoms among Vietnam-era veterans: nightmares, memory loss, time distortions, impaired thinking, an overall slowing of individual response, and diminished capacities for imagination, creativity and future planning. Like the patterns of inner control we observed in our cult investigations, Brod found evidence that, over time, people who work with high-tech systems also tend to internalize the tacit communication controls imposed by their machines. Of these symptoms he noted an obsessive desire among high-tech workers to achieve a state of "machine-like perfection," a tendency to think in absolute "yes-no" and "black-white" reasoning patterns, signs of mental overload, chronic fatigue and, at the same time, opposite signs of understimulation, boredom and sensory deprivation. Many of Brod's patients also voiced feelings of "dehumanization," "depersonalization," and an inability to relate to other human beings.

We found similar symptoms in our investigations. On a trip through Silicon Valley, we met a biomedical engineer who ticked off a checklist of his own stress responses. He described the new "disease" he saw affecting people immersed in the high-tech environments of Silicon Valley: an inability to form human bonds and enduring personal relationships. The problem was one he had experienced himself.

"After living most of my life in the Midwest—the 'heartland,' they call it—I came here with a deep longing for those human bonds," he told us. "Now I'm here and I know something is missing and it doesn't feel good."

The lack of human connection was causing deeper emotional difficulties. He struggled to articulate them.

"The only feeling I can really touch is a sense of loss, I don't know how else to express it," he said. "You want to share things with people. You have feelings that you want to talk about, but there's no one to talk with, so all those feelings end up being trapped inside. After a while it starts to put a prison around your mind. You've got all these things inside you that keep growing bigger but never get dealt with, and the mind either has to let them come out or squash them down constantly and not consider them anymore."

He put the blame, not only on the new technology, but on the pounding pace and competitive pressures of life in Silicon Valley's high-stress environment, which was becoming a template for work environments and communities worldwide. He voiced his larger, long-range concerns for the new disease of human disconnection.

"I worry that the change I've seen in so many people and have now begun to feel inside may be permanent," he confided, "but I really fear for the kids who are born here. I think they are going to get it, that will be the ultimate cost, and they won't feel the loss because they will never have known it any other way."

Childhood Developments. With little doubt, the young have already been deeply affected. A growing body of research suggests that today's youth have been affected at bedrock levels of their human nature by the overwhelming information of late twentieth-century life: by the combined personal pressures, social traumas, technological stresses and engineered experiences engulfing them at earlier and earlier ages. Entire generations have now been molded, not by rich real-life experiences that build strong minds, healthy emotions and well-rounded identities, but by information imparted electronically, via television, film, computers and other advanced communications technologies. For many, that fast-moving bitstream has become increasingly narrow, shallow and violent.

The numbers themselves have become mind-numbing media cliches: by the time they reach adolescence, most teenagers have spent 15,000 hours before various video tubes, watched 18,000 dramatized murders and many more engineered acts of violence, been exposed to 350,000 commercial messages, and filled their brains with thousands of arbitrary symbols and coded commands of meaning only to computers and other machines. After decades of debate over the impact of that inundating information, the jury is coming in with a near-unanimous verdict: more than 3,000 studies have linked repeated exposure to violent entertainment to increased aggressiveness and violent behavior in children and adolescents. Other studies have linked the drop in intelligence scores and rising rates of teenage suicide to the distorting effects of electronic media and their influential messages on malleable young minds.

The onslaught may also have profound effects on their brains and bodies. A 1992 study by researchers at Memphis State University found that children watching television for even brief periods often lapse into a "deeply relaxed, almost semiconscious state" that falls metabolically between resting and sleeping. An Australian study found that prolonged TV viewing had produced a preponderance of children with slow brain waves, impaired thinking, concentration, and a tendency to "space out" when viewing "fatuous, overly difficult or confusing" programs.

More important, in our view, are the long-term effects of so much electronic experience on their development as children and young adults. During this period when fundamental patterns of thought, feeling and social relationship are forming, the new electronic environments, for all their colorful imagery and fast-paced inputs, provide a meager experience of the world, one rich in visual information and simulated sound but poor in meaning, feeling and real-life human interaction. The cumulative impact may affect basic patterns of brain growth and organization. As the nervous system adapts to massive doses of sensory information received with little initiation or physical exertion, children may become mentally and emotionally passive. Their abilities to form mental images, to make higher connections among complex ideas and to respond to genuine emotions in real-life situations, may remain largely undeveloped. Their powers of mind and imagination, like unused muscles, may not reach levels adequate to perform elementary cognitive acts and crucial feedforward processes—such as assessing the risks and consequences of their actions.

Debate over newer electronic technologies has only begun. Advocates argue, with some supporting research to back their case, that computers and video games improve children's sensori-motor coordination, logical thinking and problem solving skills. Critics contend that the new technologies are worse than film or television alone, and some research appears to be in their favor. Those studies show that computers and related technologies tend even more to promote hypnotic attention, foster violent, sexist and anti-social behavior, provide no rewards for creative initiative or imagination, and do nothing to help young children develop emotional depth, a sense of self or other essential human communication skills.

Obviously, electronic technology is not wholly to blame for the explosion of urban violence, teen suicide, and childhood learning and communication disorders. Changes in family life, education and larger socioeconomic shifts also figure in those debates. But the trends seem to point in the same direction: away from the development of whole, healthy personalities toward a less competent, less social and increasingly vulnerable youth population.

Those developmental trends also bear strong resemblances to the larger social patterns we were observing. Despite a marked decline in their attitudes toward authority, young people from every background today appear to be more receptive than ever to the power of suggestion and more subtle psychological manipulations, to the pull of cults, gangs and other group identities, and, like the adult society around them, prone to uncontrollable urges and sudden outbursts of violence. Many appear to have become holograms of the society they inhabit, a world in which millions have stopped thinking about their lives and the other people in them, stopped feeling their inner conflicts and the consequences of their cultures' wildly discrepant messages, a world in which people and institutions have studiously avoided long-range planning and cultivation of their human resources and, instead, relegated most thinking about the future to the realm of fantasy and science fiction.

Dehumanization in Real Time. As we fit these new pieces into our picture, the larger pattern of snapping in everyday life came into view. The nineties were showing sharp increases in reported incidents of snapping, along with the first signs of a new category of generalized information stress symptoms. This cumulative, culture-wide threat carried the phenomenon of snapping across new thresholds in real terms and "real time"—not in isolated cults, social scientific theories or future projections but in the real-life facts of the American experience and the lives of people in many other places.

This phenomenon we had been observing for two decades was now surfacing among people of all ages who described to us their cumulative, slow-motion experiences of snapping in everyday life. Symptoms included a gradual overloading and breaking down of their everyday reasoning and decision-making capacities, an increased passivity, suggestibility, and disquieting weakness for prescribed programs of belief, opinion and behavior, chaotic swings of emotion, from sudden euphoria to flaming outbursts of anger, to states of burnout and an overall numbing of emotional response.

The range of real-time snapping experiences showed up in the little things of everyday life. It became clear in comments we heard hundreds of times from harried businessmen, jaded professionals, dragging homemakers and cynical students who admitted that, because of the intense mental and emotional stresses they felt themselves to be under, they had "no patience for people" or desire for intimate relations, couldn't "tolerate the news," didn't read anymore, and had no interest in larger social or political concerns—although they once did.

Often it was revealed to us paradoxically in talks with people who were dead-set in their denials, individuals caught up in patterns of withdrawal through social isolation, extended nature retreats, obsessive absorption in computers, television, sports, hobbies, and more serious means of escape through alcohol and drugs.

We also met people suffering more extreme information stress disorders and full-blown information disease symptoms: people whose capacities of choice and decision-making had been overwhelmed to the point of paralysis, people searching for meaning who had become trapped in consuming lifestyles, unbending religions and absolutist ideologies, people snapping suddenly and inexplicably, and others spinning out in widening gyres of mindless, frenzied activity. Still others appeared to have been burnt out literally, laid waste by inconsolable feelings of loss, by the shattering of their lifelong dreams, identities and ideals, and by feelings of betrayal—some real, some imagined—by family, friends, employers and society in general.

Each real-life incident of change, however slow or sudden, could be depicted, on the personal plane, by our basic catastrophe model and, in the larger sphere, by the social dynamics of chaos. In the most extreme reactions, a man or woman might lose a job or a loved one, reach a financial impasse, go through a messy divorce or simply reach the breaking point in a bad relationship, and suddenly harm himself or herself. Or, in the pattern that was becoming pandemic, a person might snap violently and lash out at other individuals or an entire community. At the new chaos point of snapping that had played out repeatedly, a confused child in an urban jungle or suburban Eden might turn a knife or gun on his parents, teachers or playmates. A disgruntled individual or group might fly off in a rage of random violence, erupt against their own deepening sense of personal powerlessness, or wage premeditated campaigns of revenge and retribution for perceived social wrongs. Or, in the manner of snapping in slow motion, people might undergo more subtle changes and follow more gradual paths around the bend.

Among these worsening instances of snapping, the cult phenomenon of the late twentieth century remained, for us, a Rosetta stone, a key to understanding the patterns of sudden change spreading over a world of constant stresses, potent communication controls, and subtle messages of surrender proliferating at an exponential rate. Over time, in a cult or any similar information environment, people are worn down, pushed over an edge. They become passive, suggestible, incapable of thinking or even feeling for themselves.

These symptoms, in our view, have become widespread in America and many cultures. The global rush toward authoritarian groups and movements that offer instant identities and absolute answers to every problem is only one indicator of how many people are having trouble thinking through life's complexities on their own. In so many places, vulnerable minds are having increasing difficulty distinguishing literal messages from metaphors, telling reality from fantasy. In others, the stress is turning believers into fanatics, lovers into abusers, fans into celebrity stalkers, frustrated citizens into haters and aspiring political assassins.

The phenomenon we have been tracking is no longer just a private problem for individuals. Like human awareness itself, snapping is a social phenomenon and fast becoming everyone's problem.

18 The Future of Personality

We have to touch people.

—*Jacob Bronowski,*
The Ascent of Man

AS WE SAT DOWN to write the final chapter of this new edition, we were staggered by the scope of change that has swept over people in the United States and every culture in the past two decades and by the dark directions so much of that change is taking.

In these years, there have been major developments in the saga of snapping. Some groups we investigated initially that began as small cults of personality, like cults historically, have run their course and dissipated with the death of their founders. Many others have grown into multinational conglomerates, global religious, political and commercial empires that proselytize, propagandize, do business, wage ideological warfare, conduct covert operations, and both court and challenge governments. Still others have become angry messengers of Armageddon, feeding chaos in the United States and worldwide. As their rumblings grow louder, the trend lines begin to emerge:

SHEPHERDING. Since the seventies, the forefront of cult activity in the U.S. has shifted away from esoteric Eastern cults and eclectic self-help therapies and, along with much of the social and political mood, tilted toward conservative fundamentalist Christianity. Sects identified with the "shepherding" movement are in the vanguard. The secretive shepherding movement, an outgrowth of the ecstatic charismatic revival that swept through Protestant and Catholic denominations in the seventies, displays authoritarian characteristics. Members are routinely required to profess total submission to sect shepherds or elders, who often exert control over every aspect of their followers' lives. Many sects are organized in an insurgent "cell-group" structure and compel their members to submit to rigid "discipling" programs. In the eighties, many shepherding churches and umbrella "parachurch" organizations formed alliances with religious right ideologues, and some remain involved, overtly and covertly, in political activities across the U.S. and worldwide.

One controversial, although largely apolitical shepherding-style sect, the Boston-based International Churches of Christ, emerged from nowhere to become one of the nation's fastest-growing religious organizations. In little more than a decade, the sect deployed strict discipling methods and arduous proselytizing demands to win more than 70,000 converts, absorb 110 smaller churches in thirty states, and establish outposts in forty-five countries. The sect has spawned droves of disillusioned members, many of whom report incidents of physical intimidation and psychological coercion by their disciplers. Among the abuses ex-members describe are: forced fasting, veiled and explicit death threats, incidents of dissenters being held in seclusion for weeks at a time, and suggestions given to some unhappy members that "suicide is from God." Several apparently have heeded that suggestion.

SATANIC CULTS. A related trend, the purported growth of satanic cults and "ritual abuse" sects, appears to be largely overblown. In the eighties, cult awareness groups reported that nearly 20 percent of their queries concerned alleged devil worship activities. Thirty-three satanic "rumor panics" spread through twenty-four states. Some of the fear was apparently fed by prominent fundamentalist sects, some by mischievous teen "devil dabblers" rebelling against their own strict religious upbringings, and some by psychotherapists and patients claiming to have recovered repressed memories of childhood ritual abuses that later proved groundless. Serious satanic practices were almost nonexistent: a 1994 survey of 11,000 public officials, police workers and mental health practitioners catalogued 12,000 allegations of group satanic ritual abuse but not one substantiated case. However, the survey did find evidence of lone perpetrators or couples involved in isolated acts of devil-worship.

OFFICIAL INQUIRIES & ACTIONS. After the death of its founder, Victor Paul Wierwille, in 1985, The Way International, which had drawn government scrutiny for its questionable financial practices and weapons training courses, had its tax-exempt status revoked by the IRS. The exemption was later restored. The cult remains organized but its activities have been largely eclipsed by those of more extreme fundamentalist sects and paramilitary movements.

In the late seventies, the Children of God, the first of the new cults to be investigated by U.S. authorities, fled the country and renamed itself the Family of Love. By the nineties, police in Europe, Australia and Latin America had arrested dozens of the sect's members and taken custody of hundreds of children in the group, many of whom were found to be underfed, poorly clothed, and showing signs of physical and sexual abuse. Charges filed against Family of Love members in the U.S. and abroad included racketeering, rape, polygamy, incest, kidnapping, draft dodging and tax evasion, some of which were later dismissed for lack of evidence. In 1993, Family members began returning to the U.S., like members of more extreme fundamentalist sects, citing the Waco debacle as the latest harbinger of the Bible's Great Tribulation, and hoping to win a last windfall of converts before Christ's prophesied second coming.

Years before Waco, members of another apocalyptic sect, the Church Universal and Triumphant, which listed centers in 120 U.S. cities and forty countries, were charged with illegally purchasing powerful military-style assault rifles and storing the weapons, along with thousands of rounds of ammunition and a small fleet of armored personnel carriers, at their secluded 28,000-acre Montana headquarters bordering on Yellowstone National Park. In 1994, CUT leaders agreed to remove their weapons cache in exchange for restoration of the sect's tax-exempt status.

In the wake of Waco, however, in response to the public outcry over the perceived persecution of the Branch Davidians, and amid a spreading sentiment that American government had grown hostile to religious believers generally, lawmakers took steps to allay the fears of other religious groups and avoid future church-state confrontations. The federal Religious Freedom Restoration Act, passed in late 1993, placed strict new burdens on government actions with respect to religion. The new law gave many cults new political allies and renewed momentum. That autumn, as the law was wending its way through Congress, the Church of Scientology emerged victorious in its 40-year battle for legal recognition as a religion when the IRS granted tax-exempt status to more than 150 Scientology churches, missions and corporations.

OTHER ENTANGLEMENTS. Ironically, since the seventies, thousands of U.S. government employees have been recruited, required or pressured into participating in varied inspirational, motivational, stress reduction and management training programs sponsored by cults, religious sects and spiritually oriented self-help enterprises. Participants include military and civilian personnel working for the Defense Department, who have long been a focus of officially sanctioned proselytizing by private fundamentalist missionary groups, and of aggressive marketing efforts by individuals and groups affiliated with Transcendental Meditation. They also included U.S. Air Force and CIA personnel, many of whom have participated in group trainings sponsored by Lifespring, an est-like group dynamic, and other new age enterprises. From 1982 to 1993, government agencies paid more than $3 million to put 5,000 workers at the Federal Aviation Administration through management and "diversity awareness" programs run by group trainers whose methods reportedly mimicked those of new age guru J.Z. Knight. Those programs prompted many complaints of psychological stress and abuse. According to participants, men were groped, women cried uncontrollably, women and minority workers were verbally assaulted with sexist and racist epithets, co-workers were required to strip to their underwear and some were physically tied to others for hours.

CIVIL ACTIONS. Some legal balance was achieved by private citizens. After years of futile efforts to find remedies through government action, casualties of snapping began to win redress through civil suits against offending cults, sects and therapies. Dozens of lawsuits were decided in favor of ex-member plaintiffs—including some multimillion dollar judgments—for damages caused by the Hare Krishna, the Church of Scientology, Transcendental Meditation, est and others. More suits were settled out of court for undisclosed sums.

However, a greater force of litigation was flowing in the opposite direction. Armed with a reported $30 million annual legal war chest, the Church of Scientology, or individuals associated with it, launched more than one hundred civil actions against sect critics, journalists, news organizations, deprogrammers, cult awareness groups and government agencies. More than forty lawsuits were filed, and later dismissed, against affiliates of the Cult Awareness Network alone. In 1992, Scientology filed a $416 million libel suit against *Time* magazine that was still pending three years later. In 1995, after sect defectors began flooding the global Internet computer network with church documents and other inside information, Scientology sued two prominent ex-members for copyright infringement and "trade secret misappropriation." The sect even enlisted U.S. marshals to raid their homes and seize their computers.

INTERNATIONAL. And wider battlefronts opened. In 1994, Scientology began a multinational media blitz assailing the German government, which had acted to inform its citizens about the sect's reported perils and otherwise to restrict its activities in Germany. In full-page advertisements in American newspapers, British-based Scientologists accused German officials of Nazi-style persecutions against religious minorities. For their part, leaders of Germany's ruling and opposition parties criticized Scientology as a "danger to democracy" and called on their government to ban the sect from operating in the German Republic. Ministers of sixteen German states called Scientology "an organization that combines elements of business crime and psychological terror against its own members with economic activities and sectarian traits, under the protective cover of a religious group." Six books were published in Germany accusing the sect of defrauding adherents, threatening opponents with violence and seeking to infiltrate private companies. "Scientology is not a church or a religious organization," said German Labor Minister Norbet Blüm. "Scientology is a machine for manipulating human beings."

REAPING "THE HARVEST." In the first years of freedom in the liberated lands of the Soviet Union, tens of thousands of Russians learned Transcendental Meditation. Hare Krishnas chanted and proselytized publicly after years of official repression. American self-help enterprises repackaged their group training seminars and stress management services as lessons in Western-style marketing and business acumen for Eastern European entrepreneurs. American televangelists, missionary sects and religious-political groups streamed into those once-forbidden lands proclaiming a "harvest" of hungering souls.

The Unification Church reigned over much of that harvest. In a speech in Moscow in 1990, Moon declared his intention to lead a coming "moral and economic renaissance" in Eastern Europe. Hundreds of Russian students were brought to the U.S. on all-expenses-paid "educational excursions" that appeared to be composed mainly of immersion in the beliefs and political ideology of the Unification Church. In 1992, two Russian students sued a Moon affiliate for allegedly employing deception, fraud, "brainwashing, sleep deprivation and coercion" during their 40-day "leadership seminar" sponsored by the group.

And in many other arenas, the Moon group emerged as the most successful multinational sect. In two decades, Moon enterprises spent sizeable sums to win global credibility in religious, political, mass media and academic domains. Beginning in the seventies, Moon's own "Master Speaks" sermons candidly expounded his plan to create a global theocracy under his rule. His Unification Church and CAUSA political network reportedly forged ties to power players in government, military and intelligence circles, to Asian organized crime figures, and to far-right political groups worldwide. In the eighties, Moon's expanding media empire, staffed by professionals and thousands of Moon followers throughout the Americas, Europe and Asia, waged theopolitical initiatives that, directly and indirectly, influenced religion, politics, economics, and governments from Uruguay to the Pacific Rim.

SAVE THE CHILDREN. Their resources multiply, their allies are many, while casualties of these mind-altering religious, political and business conglomerates continue to surface. In America and elsewhere, the elderly have become ripe targets for cult recruitment and solicitation of their life savings. Millions of children have been born into abusive cults and authoritarian groups, and many more have been brought in at young ages. The human toll is showing up in traumatic effects that can now be measured, not in months or years, but in whole lifetimes spent in the cults' closed worlds.

To date, there has been no accounting for these little ones or what their futures may hold. The first glimpses have come from studies of the children of Waco and other sects who have been raised apart from society, many without proper education or medical care, subjected to mind-altering practices and, often, to recurring physical, psychological and sexual abuses. These studies indicate that many of those young survivors may suffer basic problems of personality formation and lifelong impairments of their higher capacities for thinking, feeling, making decisions, forming relationships and becoming fully functioning members of their societies.

THE DEATH SPIRAL REVISITED. A year after Waco, another little-known sect was sucked into the vortex and ignited its own fiery mass murder-suicide ritual. In October 1994, fifty-three Canadian, French and Swiss members of the secretive Order of the Solar Temple were found dead in a series of ritual killings and group suicides carried out simultaneously at sect houses in Quebec, Canada, and four sect-owned sites in Switzerland. Some Solar Temple members were found murdered by gunshots. Some were found suffocated by plastic bags tied over their heads. In Canada, four adults associated with the sect and a three-month-old baby were slaughtered execution-style.

The Solar Temple, a multinational melange of nineteenth-century occultism, Rosicrucianism and new age mysticism, claimed to be the modern successor to the Knights Templars, a medieval Catholic military order that emerged after the Crusades. The sect's leader, 46-year-old Belgian Dr. Luc Jouret, who died alongside his followers in Switzerland, was a self-styled guru who practiced homeopathic medicine, back-to-nature religion and, like David Koresh, preached a flame-filled Armageddon theology. Like Koresh in Waco, Jouret had been arrested in Canada on weapons charges after urging his followers to assemble an arsenal in preparation for the coming Apocalypse. Later, the group became more secretive, isolated and paranoid, and ultimately removed its operations to the remote Swiss countryside.

Swiss police found farewell letters suggesting that a mass suicide

was planned by at least some members of the upscale sect, whose adherents included the mayor of a Quebec town, a Quebec Finance Ministry official and numerous employees of the province's giant
hydroelectric utility. One letter read: "It is with unfathomable love,
pure joy and no regret that we leave this world." Other evidence indicated that at least half the dead were injected with a powerful drug,
their hands bound and heads covered by black plastic bags. In both
countries, police found sophisticated incendiary devices wired to ignite
by telephone.

The carnage, reminiscent of both Jonestown and Waco, left people
on two continents shocked and baffled. Authorities speculated about
internal cult intrigues and pursued reports that sect leaders were involved in international arms trafficking and money laundering, but
they were at a loss to explain the precisely timed transcontinental
mass murder-suicide. European observers, who for years had dismissed
cult cataclysms as products of American violence and religious extremism, began to question their own historical vulnerabilities. However,
the facts conformed to the chaotic dynamics of the death spiral: apparently, an isolated cult, with a delusional leader facing public exposure
and further criminal prosecution, was consumed by its own apocalyptic prophecies and blazing visions of martyrdom.

In the closing decade of the twentieth century, there is ample evidence that America's epidemic of sudden personality change has become the world's epidemic. That evidence is visible, not only in flagrant
acts of death and destruction, but in the spread of magical thinking,
millennial mysticism, religious fanaticism and the global surge in religious-political violence. In two decades, the phenomenon of snapping,
which first appeared as an isolated outbreak of curious personality
changes among a few million Americans in a handful of odd cults and
therapies, has grown to encompass some of the most frightening and
formidable threats to peace and human progress worldwide.

Under existing laws in the United States and most countries, neither the new cult control practices nor their practitioners are subject
to any form of government regulation or consumer protection. Behind
the shield of the First Amendment and its counterparts in more than a
hundred nations, a new generation of spiritual entrepreneurs, religious-political empire builders, con men, megalomaniacs and outright
fanatics is reaching a frightening maturity. As their new mindsets
take root in the name of personal growth, religious revival and national salvation, the new technology of mind control and emotional
manipulation is leaping national borders, strewing seeds of catastro-

phe and chaos in every culture.

How does a person, or a society, devise a viable defense against a phenomenon as new and potentially destructive as snapping? It is our belief that the best way to combat snapping personally, whether in response to cults, sects, therapies, extremist political movements or the stresses of everyday life, is to understand it, to become aware of the ways each individual's inner resources of mind and personality may be subtly influenced and subverted by people and groups that promise instant solutions to every problem. On a broader plane, it is important to understand the threat to awareness posed by intense experiences of every kind and by the unprecedented stresses of life today. These new threats carried in the information dimension of our lives—in the words, images, communication techniques, technologies and other messages that reach to the organic foundations of our minds and emotions—are the new facts of life in an information age. A person who understands these complex forces will be more capable of recognizing manipulative messages, covert communication strategies, potentially dangerous technologies and damaging experiences, and of consciously avoiding them, or at least minimizing their effects.

For societies, the task of countering snapping is one of a much greater magnitude. The turn into an information age has brought the mind to center stage and given new urgency to fundamental questions of human change and control. It has also raised larger concerns for safeguarding the mind and personality, and conserving those vital resources of individuals and cultures. The spread of authoritarian groups and apocalyptic mindsets demands that every society must now begin to make basic distinctions on sensitive issues: to distinguish a person's freely chosen religious beliefs, private faith and political ideals from potentially destructive programs of control and manipulation, to distinguish responsible modes of healing, mental health therapy, personal growth, stress reduction and professional training from fraudulent or deceptive enterprises that may seek to covertly influence or control individuals and institutions for ulterior ends.

Time and again, necessary efforts by government and law enforcement to restrain the activities of destructive mind-altering groups have run into ferocious legal battles, orchestrated propaganda campaigns, outrageous countercharges, and escalating patterns of intimidation, physical assault, assassination, mass suicide and outright murder. Time and again, the explosive issue of religious freedom has become a land mine in the path of families and governments trying to protect the health of individuals, the welfare of children, and the safety of communities and societies.

Similar obstacles springing up everywhere on the world religious and political scene make potentially destructive groups difficult to detect at the crucial stages when their leaders pull the levers of closure that separate members from their societies and instill the ritualized control practices that mark the critical turn from sect to cult. Beyond those thresholds lie deeper impairments, delusions, abuses, and the final threshold of confrontation that, too often, leaves authorities powerless to act until the cycle of death begins to roll with an unstoppable momentum. These lessons learned too late at Jonestown and Waco, and in other cult confrontations, can no longer be ignored by any nation in the name of religious freedom, out of political expediency, at the hands of special interests, or in blind deference to constitutional principles that may have themselves become hostages.

Undoubtedly, in these chaotic times, any action on these sensitive issues of individual rights and freedoms is bound to cause fierce social, political and legal disputes, but the overriding imperative may be simply stated: somehow, through public guidelines, court precedents or specific legislation, Americans and citizens of every society must declare explicitly that *no individual or organization may, by means of physical duress or any overt or covert technique, impair, make captive or destroy another individual's freedom of thought.*

THE FUTURE REENVISIONED. As somber as our message has been throughout this book, our investigation of snapping has not led us to draw entirely negative conclusions. There are still hopeful signs and extraordinary promises, for if there is one thing the phenomenon of snapping confirms unequivocally, it is that the mind's higher communication capacities, our human abilities to think, feel, remember, imagine and make conscious choices, remain almost infinitely flexible throughout our lives. Although modern cultures now possess the know-how and tools to control and even destroy those capacities, that knowledge also may be used to enable people to shape their own personalities, to cultivate and command their abilities to think and feel, and to enhance, rather than impair, their power to perceive and respond to the world around them.

Since the first bursts of the consciousness explosion, some of these truly positive trends in human development have been overlooked or altogether ignored. While the new cults and therapies were capturing the attention of the public and the media, most of the founding figures of the human potential movement remained faithful to its ideals, nurturing the values of personal growth and change, shunning the fireworks in favor of more thoughtful explorations of humankind's higher powers and potentials. Until his death in 1970, human potential movement patriarch Abraham Maslow warned about the dangers of a single-minded focus on peak experience. He emphasized a wide range of potentials in his hierarchy of self-actualization, including humankind's universal needs for love, belonging, self-expression, creativity and play. Humanistic psychologist Rollo May carried those ideals forward for another quarter century. Until his death in 1994, he wrote and spoke tirelessly about society's increasing mechanization at the hands of technology and sought to calm human anxieties in the face of modern life's existential dilemmas. As an antidote, May called on people to reassert their human powers of love and will, and draw strength from their inner resources of courage and creativity.

One memorable interview that has guided us through many straits was our conversation with humanistic psychologist Carl Rogers, founder of the person-centered approach to psychotherapy which bears his name. Rogers, who died in 1987 at the age of 85, was a revered figure in the human potential movement. When we called him a decade earlier, during our first research tour through Southern California, to solicit his thoughts on the turns the human potential movement had taken, and on the many abuses of its therapeutic tools that were being reported, he granted us a few hours of his time and gave us directions to his office in La Jolla.

At seventy-five, Rogers still displayed the grace of the humanist and father figure that he was. As we laid out the themes of our investigation, he responded openly to our ideas, from the outset placing himself in firm opposition to mass-marketed therapies such as est, the prototype for so many groups that followed, which functioned on, as he put it, "intrusive" principles.

"I've read a great deal of transcribed material of Werner Erhard's. There's a lot of rather rambling talk about how great it is to discover that you make your own reality and that you're responsible for your own life—some of which I agree with, some of which I don't—but nowhere does he mention the *process* by which you're supposed to arrive at that goal. In my opinion, that process is all-important."

It was the first principle of humanistic psychology, and the contention of all Rogers' work, that the process of an individual's experience was more important than any end-product of behavior. In contrast to the intrusive style of so many cults and therapies, Rogers described his method as "facilitative." Instead of manipulating group participants, Rogers' group leaders consciously placed the power and control of the group experience, and the entire process of personal growth and change, in the hands of each individual.

Rogers acknowledged that intrusive authoritarian groups can produce equally dramatic changes in personality and that religious revivals could bring about seeming miracles of renewal and rebirth. But from his viewpoint, there was much more to personal growth than simply overwhelming the individual. He questioned the methods and intentions of those who would "use mass effects to bring about very potent personal experiences." The changes they produce, "are not self-induced, they're mass-induced," he said, adding, "those kinds of conversions don't last very long unless you keep the person in the group that brought it about."

He stated the second guiding principle of his person-centered approach. "I think that it is a terrible thing to unnecessarily exert power over another person. The more you move toward power over others, the more potential for damage there is, and the more danger there is, as in the cults, that people may get caught in something they can't get out of. The goal in the cults and groups is to attribute personality change to something outside the individual. The other kind of personality change, the kind I am concerned with, is a process from within. *I* did it. Others facilitated it, but I'm the one who did it. I'm the one who's in charge of it, and I'm the one who can determine whether it goes any further."

Rogers' insight that lasting, beneficial change rarely results from just a sudden moment of intense experience confirmed the message we had received from so many people who had learned that lesson the hard way. The remainder of our conversation was devoted to speculation about the future and the direction he foresaw for the surviving ideals of the human potential movement. We spoke of creativity, of trust, and of modern culture's movement away from the "ultra-rational" toward a new embrace of the emotional. To our surprise, Rogers' forward-looking approach incorporated an increasing interest in, and regard for, humanity's older intuitive powers. "We do have a kind of primitive wisdom that we've completely forgotten," said Rogers, "we need to get in touch with it again. In the future, I think the nonrational aspects of a person will come to be more honored and will prove to be more useful than we have any idea at the present time."

As it turned out, many younger psychologists, and some older ones as well, were moving in that direction. In our travels, we spoke with many clinicians and intrigued scientists in other disciplines who had begun delving into the domain known historically as the realm of the "paranormal." We interviewed prominent psychologists who were decoding the mysteries of "holistic healing," the secular counterpart of the faith healers' "laying on of hands." We talked with researchers working on the forefront of the new medical field of "psychoneuroimmunology," which was beginning to offer hard evidence that hope, humor, visualization and, sometimes, belief alone could produce lasting cures for dire physical ailments.

Among laymen as well, interest in alternative healing and therapeutic methods was reaching record proportions. Throughout our travels, even in casual conversations unrelated to our investigation of snapping, we heard people of all ages and walks of life recount stories of sudden, seemingly miraculous cures, uncanny "telepathic" incidents, "premonitions" that later came true, and other extraordinary experiences. Some of those reports no doubt were greatly embellished, but not all could be dismissed as a mere delusions. So many of the experiences people were referring to as "supernatural," "mystical" or "psychic" were to us completely natural. Many could be explained in communication terms as natural expressions of humankind's higher communication powers, and as organic actions well within range of the living information processes that govern the whole of the mind, brain and body.

In times to come, we believe, those higher powers will be understood in all their potentials and harnessed, actively and consciously, as everyday powers of suggestion, will, belief, touch, group dynamics, and other forms of verbal and nonverbal communication. These natural communication capacities are the most powerful tools an individual possesses, yet most people remain largely ignorant of their own higher powers of mind, unaware that they already use them all the time in their daily lives, affecting people as others affect them. As people come to better understand their natural communication powers, we are hopeful, the myths will be debunked, the frauds and charlatans exposed, and those genuine skills once viewed as miracles accessible only to an elect few will become readily available to all.

Before bringing this book to a conclusion, we drew back from our work to view our own perspective in perspective and think about the note on which we wanted to end this inquiry. After everything—the new cults and therapies, information stress and disease, catastrophe and chaos, the widening storm track of the death spiral and the growing challenges of everyday life—we thought about the larger meaning of snapping as America and the world close on a new millennium.

It's true, we both agreed, today humankind does stand poised at the threshold of a profound and potentially triumphant new age. But in our view we haven't entered that new era yet, and we may never see it, because so many people in America and elsewhere are embarking instead on a course of human abdication—on destructive and increasingly deadly new paths of manipulation, escapism and mindless reaction. Snapping, as we have come to understand it, may be summed up in a very simple definition: it is a phenomenon that occurs when an individual, for whatever reasons, stops thinking and feeling for himself, when he breaks the bonds of awareness and social relationship that tie his personality to the world and literally loses his mind to some form of external or automatic control. In that sense, the moment of snapping, when the mind shuts off, remains a moment of human decision. It takes place as some invisible switch is thrown in the infinitely flexible human brain, whether voluntarily and in good faith or unwittingly and in a state of confusion, as personality is surrendered to some religion, psychology, ideology, technology or other recipe for living that requires no real conscience and no consciousness, no effort or attention on the individual's part.

It seems clear to us that, amid the human demands of today's complex, often overwhelming global society, an individual cannot elect blissful unawareness, mindless happiness, unquestioning truth or any other pre-programmed state over everything and everyone else in his or her life. That path to fulfillment is futile for, severed from humanity, it cannot be felt, understood or shared. Indeed, our exploration has confirmed for us that the higher human powers and spiritual understandings so many people are seeking are not innate within human beings or ensconced in some hidden cosmic realm. Inside, it's all machinery—chemistry and biology. Outside, wisps of matter, energy and, mostly, empty space.

Our humanity resides in that space between. That is why we have chosen to look at snapping from the point of view of communication, for it is this social process that determines what each individual's awareness and personality will be. Communication also teaches us that an individual's sense of self can be no greater than the quality of his relationships with other people. For it is only in relation to other people that the human mind finds a pathway to itself. Even the loner or recluse who believes he is self-sufficient in his private thoughts or the world of nature has been raised by someone, given a language, and taught to think and feel.

Snapping, in all its blind detachment from the world, its disconnection, self-delusion and deadly new manifestations, is the product of a desperate attempt on the part of millions to escape the responsibilities of being human in this difficult, threatening age. In that sense, it is an act of betrayal of both one's individuality and one's society, for if our inquiry has taught us anything, it is that our human nature binds each individual organically to every other. So long as we ignore this undeniable imperative of human communication, we will remain slaves to our genes and our machines, to our culture's expanding technology of experience, and to those who seek to exploit our most fundamental freedoms.

If, on the other hand, we choose to cultivate our higher human communication capacities, respecting the new knowledge and universal values that did, in fact, emerge from the consciousness explosion, and if we come to understand how our individual personalities are bound one to another, both by our words and by our actions, we may actually reach that long-awaited millennium, that great new age of enlightenment.

Then, together, all of us will be able to cross that threshold without snapping.

Postscript: The Widening Gyre
Subcultures, Killer Cells and the Turn to Terror

The Turn to Terror. In the weeks before this new edition of *Snapping* went to press, our hopes for a more human future were dashed again, as the cycle of cult fanaticism and senseless death we had been tracking for two decades took another horrific turn: a turn to terror on a national and, for the first time, international scale.

The death spiral's arms opened wider in the spring of 1995. On Monday, March 20, as the morning rush hour in Tokyo, Japan, was approaching its peak, commuters were overcome by a mysterious gas that appeared simultaneously on five crowded subway cars bound for the city's government center. The gas turned out to be a diluted form of the nerve gas sarin, a potent toxic agent developed during World War II in Nazi Germany which paralyzes the lungs and causes death within minutes. Twelve people died and 5,500 were incapacitated by the fumes. Within hours, members of a little known religious cult called Aum Shinrikyo, or Supreme Truth, emerged as suspects in the attack. The obscure sect, which claimed 10,000 Japanese members and thousands more in other countries, mixed Hindu and Buddhist beliefs; however, like so many cults, Aum Shinrikyo departed dramatically from those age-old spiritual traditions.

Days later, in coordinated raids televised throughout Japan, 2,500 police officers, wearing gas masks and protective body suits and carrying birds in cages to serve as detectors of poison gases, descended on twenty-five Aum Shinrikyo offices around the country. Police found dozens of sect members in advanced states of malnutrition and dehydration, some barely conscious, yet most refused medical attention. Cult spokesmen, including several medical doctors, declared Aum Shinrikyo to be a peace-loving, health-oriented faith, but Japanese authorities quickly uncovered facts to the contrary. Police found staggering quantities of potentially lethal substances at cult sites. In the first week of raids, they seized 150 tons of chemicals, including large quantities of sodium cyanide, components for the explosive nitroglycerine, cultures of deadly botulism bacteria, and materials to make enough sarin gas to kill an estimated four to ten million people.

Sect spokesmen vigorously denied involvement in the sarin attacks and insisted that the chemicals were all used for agricultural and industrial purposes in sect-owned businesses. However, police found sarin by-products on the premises, along with intermediate chemicals produced in the manufacture of the gas. At the cult's sprawling Waco-like compound in a village near the foot of Mount Fuji, they found a secret doorway behind an altar that led to a modern laboratory with computer-controlled systems and sophisticated chemical analysis equipment. One police informant claimed that Aum members had hiked into the mountains months earlier and buried 25,000 plastic bags filled with sarin gas.

Nowhere to be found in those first sweeping raids was the sect's forty-year-old leader, Shoko Asahara. File photos flashed around the world of the enigmatic Asahara wearing a long beard, a shocking pink robe and a seraphic smile. The soft-spoken, nearly blind sect leader had been an aspiring scientist and amateur chemist who failed his medical school entrance exams and, in the late seventies, moved to a Tokyo suburb to work as an acupuncturist. In the eighties, he opened a shop selling Chinese herbal medicines and was promptly arrested for selling fake drugs. He took up yoga and, in 1984, launched a company called Aum that ran a yoga school and sold health drinks. He traveled to India and Nepal to study Hinduism and Buddhism and, in a familiar scenario, returned with photographs of himself beside Tibetan lamas, including the Dalai Lama, which he used to build his image as an internationally respected religious figure.

In 1987, Asahara founded the Aum Shinrikyo religion with ten followers. The sect emphasized Tibetan Buddhist teachings, yoga practices, meditation, breathing control and, at its higher levels, claimed to dispense mystical powers of levitation which, like TM's version, seemed to consist of little more than energetic cross-legged hopping. Like cults in every culture, Aum Shinrikyo reached out to educated, upscale Japanese. Its numbers included bright young college students, lawyers, doctors and scientists, many of whom were attracted by the sect's scientific claims and high-tech ritual devices. Its most intriguing and disconcerting device was a battery-operated helmet ringed with electrodes that purportedly enabled devotees to align their brain waves with Asahara's. The hot-wired hats, suggestive of more sophisticated virtual reality headgear, were worn for extended periods by sect members, including young children in the group. However, their actual effects on the brains they encircled, if any, were wholly unknown.

Aum made other scientific claims for its spiritual practices and products. In one ritual described by former members, disciples drank a special "miracle pond" liquid allegedly made from Asahara's bathwater. In another, they paid a $1,000 fee for a special "love initiation" in which sect members reportedly received 36 trillion units of Asahara's DNA—although no details were provided about how the genetic information was transferred. Cult critics cited wide use of classic brainwashing and mind control methods, including food and sleep deprivation, sensory deprivation, and physical purging through forced water drinking and weekly bowel-cleansing rituals. Many sources reported that sect members used psychoactive drugs to evoke supernatural sensations and that cult leaders used powerful tranquilizers to subdue dissident members. Other dissidents were reportedly confined in crates for weeks at a time if they tried to quit the group. The information onslaught was equally intense. In the common ritual routine, Aum members awoke at 6:00 A.M. and spent their days singing sect songs, practicing yoga, watching videos of Asahara preaching, entraining their brain waves electrically, and chanting a required 4,000 Aum chants per day.

As the story of Aum Shinrikyo and its leader Shoko Asahara unfolded, the chaotic dynamics of the death spiral swirled into view and took off in ominous new directions. With the Tokyo gas attack, the threat of cult control with its widening pattern of confrontation took a quantum leap on the geopolitical stage. The American government had consistently ignored that threat in its own law enforcement and emergency planning, and scrubbed any mention of the problem from its official inquiries into the Waco disaster for fear of offending unspecified "religious sensitivities." It soon became apparent that Japanese government officials, too, bowing to their own religious and cultural sensitivities, had made the same fatal miscalculation.

The new reality born in the Tokyo subway shifted the terms of the cult debate from the perennial defense of personal religious freedom to the growing need for societies to defend themselves against a deadly new mindset and spreading terrorist threat of religiously motivated mass murder. Like a cyclone on the move, the death spiral was sucking order from its environment, expanding in size, imperiling populations on a global scale. The Aum sect had active branches in Germany and Sri Lanka, a small office in New York City, and a large following in Russia estimated at 30,000 adherents. Days after the Tokyo attack, New York City officials held underground disaster drills to prepare for a similar terrorist act. Russian authorities closed the sect's headquarters there out of an announced concern for the safety of Aum followers.

There also appeared to be political motives to that crackdown. A Moscow newspaper disclosed that when Asahara opened the sect's Russian branch in 1992, he received assistance from high government officials acting on orders from Russian President Boris Yeltsin, whose administration reportedly sought an exchange of favors with the cult leader. With Yeltsin's help, Aum founded communes across the country and a university that served as the cult's Russian headquarters. Amid the spiritual "harvest" by foreign proselytizers reaping the liberated Soviet lands, Aum sponsored public education seminars, mass rallies across Russia, and a prime-time television show and daily radio program on Moscow channels. The foreign exchange appeared to benefit both sides: a Russian military helicopter and Russian-made nerve gas detector were seized on the cult's premises in Japan, and cult documents revealed Aum leaders had developed plans to buy expensive Russian tanks and fighter aircraft in preparation for an all-out war against the Japanese government.

In Japan, as in the U.S., the confrontation threshold was crossed long before the actual outbreak of violence. The subway gassing was only the latest and most overt act of retaliation against Japanese authorities who, a day earlier, had raided the sect's Osaka headquarters and arrested three Aum members on suspicion of kidnapping a university student who had attempted to leave the group. Other evidence indicated that the gas attack was aimed specifically at government officials: all five targeted subway trains were scheduled to arrive within minutes of one another at the station closest to the national police agency and other government offices. Police seized notebooks from sect members labeled "War with Police." Then, ten days after the subway terror, the head of the country's National Police Agency was shot four times by a masked gunman as he left his home in a quiet Tokyo neighborhood. Police were unable to confirm a suspected link between the hooded marksman, who fled the scene, and the sect.

Newspapers reported that Aum's security chief was a former underworld boss in the Japanese mafia who, after being expelled from the mob, led a secret team within the sect that kidnapped disaffected followers. Other evidence linked the cult to an earlier nerve gas incident. A year before, a cloud of sarin descended on the residential neighborhood of several judges who were hearing a land dispute case involving the cult. Seven people were killed and 200 injured, including one judge.

As in most cults, rank-and-file Aum followers appeared to know nothing of their leaders' questionable pasts and apocalyptic plans. In addition to its many members from elite families, the sect boasted a strong presence in Japanese universities and used computer networks to boost its high-tech image and attract new recruits. In Aum's first decade, according to a former high-ranking sect member, Asahara also built a business empire worth more than a billion dollars, with assets that included a computer assembly factory, coffee shops and a chain of discount stores, .

As Aum's resources multiplied, like Jim Jones during his heyday in California, Asahara tried to seize power in mainstream political channels. In 1990, he and several of his lieutenants ran for parliament in Japan; all lost. Soon after, amid reports that Asahara, like Jones in his latter days, was in deteriorating health from unknown ailments, the first signs of the sect's apocalyptic theology began to appear. One Aum tract, echoing the angry preachings of David Koresh and other endtime prophets, declared that, as the millennium advanced, the world would see "a series of events of inexpressible ferocity and terror." Special hatred was expressed for the governments of Japan and the United States. America, Asahara claimed, in the paranoid style common to far-right extremists in the U.S. and many cultures, was ruled by a cabal of Freemasons and Jews intent on dominating Japan and the world. An Aum magazine on press at the time of the Tokyo attack warned that poison gas—including sarin gas specifically—and other calamities would kill 90 percent of the people living in major cities and that the world would end by 1997.

The death dance progressed in the chaos pattern: across predictable thresholds of closure, control, building turbulence within, and intensifying friction with forces in the cult's environment. Sect leaders were publicly accused of abusing members. Asahara, married with six children, was personally accused of making sexual advances toward female recruits. The threshold of confrontation was crossed: sect leaders were charged with harassing cult critics and journalists, and with physically assaulting, kidnapping and even killing sect dissidents, their family members and other opponents.

As in Jonestown, as in Waco, a vortex formed around the cult. Residents who lived near sect enclaves filed formal complaints and organized a "Committee to Oppose Aum Shinrikyo." Concerned families enlisted a "Lawyers Group on Behalf of the Victims of Aum Shinrikyo." Asahara lashed back, charging his critics with religious persecution. Like Koresh, he began teaching that government efforts to eradicate his movement would coincide with the beginning of the end of the world. The Osaka police raid was the tiny triggering event.

The next day, the subway counterattack felled thousands. Three days later, Asahara dropped a death charge on his own followers in radio broadcasts beamed to Japan from Russian stations in Vladivostok. "At last the time has come for death," he declared, although it was not clear whether he meant his followers' death or other people's. In another statement, he issued a more explicit suicide call: "Disciples, the time to awaken and help me is upon you. Let's carry out the salvation plan and face death without regret."

In the weeks that followed, tens of thousands of Japanese police patrolled the country's public places. Noxious substances appeared repeatedly, including one burning cyanide bomb in a subway toilet that was stopped short only by chance from possibly killing tens of thousands, but police were unable to determine whether those cruder terrorist acts were the work of avenging Aum operatives or copycat crimes by other disgruntled individuals and groups. Finally, the government put a lid on the nerve gas cult. After weeks of painstaking investigation, police arrested the sect's spokesman, top chemist and main lieutenants, several of whom confessed that the sect had planned and perpetrated the sarin attack. Asahara was tracked to a deeper cache of hidden rooms in the sect's Mt. Fuji compound, where he surrendered without a fight. He was charged with murder in the subway attacks and later confessed to ordering the killing of a sect dissident.

But the terror in Japan was far from over. More subway incidents occurred. A jetliner was hijacked by a man who claimed to be an Aum member and demanded Asahara's release, then denied any connection to the group. Beyond the thousands harmed directly by Aum's attacks and the threat of further acts by Aum followers and copiers, the cult fear that gripped the country for months took a toll on the Japanese identity and legendary sense of security. In an age of lawlessness, postwar Japan had prided itself on its low crime rate and model citizenry. Now the Japanese people were forced to confront, not only a renegade cult, but their country's own cultic roots and vulnerability as a culture.

Cults were as old as Japan itself. The island nation's Shinto nature cult and Samurai warrior mindset reigned for centuries and became the base for its wartime ideology which proclaimed that the emperor was divine, that the Japanese people were descended from their ancient gods, and that acts of self-sacrifice, including suicide, were assured paths to spiritual salvation. After the war, the emperor cult was abolished, but a new legal system patterned on American freedoms made it easy for any sect to win religious recognition and tax-free status. By 1995, registries listed 185,000 religious organizations, most of them peaceful Buddhist and Shinto sects that provided strong social support to their followers. However, the country also experienced an explosion of controlling cults and new age sects. Those new sects were especially popular among Japanese youth, many of whom were emerging socially and spiritually stunted from the country's rote educational system, and among Japanese disenchanted with their culture's rampant materialism, lifelong career pressures and lethal levels of job stress. Yet the same could be said, to a greater or lesser degree, about the United States and many other cultures.

In Japan, as in America, authorities fed into a cultural climate ripe for tragedy. The government ignored numerous warning signs of Aum Shinrikyo's threat to public safety, failed to investigate charges made against the sect, and repeatedly declined to take action until the cult was out of control. Japanese scholars, like their counterparts in the U.S., closed their minds to the sect's abuses in fealty to religious freedom. Many actively defended Aum Shinrikyo and other indigenous cults. "I felt I must protect Buddhism," one professor of religious studies admitted later. As a result, thousands became casualties of an apocalyptic leader armed with powerful tools of control and portable weapons of mass destruction.

For Aum's victims, the physical and emotional pain endured. Subway survivors experienced extreme post-traumatic stress responses. Departing sect members reported their own post-traumatic disorders and information disease symptoms characteristic of prolonged exposure to mind control: mental confusion, impaired decision making, recurring nightmares, intrusive images and rhythms, debilitating fear, guilt, humiliation and suicidal thoughts. "I still have nightmares," a male sect member reported five years after he quit Aum. "I didn't want to live. I was mentally in ruins," said a female ex-member. "One subway attacker, Dr. Ikuo Hayashi, a cardiac surgeon and Aum official, later described his own powerlessness in the pull of the cult's control—even as he was committing the crime. "I kept hesitating because I realized many people would die," he told police in a guilt-filled jailhouse confession. "Again and again I tried to stop, but I was unable to disobey the sect's orders."

The new cult terror broke the last rules of engagement in the escalating war of international terrorism, injecting new elements of blind faith, unbridled fanaticism, and an urge for martyrdom without precedent in modern societies. It also added a new dimension to the problem—the information dimension—with its new realities of mind control, emotional control, religious-political propaganda, and precision tools for producing cadres of covert operatives numb to the suffering of others and even to their own instincts for survival. Now, with the first use of a homemade nerve gas on innocent citizens by obsessed members of their own society, terrorism experts agreed, it was only a matter of time before the next salvation-seeking group committed a more deadly crime using some other cheap concoction of chemical, biological or even nuclear weapons.

And the next act of terror was not long in coming.

Subcultures and Killer Cells. One month after the Tokyo attack, the death spiral came round again in a cyclone of chaos that hit the American heartland with a force no one was prepared for. Just after 9:00 A.M. on Wednesday morning, April 19, 1995, a huge explosive device concealed in a parked rental truck devastated the Alfred P. Murrah Federal Building in downtown Oklahoma City, Oklahoma. The blast blew the face off the nine-story structure and collapsed the front half of the building earthquake-style, like a stack of pancakes. One hundred sixty-seven people were killed in the blast, including sixteen small children enrolled in a day-care center on the second floor of the building. Five hundred more were injured in the Murrah building and at other blast-damaged sites as far as two miles away.

By every measure, it was the deadliest and most destructive act of terror in the nation's history.

First reports linked the crime to Middle Eastern terrorists. The bomb, an immense 4,800-pound stew of ammonium nitrate fertilizer and fuel oil, bore the signature of radical Islamic fundamentalists. Its makeup and modus operandi were almost identical to those of the 1993 World Trade Center bombing—only this bomb was ten times greater. Some feared the bombers were cadres of Aum Shinrikyo, whose leaders' whereabouts were still unknown at the time. But other clues suggested that the bombing was an act of revenge against the U.S. government for alleged crimes committed in the Waco siege that ended in its own fiery finale on the same day two years' earlier.

As it turned out, the rain of death and debris this time was not instigated by radical Islamists, Japanese nerve gassers, Branch Davidian survivors or any of the other usual cult suspects. This deed was an act of domestic terror by American citizens whose roots reached as deep into the heartland soil as those of their victims.

Within hours, tangible evidence began to mount that the terror was the work of one or more individuals associated with the budding "patriot" movement of citizen militias and allied religious-political extremist groups. The blast peeled back the curtain on this shadowy American subculture. In only a few years time, its irregular army had sprung from a fringe of far-right firebrands, anti-government activists and Christian fundamentalist zealots into a nationwide network of heavily armed, fully outfitted paramilitary units.

The network was joined by belief, ideology and advanced communications technology—cross-country telephone and fax lines, short-wave radio, computer bulletin boards, and other public and private channels. Militias were sighted in more than forty states. Their leaders claimed hundreds of thousands of armed activists and, by the mid-nineties, probably did have troop counts in the high five figures. One respected expert placed the movement and its sympathizers at five million. Many militiamen were lawful gun enthusiasts, as militia spokesmen claimed, nostalgic veterans and young reservists yearning for action, or at least to go through the motions. Thousands came equipped with camouflage and other accoutrements of guerrilla warfare: high-powered assault rifles, emergency survival packs, freeze-dried rations, water-resistant pocket Bibles and American flags. But, early on, it was clear that many in the militia subculture were not the benign "weekend warriors" the media portrayed them to be.

Some dressed like night commandos and espoused a virulent new rhetoric of God and country, casting themselves as "white Christian patriots" defending their families and communities against perceived threats to their faith and constitutionally protected freedoms. Many were militant survivalists and adherents of apocalyptic endtime theologies. Others wanted to separate themselves entirely from America's secular government and society, refusing to pay taxes or vote, pulling their children out of public schools, even going "off the grid" and cutting their links to public utilities. Still others were products of their own sudden personality changes and the worsening paranoid style in American politics and culture, obviously troubled individuals mobilizing against malevolent forces they believed were conspiring to disarm law-abiding Christian Americans, to enslave them in concentration camps being built on the sites of abandoned Army bases—even to secretly implant computer chips in their brains to control their minds and track their movements.

The new movement had old undercurrents that were all too familiar. Many of the new patriots were veterans of the Posse Comitatus movement of the eighties, which advocated armed resistance to governmental authority. Others had documented ties to historical American hate groups. Leaders of the Militia of Montana, a magnet for paramilitary activities in the upper Midwest, were reportedly associated with the neo-Nazi Aryan Nations Church in Hayden Lake, Idaho. The Texas-based Lone Star Militia was reportedly started by an Imperial Wizard of the True Knights of the Ku Klux Klan. A former Grand Dragon of the Texas Klan, Louis R. Beam, traveled the country in the eighties helping regional militias to organize. Another nationally known Klan leader, Robert Miles, head of the Mountain Church in Cohoctah, Michigan, was a father figure to militiamen in Michigan and throughout the country's midsection.

These new armed citizens groups were not cults in the strictest sense but, rather, vast extended subcultures. They had, not one leader, but many leaders and multiple centers of attraction and, on the surface at least, their power seemed to flow from more conventional psychological and social influences. The new subcultures reflected the profound changes in America life in the information age: the rolling economic upheavals, the new concentrations of wealth and power geographically, and the rapid disenfranchisement of workers in industry, agriculture and many white-collar professions, millions of whom were finding themselves abruptly cast out of the system. They mirrored the new national and ethnic tensions rising, and old ones reappearing, in the shifting global balance of power.

They also revealed a sweeping evolution of the cult phenomenon in America and worldwide. Amid new challenges and opportunities, many religious, political and personal growth groups had changed from rigidly hierarchical sects bound in closed circles around their leaders into dispersed enterprises with branching subsidiaries that functioned independently or were only loosely affiliated with their parent organizations. Others were mutating from within, forming secretive inner circles of sect lieutenants, fractious subcults, spinoffs, splinter groups and cult-de-sacs. Some subcultures had already merged symbiotically with the larger culture, like the diversified new age movement and the awakening masses of American evangelicals. Others were spawning tiny offspring "cells" that broke loose from their parent groups and floated freely into the wider social stream.

In the nineties, many of these hybrid structures began to ripen, revealing distinctive modes of recruitment, conversion and psychological control that were unleashing new forms of personality change and dangerous new mindsets in the United States and many societies.

America's patriot subculture appeared to be evolving on two tiers simultaneously: an above-ground and, for the most part, legal association of individuals and groups intent on defending their families and communities against perceived threats to their freedoms and, below ground, a secret cell network of hard-core anti-government ideologues, paramilitary tacticians, religious-political fanatics and covert operatives intent on fomenting insurrection and acts of terror against designated enemies. Of all the new social entities, to our minds, this secretive cell network was the most troubling. Small, nondescript cells were replicating like microbes in the nutrient soil of middle America, engaging in a wide array of questionable, and often undetectable, extremist religious, political and business activities. Others were becoming mobile units moving furtively through the system, armed for battle and equipped to strike without warning.

The first men arrested and charged in the Oklahoma City bombing, two Army buddies who had trained together, served together and kept in close contact back in civilian life, gave every indication of being members of a secret paramilitary cell. They were also individuals with personal histories that typified the changing face of snapping in the nineties.

The prime suspect, 27-year-old former U.S. Army Sgt. Timothy J. McVeigh, was apprehended purely by accident, flagged down ninety minutes after the explosion by a state trooper on a highway heading north from Oklahoma City, and arrested for driving a car without license plates. A computer check of his Social Security number led federal agents to his small-town jail cell only minutes before he was to be released. His comportment was familiar: a young man with a stone face and icy stare, admitting nothing and implicating no one, while investigators combed the country in search of his motives and inevitable accomplices. In court hearings, he displayed no emotion, even when confronted with photographs of the bomb damage and the dead children he was accused of killing.

The first sketchy histories portrayed a bitter young man who, by most accounts, had undergone a dramatic personality change during his time in the military. McVeigh grew up in a small town near Buffalo, New York. In school, he was a quiet one, a loner who looked meek, talked tough and claimed to excel in team sports, but even his coaches were unable to remember him. After graduating, he joined the Army and found a strong new identity. McVeigh was gung-ho from the get-go. He "played the military twenty-four hours a day, seven days a week," a fellow soldier remembered. He was the first member of his close-knit "cohort unit" to make sergeant, but he was no role model, for behind his ramrod demeanor a different, far less likeable personality was forming. This McVeigh was obsessed with firearms and became an avid reader of gun magazines. He immersed himself in survivalist ideology, mercenary movies and videos, and read extremist novels like *The Turner Diaries*, about a racist and anti-Semitic war on the U.S. government. As a sergeant, he expressed racist epithets and consistently assigned the dirtiest jobs in the platoon to black specialists.

McVeigh served with distinction in the Persian Gulf war as a gunner with the First Infantry Division, commanding an all-terrain Bradley Fighting Vehicle in the 100-hour ground assault on Saddam Hussein's armies in the southern Iraqi desert. His was not a lead unit but a second-wave support team, and accounts of his combat experiences were in conflict: some witnesses said he saw heavy fire and that, when the combat ended, his unit buried alive hundreds of wounded Iraqis in their sand-blown trenches; Army officials said McVeigh saw no traumatizing combat and denied reports that he shot surrendering Iraqis or buried any soldiers alive.

But there was no dispute that something in the desert war cut deep into McVeigh's own interior. Several of his Army comrades said he came back a changed man. A friend said McVeigh returned from the Persian Gulf believing that the Army had implanted a computer chip in his buttocks in order to track his whereabouts. In the spring of 1991, McVeigh was accepted as a candidate for Special Forces training at Ft. Bragg, North Carolina; however, a preliminary psychological screening found him mentally unfit for the elite unit, and he left the program after two days. By all accounts, the rejection was a devastating blow that ignited a rage against the military and the government. In the months afterward, McVeigh underwent a rapid physical and psychological deterioration. He lost so much weight that he looked anorexic. Acquaintances described him as cold and silent, a man who "did not have an expression 99 percent of the time" and, the other percent, was prone to explosive outbursts of anger.

The second suspect, Terry Lynn Nichols, 13 years older than McVeigh, was his peer in many respects. Both men were loners reared in broken homes, both their fathers had been auto workers, and both were leaning far to the right even before they enlisted in the Army on the same spring day in 1988. Nichols grew up on a farm in the rural thumb of Michigan. Friends recalled him as quiet and painfully shy. His lifelong dream was to become a doctor, but he found college life daunting and dropped out after his first year. His dream abandoned, he moved to Denver, where he struggled to find work as a carpenter; then he returned to Michigan to live with his older brother James on their mother's farm in Decker, an hour north of Detroit. There he floundered in farming, carpentry, real estate, life insurance, and as a manager of a grain elevator. He married a divorced woman with two sons and an active career of her own. They had a son and Nichols seemed to settle happily into the role of house husband.

Then, in the mid-eighties, a change came over Terry Nichols. As with McVeigh in the military and so many more people we had met in our travels, his personality underwent a dramatic alteration. His wife saw the peculiar spaced-out demeanor and other signs of someone pushed to a new place. "I didn't know what was wrong. I couldn't put my finger on it," she said later. "He would get up in the morning, and he would be sitting there staring into space....He was lost." The change may have been purely spontaneous, spurred by stressful life experiences or by some other unknown influence. What is known is that around that time Nichols began thinking in extremes. He became a survivalist. He read the magazines, stockpiled food and guns, and converted his savings into gold and silver bullion. Like McVeigh in the military, both Terry Nichols and his brother James became avid readers of *The Spotlight*, the newspaper of the far-right Liberty Lobby, and both shared a growing interest in guns, explosives and anti-government ideology.

In 1988, Nichols changed again. At the ripe age of thirty-three, he enlisted in the Army, becoming the oldest member of his platoon at Ft. Benning, Georgia, and fast friends with his cohort Tim McVeigh. The two were attracted to each other "like magnets," a fellow soldier recalled. Unlike McVeigh, however, Nichols stayed in the service less than a year. During his absence from home, his wife had filed for divorce, their marriage broke up, and Nichols requested a hardship discharge to care for his young son.

Quirky moves followed. In late 1990, while McVeigh was gearing for war in the gulf, Nichols traveled to the Philippines to take delivery on a mail-order bride. The next spring, he moved his new family to Nevada, claiming he planned to resume his real estate career, but there is no evidence he attempted a single sale. Then he moved back to Decker. The region was becoming increasingly extreme. Many Midwest farmers and factory workers, dispossessed by the economic upheavals of the eighties, were growing openly hostile toward the federal government, which they blamed for their troubles. The nationwide tax protest movement, the budding patriot network and more extreme groups were reaping a harvest in the heartland, and Nichols became a true believer.

In 1992, he renounced his citizenship in a letter to a county clerk, declaring himself "a nonresident alien, non-foreigner, stranger to the current state of the forum"—in language resembling that of the Posse Comitatus. A year later, however, Nichols asked a local court to void nearly $40,000 in credit card charges he had posted the previous year, but by the time the dispute was heard, the quiet, shy Nichols now angrily refused to come forward at the judge's request. In a scene that has played out repeatedly among anti-government extremists, he stood in the back of the courtroom, shouting that the court had no jurisdiction over him.

When the two men met up again as civilians, their strange attraction took on a new momentum. Their ambiguous actions, together and at a distance, seemed to revolve around some shared but never-stated agenda. In fact, much evidence indicated that McVeigh and Nichols conspired together, and perhaps with others, in quiet collaboration for several years prior to the Oklahoma City bombing.

After his discharge from the Army in 1991, McVeigh moved back to Buffalo, worked for a while as a security guard, then, in 1993, quit his job and went to live with another Army buddy, Michael Fortier, in a desert trailer park in Kingman, Arizona. That fall, McVeigh left Kingman for Decker and moved into James Nichols' farmhouse, where Terry Nichols was also residing. The three fumed together over Waco and began detonating small explosions from common chemicals. Late in 1993, Terry Nichols move to Las Vegas, then to central Kansas, where he took a job as a ranch hand. McVeigh visited him there twice that year and, in September 1994, Nichols quit his job, telling one witness that he was going into business with McVeigh selling guns and military surplus. The same day he stopped ranching, government investigators learned later, Nichols used an assumed name to purchase 2,000 pounds of ammonium nitrate fertilizer from a Kansas farmers' cooperative, which he moved to three rented storage lockers. The next month, he bought another ton of ammonium nitrate. In November 1994, as he prepared to leave on a new round of travels, Nichols wrote a cryptic letter to McVeigh saying that, in the event of his death, he would be on his own and that he should "go for it!"

Sometime during that period both men were observed at events sponsored by segments of the growing militia movement. McVeigh and both Nichols brothers attended meetings of the Michigan Militia in 1994. In January 1995, McVeigh was seen at another Michigan Militia meeting, where speakers called for action against the federal Bureau of Alcohol, Tobacco and Firearms. A month later, McVeigh attended a meeting of the Florida Militia, where he was reportedly acting as a bodyguard for nationally known Michigan militia figure Mark Koernke. Then McVeigh disappeared for six weeks.

In late March, McVeigh reappeared in Kingman where, according to a local motel clerk, he sat by himself in a barren room for twelve days. A week before the bombing, he drove to a small house in Herington, Kansas, that Terry Nichols had bought two months earlier. Two days later, McVeigh called Nichols from Oklahoma City and, immediately afterwards, Nichols drove the 500-mile round trip and dropped off McVeigh at a motel in a nearby town. Nichols claimed he was just doing a favor for an old friend with car trouble—investigators said McVeigh had gone to Oklahoma to stash his getaway car. The next day, McVeigh, using an assumed name, rented a Ryder truck at a local auto body shop. The following morning, McVeigh and Nichols had breakfast together at an area diner. Several hours later, witnesses saw a blue pickup truck similar to Nichols' parked near a Ryder truck at a lake outside Herington. After the Oklahoma blast, investigators found traces of fuel oil and dead grass at the site. They believe the two men made the bomb there. A search of Nichols' house turned up materials for a bomb of the same type as the Oklahoma device, thirty-three firearms, an anti-tank weapon, fuse cords, blasting caps, white plastic barrels with blue lids similar to fragments found at the bomb scene, along with numerous books, pamphlets and brochures on topics ranging from Waco to tax protests to anti-government warfare.

More than 1,000 government investigators joined the search for other accomplices. Michigan Militia leaders acknowledged that McVeigh and the Nichols brothers participated in their events but denied any connection to the crime. The Arizona Patriots denied any affiliation with Tim McVeigh. And, indeed, when this book went to press, there was no documented evidence that McVeigh or Nichols belonged to any militia or organized paramilitary group. However, there was ample evidence that both men embraced the movement's beliefs, language and literature, went to militia meetings, and trafficked in weapons through channels popular among paramilitary groups. For a time, McVeigh made his living selling guns at gun shows and through ads placed in *The Spotlight*. During the Waco siege, McVeigh made a pilgrimage to the battle site and came back railing against the federal government for allegedly conspiring to murder Koresh and his flock, whom McVeigh and many patriots viewed as a persecuted sect of peaceable believers and lawful gun owners, despite so much evidence to the contrary. Also around that time, McVeigh and Nichols were believed to have committed one or perhaps more robberies of guns and other valuables that may have brought them funds far in excess of their legal gun deals.

McVeigh's last words before the bombing included a veiled message written to his sister, Jennifer, an anti-abortion activist who was said to share many of her brother's extremist views, in which he intimated that "something big is going to happen." After the bombing, McVeigh's other Army buddy, Michael Fortier, admitted to triggering explosive devices with McVeigh in the sands outside Kingman and reportedly even said McVeigh had told him of his bomb plan months earlier. Fortier also told authorities that he traveled to Oklahoma City with McVeigh a week before the blast and helped him surveil the Murrah building, although in his initial interviews he denied any personal part in the bombing plot.

During those first months after their arrest, both accused conspirators maintained a warrior-like code of silence. Next, legal posturing began to soften their villainous images in preparation for the coming trial. McVeigh and his lawyers put forth a new persona of McVeigh as an all-American boy-next-door, not denying the charges but, at one point, intimating that he was a dupe of unnamed superiors. However, some evidence suggested that McVeigh himself was the point man in the plot, the one all the action turned around and ultimately threaded back to.

Other fringe players indicated that McVeigh was the focal point. In Kingman, 35-year-old Steven G. Colbern, a survivalist with a chemistry degree and his own horde of guns and ammunition, admitted meeting McVeigh. Investigators found a recruitment letter McVeigh wrote in 1994 to someone with the initials "S.C." seeking "fighters not talkers"; however, Colbern denied any role in the crime. Another Kingman resident, Walter McCarty, a local gun instructor and twenty-year Marine Corps veteran, said McVeigh tried to recruit him for antigovernment activities, but McCarty was leery of McVeigh's state of mind at the time. "He was upset about things happening in this country to the point of being disoriented," said McCarty. He knew McVeigh and Michael Fortier and portrayed both as men of ideological extremes, curiously unstable—and in perceptibly altered states. "I know brainwashing when I see it," said McCarty, a Korean war vet. "Those two boys had really gotten a good case of it."

But no one could say what leader or group the pair or any of their associates may have been influenced by. Telephone records connected McVeigh to a separatist Identity Christian sect. He called someone at the Elohim City religious community in the Ozark Mountains of eastern Oklahoma four minutes after he rented the Ryder van that carried the bomb. Like many other Identity Christians, Elohim City residents packed firearms and preached white separatism, resistance to government and the imminent coming of the Apocalypse. The sect's leader, Robert G. Millar, had ties to members of another infamous Identity sect, the Covenant, the Sword and the Arm of the Lord, and served as spiritual adviser to white supremacist Richard Wayne Snell, a far-right activist who was executed in Arkansas on the day of the Oklahoma City bombing for murdering a black state trooper. However, Millar denied that he or anyone in his group received calls from, or even knew, McVeigh.

Others surfaced as possible connections: Another Kingman man was arrested in connection with an earlier explosion, but he denied any acquaintance with McVeigh. The fuse cord used in the blast was traced to a Chicago-area gun dealer whose phone records listed numerous calls between him and McVeigh, but he, too, denied any part in the plot. McVeigh's sister Jennifer was investigated as a possible accessory before or after the fact. Also, in those first months, reports surfaced that furtive Middle Eastern figures were seen with McVeigh in Oklahoma and Kansas, but no hard facts could be found to support them. Several mysterious suspects, all dubbed "John Doe #2" by investigators, were apprehended and then released as consecutive cases of mistaken identity, although the idea of a third key figure—perhaps even a higher-up in the conspiracy—could not be discounted altogether.

Engines of Chaos. Just weeks before the Oklahoma blast, we had completed our model of the chaotic dynamics that unleashed the spiral of death in Waco. After the bombing, we could see similar dynamics at work in the mushrooming patriot movement. As prosecutors struggled to connect possible conspirators, wider investigations made clear that the new patriot cells whose furtive actions were believed to be the linking factor were not lumps of lone wackos and loose cannons thrown together. Rather, they were intricately structured, highly disciplined social groups that operated as discrete and almost wholly independent units. As new facts came to light, we learned that the practices of many patriot cells displayed elements of personal change and manipulation we had identified as cult-like methods: covert recruitment and induction, intimate group dynamics, ritualized indoctrination. They also showed more serious communication pathologies that we believed contributed to, and may have precipitated, the events in Oklahoma.

In fact, the new cell structures had their own distinctive place in the communication dynamics of the death spiral. In our initial application of chaos theory to the pattern of cult confrontations, our double-spiral chaos curve mapped the predictable points of friction where turbulence often broke out between the new sects and their surrounding societies. The spiral's inner region, depicting the internal communication dynamics of cults and other closed groups, was dotted with dimly visible circular patterns. At a higher magnification, those vague globules appeared as eerie cell-shaped microstructures. As the spiral curve rolled outward from its tight-wound center, we could see the self-contained cells form like spores, move away from the sect, and emerge as independent entities. (See Figure 6.)

The militia network's own manuals best described the form and function of these free-floating cell structures adopted by many segments of the militia movement. The manual of the Free Militia, a Midwest group, stated:

We use the term "cell" because a cell is the basic building block in any living organism. Just as all life, growth, and reproduction is based on living cells, all Militia "life" is centered around its cells. The identities of cell members are known only within the cell and by their immediate superior. All basic training is done within a cell. All codes, passwords, and telephone networks are determined by and held in confidence within the cell. All fortified positions are determined, prepared and concealed by the cell. All combat orders are executed by the cell as the cell sees fit within its own context. So the Free Militia IS its cells.

The militia's cell descriptions met our main criteria of a system poised for chaos: closure, control and confrontation. Closure: "For the most part, the men who train, work and fight together in a cell will stick together and the cell will remain in tact [sic]....[Cell members] can communicate freely and openly while shrouding the particulars of their tactics, positions, and signals to everyone outside the group." Control: "The cell leader easily conveys clear orders to a small group of men. The higher command elements can give orders to the whole Militia through the chain of command without direct contact with individual soldier [sic]." Confrontation: "Combat cells provide the patrolling and fighting capability of the Free Militia. Each...with its own leader, communications, rendezvous points, staging areas and standing orders...They are the 'arms' of the Free Militia."

Those disciplined commands took on new meaning after the Oklahoma City bombing, as Americans struggled to grasp the mindset that might have driven people with suspected ties to the patriot movement to carry out such a destructive act against their own countrymen. From our vantage point, the action of the body's real, living cells, as it was being decoded by new discoveries in cell biology, shed further light on that question.

Cells were the most fundamental units in nature, the place where

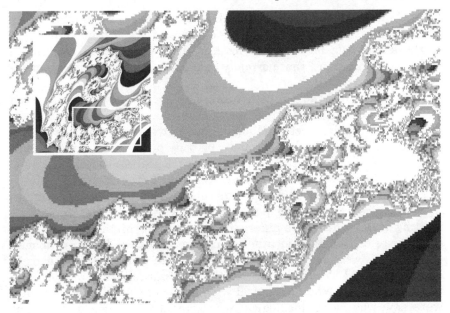

Figure 6: Magnified portion of a double-spiral chaos curve at the fringes of the Mandelbrot set, showing cell-like globules spawning in the spiral's interior and emerging as free-floating structures

life emerged, as patriot leaders had noted. However, those same life-giving cells could also become mercenary agents of death at basic levels of nature. New research in immunology had discovered an entire subclass of "human natural killer cells." Laboratory reports described in cool detail the organic process by which these killer cells form from more "naïve" precursor components, become "activated," then prowl the body and the bloodstream in search of invading viruses, malignant cancer cells and other disease-causing substances. In their normal "helper" roles, the specialized killer cells perform "lethal hits" on alien invaders that pose a threat to the body. Sometimes, however, these purely defensive cells become pathological themselves and attack the body from within—becoming indiscriminate killers of their own kind.

This submicroscopic drama of killer cells was not just a vivid scientific metaphor. Like the recurring patterns of nature revealed in chaos theory, the biological action described an organic process visible at many levels of living systems—including social systems. The new research helped to explain how vital defenders of the human system might turn into its worst enemies within: somewhere in the course of their day-to-day activities, the helper cells lock onto some distorted piece of information in the form of an odd-shaped chemical messenger. The new message alters the actions of the entire cell unit, blinding it to the identifying messages of its kin and switching off the innate biological "inhibitions" that normally stop the cell from turning on members of its own family.

The same pathological communication process could be observed in the lives of larger cells, in the self-destructive inner circles that form in closed cults, sects and ideological movements, and in the new terrorist cells roaming free through the body politic. The trail of death and indiscriminate destruction could be tracked from the early actions of the Symbionese Liberation Army and other leftist extremist cells in the sixties, to the suspected murders committed by Jim Jones' posthumous Peoples Temple hit squads in the seventies, to the apocalyptic plotting of David Koresh's inner circle of militant "Mighty Men," to the breakaway cell of Islamic fundamentalist "freedom fighters," armed and trained by Americans in the Soviet-Afghan war, who came back to bomb the World Trade Center—to the new paramilitary patriot cells manned by many who had served with honor in the U.S. military and were now waging an ideological war against their own government and fellow citizens.

In each instance, it seemed, members of these closed cliques, cells and circumscribed social units had locked onto some crazed idea, paranoid belief, or other distorted piece of information circulating in their isolated environments that perverted their guiding ideals, then switched off their inhibitions and their humanity. In such instances, the usual patterns of conflict were exacerbated, as each independent cell became a self-starting engine of chaos, capable of conceiving, justifying and igniting all manner of lethal acts against society without any outside provocation.

Religion was one source of the distorted ideas running through the minds of the new patriots, but, as in so many cults, it was not religion as most people embraced it. Many patriots were indeed devout Christian fundamentalists, but a large proportion professed the racist strain of fundamentalism known as Identity Christianity. The extreme Identity faith hailed white Protestant Americans as God's chosen people and scorned people of other races and religions as beasts and devils. And the new patriot mindset went a step farther than Identity Christianity's distortions of religious fundamentalism. At its core was a new political fundamentalism that elevated the United States Constitution itself to the level of scripture. Its absolutist, nativist mentality viewed America's founding documents written two centuries ago as sacred texts to be interpreted literally in terms dictated by patriot movement leaders. On that basis, patriot propounders had formulated their new extremist creed that decried every aspect of federal government, including taxation, public education and social welfare, opposed every effort to curb the abuses of tax-exempt religious organizations or to regulate the possession and use of firearms, and rejected every form of international cooperation.

Here was yet another device for reducing the vast complexities of late twentieth-century society. Like so many of their fellow citizens, many patriots were finding themselves without the modern skills and knowledge tools needed for life in the new global communication culture. Others were desperately seeking a grandiose new identity as Christians and Americans. Still others were being driven in closed ranks and secret associations to resist the new global consciousness with arms and unconscionable acts of violence.

Patriot leaders built elaborate rationales for their insurgent agendas. Much of the Free Militia's 100-page "field manual," *Principles Justifying the Arming and Organizing of a Militia*, appeared to have been taken verbatim from military training manuals, but for a very different mission: armed combat against Americans. Each self-contained cell was to be composed of eight to twelve "minutemen" loyal to their designated cell leader, each with its own strict chains of command and marching orders for the anticipated civil insurrection. Stated combat objectives included operations to "occupy buildings" and provide "suppressive fire" for effective "house assault" teams—although the manual gave no clear indication what buildings were to be occupied or whose houses were to be assaulted.

This manual drew heavily on the Christian Scriptures for divine justification, citing "biblical inspiration and authority" for its ideological positions, scriptural principles of "morality" and "just war" as defenses of its paramilitary objectives, and ending with a biblical "call to arms." "Jesus Christ was not a pacifist...he approved of the justified use of deadly force," one passage asserted. "Jesus Christ...commanded his followers to be armed," claimed another. This group and others sought to mobilize cell members for acts of armed "resistance" on explosive social and political issues such as taxes, gun control, abortion, capital punishment and "resisting tyranny." Quoting Christ's commandment to "Love your enemies," the manual rightly asked: "How can we love our enemies and kill them at the same time?" and self-righteously answered, "Clearly Jesus is saying...Our actions should never be motivated by hatred or vengeance but only by justice."

Other militia manuals laid out more specific plans for systematic

campaigns of domestic terror, including actions to attack federal buildings, kidnap prominent Americans, poison food supplies and execute
enemies of the patriot movement. The 200-page manual of the Montana Militia prescribed detailed plans for a domestic terror war that
included sabotage attacks designed to paralyze "the economy of the
country, agricultural or industrial production, transport and communication systems, the military and police systems"; actions aimed at
destroying "the firms and properties of people that are not Americans,"
kidnapping "known artists, sports figures" and other personalities as
"a useful form of propaganda for the revolutionary and patriot principles," "executing spies, government officials" and others who expose
the movement, raiding armories in order to seize "arms, ammo and
explosives"; and generally conducting a "war of nerves" by spreading
"false plans" with police and creating "an air of nervousness, discredit,
insecurity, uncertainty and concern on the part of the government."

One action called for specifically was "the placement of a bomb or
fire explosion of great destructive power, which is capable of effecting
irreparable loss against the enemy." Such an act, the Montana manual
stressed, "the urban guerrilla must execute with the greatest
coldbloodedness [sic]."

In some militias, those terror operations were to be run by cell
leaders acting on orders from above in a strict hierarchical chain of
command. In others, terror acts were to be carried out in conformity
with principles of "leaderless resistance" that purposely confined all
knowledge, planning and execution of specific operations to free-standing cells and smaller terrorist teams. The strategy minimized the risks
of exposure and infiltration of the cell by government undercover agents.
It also insulated militia higher-ups from discovery after the cell's acts
of terror were committed. In its initial profile, the action in the Oklahoma City bombing appeared to fit this pattern of a free-standing,
leaderless cell engaged in seemingly independent domestic terror operations.

Soldiers of Suggestion. The question of leadership, however, was largely
one of legal interpretation. Beyond the biblical quotations and military talk of cells, codes and chains of command, the real power of the
patriot movement, or so it seemed to us, was its sweeping use of suggestion to spread its new mindset, command its dispersed cells, and
even perhaps to incite violence, without issuing any direct orders whatsoever. Patriot leaders sowed the movement's insurgent ideology in
public lectures, private meetings, church services and secret sessions.
Each step of the way, their message was reinforced by mass communi-

cation: by the prolific output of patriot books, pamphlets, magazines, private-circulation newsletters, mass-produced videos, audiotapes, and the nonstop flow of extremist ideas over the nation's talk radio, shortwave and computer networks. Those channels filled the air with the movement's distorted beliefs, ideas and potentially lethal information: specific bomb-making instructions, directions on how and where to obtain raw ingredients, contraband weapons, explosives, etc. And like many recent acts of domestic terror, by aspiring assassins, anti-abortion bombers and others, the act of incitement was unprovable and usually untraceable—carried out entirely by remote control.

The germ of the Oklahoma City bomb plot itself had been in the air for nearly two decades. The idea traced back to *The Turner Diaries*, the infamous futuristic novel written in 1978 by William Pierce, head of the racist National Alliance of West Virginia. The book, widely described as the bible of the patriot movement, was read by Timothy McVeigh during his years in the military. In one scenario, a rented truck packed with an ammonium nitrate fertilizer bomb is detonated in front of a federal government building, killing hundreds of people. A more explicit plan, specifically targeting the Murrah building in Oklahoma City, was spelled out five years later. According to media reports, the plan was formulated in a series of late-night meetings in 1983 at the headquarters of the Aryan Nations sect in northern Idaho. There Aryan Nations founder Richard Butler, James D. Ellison, the founder of the Covenant, the Sword and the Arm of the Lord, Louis Ray Beam, Jr., the former Grand Dragon of the Texas Ku Klux Klan who was reportedly an originator of the concept of "leaderless resistance," and others allegedly scripted a scenario that was similar in many details to the act carried out on April 19, 1995.

In the first months after the blast, it remained mere speculation whether the alleged perpetrators were acting on, or even knew of, that earlier plan. However, one informant told government investigators that, in 1988, seven years before the bombing, James Nichols had told him the federal building in Oklahoma City could be leveled by a "megabomb" and that Nichols even drew him a diagram of the building.

To learn more about this new subculture and its clandestine cells, we made contact with several participants in the extended extremist network: far-right fundamentalists and Identity Christians, young neo-Nazi skinheads, and others who had crossed paths with the extremist movement. Our most enlightening conversation was with a man from Michigan. Dan S. was not a ringleader nor an infiltrator for any branch of government, but an investigator from the "fourth estate"—the public press. While working as a reporter for a small-town newspaper in central Michigan, he went under cover into the movement when it made its first inroads among distressed farmers and factory workers in the early eighties. For more than a dozen years, he moved freely in and out of its rarefied reaches, becoming close with some of its highest-ranking leaders and traveling to fifteen states to document their anti-government campaign in the heartland. While media and government investigators were working to uncover the Oklahoma bombers' backgrounds and ideological linkups, we probed Dan S.'s knowledge and first-hand experience for clues to the recruitment, conversion and control tactics of the wider extremist subculture.

Our source was introduced to the subculture by a local preacher who was building his own enclave within Michigan's expanding far-right network. His hook at the time was the volatile issue of taxes, which was being used by people and groups with diverse motives to arouse antipathy toward government across the country.

"In early 1980 I was in the courthouse waiting for some hearings," he began. "I met a minister who was fighting a local township over some zoning laws and we started a conversation. He had a clerical collar on and he was talking about not paying income taxes and not paying property taxes. The whole thing struck me as really peculiar. I mean here was a man of God talking about basically illegal acts. His beliefs intrigued me and at the same time scared me."

He spotted a potential story, but he did not tell his new acquaintance that he was a reporter. He listened without criticizing the minister's beliefs, then the man invited him to attend a local church service. He found it to be a church like no other.

"I went to his services for several weeks. Before long, I realized that these guys were involved in some heavy white supremacist movements. Some were involved in Klan activities, some in neo-Nazi activities, some in Christian Identity activities—which is really the religion of all of them."

The hybrid Christian Identity, or Identity Christian, movement (the two terms were used interchangeably) was the emblem of the new extremism, a blend of zealous fundamentalist Christianity and misplaced patriotism mixed in with heavy doses of race hatred. As he worked his way into the underground, our source was both intrigued and appalled by this strange new belief system.

"Initially, I was interested in it from a religious standpoint," he told us. "The twists and turns and conclusions they would jump to were just incredible to me. For example, they believed that Cain was the product of a sexual relationship between Eve and the devil, and that the Jews were the descendants of Cain; therefore, the Jews were the Antichrist. They referred to blacks and Jews alike as 'beasts.' Blacks were the 'beasts of the field' described in the Bible. Jews were the Beast of Revelation."

He recalled the disbelief he met with when he wrote his first stories about his experiences in the Identity movement. "People said, 'This is ridiculous. Nobody believes that.' They just thought it was laughable. Within a couple years, they found out that it wasn't so ridiculous and, in fact, it was the religion of those people. I saw members of the Nazi party and out and out Klansmen portraying themselves as Identity ministers."

The Identity faith was not open to just any outsider. Like hate groups historically, they were secret societies. Admission was by invitation only. Once inside, however, our source won his pastor's trust, and he was soon invited into the movement's inner circle. There he saw the first plans for terror taking shape within the burgeoning network of Identity sects and churches.

"I spent a week at an Identity compound in Shell City, Missouri," he continued. "I met people from all over the country. That's where I saw things starting to get violent, talk of killing and that sort of thing."

At the outset, however, most new recruits were introduced to the movement as Dan was, through a more palatable agenda of political and economic issues. He described one tool many groups used to fuel the anti-government climate and identify prospects who might have sympathy for the movement's more extreme ideas.

"In the eighties, we hooked up with tax protest groups and held meetings where we would tell people how to get out of paying taxes. We told them that taxation was illegal and gave out documentation showing how they could get their money back from their paychecks. We brought in speakers. We were very public. We held meetings at union halls. We posted fliers around, but nobody knew who we really were."

Similar tactics were used across the heartland to recruit displaced farmers and factory workers into wider circles of reaction. The circle our source entered was a hub for historic hate groups operating as legal tax protest organizations.

"While we were doing that, we also were involved in Klan and neo-Nazi activities," he said, retracing his own steps that led him swiftly into main arenas of extremist organizing. "I met every major Klan leader in the movement. I traveled across the country with some of them. I went to guerrilla training camps and learned how to kill people."

His testimony left little doubt that some anti-government activists were using the nation's economic distress and the public's growing frustration with government for more sinister ends. He recalled a conversation with one group leader from the Pacific Northwest who had helped to organize the white supremacist Identity sect called the Order.

"He portrayed himself as a fifteen-year tax protestor. He read in the press that Michigan had become a hotbed of anti-tax protest, and I'll never forget when I met him the first thing he said to me was 'I've been waiting for something like this for ten years. This is our opportunity. This is going to help our revolution.' "

Dan described an ongoing interaction he had with Michigan-based Ku Klux Klan leader Bob Miles. Miles, who died in 1992, was the godfather of Klansmen nationwide in the eighties and, reportedly, another avid promoter of the idea of leaderless cells. His influential writings and organizing strategies were major factors in the spread of the new anti-government mindset, but behind it, for Miles and his followers, was a hidden agenda.

"Miles' book *The Fifth Era* described how the Klan needed to become more mainstream in this new era to attract more people. Then, once they were in the network, once you had befriended them and slowly indoctrinated them, they would be more likely to accept the different beliefs you put forward."

According to Dan, Miles' advice was followed widely by the new generation of Klan leaders and people throughout the extremist subculture. He described the Identity movement's strategy of recruiting people through timeless appeals to God and country, then bringing them around to more intemperate beliefs through a process of gradual indoctrination.

"We used the tax protests to recruit. We'd hand out some religious literature that was mild, things that people were generally going to accept. We'd use catchwords—Christian, patriot—to appear as a great Christian patriot organization."

Like other cults and sects we had surveyed, the new extremist groups practiced many forms of deception. They also used varied methods of mind manipulation, including intensive regimens of individual and group indoctrination. However, unlike most cult recruiters, who swayed people with utopian visions, usually in short periods of high-pressure recruitment and conversion, the new extremist groups seemed to prefer a slower indoctrination process designed to open people by degrees to more odious beliefs.

"We would always start with some real-world fact, something the government had done that wasn't good or whatever. Then slowly, over several weeks or months, through casual conversations, the talk would evolve into other things, like guns and killing."

Dan confirmed that the extremist network also served as a major market for mass-produced print and electronic propaganda. Every meeting and retreat hosted underground entrepreneurs hawking books and pamphlets they had written, high-priced audiotapes and videotapes of various sermons, lectures, study sessions, and other indoctrination tools that spread the movement's messages over time and from a distance. At times, it seemed, each enterprising Identity sect, political group and paramilitary cell became an independent franchise in the dissemination and slow indoctrination of the new ideology.

"We would give people some middle-of-the-road literature and tell them to read it. When they came to the next meeting, we'd give them something a little harsher, or they'd be given a tape or invited to a talk, and we would always question them about what they thought afterwards."

During those years, elements of survivalist ideology were making inroads into many new age and born-again groups. Like Identity Christianity, survivalism was a staple of the extremist subculture, and it found a ready audience in the tax protest movement.

"One thing we would preach continually at tax protest meetings was to stockpile weapons, ammunition and food. We would tell people that, as the protest grew, it would bring the collapse of the government, and that blacks and Jews and Hispanics and everyone else were going to riot and come after them, and they would have to defend their families and communities from this hoard. That's when everyone in the movement began stocking up on guns, preparing for the downfall of the country."

The fear and paranoia fueled the militant mentality that surfaced in the first *ad hoc* citizen militias. Dan recalled his own induction into the infant militia movement in a chilling variation on the traditional born-again altar call.

"I went to an initiation ceremony in a church at the Identity compound in Missouri. It was odd. It was extremely religious. There were people standing along the aisles carrying weapons, rifles, a few with pistols. We all stood up and walked to the front of the church in this strange procession. We were told that it was all part of the ritual of becoming 'God's soldiers' in this holy war."

One Identity leader addressed the initiates that evening. Dan recalled the message unlike any he had heard from a church pulpit, and the congregation's reaction.

"He said 'Soon we will be asked to kill but we will kill with love in our hearts because God is with us.' Everyone was somber, everyone was proud, everyone thought they were in this special ceremony at this special occasion."

We tried to locate this violent new religious-political ritual on the scale of cult practices we had identified. We looked for the familiar codewords we had come to recognize as triggers of covert hypnotic induction. Our source described just such a ritual that seemed to mark the distinctive code of Identity—an extreme twist on the universal call to "surrender the will" issued, in one form or another, by countless cults and sects.

"You surrender to your *race*," Dan said. "You are God's chosen people. That's the whole thing in Identity. You were told that you were the white soldier of God and you had to surrender to your race and your God whenever you were called upon."

In a similar way, Identity sects replaced the typical cult mind control practice of reciting repetitive chants and mantras with a recitation of solemn oaths and other fear-filled commands that cemented the group's control from the outset.

"In the oath for the Order, you swore to uphold your race and to kill any 'race traitor' who betrayed the white race," Dan recalled. Such oaths carried implicit threats to those who betrayed the Identity movement.

"The worst thing you could ever be was a race traitor," he said. "If you are a race traitor, you are expected to die, and in fact there were people in the movement killed that I knew of—Order people, Aryan Nations people—who were executed for being race traitors."

Dan traced the turn from words to action with the emergence of the militia movement's clandestine cell groups. In the eighties, he said, cell groups were secret units within the wider extremist subculture. Only later did they surface as explicit organizing structures. Even in most militias, however, cells remained secretive and reserved for hardcore insurgent operations.

"People in cells were always referred to as the 'up-front' types, the guys who had no families and could afford to do that kind of work," he recalled.

Many early cell operatives were members of the neo-Nazi skinhead subculture. "The skinheads were the up-front guys initially. They would go out and beat up on someone and then take the heat," said Dan. However, older, more seasoned cell members were used for missions that required greater secrecy and planning. He described the internal command structure and division of labor in those early domestic terror cells.

"Each cell would be made up of different individuals who fulfilled different purposes. Some would be good at falsifying documents, license plates and automobile registrations. Some would actually perform hits on people like Alan Berg." (Berg was the Denver radio talk-show host murdered by units of the Order in 1984.)

With the rise of citizen militias, Dan explained, the basic cell model developed into a two-tiered, quasi-military system with multiple levels of overt and covert operation.

"The militias are moving in a very structured manner. They are well organized from state to state and region to region. They've set up true military structures, brigades, platoons, the whole thing, but those who 'go under' usually don't have any more public displays or public contact."

The two-tiered cell structure peeled back the public face many militias took pains to present both before and after the Oklahoma City bombing. The "out-front" face of militiamen as lawful gun enthusiasts and defenders of their communities seemed, in at least some of the new groups, to mask the "up-front" actions of the point men in floating terror cells. Dan insisted that all the field maneuvers and parading in camouflage were postures designed mainly for public consumption, and that many unwitting weekend warriors were being deceived and exploited for propaganda purposes by people higher in the movement.

"I believe that many people in the militias are being used as dupes, like we used the tax protesters. They're in it because they're gun freaks who like to play soldier or whatever, while the true white supremacists are using the militias as recruiting grounds. When people with more extreme inclinations are identified at open militia meetings, they are invited to go under and form cells and smaller subunits for secret operations."

Another gateway into the militia subculture, which leaped into the spotlight after the Oklahoma City bombing, was the nation's vast meshwork of gun shows with its thriving commerce in weapons, paramilitary paraphernalia and anti-government invective.

"Gun shows are huge in the movement," Dan acknowledged. "They're very popular in the heartland, and you can't go into one without getting the literature. They're a key dissemination point."

Looking back on his years moving among various Identity, Ku Klux Klan, neo-Nazi and paramilitary groups, Dan formed his own impression of the minds at the core of the extremist network. Some, like accused bomber Timothy McVeigh, as he appeared in the first forensic profiles, seemed to thrive on the diehard honor codes and military disciplines of the extremist underground. Yet, at some point, the minds of many extremists, from high-ranking leaders to elusive operatives out in the cold of clandestine action, seemed to spin out of control in their sealed cells and subcultures and cartwheel off in the destructive dynamics of the death spiral. Long before Oklahoma City, Dan perceived many of the new patriots, not merely as weekend warriors or strict disciplinarians, but as individuals who, by their life experiences and immersion in the murky waters of American extremism, had become dangerously vulnerable to paranoid thinking and pathological behavior.

"It happens over time," he said grimly. "They come in a little off. Then, for whatever reason, they discover something in these movements that gives them a direction, and there is a network of support there, but once they get into it many can become pathological."

His words sketched the familiar communication pathology, a spiraling pattern of runaway positive feedback that had the force to bind unstable, highly charged personalities into tight-knit cells roaming the terrain of American society.

"I'll tell you, it's downright frightening how they can pick up steam. It's like a snowball rolling downhill," he confirmed. "You hear them talk about how they read this or read that and, suddenly, 'I found all the answers to my questions!' It reinforces them and just keeps rolling and rolling. Soon they're asked to speak before the group, and then before more and more people. They take turns talking and bringing in people continually and it grows and empowers them. I saw people flip out and go into tantrums. Their eyes would become almost maniacal. They would take on an appearance of almost a religious experience and just lose control."

His concerns increased as he watched the extremist movement grow in fervor and ferocity, but his sense of its violent potential remained consistent.

"I went back under cover in '85, and again in '92, but the whole time I was in the Identity movement, I knew that someday those guys were going to commit some huge terrorist act."

With that hypothetical act now history, and the prospect of more to come, we asked our source to help us understand the changes that seemed to have turned some members of the scattered extremist groups of the eighties into the new American terrorists of the nineties. Apart from an increase in armaments and the new ease of making inexpensive weapons of mass destruction, he didn't see any major changes.

"The faces have changed. They've got a few new things to jump up and down over, like gun control and the Second Amendment, and they've got Waco, but when you get right down to it, the issues are the same. It's still the evil government, and I guarantee you that if you look into it you will find the racial aspect and the Identity aspect in there somewhere. These people haven't changed their stripes."

Of course, not all of the new patriots were racists, anti-Semites and paranoiacs. Many no doubt were sincere in their patriotic beliefs and convinced that their extreme views derived from a divine calling. However, many others appeared to have been deceived, manipulated and exploited. The spreading cell group underground raised urgent concerns about the larger patriot movement's secretive recruitment and indoctrination rituals, covert operations and long-term political objectives. It also posed new questions about the U.S. military's own intensive training programs, internal psychological climate and, for many soldiers, it seemed, grossly inadequate mustering out procedures.

The new groups posed more vexing dilemmas for lawmakers and law enforcers, grave concerns for public safety and the rule of law that, the record suggested, federal officials seemed to be anticipating and attempting to head off at the pass as early as the Weaver standoff and the shootout in Waco. With the death toll from the new terror climbing geometrically, people across the political spectrum expressed similar fears that any crackdown on extremist groups held risks of encroaching on the civil liberties of all Americans. Yet the new paramilitary groups were not just another protected religious sect or political movement. In the opinion of many jurists, the very existence of citizen militias was illegal. In fact, the Constitution reserved the authority to arm and control militias solely to state governments. Laws against insurrection prohibited individuals and groups from training to use force for civil disorder, and treason laws prohibited any person or group from waging war against the state.

However, those laws seemed to be a moot point to many patriots and many other frustrated, angry Americans. Unlike other underground movements, the patriot subculture seemed to be growing, not shrinking, in the light of public exposure. One monitoring group reported that membership in militias and smaller paramilitary units increased, particularly in the West, in the months after the Oklahoma City bombing. That fact said something about the spread of cult-like groups in the nineties and something more about the state of mind in America generally.

As the last bodies were reclaimed from the Oklahoma City rubble and the Murrah building's teetering shell was leveled by a commercial demolition team, questions hung like dust in the air: Would the bloodshed rouse the nation to really examine and root out the pathological new mindset in its midst? Would Americans reject the new anti-government extremists with their distorted ideas about their country's races, faiths and freedoms, or did many secretly sympathize with them? Would the Oklahoma bombing mark the beginning of the end of the new ideological armies—or the beginning of the end of the American experiment?

Seventeen years ago, it was much easier to draw back from our work and look objectively at the new dangers we were foreshadowing. Since then we've seen Jonestown, Waco, Tokyo and Oklahoma City. We've learned that our most precious modern resources—information and human communication—can be used to control individuals, groups and nations with frightening ease and precision. We've seen signs that some new spiritual and personal growth practices may damage the mind and body in ways that may be irreversible. In these years, we've watched a brewing storm of religious-political fanaticism gather over the United States and the world. In some places, it has given rise to new forms of mental illness and mass insanity. In others, it has given way to terror.

Our thoughts returned to the moment years earlier, when we watched the first outcroppings of this new madness and spiritual terror rising in the Middle East and in our own country. We recalled our grim projections at the time that have marked the path forward ever since. Staring at us then, as it was now and even more in the runup to the millennium, was a new peril in the life of the modern mind that, we fear, could be pushing people and nations into a darkness from which, this time, humankind may not recover.

Findings in a Study of the Cult Experience and its Effects

Summary and Profile of Initial Data Findings
Information Disease
Project on Information and Social Change

TABLE I

BACKGROUND & RECRUITMENT*	Moon	Krishna	Scientology	DLM	The Way	Bible sects	Total**
RELIGIOUS BACKGROUND							
Protestant	41%	26%	37%	33%	65%	71%	45%
Catholic	31%	32%	34%	7%	35%	19%	27%
Jewish	20%	37%	13%	58%	-	7%	21%
Other/None	7%	5%	16%	2%	-	3%	7%
MEMBERSHIP: %MALE/%FEMALE	56:44	60:40	47:53	45:55	35:65	40:60	49:51
AVG. AGE AT TIME OF 1ST CONTACT (years)	21.1	18.4	24.8	20.5	19.4	19.5	20.9
AVG. LENGTH OF TIME IN GROUP (months)	17	33	36	49	23	28	34
FIRST CONTACTED (where)							
at school/college	32%	10%	8%	45%	55%	38%	25%
at work	5%	-	11%	13%	9%	6%	8%
in private home	7%	20%	47%	24%	27%	25%	19%
city street/shopping center	49%	45%	16%	16%	9%	19%	33%
airport/train terminal	1%	5%	-	-	-	-	2%
through books/ad/etc.	5%	20%	18%	3%	-	12%	6%
FIRST CONTACTED (who)							
sibling/relative	3%	-	14%	10%	9%	8%	7%
friend	16%	24%	51%	54%	35%	38%	30%
stranger	81%	76%	35%	36%	56%	54%	63%
INITIAL ATTRACTIONS - "Very important"							
"charisma" of leader	16%	21%	13%	21%	22%	36%	24%
members' apparent happiness/fulfillment	71%	50%	66%	72%	61%	52%	66%
group's philosophy or religious beliefs	34%	40%	34%	51%	48%	60%	48%
group's social or political goals	45%	15%	32%	26%	9%	21%	35%
exciting rituals or therapeutic techniques	8%	25%	39%	30%	9%	17%	21%
attention of opposite sex group member	24%	20%	16%	21%	30%	12%	25%
desire to escape from family, society, etc.	15%	15%	16%	19%	13%	26%	20%
pressure to join from members or leaders	46%	40%	39%	9%	30%	45%	41%

*--based on nationwide sampling of 353 former members of 48 cults, sects and self-help therapies from 39 states and Canada.

**--all total % figures are adjusted frequencies

TABLE II - CULT LIFE

	Moon	Krishna	Scientology	DLM	The Way	Bible sects	Total
SLEEP (average hours per night)	5.2	5.2	5.8	6.1	6.4	6.2	6.0

DIET (% reporting)

	Moon	Krishna	Scientology	DLM	The Way	Bible sects	Total
well-balanced, no restrictions	16%	0%	50%	0%	57%	36%	26%
vegetarian/low-protein, but not unhealthy	50%	68%	14%	97%	33%	40%	50%
very unbalanced and unhealthy	33%	32%	36%	3%	10%	24%	24%

DAILY RITUALS & PROCESSES

	Moon	Krishna	Scientology	DLM	The Way	Bible sects	Total
meditation	31%	32%	5%	99%	5%	32%	37%
chanting/tongues/repetitive rituals	54%	99%	8%	15%	99%	58%	53%
"auditing" or confessional processes	43%	11%	97%	13%	9%	43%	44%
encounter/sensitivity/"training" sessions	43%	5%	41%	15%	23%	41%	35%
psychodrama or role-playing games	22%	0%	11%	0%	5%	19%	14%
guided fantasy or "closed-eye" processes	8%	5%	27%	8%	5%	23%	14%
RITUALS & PROCESSES (avg. hours/day)	4.5	5.6	3.1	4.7	3.1	6.4	4.3

ADD'L STUDY/INDOCTRINATION (lectures,

	Moon	Krishna	Scientology	DLM	The Way	Bible sects	Total
seminars, workshops, etc. avg. hrs/week)	30.1	21.8	21.4	19.9	22.3	20.8	22.3

TOTAL RITUAL & STUDY/INDOCTRINATION

	Moon	Krishna	Scientology	DLM	The Way	Bible sects	Total
(avg. hrs/week)	61.6	61.0	43.1	52.8	44.0	65.6	52.4
DONATIONS (savings/possessions)	$1058	$961	$9331	$2874	$3316	$4040	$3516
EARNINGS (fundraising/outside jobs)	$36,238	$71,630	$59,716	$6050	$1258	$6728	$25,211
NEW RECRUITS (avg. no. per member)	1.5	2.2	3.6	5.9	2.5	9.5	5.8

SEX LIFE

	Moon	Krishna	Scientology	DLM	The Way	Bible sects	Total
heterosexual	2%	5%	62%	42%	39%	23%	24%
homosexual,	7%	0%	5%	5%	0%	2%	2%
masturbation	12%	5%	32%	42%	35%	9%	22%
with leaders of group	0%	0%	8%	5%	4%	4%	6%
celibate	85%	95%	38%	70%	48%	66%	71%
PHYSICAL PUNISHMENT	22%	32%	35%	0%	0%	17%	20%

TABLE III - LONG-TERM EFFECTS

	Moon	Krishna	Scientology	DLM	The Way	Bible sects	Total
PHYSICAL EFFECTS							
abnormal weight gain	20%	22%	18%	5%	14%	10%	16%
abnormal weight loss	5%	6%	9%	-	24%	4%	18%
sexual dysfunction	23%	17%	24%	13%	24%	16%	19%
menstrual dysfunction (women)	20%	42%	17%	9%	37%	20%	22%
EMOTIONAL EFFECTS							
depression	76%	72%	76%	72%	81%	82%	75%
loneliness	62%	89%	89%	74%	57%	80%	68%
sleeplessness	21%	44%	52%	31%	33%	36%	31%
violent outbursts	16%	22%	27%	15%	14%	20%	17%
guilt feelings about leaving the group	59%	72%	58%	54%	57%	62%	59%
feelings of anger toward group leaders	56%	78%	73%	64%	90%	84%	68%
fear of physical harm by the group	36%	67%	76%	28%	38%	30%	40%
humiliation, embarrassment	56%	78%	67%	51%	52%	64%	59%
hostile feelings toward parents/family	39%	67%	24%	41%	33%	28%	37%
DISORDERS OF PERCEPTION, MEMORY, AWARENESS & OTHER INFORMATION-PROCESSING EFFECTS							
disorientation	64%	78%	76%	56%	57%	76%	66%
"floating" in and out of altered states	55%	72%	55%	67%	71%	70%	61%
nightmares	46%	61%	52%	46%	38%	52%	48%
amnesia (memory loss)	20%	44%	30%	18%	24%	34%	25%
hallucinations and delusions	12%	17%	24%	10%	19%	16%	15%
bewildering "psychic" phenomena	15%	17%	21%	13%	24%	16%	17%
inability to break rhythm of chanting, meditation, patterns of dogma, etc.	39%	61%	18%	56%	52%	40%	42%
TOTAL MONTHS LONG-TERM EFFECTS(avg)	75.7	88.6	139.1	52.9	43.5	113.0	81.5
AVERAGE REHABILITATION TIME (months)	16.6	11.1	20.1	12.3	9.5	20.8	16.0
SUICIDAL/ SELF-DESTRUCTIVE TENDENCIES	33%	25%	51%	37%	15%	34%	35%
FOLLOWUP COUNSELING (therapist, clergy, social worker, etc.)	44%	47%	41%	35%	60%	51%	59%
AVERAGE LENGTH OF FOLLOWUP (months)	9.3	7.8	13.9	18.0	4.7	15.2	10.9

TABLE IV - PEARSON'S PRODUCT MOMENT CORRELATION COEFFICIENTS ("r/p")
"r"-value = coefficient of correlation
"p"-value = significance (p = .05 or less considered significant)

RITUAL TIME vs. EFFECTS	Moon n=132	Scientology n=33	DLM n=39	The Way n=21	Total n=308
PHYSICAL EFFECTS					
abnormal weight gain	.078/.18	.025/.44	-.104/.26	.110/.32	-.001/.45
abnomal weight loss	.044/.31	*.345/.026	—	.736/.000+	.029/.30
sexual dysfunction	*.185/.016	*.429/.007	*.518/.000	.115/.31	*.1176/.02
menstrual dysfunction (women)	.032/.35	*.317/.039	.162/.16	.306/.09	.039/.22
EMOTIONAL EFFECTS					
depression	*.154/.040	*.538/.001	*.578/.000	*.402/.035	*.209/.000
loneliness	.119/.08	*.459/.004	.226/.16	*.372/.021+	*.125/.014
sleeplessness	*.207/.008	*.357/.022	*.377/.009	*.508/.013+	*.208/.000
violent outbursts	.136/.06	*.449/.005	.223/.086	*.787/.009+	.077/.09
guilt feelings about leaving the group	-.024/.39	*.530/.001	*.587/.000	*.441/.029+	.077/.09
feelings of anger at group leaders	*.172/.023	.227/.10	.243/.07	.251/.14	*.164/.002
fear of physical harm by the group	.074/.20	.049/.39	-.046/.39	.248/.16	.041/.24
humiliation, embarassment	.057/.25	.101/.29	*.647/.000	*.438/.030+	*.088/.059
hostiity toward parents/family	*.136/.059	*.403/.011	*.395/.006	.163/.24	*.121/.016
DISORDERS OF PERCEPTION, MEMORY, AWARENESS & OTHER INFORMATION-PROCESSING EFFECTS					
disorientation	*.177/.020	.163/.18	*.499/.001	*.450/.026+	*.148/.004
"floating" in & out of altered states	*.234/.003	*.403/.011	*.386/.008	*.515/.008	*.123/.015
nightmares	.106/.11	.211/.123	.147/.19	*.643/.001+	*.113/.024
amnesia (memory loss)	.103/.12	*.289/.054	:068/.45	*.352/.059	.010/.43
hallucinations and delusions	.055/.26	*.382/.016	*.619/.000	.223/.16	.070/.11
bewildering "psychic" phenomena	*.210/.007	*.490/.002	*.600/.000	*.546/.008+	*.094/.048
inability to break rhythms of chanting, meditation, patterns of dogma, etc.	.052/.27	.131/.24	.048/.385	*.486/.013	.065/.12

TOTAL MONTHS LONG-TERM EFFECTS *.251/.0016 *.515/.001 *.623/.00001 *.512/.007 *.164/.001

AVG. REHABILITATION TIME (months).109/.109 *.366/.020 *.388/.0067 *.469/.014 *.146/.005

"*" — p = .05 or less considered statistically significant
"+" — correlation includes ritual and study time combined, n=19

NOTE: refined totals, averages and correlations cover only those members in groups between 1 month and 8 years, and those who have been out of their groups 6 months or longer. Figures given are minimums and do not reflect ongoing effects. True figures may be 5 to 10% higher.

TABLE V - SEPARATION & DEPROGRAMMING

SEPARATION	Moon	Krishna	Scientology	DLM	The Way	Bible sects	Total
walked away voluntarily	32%	16%	78%	17%	13%	19%	30%
abducted or kidnapped	39%	47%	8%	55%	48%	51%	39%
came home at family's request	18%	16%	5%	22%	26%	13%	18%
legal conservatorship	15%	16%	3%	5%	13%	11%	11%
kicked out, asked to go	2%	5%	8%	0%	0%	6%	4%
PERCENT DEPROGRAMMED	78%	79%	24%	80%	91%	74%	73%
AVERAGE DEPROGRAMMING TIME (days)	4.0	3.7	2.7	6.5	3.4	5.9	3.6
RE-EMERGENCE							
sudden reawakening in a single moment	26%	26%	14%	15%	30%	26%	24%
gradual dawning over a few days	28%	37%	32%	40%	49%	36%	35%
very slow process over weeks or months	34%	26%	41%	42%	13%	30%	36%
never experienced feeling of re-emergence	4%	5%	11%	3%	0%	6%	5%
PHYSICAL INJURY DURING ABDUCTION OR DEPROGRAMMING	4	0	1	2	12	-	2.6%
(percent of injuries self-inflicted)	25%	-	100%	100%	100%	-	60%

DEPROGRAMMING OR SEPARATION
"Very important"

	Total
food and rest, physical restoration	28%
debate refuting cult beliefs/dogma/etc.	51%
deprog/counselor's threats/verbal abuse	6%
deprog/counselor's empathy and feeling	44%
testimony/support from former members	51%
empathy and feeling of parents/family	39%
help of clergy: ministers/priests/rabbis, etc.	7%
reading about brainwashing/mind control	47%
reading accounts of the cult's misdeeds	39%

REHABILITATION
"Very important"

	Total
love/support of parents/family	64%
insight/support of ex-cult members	59%
mental health counseling	14%
regaining lost money/possessions	9%
going back to school or college	25%
finding a job or new career	36%
helping others quit/recover from cults	39%
making friendships unrelated to cults	50%
getting as far from cults as possible	29%

REASONS FOR FAILURE - "Very Important"
(based on 47 reported failures)

	Total		Total
inadequate security in deprogramming	54%	further contact or pressure from the cult	65%
deprogrammer's lack of skill or knowledge	54%	too short or inadequate rehabilitation	89%
excessive verbal abuse by deprogrammer	7%	failure to seek professional followup	46%
physical abuse by deprogrammer or aides	3%	"re-entry" problems: loneliness, fear, guilt	
unavailability of ex-members for support	53%	depression, lack of confidence, etc.	71%
action of courts, police or other authorities	29%		

TABLE VI - DEPROGRAMMED vs. NOT-DEPROGRAMMED

	Moon		Scientology		DivineLight		Bible sects		Total	
	Dep.	Not	Dep.	Not	Dep.	Not	Dep.	Not	Dep.	Not
RE-EMERGENCE										
sudden reawakening in single moment	29%	29%	22%	11%	19%	0%	34%	7%	29%	13%
gradual dawning over a few days	35%	14%	67%	22%	50%	0%	39%	29%	39%	20%
very slow process over weeks or months	34%	50%	11%	52%	31%	88%	21%	57%	28%	56%
never experienced feeling of re-emergence	3%	7%	0%	15%	0%	12%	5%	7%	4%	10%
TOTAL MONTHS OF EFFECTS	79.	120.	93	139	50	76	82	116	78	121
REHABILITATION TIME (months)	17.5	20.8	14.6	19.3	12.2	12.6	14.7	23.6	14.8	19.9

T-TESTS FOR CORRELATION OF EFECTS/ NOT DEPROGRAMMED VS. DEPROGRAMMED

"t/p"	"t"	"p"
TOTAL EFFECTS (Not vs. Dep)	2.52	*.013
AVG. REHABILITATION TIME (Not vs. Dep)	2.41	*.017

"t"-value = 2-tailed variation
"p"-value = probability of significance (*-p=.05 or less considered significant)
"n"=322

TABLE VII - LONG-TERM CHANGES IN SELF-IMAGE & ATTITUDES (all members)

SELF-IMAGE				ATTITUDES
More confident	81%	Less confident	19%	Attitude toward raising a family = better 43% worse 9% unchanged 48%
More trusting	8%	Less trusting	92%	Attitude toward religion of family = better 29% worse 29% unchanged 41%
Less self-centered	61%	More self-centered	39%	Attitude toward religion generally = better 21% worse 48% unchanged 30%
More able to cope with complexity	20%	Less able to cope with complexity	80%	Attitude toward spirituality in general = better 48% worse 29% unchanged 23%
More in control of emotions	71%	Less in control of emotions	29%	

Acknowledgments

WE EXPRESS FIRST our gratitude to the many former cult and sect members, self-help therapy participants and concerned parents who helped us in our research with the understanding that we would respect their privacy by not revealing their identities.

We thank the staff and members of two organizations who aided us in researching this book and who have enhanced our work enormously over the years: William and Betty Rambur, Curt and Henrietta Crampton, Priscilla Coates and Cynthia Kisser of the Cult Awareness Network; and Dr. John G. Clark, Jr., Eleanor Clark, Michael Langone and Marsha Rudin of the American Family Foundation. We thank Marjoe Gortner, Leslie Van Houten and Maxwell Keith, Ted Patrick and Sondra Sacks, Jeannie Mills and Grace Stoen for their valuable contributions to the knowledge in this book.

We are indebted to many distinguished scientists and professional people who shared with us their thinking and research. We are especially grateful to Carl Rogers, Jack Gibb, Betty Meador and Will Schutz for their thoughts on the evolution of the human potential movement. We are grateful to John R. Pierce for helping us to separate the engineering aspects of communication from the new science's human applications; to Gilla Prizant for her thoughts on the condition of American psychiatry; to Fred Crowell, John Lyman, G.D. McCann and David Rumelhart for their views on the problems and promises of the human information-processing perspective; and to Hans Bremermann and Karl Pribram for their willingness to speculate with us on their own developing theories and related scientific research.

Special thanks to Dr. Alfred G. Smith, Professor Emeritus at the Center for Communication Research at the University of Texas, for his creative instruction and many years of thoughtful insights into the difficult questions we have set out to explore.

We thank close friends, relatives and new acquaintances across the country who have sustained us in our travels and who, in many instances, made difficult times easier and even fun: Bob Baker, Don Cameron, Holly Conway, Kacey Conway and Patrick Green, Mike and Marie Conway, Robert and Virginia Conway, Christine and Vincent Conway, Lois and Larry Davis, Mary and Dick Deich, Debbi Dudziak, Judy and Michael Einbund, Jim Fishel and B. Lynn Micale, Paula Harrington, Bob and Birchie Henderson, ReneHume, Evie Juster, Marilyn, Judy, Elaine and Bill Kanoskie, Joe Marcella, Doris Peck, Davis Perkins, Eric Rayman, Roger Repohl and Don Ross. We're also grateful to many individuals with whom we made only brief personal or telephone contact: the Crudups, the DeBlassies, Milton Erickson, Bill Farr, Sam Farry, Thelma Moss, the Randalls, Steven Smale and Irving Yalom.

We remember the many people who encouraged, helped and arranged for us to write *Snapping* initially for J. B. Lippincott Company: Donald C. Farber, Ed Burlingame, Beatrice Rosenfeld, Kathryn Frank, Katharine Kirkland and

Elaine Terranova. We're grateful to our editors at Delta Books, Christopher Kuppig and Gary Luke, and to Sallie T. Gouverneur, Sterling Lord and Phillippa Brophy for their friendship and professional support. Above all, we thank our editor at Lippincott, Peg Cameron, for her continuing belief in this book and both of us, and for fighting for our work in ways we only came to fully appreciate much later.

Profound thanks to our attorney, Melvin Wulf, to Paul Morantz and Harold McGuire, Jr. Friends and colleagues in the media helped this book to reach the public initially: Pat Lynch, G. Barry Golson, Arthur Kretchmer, Geraldo Rivera, Charles Thompson, David Hartman, Larry King, Bob Dolce and Johnny Carson. Our friends in Philadelphia sustained us: Tema and Al Levin, Bob and Esther Mezey, Marge and Harry League, Josie and Randy Zelov.

Now, too, we thank new friends and associates who made it possible for us to publish this second edition. For help with research and information, thanks to Linda Baker, Scott Barton, Juliette Bennett, David Clark, Fred Clarkson, Marilyn Dassaw, May Dooley, Dennis Erlich, Lorna Goldberg, Dale Griffiths, Steve Hassan, Galen Kelly, Liz Kelly, Steve Kent, Paul Martin, Peter McWilliams, Stan Mushaw, Ted Patrick, Rick Ross, Patrick Ryan, Dan Shriner, Joe Szimhart, Joe Trento, Robert Vaughan Young and Stacy Young. Special thanks to Maria Piro and Judith Stone for expert editorial guidance, and to Tema Levin, Lois Bell, Priscilla Coates and Kacey Conway for their invaluable research efforts.

We're deeply grateful to our colleagues at the University of Oregon Communication Research Center: Carl W. Carmichael, Ph.D., and John C. Coggins, and to Gary Cronkhite, Ph.D., Professor of Communication Studies at Indiana University, for their thoughts and supporting efforts for our work in the scientific community. Thanks to John P. Wilson, Ph.D., Gus Krauss, Dave Stein and Bob Hermann for their thoughts on PTSD. Thanks to Marc Breault, David Bunds, Dr. Robert Cancro, Mark Englund, Philip J. Heymann, Dr. Bruce Perry, Rod Rosenstein, John Russell, Richard Scruggs, Carl Stern and other sources for their cooperation with our inquiries into the Waco tragedy.

For his valued advice on literary matters, thanks to Perry Knowlton. For help with legal, artistic, research and technical services for Stillpoint Press, we thank John P. Luneau, Eric Rayman, Isaac E. Druker, Bill Kelliher, Roseanne Lentin, Mario Kranjac, John Bradley, Christine Carty, Nancy Zehner, Nina Massen, Mikki LeMoine, Skipp Porteous, Barbara Simon, John Clarke, Alice Soloway, Seth Demsey, Peter McWilliams, Ed Haisha, Grant Taylor, Betty Dodson, Eleanor Clark, Brad Searles, Denise Manno, Kerry Bruscia, Lisa Maxwell, Tim Scarbrough, Brenda Brown, Sid Buck and Mario Henri Chakkour.

For their friendship and many favors we thank again and always: Holly Conway, Katharine and John Walker, Lauren Rubin, Kim MacLeod, Don Ross, Susan Levytsky, Jerry Davis, Barbara Melser-Lieberman, Martin Price, Penny Burns, Noel Adams, Sandy Olson, Dr. Nancy Jacobs and Wendy Schneider.

Our thanks to the National Mental Health Association, the International Communication Association and the H.V. Kaltenborn Foundation for help in many ways, and to Tom Dunn and his associates at the Rusk Institute. Our deepest gratitude to Lynn Forrester for her friendship beyond compare.

Finally, we thank our parents, Bob and Helen Conway and Leonard and Arline Siegelman, for more material help, moral support and love than we could ever fully acknowledge or repay.

FLO CONWAY and JIM SIEGELMAN
New York, N.Y.
August, 1995

Resources

FOR MORE INFORMATION CONTACT:

PERSONAL/FAMILY/MEDIA:
CAN/Cult Awareness Network
2421 West Pratt Blvd. Suite 1173
Chicago, IL 60645
312 267-7777

RESEARCH/PROFESSIONAL/MEDIA:
AFF/American Family Foundation
P.O. Box 2265 Bonita Springs, FL 33959
212 249-7696

EDUCATIONAL/MEDIA:
AFF International Cult Education Program
P.O. Box 1232, Gracie Station
New York, NY 10028
AFF Message Center: 212 249-7696

CANADA:
Info-Cult
5655 Park Avenue, Suite 305
Montreal Quebec H2V 4H2
514 274-2333

COUNSELING/REHABILITATION:
Wellspring Retreat and Resource Center
P.O. Box 67
Albany, OH 45710
614 698-6277

Notes

Bracketed numbers refer to works listed in the accompanying Bibliography.

Page

Chapter 1: SNAPPING

4 ... more than ten thousand techniques: early reports in *Newsweek*, September 6, 1976, cited 8000 techniques. This figure is considered conservative today.

... six million alone had taken up some form of meditation: Los Angeles *Times*, February 13, 1977.

... three million young Americans: *U.S News & World Report*, June 14, 1976.

7 The Children of God ... New York: See "Final Report on the Activities of the Children of God," New York State Charitable Frauds Bureau, September 30, 1974.

Chapter 2: THE SEARCH

14 "sixty hours that transform your life": See Adelaide Bry's *est* [26].

... an article in the *American Journal of Psychiatry:* by Leonard L. Glass, M.D.,

19 Michael A. Kirsch, M.D. and Frederick N. Parris, M.D., March, 1977.

Est updates: *The [EST] Network Review*, January, 1985; Chicago *Tribune*, February 27, 1985; *New York Times*, February 13, 1991; see also Steven August, *Outrageous Betrayal: The Dark Journey of Werner Erhard from est to Exile*. New York: St. Martins, 1993.

Forum incidents of emotional and mental breakdown: *Minneapolis Star and Tribune*, February 18, 1987, *Washington Post*, July 16, 1992, *Washington Times*, July 16, 1992.

Charges by Erhard daughters: *Newsweek*, February 18, 1991.

Erhard legal troubles and travels to Eastern Europe: *Forbes*, November 18, 1985; *NOW*, April 4-10, 1991.

Chapter 3: THE FALL

27 The Unification Church: Our insights into Unification Church doctrines and activities come from interviews with former members and are further documented in Patrick [40], Yamamoto [47] and the references that follow.

28 ... the old New Yorker Hotel: In the *New York Times*, May 13, 1976.

... South Korean Central Intelligence Agency: On August 5, 1977, the *Washington Post* disclosed the findings of a report issued by the House of Representatives Subcommittee on International Organizations which stated: "We have received reliable information that [Mr. Moon] and organizations connected with him maintained operational ties with the government of South Korea and specifically the

Korean Central Intelligence Agency." An Associated Press article in December, 1977, reported that Moon's chief aide and translator, Col. Bo Hi Pak, was once the Korean military attaché in Washington. An earlier article in the Washington *Post* (reprinted in the New York *Post*, November 8, 1976) reported that "according to U.S. Intelligence information Pak met in the 'Blue House' presidential mansion in Seoul with South Korean President Park Chung Hee, Washington-based South Korean businessman Tongsun Park, and KCIA officials in late 1970 to discuss plans for the Capitol Hill influence buying." The article also reported that according to "informed sources in the Justice and State departments," the South Korean Central Intelligence Agency requested the massive demonstrations that followers of Moon staged on Capitol Hill in 1974 opposing the impeachment of then President Nixon." The Unification Church issued a 279-page denial of the congressional committee's charges. See also: "Investigation of Korean-American Relations, Report of the Subcommittee on International Organizations of the Committee on International Relations, (the "Fraser Report"), U.S. House of Representatives, October 31, 1978.

28   Moon conviction and prison sentence. The charges pertained to the filing of fraudulent income tax returns during the 1970s: *Christianity and Crisis*, October 28, 1985.
The Moon empire now encompasses: "Frontline: The Resurrection of Reverend Moon," PBS, January 21, 1992.

Chapter 4: THE ROOTS OF SNAPPING
34   . . . half of all adult Protestants: One early poll and other signs of the mushrooming evangelical movement were reported in *Newsweek*, October 25, 1976. Surveys of registered voters consistently show one-third call themselves born-again Christians, *Washington Post*, February 11, 1995.
36   . . . charismatic movement. . . an estimated fifteen million communities: This figure can be found in O'Connor [39].
39   The creation of a Harvard Business School graduate: I Found It figures were reported on *CBS Reports*, "Born Again," broadcast July 14, 1977.
Jesus and the Intellectual: Bright [25].
40   ". . . from all your filthiness": Quoted in American Messianic Fellowship booklet [221], p. 22.
41   Biographical material on Marjoe from our interview and Gaines [29].

Chapter 5: SNAPPING AS SOMETHING NEW
47   The first steps in that direction: The early days of the human potential movement were documented in a *New Yorker* profile on Michael Murphy, co-founder of the Esalen Institute [20]. Two other perspectives on the movement's beginnings can be found in Schutz's *Elements of Encounter* [14 and the new preface to Maslow's *Religions, Values and Peak-Experiences* [8].
50   . . . encounter edged closer to its revivalist forerunners: Ruitenbeek reports in *The New Group Therapies* [13], p. 14, that around 1930 the American psychiatrist and former minister L. Cody Marsh began employing religious revival techniques in his group work with psychotics, a method he discussed in an article in *Mental Hygiene* (1931), "Group Treatment by the Psychological Equivalent of the Revival."
51   The Hare Krishna hired its own admen . . . est gave a top position to a former Coca-Cola executive: An ex-Krishna higher-up told us that the sect hired professionals and other laymen to market the cult's commercial products. Kornbluth [33] reports that est president Don Cox had been Director of Planning for Coca-

Cola, U.S.A.. and a former instructor at Harvard Business School.

53 In the remote bush country of Australia: Pearce's discussion is in [110], pp. 125-32.

54 Anthropologists point to: Pearce cited Claude Levi-Strauss as a champion of the aborigine worldview which, Pearce said, the French anthropologist considered "an intellectual refinement as well knit and coherent as any culture's in history" [110], p. 127.
"organization men": See Whyte's *The Organization Man* [114].

55 Sally Kempton: Kempton's encounter with Muktananda is described in "Hanging Out with the Guru," *New York* [32], from which the excerpt was drawn.

Chapter 6: BLACK LIGHTNING

71 Ted Patrick update: See "The Playboy Interview: A Candid Conversation with Ted Patrick," *Playboy*, March, 1979; *San Diego Union*, July 12 and 13, 1985.

72 . . . aggressive counterattacks and disinformation campaign: After we interviewed Patrick in Orange County, we obtained copies of two anti-deprogramming tracts that were reportedly being produced and distributed on an international scale by several cults. One booklet, "Deprogramming: The Constructive Destruction of Belief," appeared to be a parody of a manual of deprogramming techniques. Prepared in Great Britain "based upon techniques as they are practiced in the USA," the manual distorted every aspect of the deprogramming process, advocating the use of "food termination," "shame-inducement through nudity" and "physical correction" ("It goes without saying that in keeping with the above approach any physical correction should be administered with as little bruising as possible"). The section on "Sex and the Deprog Tech" read: "There have been stories of subjects being hetero- or homo-sexually raped by Technicians. These would be laughable if they did not occur with such regularity. . . . Far from rape, what the subject has experienced is almost certainly the application of aggressive sex by the Technician (the beneficial aspects of which are dealt with above)."
Galen Kelly trials: In the second case, the court of appeals found that the U.S. Attorney who prosecuted both cases knowingly allowed a cult witness to perjure herself and improperly withheld evidence from Kelly's defense team. *Washington Post*, September 20, 1994, *Washington City Paper*, September 23, 1994.

Chapter 7: THE CRISIS IN MENTAL HEALTH

79 "the cult syndrome": This term was introduced in "Destructive Cultism" *American Family Physician*, February, 1977, by Eli Shapiro, M.D.: ". . . a distinct syndrome of *destructive cultism* can be defined. . . . Change in personality is the most prominent characteristic of this syndrome."

80 CAN Update: "The History of the Cult Awareness Network," Priscilla D. Coates, paper presented by former CAN Director at conference on "New Religions in a Global Perspective," Buellton, CA, May 16, 1991; newsletter from Cynthia Kisser, Executive Director, Cult Awareness Network, December, 1994.
. . . the "robot model": Ludwig von Bertalanffy, the brilliant biologist and systems theorist, was an outspoken critic of the robot model, which he saw as "theoretically inadequate in view of empirical fact and . . . practically dangerous in its application to 'behavioral engineering.'" See *General System Theory* [50].

81 Third Force psychology: See Preface to Maslow's *Toward a Psychology of Being* [9].

Chapter 8: BEYOND BRAINWASHING

85 "At Panmunjon . . . a third world war": See Schein [44], p. 288.

87   Lifton's eight thought reform criteria: see "Cults: Religious Totalism and Civil Liberties," in his book *The Future of Immortality and Other Essays for a Nuclear Age*, New York: Basic Books, 1987.
89   . . . physiological effects. . . cult members: First reported in Black [23].
91   . . . animal response to hypnotic techniques: See Estabrooks [27], p. 43. "The accepted way to hypnotize a sheep, for example, is suddenly to pull its legs out from under it, hold the animal firmly on the ground, then gradually relax the pressure. . . . [Man] simply does not respond to these methods. . . . For example, that sheep will show no 'practice effect.' It is just as easy to hypnotize him the first time as it is the fiftieth time. . . . This is directly contrary to what we would expect in human hypnotism."

Chapter 9: INFORMATION
98   Cybernetics, succinctly defined as . . .: See Wiener [85], p. 11.
. . . the vital "feedback" . . . he identified as "information": Wiener likened steering mechanisms, automatic antiaircraft guns, and human and animal reflexes to "control by *informative feedback.*" In Wiener [85], p. 113.
. . . their British counterparts preferred . . . "variety": British engineer W. Ross Ashby, in *An Introduction to Cybernetics* [49], p. 126, defines "variety" in the same terms as Shannon defines "information" in *The Mathematical Theory of Communication* [79], p. 32. Both concepts leaned heavily on notions of information introduced in the 1920s by Bell Labs scientists H. Nyquist and R.V.L. Hartley.
99   . . . the simple on-off, heads-or-tails choice: Wiener's concept of information appeared to be less discrete and more fluid than Shannon's. These varying views do not necessarily contradict each other but represent a dualism which can be as helpful (and, at times, as confusing) as the complementary wave and particle models of light. Wiener's approach has received little attention in the dfigital age, but his concept may be more applicable than Shannon's as a model of information flow in living things. In his autobiography, Wiener wrote, "I approached information theory from the point of departure of the electric circuit carrying a continuous current, or at least something which could be interpreted as continuous current. At the same time, Claude Shannon . . . was developing a parallel and largely equivalent theory from the point of view of electrical switching systems. . . . As I have said before, Shannon loves the discrete and eschews the continuum." Wiener [89], p. 263.
Wiener himself, raised such questions: See Wiener's popular works, *The Human Use of Human Beings* [88] and *God & Golem, Inc.* [87], which received the National Book Award.
100 Human information-processing/overload research: surveyed in James Grier Miller, *Living Systems*, New York: McGraw-Hill, 1978, pp. 121-202.
Information stress: *ibid.*, pp. 34-35..
101 "chunking": The notion of "chunks" of information (as opposed to single "bits") was introduced by George A. Miller in a now-famous article, "The Magical Number Seven, Plus or Minus Two: Some Limits on Our Capacity for Processing Information" (in *Psychological Review*, March, 1956, and reprinted in *The Psychology of Communication* [72]), which dealt with black box experiments in memory and learning.
Living Systems: See Bertalanffy [50] and James G. Miller, *op. cit.*
107 . . . *the hologram:* Basic principles of holography are covered in Gabor [61], Leith and Upatnicks [68], and Pennington [73]. Pribram's application was presented in articles in *Psychology Today* [75] and *Scientific American* [77].
109 In hundreds of operations: See Dr. Paul Pietsch, "Shuffle Brain," *Harper's*, May, 1972.

110   Dennis Gabor: See Gabor, "Holography, 1948-1971" [61].

113   Pribram update: See "The Relationship Between the Gabor Elementary Function and a Stochastic Model of the Inter-spike Interval Distribution in the Response of Visual Cortex Neurons," *Biological Cybernetics*, 67(2), 1992, pp.191-4; "The Cognitive Revoluton and Mind/Brain Issues," *American Psychologist*, May, 1986, pp. 507-20.

Chapter 10: THE LAWS OF EXPERIENCE

117   . . . information mixes freely: See Pribram [76], p. 16, " . . . finer nerve fibers lack an insulating fatty coating (the myelin sheath) which in large fibers prevents interaction among impulses. The slow potentials which occur in fine fibers . . . find therefore no obstacle for actual local interaction."
The metabolism of experience: Our notion of a metabolism of experience has been implied in technical terms by numerous physicists and biologists. James G. Miller refers to the "metabolism of information," Miller, *op. cit.*, pp. 53, 60. Perhaps the best known statement on the subject was by physicist Erwin Schrödinger in his historic 1943 lecture, "What Is Life?" [78]. "How does the living organism avoid decay?" asked Schrödinger (p. 75). "The obvious answer is: By eating, drinking, breathing. . . . The technical term is *metabolism* [his italics]. The Greek word . . . means change or exchange. Exchange of what? Originally the underlying idea is, no doubt, exchange of material. . . . That the exchange of material should be the essential thing is absurd. Any atom of nitrogen, oxygen, sulphur, etc., is as good as any other. . . . What then is that precious something contained in our food that keeps us from death? . . . What an organism feeds upon is negative entropy. [Authors' note: Shannon, Wiener, et al. equate information, i.e., *order*, with the *negative* of randomness—called "entropy" in physics.] . . . Thus the device by which an organism maintains itself stationary at a fairly high level of orderliness . . . really consists in continually sucking orderliness from its environment."

118   In sensory deprivation tests: Toffler discussed the dangers of sensory deprivation in *Future Shock* [113], pp. 513-16. A positive view was taken by Lilly in *The Center of the Cyclone* [7], although the duration of his isolation tank experiments is not stated. See also *Sensory Deprivation: A Symposium*, P. Solomon, ed. (Cambridge: Harvard University Press, 1965); and *Sensory Deprivation, 15 Years of Research*, John P. Zubek, ed. (New York: Appleton-Century-Crofts, 1969).

119   . . . that prize quality called genius: This figure was established in experiments conducted during World War II and has been widely confirmed in later experiments involving identical twins raised separately.
Experience literally creates . . . fundamental workings of the mind: The role of experience in brain development has become a major focus of neuroscience research and debate. Most neuroscientists, beginning with Hebb [65], hold that experience is essential for the development of even the most elementary perceptual faculties. Nearly all new research in the field confirms and extends this point of view.
. . . bedrock patterns . . . forged in the intimate relationship between parent and child: See Piaget, *The Construction of Reality in the Child* [74]; also *Psychology of Intelligence* (Totowa, N.J.: Littlefield, Adams & Co., 1966).

120   And that process is ongoing: Most neuroscientists agree that, up to age five, the brain is in its most fluid and adaptable state. In later years, however, significant portions of the brain are constantly reforming themselves. See Steven Rose, *The Conscious Brain*. New York, Vintage, 1976.

121   The Law of Requisite Variety: Ashby [49], p. 206.

122   The Law of Experience: *Ibid.*, p. 137.
123   Scientists have only begun to understand: A survey of research on this subject can be found in Pribram [76], chapter 2, "Neural Modifiability and Memory mechanisms." See also Shepherd [80], p. 57, "Within the brain itself, synapses are, of course, modifiable during the differentiation and growth of neurons in embryonic and early life; the processes concerned, however, remain among the most profound unsolved problems of biology. In the adult brain, there is more and more experimental evidence of the modifiability of synapses." (See also notes on Follow-Up, Chapter 13.)

Chapter 11: THE SNAPPING MOMENT & CATASTROPHE THEORY

128   . . . in the aftermath . . . information-processing capacities may become physicallly disorganized: Although there is at present no neuroscientific data on the snapping moment, studies of epilepsy and electroshock therapy confirm that an intense electrical "experience" may sever synaptic connections in the brain. "When strong electric currents are sent through the brain, momentarily all neural activity is disrupted and disorganized." In Wooldridge [90], p. 111.
134   Insight Seminars/Movement for Spiritual Inner Awareness (MSIA): See Peter McWilliams, *LIFE 102: What to Do When Your Guru Sues You.* Los Angeles: Prelude Press, 1994.
138   E. Christopher Zeeman: Zeeman's other applications of catastrophe theory include models of stock market crashes, prison riots and barking-dog attacks. Some applications came under criticism from the mathematical community, particularly where they were used as tools of prediction, as they were in some British prisons.
139   In an article in *Scientific American:* See Zeeman [91].
142   Thom's theory came under heavy fire: See "Catastrophe Theory: The Emperor Has No Clothes," *Science,* April 15, 1977 and Kolata [67].
         Bremermann . . . in his review of Thom's book: See Bremermann [54].

Chapter 12: VARIETIES OF INFORMATION DISEASE

148   "Psychopathology has been rather a disappointment . . . secondary disturbances of traffic": Wiener [85], pp. 146-47.
155   Physiological effects of hyperventilation: For more, see Margaret T. Singer with Janja Lalich, *Cults in Our Midst.* San Francisco: Jossey-Bass, 1995, p. 129-30.
157   Scientology . . "applied philosophy" . . . . has claimed to be largest "self-betterment organization" in the world: See Hubbard [31], p. 165.
158   Hubbard died January 24, 1986. *Los Angeles Times,* January 28, 1986.
         . . . Dianetics, employs a technique called "auditing" ostensibly to raise an individual to higher levels of being: The theory and practice of Dianetics and the auditing process were expounded by Hubbard in his voluminous copyrighted works, most of which were published in the United States by the American Saint Hill Organization in Los Angeles. See Hubbard [30], *Dianetics Today;* also *Dianetics: The Modern Science of Mental Health* (1950); *Dianetics: The Original Thesis* (1970); *Handbook for Preclears,* 7th ed. (1974); *Introduction to Scientology Ethics* (1974); *Scientology 0-8: The Book of Basics* (1970); and *Advanced Procedure and Axions,* 3rd ed. (1957).
164   Scientology updates: Scientology claims of 6 to 8 million followers reportedly inflated: *Time,* May 6, 1991 and *Los Angeles Times,* June 24, 1990; income: nearly $300 million annually: *St. Petersburg Times,* October 15, 1993 and *New York Times,* October 22, 1993; $500 million listed income for one Scientology entity: *Time,* May 6, 1991.

Scientology courses still current a decade later: *Time*, May 6, 1991 and numerous conversations with former Scientologists; Scientology methods in education, corporate consulting and professional services management: *Los Angeles Times*, June 27, 1990.

165   Psychodrama: See Moreno [10] for the original thinking behind this technique. J.Z. Knight—"Ramtha": *Time*, December 7, 1987; *OMNI*, March, 1988; *New York Times*, September 25, 1992.

167   Insight/MSIA best-sellers: See Peter McWilliams, *LIFE 101: Everything We Wish We had Learned about Life in School--But Didn't and DO IT! Let's Get Off Our Buts*. Los Angeles: Prelude Press.

174   . . . the way TM invoked alleged scientific facts to prove . . . "severely deleterious effects": See Harold H. Bloomfield, M.D., Michael P. Cain, Dennis T. Jaffe, Robert B. Kory, *TM: Discovering Inner Energy and Overcoming Stress* [24]. In chapter 2, "Transcendental Meditation: The Technique of Contacting Pure Awareness," on p. 19, the authors (two of whom were connected with the TM organization) wrote that: "some self-styled 'experts' of relaxation or other meditative techniques have been indiscriminately advocating their own makeshift mantras, unaware that severely deleterious effects can be experienced by their unsuspecting practitioners."

TM update: *Our Town*, March 25, 1993, *Washington Post*, June 9 and July 30, 1993, *Forbes*, April 12, 1993, *Des Moines Register*, November 18-19, 1990.

Popular author Dr. Deepak Chopra dedicated his book, *Quantum Healing: Exploring the Frontiers of Mind/Body Medicine* (New York: Bantam/New Age, 1989, 1990) to the Maharishi, whom he described as "one of the greatest living sages (p.2), and wrote extensively about Transcendental Meditation, its founder and its potential "quantum" health benefits (pp. 2-3, 6, 14, 182-183, 187, 217-218, 227-228).

175   Studies of adverse effects of meditation: *International Journal of Psychosomatic Medicine*, 39(104), 1992, pp. 62-7; *Natural Health*, November/December, 1993.

184   Radhasoami teachings and practices adopted by Eckankar and Insight/MSIA: See McWilliams, *LIFE 102, op. cit.*, pp. 227, 348.

Chapter 13: FOLLOW-UP: PISCES, PTSD & OTHER PROJECTS

187   fruits for life: William James, *The Varieties of Religious Experience*. New York: Longmans, Green, 1902; Penguin, 1982, p. 237.

197   . . . a new communication paradigm: F. Conway, J. Siegelman, C. Carmichael and J. Coggins, "Information Disease: A New Paradigm for Communication and Mental Health," [119].

The strength of Conway and Siegelman's assumptions: C.W. Carmichael, "Data Confirmation: Findings in a Nationwide Study of Covert Induction and Deprogramming," [115].

The distributions of the few demographic variables: J. C. Coggins, "A Critical Perspective and Questions for Future Research on Information Disease," [116].

198   reasoned action: Gary Cronkhite, "The Relation of the Concept of Information Disease to Theory and Research in Social Change," [120].

199   A study of sixty-six former Moonies: M. Galanter, "Unification Church ('Moonie') dropouts: Psychological Readjustment after Leaving a Charismatic Religious Group," *American Journal of Psychiatry*, 1983, 140, 984-989.

A 1986 study of fifty-eight former members of a West Coast psychotherapy cult: K. Knight, "Long-term Effects of Participation in a Psychological 'Cult' Utilizing Directive Therapy Techniques," unpublished Master's thesis, University of California, Los Angeles, 1986.

A second large-scale study: M.D. Langone, R. Chambers, A. Dole and J. Grice, "Results of a Survey of Ex-Cult Members." Reported in Paul R. Martin, M.D. Langone, A. Dole and J. Wiltrout, "Post-Cult Symptoms As Measured by the MCMI Before and After Residential Treatment," *Cultic Studies Journal,* 1992, Vol. 9, No. 2, page 219.

201   Vietnam Era Stress Inventory findings: John P. Wilson and Gustave E. Krauss, "Predicting Post-Traumatic Stress Syndromes Among Vietnam Veterans." In *Post-Traumatic Stress Disorders (PTSD): Collected Papers,* copyright John P. Wilson, 1983, pp. 126, 140, 272. See also John P. Wilson, *Trauma, Transformation and Healing: An Integrative Approach to Theory, Research and Post-Traumatic Therapy,* New York: Brunner/Mazel, 1989.

202   Information stress of "repeated exposure to injury and death": Wilson and Krauss, *op. cit.,* p. 141.

PTSD correlations: "Factor Analysis of Post-Traumatic Stress (Scale IV-A)," *ibid.,* pp. 185-207.

203   1992 study of forty Vietnam veterans with PTSD symptoms: "Exposure to Atrocities and Severity of Chronic Posttraumatic Stress Disorder in Vietnam Combat Veterans," R. Yehuda, S.M. Southwick and E.L. Giller, Jr., *American Journal of Psychiatry,* March, 1992, pp. 333-336.

204   Correlations in other cultures: among casualties of the 1988 earthquake in Armenia, researchers found an almost exact correlation between the severity of people's stress symptoms and their distance from the quake's epicenter. Robert S. Pynoos et al. *British Journal of Psychiatry,* August, 1993.

Dissociative disorders. . . "a state of experience": L.J. West, "Dissociative Reaction," in *Comprehensive Textbook of Psychiatry* (2nd ed.), A.M. Freedman and H.I. Kaplan, eds. Baltimore: Williams and Wilkins, pp. 885-899; also "Development, Reliability and Validity of a Dissociation Scale," E.M. Bernstein and F.W. Putnam, *Journal of Nervous and Mental Disease,* Vol. 174 (12), 727-735; Splitting: See "Splitting: The Development of a Measure," M.J. Gerson, *Journal of Clinical Psychology,* January, 1984, pp.157-162.

205   Pseudo-identity: L.J. West and Paul Martin, "Pseudo-Identity and the Treatment of Personality Change in Victims of Captivity and Cults," in S.J. Lynn/J.W. Rhue (eds.), *Dissociation: Clinical and Theoretical Perspectives.* New York: Guilford, 1994.

DSM-III and DSM-IV contrasts: PTSD, DSM-III-R, pp. 247-251, DSM-IV, pp. 424-429, 783; Dissociative Disorder Not Otherwise Specified, DSM-III-R, p. 277, DSM-IV, pp.490-491; Depersonalization Disorder, DSM-IV p. 488-499; Dissociative Trance Disorder, DSM-IV, pp. 727-729; Religious or Spiritual Problem: DSM-IV, p. 685.

207   Laboratory experiments: University of California researcher Mark Rosenzweig and his colleagues found that the brains of laboratory animals raised in "information-rich" environments had greater numbers of synapses, and thicker connections among them, than animals raised in "information-poor" environments. University of Illinois researcher William Greenough found that new synapses may form in ten seconds or less: J. Hooper and D. Teresi, *The 3-Pound Universe,* New York, Laurel/Dell, 1987, pp 63-66; Wallace, Kilman, Withers and Greenough, *Journal of Behavioral Neural Biology,* July 1992, pp. 64-68.

Numbing and endorphins. . . a "learned response": Vietnam vet study conducted jointly by Dr. Roger Pitman and other researchers at Harvard Medical School and the VA Medical Center in Manchester, NH. Pitman, Roger et al., *Journal of Abnormal Psychology,* February, 1990, pp. 49-54; see also articles by M.B. Hamner and A. Hitri, *Journal of Neuropsychiatry and Clinical Neuroscience,* Winter,

1992, pp. 59-63; and J.D. Bremner et al., "Dissociation and Posttraumatic Stress Disorder in Vietnam Combat Veterans," *American Journal of Psychiatry*, March, 1992, pp. 328-336.

1993 study of patients with eating disorders: M.A. Demitrack, et al., *Psychiatry Research*, October, 1993, pp. 1-10.

Changes in brain opiate levels among long-distance runners: Hooper and Teresi, *op. cit.*, p. 80.

209   Roles of endorphins: See *Scientific American*, September, 1979, p. 146; Joel Davis, *Endorphins: New Waves in Brain Chemistry*, New York: Dial Press/Doubleday, 1984.

Enkephalins and endorphins different origin and distribution in brain/body: *ibid.* pp. 64-66, 73, 75, 80.

. . . experiment . . . Vietnam veterans . . . "Platoon": Pitman, et al., *op. cit.*

Roles of endorphins: See *Scientific American*, September, 1979, p. 146; Joel Davis, *Endorphins: New Waves in Brain Chemistry*, New York: Dial Press/Doubleday, 1984.

Enkephalins and endorphins different origin and distribution in brain/body: *ibid.* pp. 64-66, 73, 75, 80.

Changes in serotonin may evoke hallucinations and delusions: See *Scientific American*, September, 1979; Hooper and Teresi, *op. cit.*, p. 269-271, 324-326, 331-332.

Enkephalin link to hypnosis, meditation and "floating" states: *ibid.*, p. 158.

Possible role of serotonin in floating/delusions: Hooper and Teresi, *op. cit.*, p. 133.

Endorphin role in amnesia as well as pain-killing: Davis, *op. cit.*, p. 182.

Animal studies confirm that both enkephalins and endorphins may become addictive: *ibid.*, pp. 136-138.

210   Calpain research of Dr. Gary Lynch at UC Irvine: *New York Times*, August 9, 1987, November 29, 1987; Lynch, et al., *Brain Research Bulletin*, September, 1988, pp. 363-72; Permutter, Gall, Baudry and Lynch, *Journal of Comp. Neurology*, June, 1990, pp. 269-76.

Chapter 14: SNAPPING AND PUNISHMENT

217   "Burglar, car thief": Bugliosi [94], p. 199.

Manson "appears to have developed a certain amount of insight": Bugliosi [94], p. 1969.

According to Bugliosi, the Process was founded by a former disciple of L. Ron Hubbard: Bugliosi [94], p. 636.

218   "Undoubtedly," wrote Bugliosi, "he . . .": Bugliosi [94], p. 635. Bugliosi also noted that one of Manson's chief disciples, Bruce Davis, was heavily involved in Scientology at one time, also working in its London headquarters until April, 1969. According to Scientology spokesmen, Davis was kicked out of the group for drug use, and shortly after that he returned to America, joined the Family, and participated in two brutal crimes of murder and dismemberment that preceded the Tate-LaBianca murders.

Susan Atkins, in a book: See Atkins [92].

219   "These defendants are not human beings . . . mutation.": Bugliosi [94], p. 606.

228   Leslie Van Houten update: "Turning Point," ABC News, August 9, 1994, "Larry King Live," CNN, August 10, 1994.

229   Dr. Joel Fort . . . a "maverick": New *York Times*, March 1, 1976.

Fort . . . Patty was a "willing participant": New *York Times*, March 9, 1976.

230   . . . prosecutors . . ."they wash each other out": New *York Times*, March 21, 1976.

. . . one assistant prosecutor succeeded in suggesting . . . that Lifton had a vested professional interest: New *York Times,* February 28, 1976.

231 In a network television interview: Quotes from "Patty Hearst—Her Story," CBS News "Special Report" broadcast December 16, 1976 (used with permission).

232 Dr. Martin Orme . . . stated that . . . "A totally helpless person would appear at that time": New *York Times,* February 27, 1976.
Another picture: "Patty Today," *The New York Times Magazine,* April 3, 1977, p. 100.

233 . . . man in the street . . . "brainwashing can only be done by experts": New *York Times,* March 21, 1976.
Hearst conviction/pardon request: *Los Angeles Daily News,* January 16, 1989.

234 Berkowitz . . ."no remorse": New York *Post,* August 11, 1977.
. . . doctors ruled out the possibility . . . of physical brain damage: New York *Post* August 18, 1977.

235 . . . "emotionally dead": New York *Daily News,* September 2, 1977.

236 "I said I didn't bring it to the field": Quotations from Berkowitz's letters to a high school sweetheart published in the New York *Daily News,* August 15, 1977.

237 "There seemed to be a personality change": Description by an army friend of Berkowitz's appeared in the New York *Daily New,* August 15, 1977.
"When I look in the mirror": New York *Daily News,* August 15, 1977.
"I must truly admitt": *Ibid.*
"I hope they let me go home": *Ibid.*

238 "I just asked him to go to church with me one day": From an Associated Press story in the New York *Post,* August 25, 1977.

239 Breaking his silence: Son of Sam update. According to an independent investigation of the new claims by the New York *Post,* Berkowitz had referred to himself as the Son of Sam at least two years before the killing spree began.: "Inside Edition," Fox Network, November 8-10, 11, 1993, New York *Post,* November 4, 1993, New York *Daily News,* November 8, 1993.

Chapter 15: JONESTOWN: END OF INNOCENCE

241 . . . "the story of the decade": Jimmy Breslin in the New York *Daily News,* November 23, 1978.

242 "It is time to die with dignity": *Newsweek,* December 4, 1978.
"one of the most shocking . . . outside of wartime": New *York Times,* December 2, 1978.

243 . . . Jones no longer believed in religion: *New York Times,* November 20, 1978.

249 He . . . pursued illicit relationships: "On December 12, 1973, Jones was arrested by Los Angeles police for allegedly making a lewd advance to an undercover officer in an adult theater." In *The Suicide Cult* by Marshall Kilduff and Ron Javers (New York: Bantam Books, 1978), p. 56.

251 . . . letters later were found to have been forged: *New York Times,* November 21, 1978.

253 . . . eliciting prepublication protests from . . . representatives of the American Civil Liberties Union: *Newsweek, op. cit.*

254 . . . huge supplies of psychoactive drugs were smuggled into Jonestown: New *York Times,* December 29, 1978.
"When they came out a week later . . . empty faces": *Newsweek, op. cit.*

255 "I can say without hesitation": *New York Times,* November 21, 1978.

258 Treasury Department: *New York Times,* December 3, 1978.
Federal Communications Commission: *New York Times,* November 23, 1978.
Social Security Administration: *New York Times,* November 22, 1978.
Justice Department: *New York Times,* November 24, 1978.

259 Killings of Jeannie, Al and Daphene Mills: *Newsweek*, March 10, 1980.
CIA covert operation in Guyana: Years later, the truth emerged that the CIA had a long-running covert operation in the country. The operation began in 1963, when President John F. Kennedy personally ordered the CIA to launch secret activities aimed at toppling the country's popular socialist leader Prime Minister Dr.Cheddi Jagan. Jagan was subsequently driven from office and replaced by pro-American dictator Forbes Burnham, who ruled the country throughout Jim Jones' time there. Thirty years after the covert action ended, government officials still refused to release details of the operation: *New York Times*, October 30, 1994.
House Foreign Affairs Committee conclusions on Jonestown: Associated Press wire reports, May 15, 1979.
House committee recommendation for "a concentrated program of research and training on cults": Quoted in February 20, 1980 statement of Cong. Bill Royer of California.
Dole committee hearings: "Information Meeting on the Cult Phenomenon in the United States." Washington, DC, February 5, 1979.

Chapter 16: CHAOS AT WACO: THE DEATH SPIRAL
262 Weaver case, later details: *New York Times*, July 16, 1995.
264 Francis E. X. Dance spiral model of human communication: "The spiral," wrote Dance, "gives geometrical testimony to the concept that communication while moving forward is at the same moment coming back upon itself and being affected by its past behavior." Dance [57], pp.295-297.
two or more spirals "interacting and intertwining.": *ibid.*, p. 297.
265 The "butterfly effect": See James Gleick, *Chaos: Making a New Science*, New York: Penguin, 1987, p. 322.
"will certainly produce something catastrophic": Wiener [85], p. 102.
266 . . . Wiener traces . . . outlines of Mandelbrot set: *ibid.*, p. 105.
Chaos theory applicable to personal and social change: Other social scientists confirmed our enthusiasm for chaos theory. In a 1994 article in *American Psychologist*, clinical psychologist Scott Barton, who had worked with Vietnam veterans and others at a VA Medical Center in Charleston, South Carolina, acknowledged the intuitive appeal of chaos concepts to problems of human psychology. He noted the difficulties of measuring mathematically the innumerable factors that shape human behavior but cited promising applications of chaos concepts to human problems that displayed striking parallels to those we were investigating, including schizophrenia, post-traumatic stress and multiple personality disorder. "If it is feasible. . . modelers should by all means attempt such strategies," he wrote. See Scott Barton, "Chaos, Self-Organization and Psychology," *American Psychologist*, January, 1994, 5-14.
269 Koresh/Branch Davidians facts and background: *New York Times*, New York *Daily News*, New York *Newsday*, *Newsweek*, *Time*, February-May, 1993.
270 Koresh plans for acts of insurrection: Cleveland *Plain Dealer*, July 12, 1995. See also testimony of Texas Department of Child Protective Services worker Joyce Sparks and ATF agent Robert Rodriguez, Hearings of House Government Reform and Judiciary committees, Washington, DC., July 21 & 24, 1995, *New York Times*, July 22 & 25, 1995..
A consultation that . . . entirely legal: Legal reviews by the Departments of Defense and Treasury confirmed that law enforcement consultations with military advisors were conducted routinely and that the Army-ATF interaction in no way violated federal *posse comitatus* laws against military involvement in domestic law enforcement operations. No military personnel were on the scene during

raid and none participated in the operation. Hearings of House Government Reform and Judiciary committees, Washington, DC., July 20, 1995; *New York Times,* July 21, 1995.

272   Children and adults instructed in commiting suicide with a gun: Testimony of Kiri Jewell, hearings of House Government Reform and Judiciary committees, July 19, 1995, *New York Times,* July 20, 1995.

284   No possibility of suicide. Attorney General Reno said later, "Obviously, if the chances were great of a mass suicide, I would never have approved the plan": *New York Times,* April 22, 1993.

285   Behavioral sciences subunit. . . memoranda: Memoranda prepared by special agents Peter Smerick and Mark Young, dated March 5, 7, 8 and 9, 1993. In a later memo, Smerick seemed to reverse course and drop his opposition to the tactical pressure, but only after learning that his superiors—including the FBI Director—were unhappy with his earlier views. In the 1995 congressonl hearings, Smerick attributed his seeming reversal, not to external pressure, but to his own bout of groupthink, what he called "pressure from within to be a team player." Testimony of Peter Smerick, hearings of House Government Reform and Judiciary committees, July 25, 1995.

286   A 1995 congressional hearing . . . powerful national gun lobby: Roles of paid National Rifle Association experts and consultants in 1995 Waco hearings: *New York Times,* July 13,17 & 30, 1995.

288   Factual errors. . . extent of FBI contacts with cult experts and former Branch Davidians: "Report to the Deputy Attorney General on the Events at Waco, Texas, February 28 to April 19, 1993," Washington, DC., October 8, 1993, pp. 190-193. The report states that Breault was not contacted by the FBI and misrepresents the nature and extent of consultations with deprogrammer Rick Ross. Documentation supplied to us confirms that FBI negotiators in Waco contacted Breault in Australia after the ATF raid, and that bureau personnel initiated contact with Ross in Dallas on March 4, 1993 and had at least eighteen discussions with him during the siege, the last on April 13. Personnel communications with Marc Breault and Rick Ross, 1994.

One outside expert: Nancy Ammerman, a sociologist affiliated with the Candler School of Theology at Emory University in Decatur, Georgia, claimed to have studied the factual evidence, consulted with academic colleagues and "reviewed. . . academic literature on 'New Religious Movements.'" She also admitted to receiving unspecified information from "various political and lobbying groups." Nancy T. Ammerman, "Report to the Justice and Treasury Departments regarding law enforcement interactions with the Branch Davidians in Waco, Texas," September 3, 1993, pp. 1-10.

290   Groupthink: Irving L. Janis, *Victims of Groupthink,* New York: Houghton Mifflin, 1972.

Cognitive dissonance: See Leon Festinger, *A Theory of Cognitive Dissonance,* Evanston, IL: Row, Peterson, 1957.

"Psychological discomfort": Cronkhite discussed the subject in his paper on information disease for the International Communication Association. Writing years before the Waco crisis, he descibed the psychological discomfort that motivates dissonance reduction as "the need to avoid blaming oneself for the negative consequences of irreversible decisions one perceives oneself to have made freely, with inadequate justification." See G. Cronkhite [120].

291   . . . or, in our perspective, information stress: See James G. Miller on information overload in governmental systems and pathology at the level of groups and organizations, Miller, *op. cit.,* pp. 160-163, 169.

Chapter 17: SNAPPING IN EVERYDAY LIFE

299 . . . effects of "future shock": See Toffler's *Future Shock* [113].

. . . effects of information revolution: See McLuhan's *Understanding Media* [108] for the classic perspective. Psychiatrist J.A.M. Meerloo described this phenomenon years before *Future Shock*. In "Contributions of Psychiatry to the Study of Human Communication" (Dance [57], pp. 130-59), Meerloo wrote, "Indeed, there exists a positive communication explosion, a prelude to an avalanche. I have already observed in some patients the breakdown of their communication systems as a result of this overloading. We are in danger of being crushed under a mountain of information debris."

302 . . . consumers conditioned . . . advertising appeals: See Packard's classic, *The Hidden Persuaders* [109]; also "The Gilded Bough: Magic and Advertising," by Howard Luck Gossage, in *The Human Dialogue* [107], p. 363, and "The Folklore of Mass Persuasion," by Floyd W. Matson, *ibid.*, p. 371.

. . . the more suggestible he may become: Marcuse discusses the "confusional technique" of hypnosis [37], p. 57.

305 . . . remained literally immobilized: See Terry Buss, F. Stevens Redburn, Joseph Walrom, "Psychological Impact of a Plant Closing," in *Mass Unemployment, Plant Closings and Community Mental Health*. Beverly Hills, CA, Sage Publications, 1983.

306 . . . three quarters of people who work around computers experience stress: *Harvard Medical School Health Bulletin*, 1984.

information sickness: Denver *Post*, September 19, 1982.

NIOSH cites computer work as most stressful: *Forbes*, July 2, 1984.

307 Greenfield and Raskin high-tech personality stress symptoms: *Computerworld*, June 18, 1984.

Technostress: Craig Brod, *Technostress: The Human Costs of the Computer Revolution*, Reading (MA): 1984. The term technostress was used earlier in an article in *Time* magazine by Thomas MacDonald of Transition Associates, La Jolla, CA. Findings in white-collar stress study: *ibid.*, p.68.

similarity of technostress and information disease symptoms: *ibid.*, pp. xi-xiii, 7, 9, 17, 23, 26, 41-43, 49-50, 104, 76-78, 81, 90-97.

similarity of technostress and PTSD symptoms: Wilson and Krauss, *op. cit.*

308 . . . today's youth . . . affected at bedrock levels: See "What TV Does to Kids," *Newsweek*, February 21, 1977; also "Television and the New Image of Man," by Ashley Montagu, in *The Human Dialogue* [107], p. 355.

TV watching figures, California study link to increased violence: *New York Times*, January 21, 1987.

Teen suicide rates doubled from 1960 to 1987: *New York Times*, August 19, 1990.

National Assessment of Educational Progress: *New York Times*, December 3, 1987; *New York Times*, August 28, 1991.

309 TV and metabolism: study by Dr. Robert Klesges, Memphis State University, *New York Times*, April 1, 1992; also Klesges et al., "Effects of Televison on Metabolic Rate: Potential Implications for Childhood Obesity," *Pediatrics*, February, 1993, pp. 281-6.

Computer/video games: *New York Times*, December 22, 1991.

Australian studies of TV and children: See Jane M. Healy, Ph.D., *Endangered Minds: Why Our Children Don't Think*, New York: Simon & Schuster, 1990, p. 204.

Newer electronic technologies effects on children: Brod, *op. cit.*, pp. 122-125.

. . . young people. . . more receptive to group identities: See "Deviant Adolescent

310 Subcultures: Assessment Strategies and Clinical Interventions," *Adolescence*, Summer, 1992, p. 283-93.

Chapter 18: THE FUTURE OF PERSONALITY

314   International Churches of Christ: *Des Moines Register,* August 15, 1992, "20/20," ABC News, October 15, 1993.

Satanic panics. Nationwide estimates of satanism practitioners tripled, from 500,000 in 1976 to 1.5 million by the late eighties: *National Sheriff,* February-March, 1987; nationwide Satanism survey conducted by National Center on Child Abuse and Neglect: *New York Times,* October 31, 1994.

The Way tax-exempt status revoked in 1985: *Cult Observer,* May/June, 1987; exemption reinstated, Emporia (Kansas) *Gazette,* October 14, 1987.

Children of God change to Family of Love in 1978; use of sex for evangelizing, the practice was banned in 1987, partly in response to fears about AIDS: *Washington Post,* June 2, 1993; *New York Times,* September 9, 1993.

315   Church Universal and Triumphant: *New York Times,* November 9, 1989; IRS settlement, New York *Times,* June 5, 1994.

316   Lifespring and U.S. Air Force, CIA personnel: *Air Force Times,* February 18 and September 8, 1980; *Look,* June 11, 1979.

FAA trainers patterned on J.Z. Knight: *New York Times,* April 1, 1995.

Cult lawsuits: Hare Krishnas, *New York Times,* April 9, 1990; Scientology, Los Angeles *Daily Journal,* July 21, 1989.

Scientology-IRS settlement: *St. Petersburg Times,* October 15, 1993; *New York Times,* October 22, 1993.

Scientology sues *Time*: *Washington Post,* December 10, 1994.

Scientology in Germany: *New York Times,* October 13, 1994.

317   European cult/self-help therapy trends: TM in Russia, *Des Moines Register,* November 18, 1990; Krishna in Moscow, *Des Moines Register,* August 14, 1990; U.S. born-again Christians in E. Europe: *New York Times,* October 7, 1991.

Moon Moscow speech, *Washington Post,* July 26, 1990; Moon recruiting in Russia, *New York Times,* November 14, 1990; two Russian students sue Unification Church affiliate, *New York Times,* February 23, 1993.

Moon political action and ties to organized crime: "Frontline: The Resurrection of Reverend Moon," PBS, *op. cit.*

318   Dr. Luc Jouret/Solar Temple: *New York Times,* October 6, 9, 14 and 16, 1994; *Washington Post,* October 7 and 8, 1994.

POSTSCRIPT: THE WIDENING GYRE

327   Aum Shinrikyo: *New York Times,* March 26, 1995

328   . . . sarin to kill four to ten million people: *New York Times,* March 25, 1995.

. . . reportedly buried 25,000 plastic bags filled with the gas: *New York Times,* April 6, 1995.

329   Aum rituals "miracle pond". . . "love initiation": *New York Times,* March 24, 1995.

tranquilizers to subdue dissidents *New York Times,* March 26, 1995.

Aum dissidents confined in crates: *New York Times,* March 27, 1995.

Japanese government deference to religious sensitivities: *New York Times,* April 1, 1995; "Japanese authorities are particularly sensitive to charges that they are persecuting religious groups": *Time,* April 3, 1995.

330   Aum in Russia, links to Yeltsin government: *New York Times,* March 30, 1995.

Aum plan to buy Russian tanks and aircraft: *New York Times,* April 20, 1995.

Aum alleged crimes: accused of abusing members, harassing critics and journalists, attacking, kidnapping and even killing dissidents, sect family members and other opponents. *New York Times,* March 26, 1995.

Aum security chief a former underworld boss: *New York Times,* April 7, 1995.

331   Aum empire worth over $1 billion: *New York Times,* May 22, 1995.

332 "At last the time has come for death": *New York Times*, March 24, 1995.
Asahara arrest and confession: *New York Times*, June 15 & 23, 1995.
Jetliner hijacker claims, then denies, Aum connection: *New York Times*, June 22 & 23, 1995.

333 "I felt I must protect Buddhism": statement by Shinichi Nakazawa, professor of religious studies at Chuo University. *ibid./New York Times*, April 1, 1995.
Ex-Aum members symptoms: *New York Times*, June 5, 1995.
Aum subway attacker confession: *New York Times*, May 22, 1995.

335 Militias sighted in forty states: *New York Times*, June 18, 1995.
Militia movement high five figures . . . estimated five million sympathizers: *New York Times*, May 15, 1995.
Alleged plan to disarm and enslave Americans: *USA Today*, January 30, 1995.
Militia links to extreme fundamentalists and historic hate-groups: *USA Today*, January 30, 1995.

336 Texas Klan leader traveled the country: *New York Times*, April 26, 1995.

338 McVeigh personality change: *New York Times*, April 29, 1995.
Terry Nichols background: *New York Times*, May 28, 1995.

340 Log of Nichols-McVeigh activities: *San Jose Mercury*, (Knight-Ridder News Service), June 7, 1995.

341 McVeigh gun business and advertising in *The Spotlight* newsletter: *New York Times*, April 29, 1995.
McVeigh, Nichols suspected in gun robbery: *New York Times*, June 19, 1995.

342 McVeigh quote "something big": *New York Times*, May 15, 1995.
Elohim City sect, Robert G. Millar and white separatist Richard Snell: *Rochester Democrat and Chronicle*, May 23, 1995; *New York Times*, May 25, 1995.
Michael Fortier tied to Oklahoma trip: *Chicago Tribune*, June 2, 1995.
Colbern, other possible connections: *Dallas Morning News*, May 14 & 18, 1995.
McCarty statements about McVeigh/Fortier: *Arizona Republic*, May 28, 1995.

344 Militia manual on cells: *Principles Justifying the Arming and Organizing of a Militia*, Copyright 1994 by the Free Militia, p. 78-80.
secrecy in cells: *ibid.*, p. 78-96; "Secrecy Key to Patriot Movement," *Denver Post*, January 23, 1995.

345 Breakdown of inhibition in human natural killer cells: *Science*, April 21, 1995.
"naïve" cells activated into killer cells. . . "lethal hits": *Journal of Experimental Medicine*, March, 1982, pp. 783-96.
"lethal hit": *Cell Immunology*, January, 1984, pp. 43-51.

347 "Jesus Christ was not a pacifist": *ibid.*, p.8.
"Love your enemies": *ibid.*, p.9.

348 Montana militia manual: *New York Times*, April 29, 1995.

349 *The Turner Diaries* link to bombing ideas: *New York Times*, April 26, 1995.
Alleged extremist plans to blow up Murrah Building: *New York Times*, June 13, 1995.
"Leaderless resistance": *New York Times*, April 26, 1995.
James Nichols' earlier talk of bombing Murrah building: *New York Times*, May 26 & June 15, 1995.

357 Insurrection and treason laws: Denver *Post*, January 23, 1995.
Militia membership grew after Oklahoma bombing: *New York Times*, May 18, 1995.

Selected Bibliography

THIS LISTING of books, magazine articles and scholarly papers is not intended to be complete, but it will provide the reader with references to the main sources cited in this book, along with some of the key texts and seminal works used by the authors in the formulation of their perspective. Entries are grouped under headings that do not necessarily indicate the main subject matter of the work but rather the context in which it was found to be most valuable in this book. All newspaper articles and many other magazine articles are described in the accompanying Notes.

Topics in Modern Psychology and the Human Potential Movement
1. Freud, Sigmund, *Civilization and Its Discontents,* trans. by J. Strachey. New York: W. W. Norton, 1962.
2. _____, *New Introductory Lectures on Psychoanalysis,* trans. by J. Strachey. New York: W. W. Norton, 1965.
3. Gibb, Jack R., "Climate for Trust Formation," in L. Bradford, J. R. Gibb, and K.D. Benne, eds., *T-Group Theory and Laboratory Method.* New York: John Wiley & Sons,]964.
4. Jung, Carl G., *Modern Man in Search of a Soul,* trans. by W. S. Dell and Cary F. Baynes. New York: Harcourt, Brace & World, 1933.
5. Koch, Sigmund, "The Image of Man Implicit in Encounter Group Theory." *Journal of Humanistic Psychology,* 11:109-27 (1971).
6. Lieberman, M. A., I. D. Yalom, and M. B. Miles, *Encounter Groups: First Facts.* New York: Basic Books, 1973.
7. Lilly, John C., *The Center of the Cyclone.* New York: Julian Press, 1972
8. Maslow, Abraham H., *Religions, Values, and Peak-Experiences.* New York: Viking Press, 1970.
9. _____, *Toward a Psychology of Being.* New York: D. Van Nostrand, 1968.
10. Moreno, Jacob L., *Who Shall Survive? Foundations of Sociometry, Group Psychotherapy and Sociodrama,* 2d ed. Beacon, N.Y.: Beacon House, 1953.
11. Rogers, Carl R., *On Becoming a Person.* Boston: Houghton Mifflin, 1961.
12. _____, *Carl Rogers on Personal Power.* New York: Delacorte Press, 1977.
13. Ruitenbeek, Hendrik M., *The New Group Therapies.* New York: Avon Books, 1970.
14. Schutz, William C., *Elements of Encounter.* Big Sur, Cal.: Joy Press, 1973.

15. _____, *Joy: Expanding Human Awareness.* New York: Grove Press, 1967.
16. Siroka, R. W., E. K. Siroka, and G. A. Schloss, *Sensitivity Training and Group Encounter.* New York: Grosset & Dunlap, 1971.
17. Skinner, B. F., *Beyond Freedom and Dignity.* New York: Alfred A. Knopf, 1971.
18. _____, *Science and Human Behavior.* New York: Macmillan, 1953.
19. Solomon, Lawrence N., and Betty Berzon, *New Perspectives on Encounter Groups.* San Francisco: Jossey-Bass, 1972.
20. Tomkins, Calvin, "New Paradigms" (a profile on Michael Murphy). *The New Yorker,* January 5, 1976.
21. Wann, T. W. ed., *Behaviorism and Phenomenology: Contrasting Bases for Modern Psychology.* Chicago: University of Chicago Press, 1964.

Topics in Religion, Religious Cults, and Self-Help Therapies
22. *There Are Some People Who Really Care About You!* Chicago: American Messianic Fellowship, 1974.
23. Black, David, "Why Kids Join CULTS." *Woman's Day,* February, 1977.
24. Bloomfield, H. H., M. P. Cain, and D. T. Jaffe, *TM: Discovering Inner Energy and Overcoming Stress.* New York: Delacorte Press, 1975.
25. Bright, Bill, *Jesus and the Intellectual.* San Bernardino, Cal.: Campus Crusade for Christ, Inc., 1968.
26. Bry, Adelaide, *est: 60 Hours That Transform Your Life.* New York: Harper & Row, 1976.
27. Estabrooks, G. H., *Hypnotism,* rev. ed. New York: E. P. Dutton, 1943, 1957.
28. Fenwick, Sheridan, *Getting It: The Psychology of est.* Philadelphia: J. B. Lippincott, 1976.
29. Gaines, Steven S., *Marjoe.* New York: Dell, 1973.
30. Hubbard, L. Ron, *Dianetics Today.* Los Angeles: American Saint Hill Organization, 1975.
31. Hubbard, L. Ron, *When in Doubt . . . Communicate,* Ruth Minshull and Edward M. Lefson, eds. Ann Arbor, Mich.: Scientology Ann Arbor, 1969.
32. Kempton, Sally, "Hanging Out with the Guru." *New York,* April 12, 1976.
33. Kornbluth, Jesse, "The Fuhrer Over est." *New Times,* March 19, 1976.
34. Lifton, Robert J., *Thought Reform and the Psychology of Totalism: A Study of "Brainwashing" in China.* New York: W. W. Norton, 1961.
35. Litwak, Leo, "Pay Attention, Turkeys!" *The New York Times Magazine,* March 2, 1976.
36. Malko, George, *Scientology: The Now Religion.* New York: Delacorte Press, 1970.
37. Marcuse, F. L., *Hypnosis, Fact and Fiction.* West Drayton, Middlesex: Penguin Books, 1959.
38. Marin, Peter, "The New Narcissism." *Harper's,* October, 1975.
39. O'Connor, E. D., "Pentecost and Catholicism." *The Ecumenist,* July-August, 1968.
40. Patrick, Ted, with Tom Dulack, *Let Our Children Go!* New York: Thomas Congdon Books/E. P. Dutton, 1976.

41. Prabhupada, His Divine Grace A. C. Bhaktivedanta Swami, *Bhagavad-Gita as It Is*. Los Angeles: International Society for Krishna Consciousness, 1970.

42. _____, *Easy Journey to Other Planets*, rev. ed. Los Angeles: International Society for Krishna Consciousness, 1972.

43. Sargent, William, *Battle for the Mind: A Physiology of Conversion and Brainwashing*. New York: Perennial Library/Harper & Row, 1957, 1959.

44. Schein, Edgar H., with Inge Schneier and Curtis H. Barker, *Coercive Persuasion*. New York: W. W. Norton, 1961.

45 Sontag Frederick, *Sun Myung Moon and the Unification Church*. Nashville, Tenn.: Abingdon Press, 1977.

46. Wolfe, Tom, "The 'Me' Decade." *New* York, August 23, 1976.

47. Yamamoto, J. lsamu, *The Moon Doctrine*. Downers Grove, Ill.: Inter-Varsity Press (Inter-Varsity Christian Fellowship), 1976.

Topics in Communication Science

48. Ashby, W. Ross, *Design for a Brain: The Origin of Adaptive Behavior*. London: Chapman & Hall, 1952.

49. _____, *An Introduction to Cybernetics*. London: Chapman & Hall, 1956.

50. Bertalanffy, Ludwig von, *General System Theory: Foundations, Development Applications*, rev. ed. New York: George Braziller, 1968.

51. Bohm, David, "Some Remarks on the Notion of Order," in C. H. Waddington, ed., *Towards a Theoretical Biology*, vol. 2, *Sketches*. An International Union of Biological Sciences symposium. Chicago: Aldine, 1969.

52. Bremermann, Hans, "Complexity of Automata, Brains, and Behavior," in M. Conrad, W. Guttinger, and M. Dal Cin, eds., *Physics and Mathematics of the Nervous System*. Berlin and New York: Springer-Verlag, 1974.

53. _____, "Limitations on Data Processing Arising from Quantum Theory, Part l," in M. C. Yovits, G. T. Jacobi, and C. D. Goldstein, eds., *Self-Organizing Systems 1962*. Washington, D.C.: Spartan Books, 1962.

54. _____, "A Universal Topology" (a review of René Thom's *Stabilité structurelle et morphogénèse*). *Science*, vol. 192 (August 10, 1973), pp. 536-38.

55. Brillouin, Leon, *Science and Information Theory*, 2nd ed. New York: Academic Press, 1962.

56. Cherry, Colin, *On Human Communication*. Cambridge, Mass: M.I.T. Press; New York: John Wiley & Sons, 1957.

57. Dance, Frank E. X. ed., *Human Communication Theory; Original Essays*. *New* York: Holt, Rinehart & Winston, 1967.

58. Dechert, Charles R., ed., *The Social Impact of Cybernetics*. New York: Simon & Schuster, 1967.

59. Elsasser, Walter M., *Atom and Organism: A New Approach to Theoretical Biology*. Princeton, N.J.: Princeton University Press, 1966.

60. _____, *The Physical Foundation of Biology*. New York: Pergamon Press, 1958.

61. Gabor, Dennis, "Holography, 1948-1971." *Science*, vol. 177 (July 28, 1972), pp. 299-313.

62. Gilbert, E. N., "Information Theory After Eighteen Years." *Science,* vol. 152 (April 15, 1966), pp. 320-26.
63. Hall, Edward T., *Beyond Culture.* New York: Anchor Press/Doubleday, 1976.
64. _____, *The Silent Language.* New York: Doubleday, 1959.
65. Hebb, Donald O., *The Organization of Behavior: A Neuropsychological Theory.* New York: John Wiley & Sons, 1949.
66. Helvey, L. C., *The Age of Information: An Interdisciplinary Survey of Cybernetics.* Englewood Cliffs, N.J.: Educational Technology Publications, 1971.
67. Kolata, Gina Bari, "Catastrophe Theory: The Emperor Has No Clothes." *Science,* vol. 196 (April 15, 1977), pp. 287, 350-51.
68. Leith, Emmett N., and Juris Upatnicks, "Photography by Laser." *Scientific American,* vol. 212, no. 6 (June, 1965).
69. MacKay, D. M., "Cerebral Organization and the Conscious Control of Action," in J. C. Eccles, ed., *Brain and Conscious Experience.* Berlin and New York: Springer-Verlag, 1966.
70. McCulloch, Warren S., *Embodiments of Mind.* Cambridge, Mass.: M.I.T. Press, 1965.
71. _____, "The Reliability of Biological Systems," in M. C. Yovits and C. Scott, eds., *Self-Organizing Systems: Proceedings of an Interdisciplinary Conference.* New York: Pergamon Press, 1960.
72. Miller, George A., *The Psychology of Communication.* New York: Basic Books, 1967.
73. Pennington, Keith S., "Advances in Holography." *Scientific American,* vol. 218, no. 2 (February, 1968).
74. Piaget, Jean, *The Construction of Reality in the Child.* New York: Basic Books, 1954.
75. Pribram, Karl H. "The Brain." *Psychology Today,* September, 1971.
76. _____, *Languages of the Brain; Experimental Paradoxes and Principles in Neuropsychology.* Englewood Cliffs, N.J.: Prentice-Hall, 1971.
77. _____, "The Neurophysiology of Remembering." *Scientific American,* vol. 220, no. 1 (January, 1969).
78. Schrodinger, Erwin, *What Is Life? and Mind & Matter.* Cambridge, England: Cambridge University Press, 1967.
79. Shannon, Claude E., and Warren Weaver, *The Mathematical Theory of Communication.* Urbana: University of Illinois Press, 1949.
80. Shepherd, Gordon M., *The Synaptic Organization of the Brain: An Introduction.* New York: Oxford University Press, 1974.
81. Sokolov, E. N., "Neuronal Models and the Orienting Reflex," in M.A.B. Brazier, ed., *The Central Nervous System and Behavior.* New York: Josiah Macy, Jr. Foundation, 1960.
82. Smith, Alfred G., ed., *Communication and Culture.* New York: Holt, Rinehart & Winston, 1966.
83. Waddington, C. H., ed., *Towards a Theoretical Biology,* vols. I-IV. An International Union of Biological Sciences symposium. Edinburgh, Scotland: Edinburgh University Press; Chicago: Aldine, 1968, 1969, 1970, 1972.

84. Walter, W. Grey, *The Living Brain.* New York: W. W. Norton, 1953.
85. Wiener, Norbert, *Cybernetics: or Control and Communication in the Animal and the Machine.* Cambridge, Mass.: M.I.T. Press, 1948.
86. _____, *Ex-Prodigy: My Childhood and Youth.* Cambridge, Mass.: M.I.T. Press, 1953.
87. _____, *God & Golem, Inc.: A Comment on Certain Points where Cybernetics Impinges on Religion.* Cambridge, Mass.: M.I.T. Press, 1964.
88. _____, *The Human Use of Human Beings.* Boston: Houghton Mifflin, 1950.
89. _____, *I am a Mathematician: The Later Life of a Prodigy.* Cambridge, Mass.: M.I.T. Press, 1956.
90. Wooldridge, Dean E., *The Machinery of the Brain.* New York: McGraw-Hill, 1963.
91. Zeeman, E. Christopher, "Catastrophe Theory." *Scientific American* vol. 234, no. 4 (April, 1976).

General and Miscellaneous References
92. Atkins, Susan, as told to Bob Slosser, *Susan Atkins: Child of Satan-Child of God.* Plainfield, N.J.: Logos International, 1977.
93. Bronowski, Jacob J., *The Ascent of Man.* Boston: Little,Brown, 1974.
94. Bugliosi, Vincent, with Curt Gentry, *Helter Skelter: The True Story of the Manson Murders.* New York: (W. W. Norton, 1974) Bantam, 1975.
95. Burgess, Anthony, A *Clockwork Orange.* New York: W. W. Norton, 1963.
96. Cassirer, Ernst, *An Essay on Man.* New Haven: Yale University Press, 1944.
97. Cummings, E. E., *73 Poems.* New York: Harcourt, Brace & World, 1963.
98. Dewey, John, *Experience and Education.* New York: Collier Books/Macmillan 1938, 1963.
99. Drake, Stillman, trans., *Discoveries and Opinions of Galileo.* New York: Anchor Books, 1957.
100. Fosburgh, Lacey, "Patty Today." *The New York Times Magazine,* April 3, 1977.
101. Eliot, T. S., "The Rock," in *The Collected Poems of T. S. Eliot* New York: Harcourt, Brace, & World, 1963.
102. Heisenberg, Werner, *Across the Frontiers,* Ruth Nanda Anshen, ed., *World Perspectives,* vol. 48. New York: Harper & Row, 1974.
103. Hoffer, Eric, *The Ordeal of Change.* New York: Harper & Row, 1963.
104. Kogan, I. M., "Information Theory Analysis of Telepathic Communication Experiments." *Radio Engineering and Electronic Physics,* vol. 23, March, 1968.
105. Kuhn, Thomas S., *The Structure of Scientific Revolutions,* 2nd ed., International Encyclopedia of Unified Science, vol 2., no. 2. Chicago: University of Chicago Press, 1962, 1970.
106. Langer, Susanne K., *Philosophical Sketches.* Baltimore, Md.: Johns Hopkins Press, 1962.
107. Matson, Floyd W., and Ashley Montagu, *The Human Dialogue. Perspectives on Communication.* New York: The Free Press, 1967.

108. McLuhan, H. Marshall, *Understanding Media: The Extensions of Man.* New York: McGraw-Hill, 1964.
109. Packard, Vance, *The Hidden Persuaders.* New York: David McKay, 1965.
110. Pearce, Joseph Chilton, *The Crack in the Cosmic Egg.* New York: Julian Press, 1971.
111. Riesman, David, with Nathan Glazer and Reuel Denney, *The Lonely Crowd,* abr. ed. New Haven: Yale University Press, 1961.
112. Targ, Russell, and Harold Puthoff. *Mind-Reach: Scientists Look at Psychic Ability.* New York: Delacorte Press/Eleanor Friede, 1977.
113. Toffler, Alvin, *Future Shock.* New York: Random House, 1970.
114. Whyte, William H., *The Organization Man.* New York: Simon & Schuster, 1956.

Articles and Papers on Information Disease
115. Carmichael, Carl W., "Data Confirmation: Findings in a Nationwide Study on the Effects of Covert Induction and Deprogramming." Paper presented at the conference of the International Communication Association (ICA), Honolulu, HI, May, 1985.
116. Coggins, John C., "A Critical Perspective and Directions for Further Research on Information Disease," ICA, *Op. cit.*
117. Conway, Flo, "From the Marine Corps to Madison Avenue: The Social Implications of Information Disease." ICA, *Op. cit.*
118. _____, and Jim Siegelman, "Information Disease: Have Cults Created a New Mental Illness?" *Science Digest,* January, 1982.
119. _____, James H. Siegelman, Carl W. Carmichael and John C. Coggins, "Information Disease: Findings in a Nationwide Study on the Effects of Covert Induction and Deprogramming," *Update,* Aarhus, Denmark, June & September, 1986.
120. Cronkhite, Gary, "The Relation of the Concept of Information Disease to Theory and Research in Opinion Change." ICA, *Op. cit.*
121. Kilbourne, Brock K., "The Conway and Siegelman Claims Against Religious Cults: An Assessment of their Data," *Journal for the Scientific Study of Religion,* December, 1983, 22 (4): 380-385.
122. Kirkpatrick, Lee, "The Conway-Siegelman Data on Religious Cults: Kilbourne's Analysis Reassessed (Again)," *Journal for the Scientific Study of Religion.* March, 1988, pp. 117-121.
123. Maher, Brendan A. and Michael D. Langone, "Kilbourne on Conway and Siegelman: A Statistical Critique," *Journal for the Scientific Study of Religion.* Sept, 1985, pp. 325-326.
124. Siegelman, James H., "Information Disease: A New Paradigm for Communication and Mental Health." ICA, *Op. cit.*

Index